Karate Dō
My Way of Strife

Norma Foster

Serial Number: P2446170252
Title: Karate Dō My Way of Strife
Author: Norma Anne Foster
Layout: Merry Oskooei
Cover Designer: Mah Laalpour
English editor: Patricia Kyle
ISBN: 978-1-77892-221-3
Subject: Karate, Memoir, Inspirational
Book format/Size: Paperback, 9 by 6
Pages: 424
Publication Date: November 2025
Publisher: Kidsocado Publishing House

Copyright © 2025 By Kidsocado Publishing House
All Rights Reserved, including the right of reproduction in whole or in part in any form.

Kidsocado Publishing House
Vancouver, Canada

Phone: +1 (236) 333-7248
WhatsApp: +1 (236) 333-7248
Email: info@kidsocado.com
Website: https://kidsocado.com
Address: 2100-1055 West Georgia St,
Vancouver, BC V6E 3P3, Canada

In memory of those whose paths I have crossed and are no longer here but never, ever forgotten:

Fusajiro Takagi
Osamu Ozawa
David Akutagawa
Toru Arakawa
Robbie Smith
Hideho Takagi
Diogenes Cepeda
Katsumi Hakoishi

Contents

Acknowledgments..7
Disclaimer:..7
Preface..8
Introduction...9
Aberdeen, Scotland, 1969..13
The fight to start practicing karate...16
Edinburgh, Scotland, 1952-1966..18
Aberdeen 1966-1971..33
9th Kyu Exam 1970..38
Sensei John Allen...39
The Invisible Student..41
8th and 7th Kyu (grade) exams...42
Finally, real training..43
6th Kyu Green Belt April 1972...44
Acceptance..45
Self-defense..47
Street applications: a normal Saturday afternoon in Union St.....48
Training Methods in Aberdeen - early 1970s.................................51
Training at Crystal Palace 1973..55
Abuse of power and vulnerability 1973..61
Competition in Shotokan Scotland for women, 1969 – 1987.......68
Shodan..73
Last Months in Aberdeen 79
Houston, Texas, United States of America 1975–77.....................85
Cha Yon Ryū Taekwondo..91
Waco, Texas 1978...95
Fukuoka, Japan 1977–78...98
Little Rock, Arkansas, 1978..128
Aberdeen and London, UK, 1979 141
London, 1980...154
Vancouver, BC, Canada 1979–1981...158
The West End, Vancouver..168
Chinatown..170
Women in the Naha Te *Dōjō*...172
Cypress Bowl, West Vancouver..177
All Canada Karate Association (ACKA)..180

Attacked in Hawaii..182
Possible Dreams..187
Vancouver 1981-1988..188
The Shiseikai...189
Miz Nawma Resurfaces 1982...194
Provincial Championships 1983...197
Canadian National Championships 1983...200
Vancouver 1983...205
Carnegie Recreation Center, Vancouver 1983..208
Hidetaka Nishiyama sensei, San Diego 1983..215
Mother, Vancouver 1984...216
Mother, Seaton, Aberdeen 1936..226
Meanwhile back in Kitsilano..227
William Amos Jr., Aberdeen, 1984...229
JKA instruction, Vancouver, 1984..231
The Top, 1984-85..237
Fort St. John 1984...239
Repeat Nidan Exam, 1984...242
Osoyoos-Oliver, 1985...245
Guernsey, Channel Islands, 1985..248
James Johnson 1985..252
Stress test, 1987...254
Las Vegas, 1985...257
Sydney, Australia 1986..261
Reflections, 1988...264
Chicago, IL, USA 1988..265
International competition as an official; New Orleans 1988..................................269
First Fukuoka Women's World Cup 1990..271
Tōkyō 1989..274
Training in Japan, 1989...280
The Japan Karate Association, Ebisu, *Tōkyō* 1989..283
Buddhism and Yamanashi; JKA 1990...288
Next step on the Way..298
Arakawa *Dōjō*..299
Referee Clinic, Nagoya 1989..303
Competition in Japan..311

Guseikai (Serendipity) *Dōjō*, Sugamo, 1990	313
Tanya's Wedding 1995	320
WUKO World Championships Mexico City 1990	327
APUKO Championships, Auckland, New Zealand, 1991	336
JKF 4th Dan exam 1992	338
World Championships, Granada, Spain, 1992	339
JKF Wadō Kai 4th Dan Examination 1993	342
JKF 5th Dan Exam 1995	353
The Tōkyō British Club *Dōjō*	357
One of The JKAs' 1994	368
Farewell party for Beverley, Tōkyō, 1995	373
Wear and Tear, 1995	375
International Budō Seminar, Katsuura	377
Tōkyō, 1996	379
Pusan, Korea 1994	380
Reflections on Meiji Dōri beach, Sugamo	390
Takushoku University	394
Tōkyō, December 1995	404
Tōkyō, January 1996	409
Tōkyō, Spring 1996	410
Sun City, South Africa, 1996	413
Time out with Dr. and Mrs. Takagi	415
Time out with Hakoishi sensei	417
Vancouver 1997	420
Explanation	421

Acknowledgements

I am grateful to all the teachers I met throughout my life. You all pointed me towards the Way and kept me on a better road: Donald Matheson, William Sinclair, Ronnie Watt O.B.E., John Allen, Hirokazu Kanazawa, Osamu Ozawa, Cedric (Bull) Rodgers, Jeannie Parker, Tanja Petrovic, Hiroko Noguchi, Mike Scales, Andy Holmes, James Johnson, Fusajiro Takagi, Toru Arakawa, Dr. Hideho Takagi, Tommy Morris, Reza Salmani, Toby Threadgill, Bob Nash, Antonio Espinos.

I am indebted to many human and other friends who have supported me throughout this journey, including, but not limited to, Nicky Gavin, Ronnie Herd, Tim Pulman, Barbara Gordon Pulman, Lorraine Milne, Margaret Amos, William Amos Snr., Michael Hendry, Suzanne Jean, Yasmin Merali, Emma Baker, Shawna Escher, Katsuyuki Kawano, Alan Tanzadeh, Sooty, Sammy, and the Doglets, Jackie and Molly.

Thank you all and the hundreds of others I have studied, trained, laughed, lived, cried, sang, and danced with, including those who punched, tripped, threw me on the ground, or kicked me along the way. Without you, nothing might have been achieved.

Disclaimer

Some of the names of individuals in this book have been changed to protect the guilty.

Preface

I was compelled to start writing this book while in Japan, upon the recommendation of Patrick McCarthy. I had met him many years before, when he lived in Vancouver, and bumped into him at the Budokan Gakuen seminar for foreigners in Katsuura, on the southeast coast of Chiba Prefecture, Japan. Women have been involved in martial arts (Budo) throughout history, wielding weapons in ancient and more recent wars, fighting for their lives and country, and more recently participating, teaching, training, administering, guiding, officiating, and coaching the sporting facet of "modern" Budo, such as Judo and Karate. However, the stories of women who have spent decades in any martial art remain largely untold. I hope this book will encourage women to document their experiences that will continue to contribute to the growth and development of women and girls in Martial Arts across the globe.

It has taken a long time to finish this book; an editor does not make a writer. But eventually, the editing had to stop to let the tale unfold.

Introduction

This is the autobiography of a woman who fought for the right to learn karate in Aberdeen, Scotland, in 1969. Those early days marked the beginning of a lifelong struggle to achieve personal goals through participation in all aspects of karate. She is not alone. Thousands of others across the globe have unique experiences to share and stories to tell. Hopefully, women in today's more enlightened world will never have to endure the public and private humiliation, condescension, sexism, disrespect, denunciation, and financial hardship that Norma Foster overcame with tenacity and dignity.... but never alone. The support and encouragement of remarkable teachers and close lifelong friends gave her the strength to navigate a persistently convoluted path full of unforeseen obstacles, U-turns, and dead ends, and to permanently change the roles of women involved in mainstream Karate forever and for the better all over the world.

Princes Street Gardens, Edinburgh 1954: shopping day

The black and white photograph, taken on a summer day around 1954, shows a chubby two-year-old girl with a halo of blond, curly hair, dressed in dungarees and a T-shirt. She strides purposefully along Princes Street, which stretches for a mile along the base of Edinburgh Castle. Her mother, Helen, and her aunt, Agnes, had taken her to Princes Street Gardens for a picnic.

Centuries ago, the Gardens were the moor of Edinburgh Castle that sits atop a massive chunk of volcanic rock. Opposite the Castle and parallel to the moat that evolved into manicured gardens lies busy Princes Street, the elegant, upscale shopping centre of Edinburgh, bustling with tourists from all over the world, double-decker buses, taxis, cars, and all sorts of other wheels. The Gardens feature a nine-hole crazy golf course, a floral clock to the East, and a stage for summer shows, accompanied by an elaborate bronze fountain that cascades water to the West. Other attractions include the Scott Monument, a Gothic tower beneath which Sir Walter Scott is said to recline, forever contemplating his next novel. The West End of Princes Street at Lothian Road is anchored by the Caledonian Hotel. In contrast, the East End at The Bridges is graced by the North British Hotel, which overlooks the gully of Waverley Railway Station and the 18th-century "New Town" to the North. Since the railway tracks to and from all parts of Britain run directly along the base of the castle, locomotives constantly chuffed and puffed steam as they lumbered with much squealing of brakes and lightning bolts cracking from the wheels upon approaching or departing the station, for the run up the east coast to Aberdeen.

Everything is very nice and is not at all noticeable to the little girl in the picture. She did not flinch when the daily one o'clock gun blasted its empty shell from the castle battlements and was not at all frightened by the trains. She has places to go, things to look at, and flowers to smell.

Eight hours or so after the camera clicked, two policemen found the little girl happily wandering about a busy shopping area at the South end of The Bridges, two miles away, examining toys in windows.

"*Hello, little girl,*" said one of the two bobbies in their smart blue uniforms with funny hats and lots of shiny gold buttons.

"*Hello, Mr. Policeman,*" replied the tyke with a big smile. (She knew policemen were nice people from her Noddy books.)

"*What's your name?*" The policeman to the right asked.

"*Norma Anne Amos,*" she responded.

"*Do you know where you live?*" asked one of the two policemen.

"*9 Brougham Street, Edinburgh 3,*" she replied.

"*Hmmm. It's her, Alec.*"

They delivered her to her somewhat distraught mother.

Independent, adventurous, curious, stubborn, and self-confident, and wearing dungarees instead of a frock, the nice policemen might have found these qualities questionable in a three-year-old girl.

Avid reader of Noddy books 1955

Aberdeen, Scotland 1969

The lads in the Blue Lamp

All the good-looking lads seemed rushed into the Blue Lamp pub 30 minutes from closing time on Tuesdays and Thursdays, enthused, excited, animated, and sweating, and downed as many pints of beer as possible. They spoke a peculiar language that included words such as "noida, kaytoe, washin', canny sawa, sookie, kara'ay, kerries", then driving home.

Robert was a fish worker. His father owned a family business, which Robert, his two sisters, and his younger brother Michael helped. They lived in a council house on the No. 25 bus route, attended Catholic schools, and left at sixteen (girls) or eighteen (boys) to work filleting fish for their dad from 6 am until their (and/or their Dad's) lives ended. Robert had a car, looked a lot like Redford, and was very good-natured and shy. He was about twenty-three and a Brown Belt in karate. Likewise, his brother Michael. Robert's closest...... friend, also known as Mike, had tried karate once, but due to a slight leg deformity from childhood polio, he found it difficult and quit around the Yellow belt. Ronnie W. shopped for clothes in London, drove a Ford Cortina, lived in a tenement with his parents, and was about twenty-four. His dad was a construction worker, and Ronnie worked in the same paper mill across the street from where he lived. He had left school at fifteen to work in the mill. He had a girlfriend with dark hair down to her waist, an unusual sight in Aberdeen. He had just recently become a .... Black Belt.

Brian B. seemed more mysterious, deep, and somewhat scary. He had sparkly, clear green eyes, a dazzling smile, and perfect white teeth that shone through a large bushy beard seemingly attached to a tangled mass of shoulder-length hair. A heating engineer, he was close friends with Ronnie, and his girlfriend, Joan, was considered by some to be the most beautiful girl in the city. Long, straight blond hair shimmered in a waist-length curtain; she wore the latest fashions from London. She was seventeen, the same age as me. Brian was a Brown Belt.

The crowd was completed by Ronnie H., whose alter ego was also called Ronnie F., and both of these Ronnies had also practiced karate but quit at around the Yellow Belt level. These two, along with most of the others, were more concerned with soccer, the politically correct sport for young Scots.

What also helped to differentiate this group was that they all had cars.

The most advanced form of personal transportation for a high school senior at the time was a scooter, and most young adults and teens relied on buses for city transport and trains for longer hauls.

These lads attracted attention wherever they went. They were an "In Crowd." Who didn't want to be a member, to drive up the main street of the city in a private car instead of standing at bus stops in howling winds and sleet, looking miserable, frozen, and poverty-stricken? Everybody wanted to buy clothes from anywhere but Aberdeen, and preferably not in Scotland at all. It was 1969, and the city danced to Motown. The girls drank blue lagoons, and a peculiar Scottish vision of California Flower Power was in vogue. Everyone seemed to be in their late teens and early twenties. I had a job, my flat, and the freedom to make and bend my own rules. The social life in Aberdeen at that time for people in this age group centered around specific pubs.… all of which closed at 10 pm Monday-Saturday and did not open at all on Sundays. The way around this licensing inconvenience was to drink in hotel bars on Sunday, from lunchtime, which seemed to extend into the evening. The Lamp on weekdays, the Star and Garter on Saturdays, and the Dutch Mill Hotel on Sundays.

Entertainment seemed limited to the "pictures" (movies) or scintillating conversations at smoke-filled bars, sneaked into on the arm of a male of legal drinking age (eighteen years) when underage.

One Tuesday evening, I threaded my way through closely packed tables at the Lamp and stood at the bar, waiting for attention from the barman. The conversation buzzing around among Ronnie W, Robert, Mike, and Brian was essentially indecipherable due to the Motown sounds throbbing from overhead speakers and the odd words, in addition to the Doric speech of Aberdeen spoken by the lads.

"Did ye see 'e boy deein oan washin' gerry tae the ither boy's heed?"

"Aye, it wiz nae real min."

"Aye but yiv nivver seen Noida deenit."

"I ken, but oans a f ------n tiger. Vicious min."

"Takahashi's nae bad."

"Aye he's cumminhere tae dae a coorse."

"Fit'll we dae wi' im efter trainin."

"I d'a ken. Mibbe tak him oot duncin."

"Bit, ee'll no hae a trap."

"Aye, bit we can aye ask oan wee thing Norma tae come wi' us."

Which was how I ended up dancing with Takahashi at the Beach Ballroom and hearing even more of these strange words. Sometimes, a punch would materialize out of nowhere, which would incite another round of strange words.

Visit to Aberdeen 1979

The fight to start practicing karate

Three topics usually dominated the conversations among any crowd of plumbers, electricians, fish and mill workers in Aberdeen: soccer, sex, and politics. Sometimes religion, but in this In Crowd, the key word was *kara'e with* a glottal stop.

I thought it sounded interesting. So, I asked one of the lads a question.

"Robert, would you explain more about what you lads are talking about?" Kara'e.

"Yes, I know that. Haven't I danced with Takahashi? But what exactly do you mean? Tell me about it."

"Ach Norma, dinna ask such stupit questions. It's somethin' we loons dee 'at comes fae Japan, as ye weel kayen."

"Fine, but what exactly is it? Explain. My uncle was a boxer; you know; I think I can understand a bit of pugilism."

"Ronnie, fit's pyoojilisim? Heh. Robert. Geess a fag."

"I d'na ken fit pyoogilisum is an I dinna smoke onymair."

"Oh come on; what is it about karate that gets you guys so fired up and animated that you can't even see all these girls sitting over there just drooling in your general direction?"

"We're talkin' aboot kickin and punchin 'i' boy's lights oot. We're talking aboot ka'aa and fightin'. It's nithin' tae dae wi' girruls."

"As I said. Sounds so interesting because you lads are always so enthusiastic. I'd like to try it."

"Aye aye, Norm. D'ye wa' a drink?"

"Aye. A brandy and lemonade, please. I'm serious. I want to start training in this karate, as it seems interesting."

"Dinna be silly, Norm. "Yi hif t' dee press-ups."

I've been doing pushups since I was seven. I was a competitive swimmer."

"Yi might get hurt."

"I understand that. It is a martial art, not playing the violin."

"Yi might get a black eye or a thick lug, yi'd look ugly and yi'd start greetin' because i' wid hurt."

"I doubt it. I've seen worse and been humiliated by better people than you."

"Yi hif te hae disiplin 'cause yi hif tae dee trainin' a' the time."

"I swam for seven years and did land work 3x per week and water work 4x per week. What's new?"

"Er's nae girruls trainin'."

What about Gail?

"Aye, Gail wiz good richt enough, but she couldna stick it past yellow belt. She gave up."

I wouldn't give up.

Aye aye Norm......

I joined Warrender Baths Club in 1959 and became an avid, if not a remarkable, member of their beginners' division. I had taught myself how to swim, and I loved hurling myself off a springboard with total abandon. I also taught myself how to dive and studied swimming form from a book while supported by a bar stool at home. My mother refused to pay for lessons for anything, but I was hooked, and that minor detail was not going to deter me. Thus, I began a seven-year love affair with swimming. I loved everything about it. The smell of the chlorinated water from way down the street, the quiet of an empty pool. The Speedo logo and the Jantzen diving girl trademark were endless sources of fascination.

Circuit training three times a week, with stretching and strengthening exercises, and pool work four times a week, including frigid 5:30 Saturday mornings, before the water heater was switched on. Impossible to break a sweat in that water, no matter how hard the training.

Seven years and a lot of invested pocket money later, Coach Frank informed me that, as I was no longer beating the clock, I would have to move on to make room for more talented kids who were waiting to join the program.

Bitterly disappointed, my first love affair ended at age fourteen.

I tried diving. Studied for six months and managed to pass the bronze test of the Scottish Amateur Diving Association. However, for the silver test, a one-and-a-half somersault was required from the 1m board. In a practice session, I performed a one-and-a-quarter somersault, landing flat on the surface of the water from a 3m height off the spring. I have never felt such intense, total pain. Maybe a whole-body jellyfish sting would come close. Scarlet from toe to forehead, my second attempt at a relationship ended that very evening, and there I was, with nothing to do in my free time for the first time at age fourteen.

Later, I learned to play squash and did so regularly, but nothing seemed to offer the self-discipline of training to be a competitive swimmer. When I first started hearing about karate from the boys in The Blue Lamp, it seemed reasonable that I would be able to cope with the training.

However, the past seventeen years had left its mark; regardless, I refused to accept the notion that I could not study karate…. or anything for that matter, just because I was a girl.

Edinburgh, Scotland, 1952-1966

Sometimes, Scotland seems like a beautiful, wild, and inhospitable place to me. However, others find it friendly and warm. A great deal of the North is unsuitable for growing anything other than sheep, deer, or highland cattle and heather due to the acidic moraine soil.

The weather is often unpredictably bleak due not only to the latitude, which is similar to that of Hudson's Bay, Canada, but also to being perpetually in the middle of an elemental battle for supremacy between the North Sea and the Atlantic Ocean, mediated by howling Arctic winds. Being surrounded by those grey seas, looking up at grey skies, and looking forward to a grey future of headscarves and shopping bags, the people often seemed dour, negative, and complaining to me. The class system was glaringly obvious in the 50s, and there always seemed to be someone further up or down the class scale than you. The men were macho, and talk of World War II was still rife. Reminiscences often started with "During the War, I ……" Women talked about eating real butter and drinking real instant coffee. A great oxymoron. Some still collected food coupons, and words like demobbed (released from military duty) were still heard. They knew their place, these working women of 50's Scotland, and though tinged with a Marilyn Monroe romance of the wartime years, their place remained essentially unchanged since the dawn of written Scottish history. An expression I heard in relation to Kyushu also seems to fit the Scotland I knew: men are men, and sheep are nervous. I wasn't aware that I was functioning in chauvinism. The word was not even in my vocabulary.

I was raised in Tollcross, Edinburgh, 25 yards from a major five-way intersection. The grimy sandstone tenement that my mother and I lived in had been built in 1879. The area is central, located within walking distance from the omnipotent Castle and Princes Street. It was also relatively near the university and several major hospitals, one of which, the Royal Infirmary, hadn't changed much either decoratively or structurally in 400 years.

Tollcross was a working-class area in the 1950s that also contained a few 16th-century slums that were inhabited by spooky, unsavory characters, drunks, and armed gangs of street kids. Drunks occupied parts of the area, collapsing in, bottles of methylated spirits and other flammable liquids leaking fumes as noxious as those emanating from their own persons. This is the area where not only I, but Sean Connery also grew up, but I didn't know that. I didn't like it much because my freedom was restricted. I was not allowed a bicycle to get to school because of the traffic, no ball games in the street, no places to chalk pebbles (hop/skip/jump game involving an empty shoe polish tin). I knew there were better places in which to grow up. Individual private homes with terraced homes consisting of several storeys with basements, gardens, garages, sculleries, and back doors. However, I also knew that other areas were considerably worse. So, I was thankful that I could walk within five minutes to play in the Meadows (grass, trees, and rolling hills (great for winter sledging and rolling eggs at Easter), playing par three golf, cricket, lawn bowling, tennis, or rounders (kids' baseball) or in the back greens of the tenement. Unfortunately, playmates were scarce as my mother (doing her best to aim for higher things) would not let me play with local kids. I had no brothers or sisters (to my knowledge!), so I became adept at entertaining myself.

I taught myself to play tunes on the upright piano that my mother had in the "Front Room." This room contained all my mother's treasures, and I found it fascinating. She had placed a pair of huge Kutani porcelain vases on the marble mantelpiece, decorated with the "thousand buddhas" and cobalt blue rims. An ornate 19th-century Japanese sideboard overwhelmed with gilded ormolu curlicues, drawers, and doors displayed two fragile Japanese tea sets and my uncle's amateur boxing trophies. A mahogany whatnot displayed ivory elephants from India, brassware from the Middle East, fascinating Chinese dolls, and lacquer music boxes that played the strangest tunes. "China Night" was one of them. Most of these intriguing items were brought back from exotic places by my seafaring father. The floor was carpeted in an Oriental design, and comfortable chairs flanked a mahogany coffee table covered with current issues of Vogue and Harper's Bazaar. A Victorian bookcase housed encyclopedias, and a radiogram stood in a corner, playing mother's substantial collection of 78 rpm records during her occasional, rather elegant soirées.

A black and white portrait photograph of my mother wearing a pendant and matching earrings in the style of a Sri Lankan Buddha face dominated the room. Overall, the room reflected her good taste and appreciation for fine arts, fashion, and her limited financial means. Many of the items in the Front Room were gifts from a woman who admired my mother's spirited attitude in difficult times. I was allowed to play the piano and enjoy the encyclopedias, but not to touch anything else in the room.

My mother raised me almost entirely by herself, as my father was always absent, sailing to interesting and far-flung places. During the 1950s, he was an engineer on whaling ships that plied the Newfoundland and Greenland coasts, and he was absent for six to nine months of the year.

Mother was an attractive redhead, as that shade was described then, with fair skin that freckled easily. She was attractive, gregarious, and at 5'0", had much of her clothing tailored to fit. Her prized possession was her 22" waist, which was often emphasized with flair for the benefit of anyone who turned their head in her direction, which happened often.

Lonely, attractive, intelligent, and witty, my twenty-four-year-old mother with an absent husband and a toddler, started to look for a more mature company. By the time I was four, she kept regular company with an individual who became a surrogate father until he tried to molest me at the age of thirteen. Time to stop trusting adults and giving them unconditional respect.

Which was too bad since I had been brought up with common-sense values. Mother and my schools saw to that. I respected uniforms, adults, secondary school children older than myself, teachers, and all authority figures without question. Discipline throughout my schooling was strict but reasonable, and I was fortunate to have had teachers who sincerely cared about educating children during my primary school years. I had two male teachers throughout most of my primary education, and they were truly remarkable human beings. Donald Matheson and William Sinclair taught with compassion, respect, humor, and sensitivity. These men were probably key in shaping my attitudes to people in positions of authority, particularly teachers.

I started primary school at the age of four. I was given an oral test by William Robertson, the headmaster, to see if I could make it, as my classmates would be aged five and six. The joys of an inconvenient

October birthdate.

"Can you tie your shoelaces, Norma?"

"They are tied, sir." I replied.

A glare from my mother, followed by some scowls. I untied them and tied them again. What a silly thing to ask, I thought.

"Very good. Can you count to 10?"

"1,2,3,4,5,6,7,8,9,10. 10,9,8,7,6,5,4,3,2,1" I counted with a glitch.

"Well, yes, Mrs. Amos, I think that she will be capable of keeping up with the class," he stated.

I was thrilled. As an only child, I had to keep myself amused a lot, and here was a whole building full of kids!

Mother soon became fed up with walking with me to Sciennes (primary) School every morning, and I wanted to prove my independence. I wanted to show her I could be trusted and that I had grown up. So, I campaigned as a five-year-old can for the right to do something I wanted so badly to do: walk to school by myself. After all, I'd already been doing errands and shopping for a year. Finally, I received permission. What a feeling! Freedom and independence. I didn't talk to strangers. I walked in the middle of the path. I asked a policeman to help me cross Marchmont Road, a busy intersection for a five-year-old. After a few tries, I actually made it to school by the bell after learning about Time.

Once I could be trusted to actually make it to school on time, my mother started working. I would come home after school, let myself into the flat with the key around my neck, and behave myself by doing homework until she came home. In the winter, getting home meant dealing with the early darkness and navigating the hilly parts of The Meadows, then walking by rows of forbidding Victorian tenements. These three-to five-story structures all had dark stairwells and corridors that emptied into rabbit warrens that led to back greens (backies) located behind the tenements. These were full of broken-down walls, unkempt grassy areas full of weeds, stinging nettles, and washing hanging out to dry. The area behind the butcher shop smelled of rank blood and greasy rotting meat, so there was a perpetual fear lurking in the back of several children's minds that a bogeyman would grab them, secrete them into one of these dank corridors, do unspeakable things, then fling them into the butcher's backyard to be minced. After all, not too long ago, this was the very city where people had been murdered to supply the medical school up the road with cadavers. Some of the tenement passages smelled very strange. It was a while before I learned it was stale urine. Cats, dogs, humans.

Charles Dickens, Robert Louis Stevenson, and Sir Walter Scott were always with us, children of Edinburgh, who helped to advance the Industrial Age. For example, five-year-olds were enslaved to work as chimney sweeps. Witness the soot that puffed straight out of the Industrial Age that grimly clung to the sandstone tenement walls until 1993! My grandfather remembered horse-drawn carriages and talked about Queen Victoria! The point is that children grew up steeped in history, naturally.

A fertile imagination was fueled by Scottish history studied even at school, childhood horror tales, and labyrinthine architecture; I made it my business to understand where every one of the tenement passageways led. I also enjoyed playing imaginary games with bogles, beasties, and gremlins. I scrambled about the rabbit warrens and learned not to be afraid of the butcher's smell. I became familiar with every toe and hand hold in every crumbling wall in the backies and memorized which doors were always, sometimes, or never locked. I roller-skated on noisy metal wheels and knew which sidewalks had the least cracks and holes. The best skate courses were always occupied by drunk and drugged men. These "alkies" (alcoholics and glue sniffers) provided a human obstacle course to skate around or jump over. They posed no threat because they were too slow to react.

Some skills were a natural adaptation to the environment. By the age seven, I was not afraid of dark recesses lurking in tenements. I was comfortable knowing their layout, and it became second nature to consider the chances of escape from some bogeyman bent upon stealing my marbles by vanishing into a dark stairwell. By about the age of ten, I started delivering newspapers, running up and down flights of stairs in a broader circle of tenements, so I began to know the names of the tenants on every landing of every tenement in the Bruntsfield and Tollcross areas. Knowledge was power.

Summer holidays were spent in a street called Seaton Place East, the home of my maternal grandfather in Aberdeen. This city was in a different world. Only 112 miles north of Edinburgh, the terrain, the weather, the accents, and the immediate environment were totally unlike those of the capital.

In Auld Reekie ((Old Smokie; nickname for Edinburgh based on the belching sooty chimneys of the Industrial Age), school occupied weekdays, and the weekends were opportunities to escape home by exploring the Royal Scottish Museum, roaming all over Edinburgh Castle (free of charge), the areas around the Royal Mile to Holyrood Palace or to spend a rainy day in the George IV library, or climb Arthur's Seat one of the seven hills surrounding Edinburgh) In Aberdeen, where even tenements were built of sparkly granite, you could play all day long for seven summer weeks with local kids and study how to be street-smart.

Every summer, I arrived with an Edinburgh accent and left with the Aberdonian patois, which is called Doric, and a whole new vocabulary. Scottish regional dialects differ not only in accents, but also in the words used to describe the same things. Doric includes corrupt French, which had been the court language of Scotland during the short-lived reign of Mary Queen of Scots: Dinna fash yerse'l (calm down; from facher to be angry), minker (disgusting, ugly, drunk). Nordic words include hame (home) oot (out), bide (lives, stays), breeks (trousers), claes, (clothes), een (eyes), greet (cry/weep)

Seaton Place East was in one of the poorer council-subsidized districts of the city. Seaton Primary School, which my mother had attended, occupied one side of it. The opposite side consisted of three-storey granite tenements that looked dreich (gloomy) and depressing in the rain, but sparkled in sunlight. Tollcross in Edinburgh was black and depressing all the time. The council flats in Aberdeen seemed to be full of scullery maids and fishwives who were abused by their spouses, and passed such behavior not only on to each other but towards their broods of vaguely malnourished and unwashed children with green teeth that bled at the sight of a toothbrush and wore ragged, hand-me-down clothes.

The dialect was important because it was a class differentiator. I spoke with a "cultured" Jean Brodie accent that marked me as a child of the capital and, therefore, in a different class from the Seaton kids. I usually arrived in a taxi, wearing a clean school uniform, which was sufficient to draw crowds of children onto the street and residents to poke their heads out of tenement windows to stare. Usually, traveling by taxi was the norm as my mother sent me unaccompanied on the three-hour train journey to Aberdeen from about the age of seven, with strict instructions to catch a taxi as soon as I exited the railway station. Those were, indeed, special times.

After an initial test, the local children overcame their awe and realized that despite my accent, the taxi and the clean-pressed school uniform, I was just a kid like them. In addition, they soon discovered that my maternal grandfather was "aul' Wullie Wyllie". He had lived there for forty years, and everyone knew his story. A card-holding member of the Communist Party, his wife was a psychopath who was currently incarcerated in the local psychiatric hospital, Kingseat. She escaped several times, and once, I had the opportunity to see her from a safe distance. She looked like a witch, with a grey and white disheveled, matted thatch for hair, a filthy old coat, and downtrodden shoes. She wielded a long-bladed kitchen knife, and she was hurling a stream of unintelligible abuse as she tried, unsuccessfully, to stab my grandfather. The local street kids kindly tried to shield me from this spectacle, but I wanted to see it because it was my grandmother, after all—and I thought it was quite exciting. A police car and an ambulance arrived at the same time. The police restrained her, and paramedics gave her an injection of something, then bundled her into the ambulance, still writhing and howling. When I read Robert Burn's famous lyric poem, "Tam O' Shanter", this vision of my grandmother always seems to merge with the witches at the Kirk of Aulderne.

The children befriended me, and I easily changed my accent and body language to emulate their ways. I became best friends with two boys. Ian was small, thin, and sharp, and John, his best friend, had fascinating green teeth. Ian lived with his parents and seven other siblings in a two-bedroom flat, and John lived with his grandmother. John said that he never brushed his teeth because they bled when he tried, but they didn't bleed if he left them alone. I thought this was some sort of magic because I was led to believe by the "Happy Smile Campaign" for Lothian schoolkids, that if you didn't brush your teeth twice a day, they would fall out.

The three of us were always together most of the long summer days during consecutive years of school holidays. Aberdeen is far enough north that summer daylight extends until about midnight, so we could make mischief for almost 18 straight hours every day of the summer, in the event that the weather permits us. We climbed washhouse drainpipes, we threw stones at windows, wifies, wellies - anything was good as a target. We climbed in and around the air raid shelters left over from the war. Learned to ride a bike! But the greatest treat was that Seaton Place East dead-ended onto the rough right at the beach near the estuary where the River Don flows into the North Sea. We collected scrap metal washed up on shore (from the war) and carried it to Scrappy Ross, who weighed it and rewarded us with money that would quickly be spent on a wealth of shared treats. On warm days, we could stay at the beach all day and play "Japs and Commandos" in the enormous sand dunes and coarse coastal grasses bordering the golf course. We would jump and roll in these immense dunes, playing dead and dying, then miraculously resurrect to become yet another commando. Only commandos could resurrect because they were "*good*". On the other hand, only those who could "die" dramatically ever wanted to be "Japs", because you had to throw yourself off the lip of a 20-foot dune in a convincing manner. So, we practiced our "death skills". We stole golf balls to play putting or go to a par three-course, having rented a nine iron and a putter from the "parkie". We stole gooseberries, raspberries, or strawberries from small plots of cultivated land not far from the bottom of the street. Then, to cover up the crime, we stole the bamboo supports to make bows and arrows.

"Ach, 'at's I mannie Dow's plottie. He's aye too drunk ti mind if he pit fit kindso' berries oer here or nane at a".

At the end of the summer in this paradise, I would put on my primary school uniform, along with my Edinburgh accent, and cry as I left all my friends behind. However, I couldn't let them see that because they would think I was a sissy, and everyone knew I was one of the boys. After all, I could run as fast, jump as high, throw stones as accurately, and perform wheelies on big girls' bikes just as well as they. I could collect, carry, and sell scrap for as much as they could and steal as many golf balls as they could.

Off I returned to the capital to be a "*lady*" for another year, during which these skills would remain hidden.

These kids showed me a different perspective on life and supplemented my formal education. They helped me overcome fears such as heights (jump Norma, it's nae that far), bullies (ach he's nae that big), alcohol abuse (ach, dinna mind him he's just pished), threats (dinna believe him he's spikkin shite). They taught me how to ride a bicycle, climb, play golf, throw stones, sing local songs, and make up slang rhymes. In a way, they also taught a kind of self-respect and dignity. Some were regularly beaten by both parents. Fathers were usually drunk during waking hours, and abuse was the normal modus operandi. Abused elder children, who shielded their younger siblings, eventually abused and terrorized the younger ones themselves. These kids shrugged off the abuse at least for a few hours by playing outdoors, where it was never alluded to. Big brothers or sisters often had to be surrogate fathers or mothers to a brood ranging in age from mere babes to teenagers. These families owned next to nothing, and the children were always dirty and unkempt because no one cared enough about them. Yet, through all this poverty and lifelong abuse, they could befriend a stranger and share whatever they had left to give—their hearts, feelings, jokes, secret hiding places, treasured golf balls, or favorite stones.

Sadly, John and Ian both became heroin addicts, and John died around the age of twenty-five of an overdose. I don't know what became of Ian to this day.

Throughout the 1950s until about 1961, all was reasonably secure at home. Mother went out with her chiropodist on Tuesdays and Fridays, usually returning home around 9 pm. She worked in various jobs, often in the fashion industry. I did not see my father very often, perhaps about once or twice each year for a week or so. I was doing well academically in primary school, being in the top 3 of 35 kids throughout my primary years. I was reasonably competent in sports, having been on the netball team and swimming team, and won the gym prize for one year. A regular joiner, I was also a member of the choir and the Edinburgh Primary Schools String Orchestra (Leader, 1st Violins). The playground found me skipping with the class, swapping scraps, and playing jacks. Of course, I was also training after school hours for the glory of Warrender Baths Club.

Migraines kicked in at age nine, coincident with mother's fall into alcoholism and promiscuity.

She often went out at night and returned home very late with various men, picked up at local bars. Her behaviour was predictable, and the early morning usually found her kicking out the unfortunate man after he had taken care of her needs. Sometimes they left quite discreetly; others would not go without a fight. After slamming and bolting the door on her luckless date, she would go back to bed and demand that I get up and make her a sandwich, fix her a drink, and make her some tea, usually well before dawn.

I would go to school exhausted from the tension of waiting alone in the flat until she arrived home, then being unable to sleep through the records she played or the sounds of the repeated assaults on the bedsprings and her heavy breathing. My room was sandwiched between the living room, where she did her initial entertaining, and her bedroom, where the grand finale occurred night after night.

Finally, in 1963, the effort required to pretend that all was normal and well-adjusted at home became too much. I ran away. (I was only 13, and no one believed that my mother had become a belligerent, aggressive, physically abusive harridan when she was inebriated night after night, or that she was acting like a whore. I never told anyone about her chiropodist lover's attempts to have sex with me in his car until many, many years later because, instinctively, I knew that wouldn't be believed either. By the time I told my mother about it, he had long since been buried.)

A social worker found me and brought me back to my mother, who whipped me with the buckle end of a fat brown leather belt. I went to school the following day with bruises on my thigh the size of grapefruits. They attracted the attention of the gym teacher, who questioned me about them as they were below the navy-blue knickers girls wore for gym class.

Fell down the stairs, Miss.

Migraines had kicked in at age nine, coincident with the start of mother's descent into alcoholism and wanton debauchery.

I became adept at compartmentalizing thoughts and realities. I would save a particular thought or event that gave me pleasure until I was about to go to sleep at night, when it would be accessed from an imaginary file and rolled about in my mind like a favorite sweetie in a kid's mouth. I played the role of a happy, well-adjusted kid with two parents at home who said grace before meals, whose mother cooked, washed, cleaned, and shopped for groceries. I dreamed of a better toaster whose father was home every night and who helped with the math homework. I used to love visiting my friends' homes and pretending I lived there—actually, anywhere other than reality.

I would return home, dreading with each step that mother would be in, that she would be out, that if she were in, she would be totally gone. She was still vivacious and witty when sober, sharp of tongue, but also of humor. However, after a seemingly minimal amount of alcohol, her personality and her face would change, and she would become a mask of hate, rage, and frustration. I was the most convenient target for her spite and venom, and it was partially explained by my resemblance to my father.

By 1965, school grades began to suffer. Though I had passed with honors from primary school into the elite Boroughmuir Senior Secondary School with a direct line into university, I could no longer maintain the same standards and had sunk to the mediocre level of 18th among a class of 40. Life at home was becoming unbearable due to sleep deprivation. I could not concentrate at home or any other place due to being deprived of sleep. Here is an example of why. My mother would go to the local bar alone and sober and return inebriated and accompanied by random men. The 78 rpm records would start, more alcohol was consumed, and conversation started. Thereafter, the conversation dwindled, heavy breathing started, and a stack of 78s stopped playing. Words stopped, and heavy breathing became louder. Since I was next door to the kitchen, I heard every breath and every grunt associated with boisterous sex on the kitchen floor. So, one night, I could not sleep and I could not stand all this for one second more, so I slammed the door and stepped into the kitchen to see a naked male stranger bouncing about on top of my mother. So that was, of course, when I turned on the tears and screamed at the top of my lungs…. deliberately. Both adults were shocked and horrified and starting yelling. The man stood up proudly to announce, using as much profanity as possible, that he would "get me in the tenement stairs" and "show me what's what". I actually was not the least bit afraid of this creature or his appendage that had suddenly become smaller, but they did not know that, of course. So, I started screaming. That seemed to resonate somewhere in mother's psyche as maternal instinct. She got up from the floor, cursing and fighting, yelling at him to leave, then threw him out as he was struggling to put on underpants, socks, and trousers. The scene was ironically comical, except it was real. I have to admit that I considered his threats and looked over my shoulder for a while, but though nothing ever happened, I felt that the possibility of someone getting back at my mother through me might be quite high.

I was a fourteen-year-old in a class of sixteen-year-olds. I was already channeled into a science program that could eventually lead to a career in that field, and I loved it. I knew that my future depended upon passing the "O" level exams, which were the lowest prerequisites for university entrance. I also knew that if I stayed with my mother, I was going to have a very rough time doing this.

I couldn't see a way out of this dilemma. I needed to escape to survive. Running away would not do it. The previous attempt resulted in me telling all to a friend's mum, who summoned social services. They immediately called Mother, who graciously told them I was a problem child who tells lies, then gave me a hiding (battering) that left a grapefruit-sized black and blue mark on my right thigh that attracted the attention of the gym teacher. Who asked how that happened? "Fell down the stairs, miss." So, there was nowhere to turn for help. However, fate intervened and sent Mother out for a "wee drink" with her elder sister, Isobel, who was visiting from Aberdeen. I decided to try to explain to Isobel what a day and a night in this pit of depravity were like. Isobel could not believe it. She was kindly, overweight, and benevolently disposed towards her attractive, younger sister—until that night.

Isobel arrived home well before Mother, flustered and mortified. Mother arrived home accompanied by a man after the pub closed. She was so intoxicated that she could not stand upright, but dismissed the man at the front door. She snarled a stream of verbal abuse at Isobel and told us both that if we didn't like it in her house, to f*** off. All this venom shocked Isobel, who could hardly comprehend the demon before her, unlike the angel who used to be her cute little sister, but very much like her own psychopathic mother. She gave the same advice to Isobel, who told me to pack what I could carry. My luggage included the clothes I was wearing, my schoolbag, and not much else. Isobel and I stayed at a bed and breakfast that night and caught the first train to Aberdeen the following morning.

Duthie Park, Aberdeen, 1975

Aberdeen 1966-1971

After living with Isobel, her husband, and son for a year, I realized I could not live there any longer. There was something seriously wrong with her. A younger brother, Oliver, became an alcoholic after he returned intact from the army and a short career as an amateur featherweight boxer. An elder brother, Bill, was unlike his siblings in that they had red hair and brown eyes, whereas he had jet-black hair and green eyes. In fact, his father was someone else, and my maternal grandfather adopted him. He never did develop any of the symptoms as his half-siblings, although he too enjoyed the Scottish national sport of alcohol excesses.

Isobel started to change during the first year at her home. She became slow, dull-witted, and hardly spoke to her husband Joe, or their son, Joseph, who was seven years younger than me. I had no clue what was wrong with her. She would sit in the same place for hours, staring at nothing, and chain-smoking cigarettes.

But at least I could sleep the whole night through without interruption.

My father sent money to Isobel each week to pay for my expenses. I was humiliated when Isobel brought me to a secondhand shop to buy a green blazer for my new school, Aberdeen Academy.

I was doubly mortified because I was quite proud to go to this school. My father had been a pupil there, and his elder brother Alex, who had died on Mountbatten's boat, the Kelly, was listed on the carved honour roll of those former pupils who had laid down their lives in the war. History! And here I was in someone's cast-off, frayed old blazer with a faded school badge. The school motto was, "*Ad Altiora Tendo,*" which is Latin for "Aim for higher things." I grimly thought that this should not be difficult when starting this low.

Despite the humiliating blazer, I started to make friends, play field hockey, participate in athletics, study, and discover boys in a different way from those at Seaton. Like the Edinburgh schools I had attended, it was co-ed, which was useful for that sort of transition, I suppose.

Isobel became increasingly withdrawn and gained a substantial amount of weight. She did not work (having been a nurse) and did no housekeeping, so Joe became the cook, and I was the housekeeper. I already knew all about this because it was part of life with Mother, along with the weekly grocery shopping, cleaning, washing dishes and clothes, and ironing. I just could not grasp why Isobel behaved so oddly.

Finally, I had a bout of tonsillitis, and Isobel refused to take me to the hospital, saying I was faking it. I thought this comment was a function of her condition. Her husband said that tonsillitis could be cured by tying a sweaty sock around my throat. So that was the only option on offer. Wearing Joe's socks all sweaty from working as a blacksmith, Eeeeeoooow! I was totally disgusted. This concept of a cure led to recurrent attacks of tonsillitis for the next two years, which finally ended in surgical removal due to antibiotic resistance and constant pain.

I finally complained to my father that this was not the most suitable arrangement for me after all, as Uncle Joe had started to blame me for Isobel's condition. My father promised to find me somewhere else to live.

However, my absence did nothing to alleviate Isobel's condition as she rapidly spiraled down a rabbit hole of intractable severe depression that required lifelong hospitalization, ironically, in Kingseat, where her own mother died. Isobel left that institution only twice. Once to attend Joe's funeral and once to attend her own.

My father had four living siblings, Margaret (Margie), Elizabeth (Betty), Grace, and Linda three of whom had married well, lived middle class lives, raised polite, mannerly children, imposed standards, did not use profanity, did not sell the use of their bodies, and were not alcoholics, psychopaths or depressed.

They lived in stand-alone granite houses with gardens and had front and back doors.

However, not one of the three families would take responsibility for a fifteen-year-old. I had thought that they just did not like me, but I did not know the backstory until thirty years later. My mother would fortify herself with a mickey (375 mL) of brandy on the train from Edinburgh to Aberdeen, station herself in the street at the front door of her sister-in-law's home, and scream profanity about them at all hours of the night until the police would come and remove her. The last thing they wanted was an excuse to attract this type of trouble near their whitewashed doorsteps. I didn't blame them really, but I had difficulty digesting the fact that the opinions of neighbors mattered more than helping a destitute child of their own family. They were afraid of my mother and of what the neighbors would think. They turned a blind eye to the horrors I had faced night after night for years.

I later learned that my Uncle Tommy, husband of Auntie Betty, had offered to adopt me because I was only two years younger than their daughter, Lorraine, but my mother refused to let go…

The burden of my care fell by default, upon the shoulders of the people least equipped to do it, my paternal grandfather (Granda; William Amos), aged 86 and unmarried Auntie Margaret who lived with him in a two- bedroom council house in Mastricht, at the edge of a council estate (run by the municipal government).

I liked and respected Auntie Margie and Granda, who was a staunch Scottish Nationalist who could, on occasion, tell prewar tales of Aberdeen and recite Robert Burns' epic poetry by heart. Margie had served in the war and had been stationed in Aden (present-day Yemen) and had experienced life outside Aberdeen. She worked as a secretary in a shipping company. Granda was a Freemason with three loves: Robert Burns, the Bible, and his "lady friend" Lynn, whom he would meet in town once a week for a polite dram of dark rum and return home by bus. Margie and the other sisters were quite derisive about it, but I thought it was great, considering he could hardly get out of his chair to go to the bathroom, and 30 minutes was required to hobble from the house to the bus stop 50 yards down the street. I liked the twinkle in his nearly blind blue eyes and the way he kept his full head of snow-white hair tidily crew-cut.

They got on with the burden of feeding, clothing, nurturing, and sheltering a fifteen-year-old and did quite a good job of it, too, considering the circumstances. He was a strict disciplinarian, but my aunt said he had mellowed over the past fifty years. He had worked on the railways for sixty years, renounced cigarettes that he had smoked since the age of ten, and replaced them with a pipe at the age of sixty-four years. It was a miracle to learn that he died at the age of ninety-two, not of emphysema, which he certainly had, but of accumulating stroke. Quite a character. My aunt was firm, and although I chafed at their rules, I understood their rationales for them and tried not to complain. It was a small price for a teenager to pay for a sane and stable environment.

I sat the O-level exams the following summer and passed all eight courses that I tried. You needed three higher (H-level certificates of education) and five ordinary (O-level certificates of education) levels for university entrance, so I was off to a good start. Only five each of highers and O levels were needed to enter the faculty of medicine.

However, I decided that I had had enough of being shunted around relatives and, at the age of fifteen, figured out that when I wore out my welcome with Margaret and Granda, I would have nowhere else to go. An idea formed, accelerated by an advertisement I saw in the Evening Express newspaper early in October 1968.

It was for a job as a Scientific Assistant in the Lipid Biochemistry Department at the Rowett Research Institute, just outside Aberdeen. The requirements were O (ordinary) levels in science. The successful candidate was expected to pursue further studies at Aberdeen Technical College, which would be funded by the Institute as long as the exams were passed. I didn't know what a lipid was, but I applied for the job anyway because of the magic word 'biochemistry'.

I arrived for an interview with Alan Garton, the head of the department, wearing my school uniform. I got the job. £8 a week, plus a daily lunch subsidy at the 17th-century baronial mansion owned by the Earl of Strathcona, occupied by the institute.

Sounded like a great deal. One month after my sixteenth birthday, I left my grandfather's house and moved into my own rented room in a boarding house. Finally, Independence at last!

I reasoned that there was no need to attend university if I could work in a lab and gain experience while continuing my education. After four years, I would have a higher qualification and four years of experience as opposed to the glut of university graduates with no experience competing for jobs.

So, by the age of sixteen, I was a wage earner and taxpayer, living alone and aiming for higher things. I was of the legal marrying age but not old enough to drink alcohol or to drive. I felt that I had escaped from some kind of hell, with all my parts still functional. I was cynical, but then I was cynical when I was nine years old, according to one of my primary school teachers. I had plans. I had a future. And it was going to be much better than my past.

If the boys at The Blue Lamp thought I was going to give up so easily, they had no idea what I was made of. Actually, I wasn't sure myself.

I was now in sole control of my destiny.

The boys at the Blue Lamp who thought I would give up so easily had another thought coming…

Michael Turnbull gave me a *karate gi* jacket (top part of a karate uniform 空手着). I was thrilled, even though the jacket somehow didn't seem to fit as well as everyone else's. Nevertheless, this slight of elegance was offset by the red Chinese writing embroidered on the front of it! His elder brother Robert gave me an old pair of gi pants. Someone gave me a white belt. I later found out that the Chinese characters said *kara* and *te*.

"*Doon yer body, up yer hips, aye 'at's fine Norma.*" thus spake Sensei (teacher 先生) Ronnie Watt, shodan (1st degree black belt).

Purple belt instructor Sandy M ignored me completely, as did several of the boys in the class of 20–30 students. I later discovered that they thought I was Ronnie's latest bit of fluff and would stop training as soon as Ronnie's fling with me was over.

Those who did not ignore me laughed and joked and condescended with pats on the bum and head—as if everything I did was fine. It was not, and I knew it, so I kept doggedly trying to "get it right."

9th Kyu Exam 1970

After six months of this treatment, an examiner came to Aberdeen to conduct a grading examination. Despite being late, permission was granted to attempt the 9th kyu exam. Alone. I had difficulty understanding the examiner's commands, which was obviously due to the fact that he was Japanese, and this is how these words are typically pronounced. The small but ferocious-looking man with jet-black hair scowled in my general direction and waited patiently as Ronnie translated the commands from Japanese into Scottish Japanese. Miraculously, I passed the test, and it was not until I presented my little red Karate Union of Great Britain (KUGB) record book for signing that I realized that the examiner was not Japanese at all but Andy Sherry. Also, the reason I did not understand his commands was his wickedly nasal Liverpool accent!

We were training in the "62 Club", a downscale social club patronized by bikers wearing black leather and tattoos describing their loved and hated ones. The location was not well-suited for maintaining members or attracting new ones, and Ronnie's club began to dwindle, with only about five members, including me. Since space was very difficult and too expensive to rent for training, he decided that there was only one thing to do.

We were going to merge with the notorious John Allan, of dubious personal reputation and inferior karate skills.

John was about ten years older than Ronnie and a nidan (2nd degree black belt).

Boy, I was scared.

Sensei John Allen

John was about 5'5", a little, wiry mass of bone and sinew. He had survived the usual dysfunctional home, a target of much violence and destruction.

He had boxed in a circus booth for £1 a fight, win or lose. He usually lost. His adult life was a vicious circle of employment in jobs that bored his mind or wore out his body, followed by unemployment, followed by despair, alcohol, drugs, suicide attempts, rescue, rehabilitation, and yet another mindless job. Although he actually possessed a quite formidable intellect, he left school at the age of thirteen, so he had no formal academic qualifications. He loathed manual labour, which was one of the few jobs available to him but for which he was physically unsuited, and factory jobs numbed his mind. He had been married at least three times and had children somewhere he was unable to support, but he was currently married to Yvonne, an attractive, intelligent, and compassionate socialist whose pale skin, black hair, and green eyes suggested Celtic ancestry. Many voiced the opinion that she was wasting her life with John, as she had all sorts of potential, being a university student and was at least fifteen years younger than him. However, she was compassionate and a good match for John's thwarted intellect.

In the early 1960s, John started judo as he quit the boxing booth and looked for some other way of protecting himself. Unfortunately, this was not a great success, as he kept breaking all sorts of bones rather easily.

But judo piqued an interest in Japanese martial arts, and he was thrilled to discover a book about karate. He diligently studied this book, and when Hirokazu Kanazawa of the JKA visited Scotland in 1964, he gave John a 6th kyu and fixed his Japanese pronunciation. John found that "*age uke*" was not pronounced "agg ook" after all and that *mae geri* was not "may jerry".

By 1970, he seemed quite menacing. Brown button eyes in a Crocodile Dundee face would X-ray you. When tiny John entered a *dōjō* wearing a gi, far bigger and tougher men would suddenly tense, lower their stance, straighten their backs, and correct whatever imaginary fault they thought John was pointing out. Such fearsome charisma!

I watched him teach. He had long, low movements that required considerable flexibility and strength. He was strict but has had charisma that made it all acceptable. His teaching and technical style were completely different from Ronnie's, and he possessed a depth of knowledge that spoke to experience beyond that of anyone in the class. Whatever it was, I wanted to train and study with him because I felt that he could take me further than Ronnie at the time.

Ronnie was still not thrilled about the idea of merging. The clash of egos and personalities was a little too much.

I asked if I could join John's club.

John's face tightened up, and he scowled at me as though I had uttered some unspeakable curse.

"No." John replied sternly.

"Well, can I watch the class?"

"Certainly." He replied.

After weeks of watching, I started to ask him again every class. Same answer. Then, one day, when he was probably getting tired of having this blind spot in the corner of his eye, I asked again.

"Please, can I practice here?"

"No."

"Why?" I pressed further.

"Nae women in my dōjō" he said.

"Why not?" I asked.

"They wouldna' put up wi' it."

"Eh???"

"Would distract the men," he said.

"In a gi??" I asked.

"You don't know anything about karate."

"I have been training for six months already. I am a 9th kyu."

"No changing rooms for women."

"Is there a toilet"? I asked.

"Yes."

"If I change in the toilet, can I train?" I asked again.

"Oh, for heaven's sake, I suppose so." Finally, he gave in.

That was the most he had said directly to me for weeks.

The Invisible Student

John was a perfectionist who corrected everyone in the class .... except me.

He walked down the line of about 30 people, from black belt to white, giving everyone feedback. Come to me, he would do a U-turn.

But I could learn from him. If he fixed someone's retracted fist position, I would alter my own. If he adjusted another person's stance a fraction, I adjusted mine. This instruction by proxy continued for another three months. I paid the *dōjō* fees, and I showed up for class three times a week. I could see that John did not like Ronnie any more than he liked me, though it had to have been for different reasons. Ronnie chafed at training under someone he clearly did not respect. So, I had work to do.

8th and 7th Kyu (grade) exams

The 8th Kyu test was finally administered by a genuine Japanese instructor. His name was Sakunosuke. Wow! Real Japanese sounded nothing at all like Andy Sherry.

I passed, but this grade was not indicated by a color. Not serious enough, so I began to clearly visualize a target, over and above simply proving something to the boys.

I aimed for 6th kyu Green Belt, then I would quit, having surpassed Gail and proven myself to me and the boys.

I continued trying to fix my errors based on John's indirect correction, and on December 21, 1971, Andy Sherry made another of those profitable sweeps through the Northeast of Scotland and passed me for 7th kyu.

Yellow Belt!!! For a Christmas present and personal award of achievement, I decided to buy myself a Tokaido gi. It had to be ordered from London as there were no gi suppliers in Aberdeen. In fact, I do not think there were any gi suppliers in the whole of Scotland. The gi cost £ 6.15, which was over 80% of my weekly wage, and it took three weeks to deliver. This milestone was also commemorated by inheriting a Yellow Belt from Tom Byrne, secretary of the club, who had just passed his 5th kyu, Purple Belt. I gave him my white belt, and he dyed it purple. The only way to get colored belts was to dye them yourself, and the only way to get a black belt was for a Japanese person to give you one.

Colored belts were much respected in those days, not only because they indicated slow progression up the kyu ladder but also because they were handed down to you by a senior in the hierarchy. It was a great thrill to receive an old belt from someone you really respected. When Robert T passed his Shodan, Hirokazu Kanazawa gave him a belt. Robert then went about proudly saying that is *Kanazawa's belt*. I remember thinking that it was terrifically kind of Mr. Kanazawa to give Robert his belt, as the thought never occurred to any of us then that he might have more than one belt or students other than Robert. Later, I met several people with the same claim, so I concluded that Kanazawa must have had an awful amount of belts to be giving them away like candy. About twenty years after that, Kanazawa told me that people used to steal his belts all the time, so he never had one long enough for it to become ratty. So, he only wore a plain black belt without his name embroidered on it.

Nice chance to reflect upon the paradox of showing your respect for a man by stealing his belt.

Finally, real training

I trained for Green Belt in deadly earnest. Training in rough wood floors worn smooth as ice and just as cold (St Katherine's Hall), stone floors, 19th Century primary schools, church halls built in the 18th Century, grit and splinters, just about anywhere. Frozen in winter and not even warm in summer. The quest was always "to Find a Hall."

John decided that I really was serious about training after all and started to include me in his teaching vista. The 7th kyu and Tokaido karateka were the outward symbols of *"Serious Training"* and I had achieved the standard investment milestones: identifiable effort in and money parted with.

I never realized everything I did was so wrong! Every single movement I made had several problems. Not enough kite (decisive moment when a technique impacts a target with maximum physiological force combined with mental focus 決め), stance too short, punch too weak, feet not fast enough, everything off target, blocks too slow, kick retraction too slow, arse sticking out. Why couldn't I do a back stance like him? But I loved it. I persevered because this was what I had asked for. The right to the same treatment as the male members of the *dōjō*.

6th Kyu Green Belt April 1972

Happily, I swapped my yellow belt for a white one belonging to someone who had just passed yellow belt. The following day, at lunchtime, I rushed to the haberdashery shop and, after much deliberation, selected just the right shade of emerald with which to dye the belt. The remainder of the lunch hour was spent in the lab immersing the belt in a 5-liter conical flask containing bright yellow dye and boiling it over a Bunsen burner in the fume cupboard. After it reached saturation, the dye was fixed in a cold diluted solution of acetic acid. The belt was rinsed and dried in the glassware oven. It was important to get the dying process just right, otherwise your gi would develop a ring of tie-dye around the waist and hip so that a belt was not required to advertise your level of competence.

After the fact finally sunk in that I had just achieved my objective, and I could challenge the dizzy heights of Heian Yondan (The fourth of five *kata* [forms] required to pass belt rank exams) apprehension kicked in. You have done it Norm, give it up now while you're ahead. How could you remember the sequences of all those *kata?* How is it possible to do a whole *kata* in horse stance, namely the *Tekki kata* required for Brown belt? More mountains are seen from the top of the one just climbed. Yet, Heian Yondan seemed like fun, and what was the point of worrying about horse stances when I might never get past Heian Godan (The fifth *kata* required to pass belt rank exams), a requirement for one of the two Purple Belt levels between Green and Brown.

Maybe I could set a new target. I was the first female to hold a Karate Green Belt in the city, an achievement significant enough to be reported by the Press and Journal, Aberdeen's morning newspaper.

Maybe I could even aim as far as Brown Belt. After all, since there were three grades of Brown Belt, no one would really have to know if you were a 3rd kyu, or nearly an awesome BLACK BELT! On the other hand, a Black Belt seemed too high to reach, as those wearing them were very rare. Maybe a Brown Belt would be doable.

Acceptance

By then, I was one of the boys. I went to the pub with the club members after training, and they became quite protective, as though I represented a fragile trophy. Yet they seemed a little confused as to how to really deal with it all, as if my being among some of them somehow devalued their images in karate. After all, if a wee girl of 5'2" could progress, it could not be that difficult, dangerous, or macho after all. But generally, I was accepted. I had passed the tests for entry into this—hitherto exclusively male domain and was quite comfortable in it.

There was no active recruiting for new people, no advertising, and we behaved like a cult that knew special secrets. People came to us; we did not go to them. Advertising was bad form; it was rather considered as boasting. We wore no badges, had no club name, sought no spotlights. Karate was not even discussed unless it was with other practitioners. It was just avoided, as in:

"Farr ye gan 'e'nicht Robbie?"

"Ahm awa' tae ma Trainin'"

Eventually, it became known as the Aberdeen Karate Club as opposed to Ronnie's Scottish Shotokan Association, which later underwent an *Enoeda*-inspired name change and mushroomed into a very successful business. That was really the fundamental difference in philosophy between John, who wanted intellectual exclusivity and uniqueness, and Ronnie, who wanted a way out of the factory with something identifiable, tangible, and growable. In a way, one could say that Ronnie represented early organized sport, whereas John represented tradition.

John's club eventually constructed crude membership cards, and we always had a spiffy red "license" book with a rising sun symbol on it. It said KUGB, and the joke was that it was a "license to kill" issued by the KGB. Into this book was the signature of the examining instructors along with the dates upon which grades were achieved, records of courses attended, and a "license" receipt that showed you were a fully paid-up member of the KUGB. It all seemed very selective and added to the sense of membership in an exotic Eastern cult. The list of spaces for recording grades started at 9th kyu and ended at 3rd Dan. I had two concerns about this at the time. One was that there must be a joke in leaving that much space, as a 3rd Dan was as rare a sight as bikinis in winter, let alone a female 3rd Dan. The second was the notion that somehow, no one who held this license could ever pass beyond 3rd Dan, since the ceiling was already defined. I could imagine groups of Japanese designing a record book for *Enoeda's* organization and deciding that no Brit could ever understand enough to progress beyond 3rd Dan (3rd degree black belt). Indeed, no one at that time training under the JKA system in Scotland had achieved this rank

Our club membership card had socio-cultural merit. The JKA has this high moral tone in its *dōjō* kun:

Jin kaku kansei nitsutomeru koto!

Makoto no michi o mamoru koto!

Doryoku no seishin o yashinau koto!

Reigi o omonzuru koto!

Keki no yu imashimeru koto!

Karate ni sentenashi!

Roughly translated as:

Seek to perfect your character

Follow the way of truth

Be faithful

Respect others

Control your emotions

Never attack first.

Although followers of the same school, our *dōjō* rules were:

No smoking, swearing, chewing gum or spitting inside the dōjō.

Self-defense

John decided to start teaching me self-defense. I hated it. I was only getting taught this because I was a girl. No man in the class ever practiced anything as feeble as self-defense! I wanted to learn *kata* and *kumite* skills, not the graceless maiming skills that seemed to be the focus at the time. I just couldn't get the hang of the alien's twists and turns and close body contact. Also, the stuff could not be practiced as no-one wanted to be my partner because it was obviously *girruls stuff*, like eating vegetables, or drinking cocktails, and not suitable fare for fighting men of the tartan (patterned cloth [originally fine wool] consisting of horizontal and vertical bands of different colors. Represents Scottish clans, families, or regions. What kilts are made of). However, John persisted, and I figured I should at least learn some self-defense, as it looked like I might stay the course after all and actually reach a stage in the examination process where a choice between free fighting and self-defense would be given to demonstrate understanding of applications. Men were not offered this choice at that time.

I was rather lackadaisical in practicing my virtual self-defense routines without help from the class. Anyway, I could not understand how it could be practiced effectively, without causing serious harm to the "attacker." How would you know if it would work? John realized this and said that he was going to grab me in a choke hold as fast and hard as he could, and he was not going to let go until I executed something potentially lethal. I believed him. I did everything he told me, in the sequence and manner that he desired.

As he told me, I thrust one hand over the front of his neck, and the other behind his knees, and dumped him on his head.

He did not tell me to break his neck.

End of self-defense training.

It was not the first time John's neck had been broken, but I didn't know that at the time. We were a very cruel crowd. After rushing comatose karate instructor from practice to the hospital with a broken neck, and seeing that he was going to be OK with a cast for a few months, the jokes could not stop flowing.

"Wee Norm broke Johnny's neck? Gwa!"

"Aye! She did that!"

"Dinna be stupit. Ah thocht kara'e wiz aboot breakin bricks, nae heeds."

"Aye, but John's nae affa smart. His heid's thicker 'an ony brick."

And other flashes of black humor.

John suffered from depression and ventured deeper into drugs as a way to combat alcoholism, and became suicidal. During his teenage years, he had a history of depression and had spent some time in and out of psychiatric hospitals. It was not unusual to drop by his apartment and find him comatose in front of an unlit gas fire that filled a tiny room with lethal odors. Nor was visiting him in Kingseat psychiatric hospital, where he would be given therapy and released upon visible signs of attitude improvement. One such sign was when he started teaching karate to some of the more able inmates of the hospital. He ran a class there once for several months, and some of the staff even joined in.

Street application: a normal Saturday afternoon in Union St., Aberdeen

A bright sunny Saturday afternoon—a rather rare spectacle in Aberdeen. We had tumbled out of the Star and Garter pub at closing time, to go shopping, strut up and down the main street of the city, have tea in the Falkland restaurant about 4 p.m., where essentially the same people we had met for drinks with at lunch time, would gather again, to catch up on any news they had missed during the last two hours.

On my way back to the Star & Garter, I felt a tug at my left shoulder. Someone is trying to steal my shoulder bag! Without thinking, I stepped to the right, raised my left hand, and blindly arced the edge of it down in the general direction of a groin, somewhere behind me and to my left.

A karate chop! Contact! Bingo!

Scream!

Success! I had just successfully defended myself against a pickpocket!

Wrong. The screaming finally became coherent. My name seemed to be part of it. A slow turn with great trepidation and revealed friend Waldo, also on his way back to the Star & Garter, staggering about with his hands cradling the bit where his legs joined the rest of him.

Tears in his eyes.

"Ach Norma, I wiz only joking."

I was mortified. What could I do to help? Apologies just were not enough, and I certainly couldn't do anything for the afflicted parts. Fortunately, the pain was not totally crippling, and by 4 pm, the entire Falkland restaurant staff greeted me with a smile when I walked in. I felt pretty bad and embarrassed, but when Waldo arrived, he was razzed even more for letting wee Norma stop him in his tracks. Fortunately, Waldo was a good sport, no doubt partly because his reproductive capacity remained intact and many a chuckle was enjoyed over the incident.

I learned that self-defense could be dangerously effective when applied correctly, and although my response was trained, I had reacted instinctively. That is, a lack of decision-making before action. Later, I learned that this event had shown me exactly what I had learned, and the effect that training had on my responses. Two years of training and a month studying one specific sequence? Scary stuff, as I couldn't subjectively tell if I had changed, progressed, regressed, or was just fooling myself about learning in the controlled *dōjō*, working in reality. Another situation involving self-defense arose ten years later, with results that were quite different.

I still dislike self-defense training. I find it extremely difficult to be realistic, and if it is practiced "safely", then I think it can lead to a false sense of security. Furthermore, I do not believe that any style of karate, if practiced in a classical manner, is useful for self-defense. After all, we spent a lot of time smacking air or well-muscled targets with closed fists rather than worrying at soft spots with open hands and not a *mot* about pressure points, cause and effect, or nerve endings.

Better strategy against two lads from Glasgow

Another opportunity for some local survival choices came around late on an autumn Friday night. I had caught the last bus home alone as usual. Two boys from Glasgow jumped off the bus at the same time and took up positions on either side of me. At that time, Glasgow had a reputation for being the most violent, dangerous, and volatile city in Scotland, and two syllables of a Glasgow accent were enough to summon goose bumps and vertical hairs.

"Fair ye gan hen?"

"Some place different from you."

I looked at each of them straight in the eye and figured out the what-ifs.

They were not much bigger than me, so physically speaking, I was not too afraid of either of them. But their accents conjured up rape and pillage. And they were two, and I was one.

"Ach, cumoan hen. Why no jist invite us up tae yer hoose fur a wee bit o' fun."

"I don't think so."

With all the hauteur, the full 157 cm and an Edinburgh accent could muster, I continued walking, mind churning and scheming.

If I get to my stair door and they are still here I will exhaust them by walking and walking until they become bored with the lack of desired response.

Don't fumble for key right now, they will seize the opportunity and know you live nearby.

If you make it to the door, run like the wind up the three flights of stairs.

Damn. Where is the key.

Hah. It's in your right pocket.

Hold onto it tightly and use as a weapon.

They continued walking and taunting. I looked up to the top of the corner tenement. They followed my gaze and spied a light and a figure in the window.

"Whatr yi lookin at hen?"

"Is that yer maun in there about tae beat us up? Ha ha ha . . ."

A chance worth grabbing.

I responded with a precise snobbish Edinburgh accent Maggie Smith portrayed in the movie entitled The Prime of Miss Jean Brodie (1961); Ts crossed, I's dotted.

Well, actually, my boyfriend might not like it if I came home with two new boyfriends. I really do not know what he might do.

The two discussed my future and decided to "let me off" because they had better things to do after all (they were afraid of who might be waiting for me) up there by the window. Which was just as well. The figure they saw framed in the window three stories up was that of a wax 1930s half mannequin that I had bought at an antique auction. Her ruby lips parted in a smile just wide enough to show her perfect porcelain teeth, and her new ling blond wig beautifully complemented her big blue eyes.

Training Methods in Aberdeen-early 1970s

We had no books, videos, magazines, or examples about karate other than publication "Karate and Oriental Arts" (KOA), which occasionally made its way as far as the Northeast of Scotland. It regularly featured the Red Triangle boys from Liverpool, Andy Sherry, Steve Cattle, Terry O'Neill, and people who seemed to do odd things like Ticky Donovan from London, or Hamish Adam, who was in Edinburgh. There was a woman too, called Pauline Fuller, who was a nidan in the KUGB. She had blond waist-length hair, but it was black at the top, and she seemed to be built like a truck. She had a space between her front teeth, and she looked mean and physically powerful. An article about her in The Times said, "she could have her teeth drilled without the needle". I believed it. A fearsome woman. I wondered whether it was a function of training with Mr. Enoeda.

We would not have conceived of studying the coaching or teaching methods of other sports, as what we were doing was so far removed from coaching mere sport. Still unique, exotic, Japanese.

A little magazine was how I discovered what the boys from the Blue Lamp really meant when they uttered Japanese-sounding words. Noida was *Enoeda,* and washing was *mawashi geri.* The Doric tongue did not sit well with the mysterious Japanese argot of karate. I learned that what Hamish Adam did was called Wadō Ryū, and what we did was called Shotokan. Not a bad realization after about three years of training. There was also something called Taekwondo, and practitioners of this wore strange gi with a black diagonal strip on the folding edge. They did a lot of stuff for charity, such as thousands of push-ups or sit-ups, or demolishing a building with bare hands and feet. I asked Ronnie what Taekwondo was. *Mickey Mouse kara'e.* Well, that explained everything. I had been training for about three years before I discovered that there were apparently other ways of doing the same thing. I had just thought we were practicing karate. Now, I took some kind of pride in the new knowledge that I was practicing not just mere karate, but Shotokan! No Minnie Mouse was I, and Ms. Fuller couldn't possibly be mistaken for anything cute!

Training in karate at that time was barbaric. Some students had to leave class for the hospital with ripped tendons and other horrors. We bounced like Tigger and were punished with bunny hops, walking around the gym in a low front stance while bearing the weight of someone on your shoulders who outweighed you. Even Japanese Shotokan instructors of the 60s and 70s all graduated from Takudai with bachelor's degrees in economics. They were inexperienced new graduates of the JKA

Instructor program, used to bullying younger Japanese undergrads with physical power, flexibility, stoicism, and a militaristic hierarchy of belt ranks that nurtured culturally imprinted stupidity. We did not realize we were being bullied. After all, we were busy being samurai, and that meant we were warriors. We were perfect fodder for these newly minted godan (5th degree black belts).

All our social lives still revolved around the pub, so every day found us drinking many rounds of something alcoholic and smoking packs of cigarettes. What was that doing to us while we smugly considered ourselves fit? Now we know otherwise. At least if one wishes to live that way now, it is an informed choice. But it was just peer pressure. This quasi-militaristic type of training, coupled with that lifestyle, doubtlessly hindered rather than progressed our understanding of karate.

We were also very insular, never receiving any other input but the JKA of Takudai, who encouraged us in our excesses. We were serious, committed, and unique. Samurai of Scotland. Only Ronnie W. would socialize without drinking. Of all of us, he really had the best ideas. We thought he was loony at the time. He went on a brown rice diet. He would lose weight, refuse proffered drinks (usually a social no-no in Scotland), and talk endlessly about kara'e and women. Mostly karate. He was never overweight to begin with, so we all thought he was just daft. But oh yes, he was truly serious. He lived for HIS karate.

His father later collapsed and died of a heart attack at work around the age of 54 .... and Ronnie looked a lot like him.

Ronnie shared a two-bedroom flat with his parents in Woolmanhill, opposite a paper mill where he worked. The tenement had outside toilets on each landing that were shared by two families.

However, Ronnie's half of the flat was full of dreams that were somewhere far from the mill. Ronnie was fascinated by the Orient as his part of the Back Room. Japanese swords, fans, symbols, any books about samurai or Japan, a model of the WW II battleship, Yamato, sailing on top of his mum's China cabinet. All this fought for supremacy with Marilyn Monroe, tigers (Enoeda, the tiger of Shotokan), and a huge bedspread with a tiger print. His mum's decor included glass and ceramic knick-knacks and bright colors that differed among the floral carpet, wallpaper, curtains, doilies, and good China. The 14 ft2 room was cluttered and bursting at the seams.

But I was so grateful to have a room over my head, and I will never forget the warmth and kindness of Ronnie's parents. They slept in an alcove in the Front Room in which a kettle boiled over a fire, and about a 6 ft2 area served as a kitchen. Ronnie occupied the Back Room. Ronnie, always chivalrous, slept on the floor during my occupancy. Despite their living situation, they acted in a way that none of my family members were able to do.

Shoto, the Siamese cat, would occasionally deign to appear and elegantly ignore the clash of culture and colour that Ronnie returned home to every night. Ronnie stirred up considerable dismay in deciding to stop working at the mill and teach karate "professionally." He finally split from John, taking with him, not a lot of supporters. Ronnie seemed driven by a profound need to better himself socially, economically, and aesthetically.

Karate in Aberdeen was associated with a "blue collar mentality". More than one person questioned what on earth I could be getting out of such a low-class activity. John once said that he found it difficult to teach at the university, where he had just opened a club, because people kept asking questions and wanted to intellectualize and analyze karate instead of just training.

Looking at the *dōjō* membership, there were few professionals among us, or even people with pretensions of becoming professionals. For the most part, we were indeed a class of workers. Karate was cheap. One gi could last a long time, perhaps partly because it was often too cold to sweat, and the gi was never washed often because you had to go to the laundry. Who had a washing machine in their house? Regardless, Karate was affordable, and those who persevered seemed not to be the intellectual movers and shakers of the city.

This all changed with the movie "Enter the Dragon", our introduction to a martial art created by Bruce Lee called Jeet Kune Do, which was not Shotokan Karate.

History! Culture! Asian Mystery!

Suddenly, people wanted to join Karate clubs. It didn't matter that Shotokan was nothing like Jeet Kune Do; they wanted to understand how to gracefully fight evil and embrace Eastern philosophy. Karate *dōjō* started to fill up with beginners from a far broader socio-economic spectrum and educational level than ever before.

But they were still all men.

Training at Crystal Palace 1973

I began to think that maybe I should venture down to London and worship at the Shrine of British Shotokan, the summer course at Crystal Palace. I also wanted to compare myself as I had seen nothing other than Yvonne in Aberdeen, so I had no way of really knowing for sure whether my little red KUGB book represented anything real compared with other karate practitioners in the UK. The first week was a study of all aspects of karate, and the second mainly concentrated on *kata*. I asked John about whether or not I should go and voiced concerns over my puny level of Brown Belt. Would I be comparable to Brown Belts from other parts of the country? I had only Sakunosuke's opinion that I was a 2nd kyu, no other women and no men outside my *dōjō* for comparison. I was a little apprehensive about going all the way down to London just to find that what I had learned wasn't sufficient, and that I should really be a yellow belt or just give up.

John rather grimly replied with narrowed flinty eyes that anybody training in his *dōjō* had nothing to fear regarding standards and that I would be just as good, if not better than anyone wearing a Brown Belt at Crystal Palace. I did not quite believe him, but his attitude towards my question was reassuring enough to secure a space at the Crystal Palace residence.

The crowd at Crystal Palace, the U.K. National Sports Centre, was awesome. There were over 300 people there for the sole purpose of practicing karate, and the instructors were all those legendary names I had only read about in KOA! There were even women! In fact, there was Pauline Fuller in the flesh, with a baby no less, whose husband, Ray, looked after in the stands. She would go and feed it and take care of it during breaks! I had never seen such behaviour. She was the only woman among the group called Sandan (3rd degree black belt) and above. She was simultaneously fearsome and inspiring. There was Steve Cattle, Terry O' Neill, Keinosuke Enoeda, and other names I had only seen in print, such as Asano, Kaze, Shirai, and Ochi. Blue Belts! I had never seen a Blue Belt before. Wondered what they were.

I was invited to see a Japanese movie with all the instructors. It was called Tora-san. This was a comedy about a Japanese man nicknamed "Tora" which means "tiger" I could laugh at all the right bits without subtitles. No one could understand why. I explained that the movie did not require understanding of the Japanese language, as it was rather obvious and slapstick. Unfortunately, all the instructors of the course went to a Japanese restaurant, where I had the distinct feeling that I was on show for the general amusement of the group. See this young girl from Aberdeen. She is simple and stupid and has never been to a Japanese restaurant before. Watch this. And with a sly look, something unspeakable was ordered from the sushi bar and plunked in front of me, and I was told:

"Hora!" You eat.

I shrugged, picked up the chopsticks, dipped a piece of this unknown substance into some soy sauce, and put it in my mouth. I chewed it and chewed it until I could finally swallow it while exercising every vestige of self-control not to gag, throw up, and keep a straight face. All were shocked.

"Hah! You eat?"

"Yes, I eat."

"You know what it is?"

"Octopus," I replied.

"How do you know?"

I point to the octopus on the ice behind the glass at the sushi counter.

Naive, perhaps, but not totally stupid.

"You like?"

"No"!

They were also amazed that I was adept with chopsticks. Well, that was because I had practiced picking up individual peas and grains of rice from Cha Ho Fan served by the local Chinese carry-out at every chance I could get.

I loved the training at Crystal Palace and the gatherings afterward. Accents from different parts of the country and a wealth of anecdotes. It was more than reading a tabloid. I also went with Ronnie to see Raymond's Revue Bar, of Penthouse magazine fame. Ronnie was an avid subscriber to the publication. Debbie does Dallas, Paula does Paris, and Ronnie does Crystal Palace.

Disrespectful stories circulated like used pound notes and were terrifically funny. A great deal of those were concerned with the level of English spoken by these Japanese gods and their ability to make people shake with fear. This is a typical anecdote.

At Crystal Palace, Enoeda taught approximately 100 brown belts Tekki Shodan, a kata performed exclusively with lateral movement from a single stance, known as Kiba Dachi, or the horse-riding stance. The last movement consists of a double fist strike or a simultaneous left middle-level block and right-hand strike, depending upon the interpretation. Regardless, the *kata* finishes in the same horse-riding stance (like a squat, with feet facing forward) with both arms extended towards the right, with the face turned precisely towards the right. Approximately 99 people were posing in something like that, but one individual had the stance correct, although his head was turned to the left.

Enoeda, the feared Tiger of Shotokan, padded stealthily up to the gentleman and told him to:

"Change yooa hace."

Unfortunately, English was not this person's native language either, so he had no idea what Enoeda wanted him to do.

Enoeda scowled at him and repeated his command.

No reaction.

Enoeda began to lose patience, and sweat started trickling down the poor fellow's face as his legs began to shake (as well as those of 218 other legs) due to holding the low squat for too long. He was so overcome by fear and desperate to do whatever Enoeda wanted, if only he could figure it out.

Enoeda put his own face about one inch from that of the man and started a low-pitched growl that rapidly reached a deafening howl and barked once more:

"CHANGE YOOAH HACE!!!"

By now, all the other brown belts were having a hard time maintaining their stances and controlling their impulses to burst out laughing, glad it wasn't happening to them. But they dared not laugh in case Enoeda singled them out for some kind of nasty punishment before their legs gave out with tension.

The long-suffering, humiliated brown belt started to rearrange his features into something between a tentative smile and a grimace, which clearly mortified Enoeda.

He decided that he would never be able to get this person to understand his English, so he employed a different method of communication.

He slapped the brown belt's face with sufficient force to turn it 180° to the right. Satisfied with the kill, Enoeda, the Tiger of Shotokan, walked away bellowing.

"I awreddy say you tree time: CHANGE YOOAH HACE!"

I tried the 2nd kyu test at the end of the first week with about 50 other people and passed it, confirming what John said was true, considering that I dared present myself for an examination only two months after passing 3rd kyu. A new signature on my grading record is that of the Tiger himself. And on the right side of the book!! None of my fellow Aberdonians passed their exams. Ronnie and Brian were attempting 2nd-degree black belt exams, and they were not happy about failing. My elation at being a rung higher up the ladder to Shodan (1st degree black belt) had to be suppressed all the way to his home in north west England, as Sakunosuke decided that he could save us all money by driving us halfway home in his Jaguar. That journey was quite possibly the most oppressive experience this newly minted 2nd Kyu had ever encountered. Being crammed into a car for five hours with such dismally depressed and gloomy people rendered keeping my mouth shut and my face straight was even more difficult than swallowing an octopus.

We spent the night at his home, where his collection of Japanese swords was matched only by his collection of Scotch whisky and other potables. He ordered us all to drink. None of us drank whisky and had no clue what sake was.

Ronnie, you no good. Drink. You fail. You rubbish. More training, better getting."

"Brian, Keith, you same. Drink. You happy getting."

"Norma. Drink. You very happy you pass."

So, we all consumed hot sake prepared by his wife, Haruko. Ronnie did not consume alcohol, Brian liked beer, and I would drink brandy with lemonade (7-UP). But, no escape. Haruko walked into the room bearing an untouched bottle of cognac and filled a half-pint glass with it. I did not usually drink straight cognac, but could handle a sip or two… but the one sip of the hot sake was nauseating. During the night, I was too weak to get out of a cot that lay 6 inches off the floor, and ended up filling several of the empty pint mugs strewn all over the floor with gastrointestinal contents. We all boarded a train for Glasgow and Aberdeen with hangovers and green faces, and I never touched sake (until 40 years later in an unscheduled initiation ceremony for Shindō Yōshin Ryū Jiu Jitsu), nor, for that matter, much brandy.

Hirokazu Kanazawa   Hidetaka Nishiyama   Masatoshi Nakayama   Keinosuke Enoeda

Shiro Asano   Hiroshi Shirai   Taiji Kase

I trained with these JKA instructors at seminars. Signatures from three of them are in my KUGB license and record book.

Abuse of power and vulnerability 1973

Two months later, the communal phone rang in the corridor outside the lab, and someone came running in, shouting that I had received a long-distance phone call from a foreigner. I had no idea what it could be about or who. I became a bit apprehensive, as the last time a "foreigner" had called, it was the Royal Infirmary in Edinburgh telling me that my mother had been admitted with several stab wounds, one of which had punctured her lung. I had enquired as to her condition, and her attending physician assured me that she would be released by the end of the week. Upon discovering that Mrs. Amos did not know how she acquired the wounds, I decided not to go to Edinburgh to visit her, as it all indicated a downward slope, I did not wish to be involved in.

However, the voice on the phone belonged to Sakunosuke, and he said

"You going, Sweden?"

"I don't think so." (I earned £10 each week and paid £6 for rent). I laughed. Preposterous.

"No. You going Sweden"

"No, I don't going Sweden. What kind of joke is this? I don't even going Stonehaven (15 miles away), never mind Sweden."

"Why no going Sweden?" He asked.

"I laughed. Please be serious. NO MONEY. NO REASON"

"I pay," he said.

"I laughed. For what?"

"Training course. You go Sweden Monday," he said.

"I laughed. Can't. No money and No passport." (it was Wednesday, and I had never been outside the UK).

"Get passport," he ordered.

"It takes six weeks," I replied.

"Get short time passport. Easy getting. Only one day," he said.

"Who else is going?" I asked.

"Steve Cattle and Sandy Hopkins. You go. I already fix from London. You only pay Aberdeen London."

I didn't know whether to laugh or cry. This was insane. I was a lowly 3rd kyu. Why take me to Sweden? Sandy was famous for kata and winning the KUGB national championships, and Steve was already a noted practitioner with many titles under his 3rd Dan belt. Sakunosuke had been married to Haruko for a short time, and they had just had a baby girl. Presumably, he was happily married.

Haruko was beautiful, charming, dignified, and reserved. No one knew what she was suffering, how Japanese marriage works, or what their relationships were like

"Why not take Haruko?" I asked.

"She only wife."

Sakunosuke had sent me, about a month or so before this, a postcard from Ireland, where he had been teaching a seminar. He had drawn a cartoon Japanese face with slanted eyes and buck teeth, smoking a cigarette, and wearing a WW II helmet. He had also written something on it, and I did not know what it meant or what language it was. I was horrified when I learned the meaning, but I thought that people do not commit words like that to paper if they are not sincere.

Still holding the phone, I mused over the expectations implicit in this offer. I understood. I would have my way paid to Sweden for two weeks so that I could train in their summer course at Malmö, and was expected to get a passport, take two weeks off work, train every day, and have a chance to see something of Scandinavia Hmmm.

"OK. I'll go if I can get time off work and if I can get a passport."

I hoped that it would not happen.

I put down the phone. Think about this. Are you willing to pay the price?

Wow! Sweden. Oh my god, what have you done? Ah, to hell with naysayers.

So, I went.

Photographs show a slightly uncomfortable, very young-looking girl with bell-bottomed pants, high platformed Mr. Freedom boots, and a face hiding behind an enormous pair of Christian Dior sunglasses. Traveling with Steve and Sandy was no slice of cake either. I knew that both he and Sandy had classified me as inferior for at least three reasons:

I was Scottish, not English.

I was a mere brown belt.

I had incorrect table manners.

"Why don't you cut your steak with the fork, piercing the portion of meat that will remain on it after you have cut it from the larger piece with the knife? That way, you will not have to spear the meat twice because you cut the larger portion first".

Typical of humiliating meals with Steve Cattle.

Embarrassed and chastened, I had nothing to say because he was a Sandan, my Sempai (senior). He was arrogant and condescending.

I had the chance to remind Steve of this about 20 years later when he was a 6th *Dan* authority and taught a seminar in Vancouver, Canada. He laughed and said he had no memory of it, but that it sounded like him. And that if he could not spout his opinions, he'd probably be dead because that was part of his being Steve. Ironic that Steve died in 1995 on a train on the way to class. He had suffered an epileptic seizure and choked on his tongue. Poetic justice?

However, in 1973, I did not know that Steve was nicknamed Stumpy due to his not being very tall. We alighted from the ferry at Ostend and drove in the Jaguar to Hamburg, where we all spent the night in the home of a person called Kawasaki, whom Sakunosuke knew from university. This person did not study karate. But first, we had to eat pizza and walk down the Reeperbahn, the red-light district of Hamburg. My parochial eyes were shocked at the overtness of it all. Scantily clad women demonstrating their wares in ground-level windows, Lewd and noisy and alive with guttural German voices. Sakunosuke seemed in his element, but Sandy and I were uncomfortable with it all.

The next morning, we drove through Germany to Darmstadt. Sakunosuke found the German word for exit, *"Ausfahrt"* highly amusing, and kept erupting in convulsive laughter every time he passed a freeway exit. This was rather often, considering we were cruising along autobahns at speeds that varied between 100 and 140 miles per hour. None of us Brits felt very safe…

We boarded a ferry for Malmo on the other side of the Baltic Sea. Visions of Vikings. How does Swedish sound? What do they eat? How will we understand them?

"Just Ossu enough."

"What exactly is the meaning of Ossu, sensei?"

"Karate training people saying Good morning. Cheers. Hello. How do you do. All Ossu."

"Pushing spirit. Ossu."

"Right. I see. Thank you, sensei."

The Swedish summer course was the first time I had ever trained outdoors. It was the first time I saw men and women changing in the same rooms, such tall women! Marguerite, a striking girl wearing a green belt, was around 6'3". Other "firsts" included drinking instead of spooning yogurt, gambling in a casino, seeing four countries in two days, learning the kata *Chinte* (unusual hands 珍手), and an informal, but structured competition.

I was not happy about this friendly competition among the participants. I was looking forward to watching the kata event. A kind of small reward, relaxing and watching the competitors toe the line, two by two, and perform whatever *Heian* (calm/peaceful mind 平安) *kata* (form 型) that Sakunosuke picked out of a hat. The judges would raise red or white flags according to their choice of the winner. I would see real kumite matches according to the Rules.

Just before the colored belt kata competition, I was shocked to hear my name being called out. I did not enter my name for this, and I had no intentions of competing. I was not in a calm, peaceful mindset. I waved my arms to indicate "no". Not me. I am NOT doing this.

"You must" said Sandy, who would, of course, perform a flawless performance of *Kanku Dai* (viewing the sky 観空 big or large 大) in the finals, and a mere 3rd kyu really had no business refusing to demonstrate incompetence.

I refused. She told me that Sakunosuke had entered my name and, so I had no choice. Sandy urged me and threatened, cajoled and argued. I would not budge.

She said that Sakunosuke was furious.

"What you doing?"

"Watching the tournament," I replied.

"You competing. Heian kata. I enter name," he said.

"No. I am not ready for this."

My face turned scarlet even at the thought of performing in front of a hostile audience, and that I was defying some Karate deity.

"No! No! NO!"

I competed.

I had to perform Heian Nidan (number 2). I did it in the most lackadaisical manner I could, in a deliberate attempt to sabotage myself. I was doing just fine until terror overcame my opponent, and he stopped dead in his tracks, four movements from the end. Since I finished the *kata*, despite the absence of spirit, *kiai*, or even effort, I won the round and went to the next round.

Good heavens! More torture by *kata*.

Sakunosuke was on the verge of apoplexy by then.

"What bloody hell you doing"? He asked.

"I told you. I am not interested in competing". I replied.

"You do better kata next round" he said.

"He walked away, glowering."

I repeated the show in the next round. A shame because it was my favorite *Heian* Yondan (number 4). But no, I ho-hummed my way through it and waited for the losing decision.

A draw! What is the matter with these judges? My opponent must have been as excited about the event as I was. O hell. Another kata pulled out of the box. *Heian Godan* (number 5). My least favorite. Finally, I just let my mind wander off into a vacuum and came to a dead end in the middle of the performance. Finally, I was able to sit down and enjoy the tournament and the demonstrations.

Marguerite kindly asked me if I was feeling OK, as she had seen me perform better *kata* during the training sessions. I told her I was feeling just fine since, with this show of defiance, the wrath of Sakunosuke was quite tolerable. I had gained some self-respect. Pretty silly, really. I should have just performed the kata as usual.

After this grand finale, we traveled to Copenhagen by hydrofoil, accompanied by Ted H, an American draft dodger from Chicago who spoke fluent Swedish, and Lief, a brown belt with a wicked sense of humor.

We were welcomed by Bulla, the national coach in Denmark. Aptly named, I thought. He was in his early 40s, with a shiny bald head, bright blue eyes, an even tan, and no neck. He was a 3rd *Dan*, and we all stayed at his beautiful house, which consisted of floor-to-ceiling teak walls and furniture and was occupied by his current girlfriend, a stunning, languorous sixteen-year-old blue-eyed blond, whose role in life at that moment was to serve Bulla. He said that when he was tired of her, he would replace her immediately. Would we like to visit his brothel? Sandy and I were suddenly nervous.

Bulla had two sources of income. One was a *dōjō*, and the other was a brothel. He said that because brothels were plentiful in Copenhagen, he made most of his income from karate.

"Sex on five floors," said the ad for Bulla's brothel. The entry-level contained a reception area and a movie theater. The services offered by the other levels were listed in the brochure. Swedish massage, S&M dungeon, Turkish baths.... any whim was catered to somewhere in that building.

The beauties at reception looked down their proud noses at Sandy and me. They scoffed at us "Amateurs" as they herded us into the full-colour pornographic cinema, in which a solitary male sat fantasizing with his right hand. We didn't want to watch this movie in which the main color was pink. Still, we were sternly told to stay where we were while Sakunosuke, Steve, and Bulla disappeared into the bowels of the establishment, where whips, spikes, and ropes were available. I don't know what they did, because they never talked about it. We couldn't quite get the movie because not only was the dialogue scant, as the actors were busy, but the grunts were in Swedish.

We drove west across Denmark, and I was surprised to see how much it looked like England: gently rolling, emerald hills and miles of farmland.

At Esbjerg, we boarded the ship for Harwich, England, and 18 hours later, we arrived in the UK. Back to Aberdeen, with a mixed sense of adventure, dismay, regret, satisfaction.... but with enthusiasm for training in no way diminished. I had seen karate practitioners from other countries, and I understood my level to be as Sensei John said it was.

Haruko's wife kindly collected photographs of the trip and gave him hell. There was a God, after all.

Competition for women in Shotokan Scotland, 1969–1987

It didn't exist.

We were all brought up in our passage through the kyu grades to believe that the only competitor is yourself. There was no one else. There wasn't any known competition in Aberdeen, not even for men.

Around the time I was a green belt, we in Aberdeen heard of a competition to be held in Dundee that would attract people from all over Scotland. We went down to enter. Me too.

There were no women in sight. That was not a total shock, as all my training had been with men. It was reasonable that in a competition, I should fight one.

There were no gloves, no pads, no mouth guards. I'd never seen such things anyway.

My name was called for my first fight. I was nervous as hell.

My opponent materialized at the opposite line. He was a Sikh.

"*Rei*" (bow; Two opponents bow to each other before and after a match) said the center referee. I bowed. The Sikh fellow did not. He backed off and renounced the match because his religion forbade him from fighting with women.

So, I won my first fight by default and sailed into the next round.

I sailed out of it just as quickly. My opponent didn't like fighting women any more than the Sikh, but he certainly wasn't going to be beaten by one.

Every time I punched, he grabbed some joint and twisted it so that I would be hurled to the ground. Every time I stepped, he would trip me up and hurl me to the floor. But I was stupid and determined, so I kept attacking him, and he kept throwing me about. The referee stopped the match when he figured I'd had enough and pronounced my laughing opponent the winner. He was a brown belt in jiu-jitsu.

This was my only voluntary competition in five years of training. By 1974, we had opened a club at Aberdeen University, and I was the "Captain" of it, being employed by the University and a Black Belt. We had joined the new British Universities Karate Federation, and they were having their first championship in Hull, England, about eight hours by train from Aberdeen. A few of us had decided to enter, and upon finding out that they had a women's *kata* division, I visualized loads of technically superb women from all over the country that I could gaze at in awe. If Sandy Hopkins was anything to go by, then I reckoned that there should be some great karate to see at this event. I entered, along with some other members of the University Club, and we sent the forms off.

But - a slight inconvenience. I was scheduled for minor surgery on the day we were supposed to travel to Hull - the day before the competition, and I was told I would have to be in the hospital for three days. I kept quiet about this, as I had no intention of missing this tournament, and I didn't want to explain it to the guys because it was "women's stuff" and I was embarrassed. So, on the day before their departure, I explained that I was going to be delayed and that if I didn't make it to the train station, please leave without me.

I went to the hospital and fasted overnight. In the morning, I had the surgery, and by the afternoon, I was sitting up, fully clothed, gi in the closet and ready to go. I was not staying in the hospital one minute longer, but I had to have a doctor's permission to leave. Finally, he arrived at 3 pm. Yes, yes, YES! I feel FINE. OK, he said, you can leave, but please have someone pick you up from the hospital. Don't move around too much and stay off work for a week. I promised faithfully to do what he said, grabbed the bag with my gi, and raced down to the train station. No more trains to Hull, but there was a train to Glasgow, and I could connect with a mail train that arrived in Hull around 1 am. With a second thought, I took it.

Arriving in the middle of the night, alone, not knowing where my teammates were staying, with no idea of the city. All I knew was that Hull University was the venue. I hailed a taxi and told the driver to drop me off in front of a respectable bed and breakfast (B&B) near the university. He did, and they had a room. I thankfully closed my eyes, secure in the knowledge that I hadn't yet had a major setback and would be OK.

The next morning, fortified by an English breakfast of cold toast, cold kippers, and hot tea, I asked the B&B owner how to find the University. I started walking. A blindingly sunny day. A good sign. A car pulled up, and the driver rolled down a window to ask me where I was going. I told him, and he said he was going to the same place and that he would take me. I got in the car.

He dropped me off in the parking lot in front of the gym, where people were rolling out of tour buses and all kinds of vehicles. I spotted my teammates and sauntered over. They were surprised but happy to see me.

There were only nine athletes in the women's kata *division*, and some were brown belts. A bit disappointing. Maybe others would arrive later? No. That was it: Nine competitors. So, there was only one round of competition, and I performed Bassai Dai (breach/destroy a fortress). They gave me a silver cup for 1st place. The girl who took second place performed the same *kata*. Yikes! Unbelievable!

That night, I stayed in the same boarding house as my teammates, some of whom won cups, too, so we all celebrated in the usual liquid manner and remained boisterous and motivated until the wee hours. I returned to Aberdeen none the worse for wear.

The following year, that tournament was held in Bristol. I entered again, this time with the *kata* Chintei, and received another 1st place trophy. The girl who placed runner-up last year also performed Chintei and again finished in the same position. I never competed again anywhere near the UK until 1985, at the 2nd Commonwealth Karate Federation Championships in Guernsey.

Around 1987, I visited Aberdeen, where Ronnie's successful organization had grown to the thousands, and he seemed to have a *dōjō* in every city, town, village, and hamlet in Scotland. But he did not have a kumite competition for women. I asked him why, and his reply was, "The women wouldn't like it". I inquired as to whether this was the opinion expressed by the women themselves or Ronnie's opinion. I pointed out that women all over the world were participating in competition and that there were three weight divisions in international competition, so perhaps he should ask them what they thought.

He did. He was astonished at the response, and another small obstacle to women's karate in Scotland was trampled on.

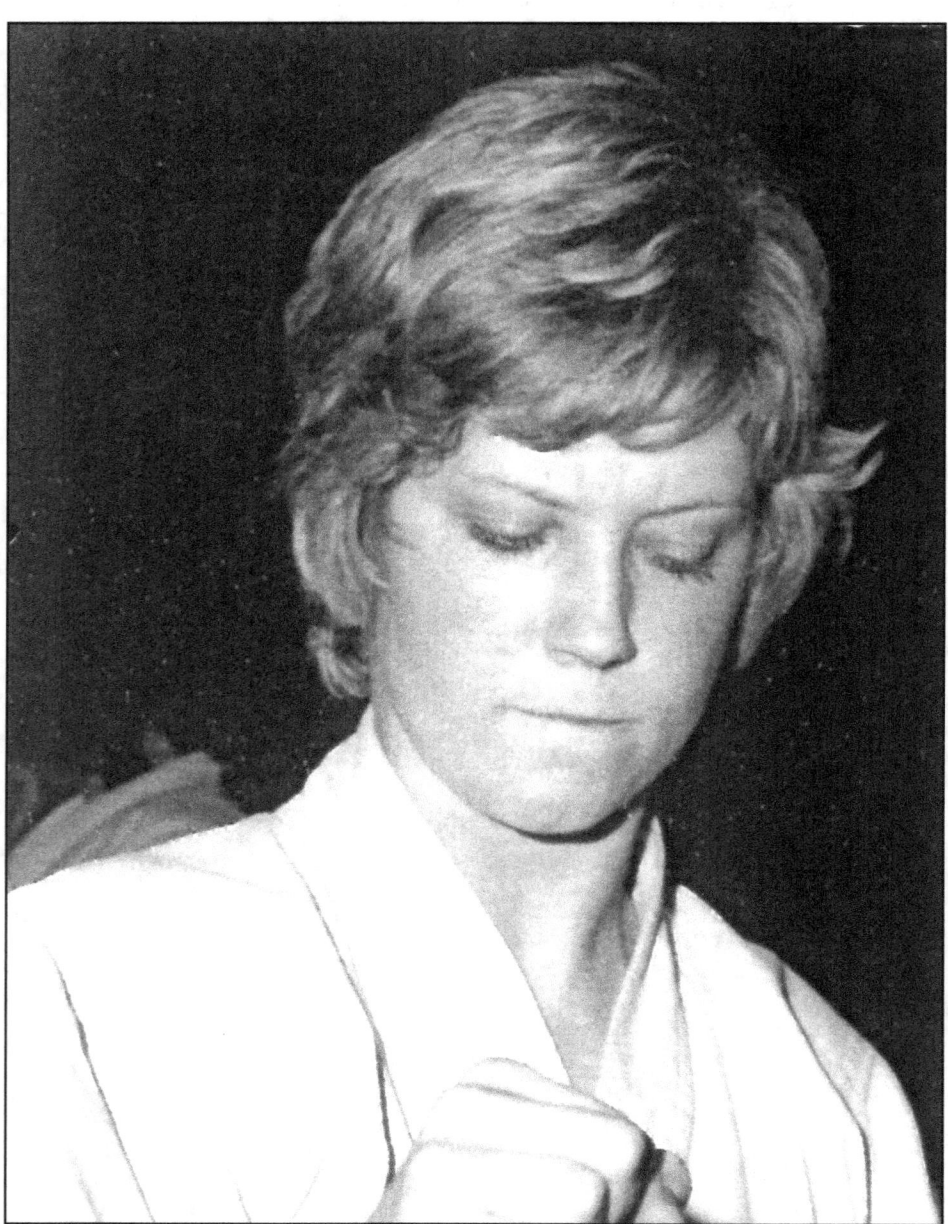
Training, one day before the Shodan test. Aberdeen, 6 February 1974

Shodan

Three months after passing 2nd kyu at Crystal Palace, I passed 1st kyu under Sakunosuke's scrutiny. There was no stopping me now! The fast track to Shodan!

In terms of organizational affiliation, I had vacillated between Ronnie's group, of which I was secretary for a while, and John's club. Ronnie's Scottish Shotokan Karate Association had Keinosuke Enoeda as the figurehead, and John's Aberdeen Karate club decided to stay with Sakunosuke Nothing like karate clubs with differing viewpoints to stir up resentment and isolationism! Although John and Ronnie remained at opposite poles for the rest of time, overall, I had managed to remain fairly neutral and remained on good terms with both. However, as the New Year of 1974 rolled in, I was training with John and was not on Ronnie's guest list.

This year marked a milestone in Scottish Shotokan karate, as it was the 10th anniversary of the introduction of karate into Scotland by Hirokazu Kanazawa.

Because Kanazawa was politically neutral, having not lived in the UK for several years, and because many people still revered him, Sakunosuke stirred up enthusiasm for a joint course, with himself and Kanazawa as instructors, and all practitioners of Shotokan, regardless of their political affiliation, were welcome to attend. Everyone was excited, even those who had hung up their belts years ago. All kinds of people started appearing from the woodwork, "getting in shape" just to train with the legendary Kanazawa. A weekend was selected in February 1974, and the burden of organizing a great deal of this course seemed to rest on my shoulders. I worked at the University, so I had access to rentable space in the Student Union building. I helped spread the word to people that the great man would be visiting. I was tasked with collecting course fees, maintaining attendance and payment records, being part of the welcoming committee, arranging hotels and transportation, and, of course, attempting the Shodan exam. Norma, Jill of all trades.

A clutch of us went to the railway station to greet The Man. Nothing had prepared us for the sight of an unassuming person with long sideburns wearing a navy-blue blazer, grey pants, a white shirt, and a tie. Gods are supposed to be easily identifiable. Nothing from the British schoolboy clothes hinted at the awesome machine in the book "Dynamic Karate". Photographs show a young Kanazawa that could be used as an anatomical diagram to instruct medical students. Sakunosuke immediately relieved him of his minimal luggage in a manner befitting the *kohai* (junior 後輩) of such a famous *senpai,* person above another in rank, age or experience 先輩) and promptly forgot that the rest of us were standing there, unintroduced and ignorant of the language (certainly Japanese) the two men were rapidly conversing in.

We followed them to a Chinese restaurant. All protests about training within an hour were ignored. Finally, we arrive at the course venue. A few black belts with unusual accents showed up and expected to train for free. After all, they considered themselves *deshi* (students, pupils, disciples 弟子) of Kanazawa sensei and thus special enough not to have to pay like us mere locals. I was advised to let it be. So, they did receive special treatment, just as they felt they deserved, thus confirming their belief in their uniqueness. I was a bit upset about that because, after all, they hadn't come off the train with Kanazawa, so the relationship couldn't be that close. But I soon forgot this in the midst of all the other trivial details involved in running a course. There were over 100 people, none of whom seemed to have the correct sum of money. There were lots of "I'll pay you later", "Give me my change later/now", or "I already paid through so and so". Such was Aberdeen in 1974. We were all struggling.

The first day of the course was interesting, and those of us who had never seen Kanazawa before joined the Awe club. Kanazawa had a very different teaching style from that of Sakunosuke He seemed more analytical and philosophical, and he did some unusual things that we had never seen before.

In the pub later that night, Kanazawa explained that those things were from *Tai Chi Chuan*, for which he had great respect. He was only showing us breath control, but it was awfully deep and alien to us. Also, having dismissed Bruce Lee as a celluloid actor, we had to revamp our attitudes about Chinese martial arts, because Kanazawa, the great proponent of Shotokan, which is real karate, believes that Chinese martial arts are a Good Thing and have much Merit. Of course, few of us had ever seen any live Chinese martial arts, let alone *Tai Chi*.

Kanazawa gave us the frog story, about how he could hold a frog in his hand and prevent it from jumping off by depriving it of the force to push against to take off. We thought Kanazawa sensei was from another planet.

Someone asked him to recount the story of his renowned fight with Takayuki Mikami in the first All-Japan JKA championships, which took place during the late 1950s. It went something like this. He and Mikami were roommates, and here they were, fighting for the gold medal. Kanazawa sensei was taller and had a longer reach, but Mikami was very fast, and they had already tied one match and were into overtime. The rule was *shobu* (sudden death match 勝負), so the first to score would win the gold. This was in the era of bare fists and no groin protection. Mikami threw a powerful kick, which Kanazawa sensei blocked, but experienced excruciating pain. The hand used to avoid the kick was broken. However, he carried on to a draw and stoically endured the overtime without a single technique being thrown. Both were eventually awarded 1st place trophies. Many years later, he told me that he could not lose in front of his mother, who was in the audience. Regardless, this fight went down in Shotokan lore as a classic tale of samurai engaged in psychological warfare so intense that it transcended mere technique (or was it just a wee boy wanting to do his best for his mum).

We all sat around, alcohol flowing freely as usual, establishing some kind of rapport with Kanazawa sensei and engaging in stimulating discussions about techniques, people, and urging him to share more stories of the "old days". The entertaining evening wore on, and as closing time approached, Sakunosuke took me aside and asked with great sincerity if I would consider a threesome with himself and Kanazawa.

"*Excuse me?*" I didn't believe my ears

"*You know.*" One girl, two boys, ne?

"*What?*" I was incredulous

"Only Kanazawa sensei and me." Then you go home OK.

My skin started to crawl with disgust. Bile rose in my throat, and my knees turned to jelly.

In shock, I tried to figure this one out.

Did Kanazawa ask for this?

Was this Sakunosuke's idea?

Did Kanazawa know about this and sanction it?

What is going on?

I have to try the Shodan test tomorrow.

Does this have anything to do with it?

What if I refuse?

Will I fail?

What if I did it?

Would I fail?

Why me.

There are lots of other girls around.

"*Go ask someone else, you bastard,*" I spat through tears.

"*You've done it now, Norma—no black belt for you,*" said the voice in my head. "*Five years of effort for nothing. If that is the value of a black belt, maybe you do not need it*".

However, the next day, I showed up at the course anyway, having decided that I would look at the test as a practice Shodan exam. I tried to behave as though nothing was amiss. Compartmentalizing my thoughts again as I did many years ago. Practiced during the day-long seminar, but could not regard Kanazawa with the awe of the previous day, and also could not look at Sakunosuke.

When the time for the test arrived, the whole of Aberdeen seemed to be either taking the test or watching. There was standing room only for the spectators crowding into the hall, and most of the people testing seemed to be from Ronnie's organization.

I decided to try the exam. My name was called up with Keith Crichton, a quiet, unassuming, and dedicated practitioner who had failed the Shodan test multiple times for no apparent reason. Keith and I went through our paces. Basics, followed by a *kata* of our choice. I did *Bassai Dai* as the *kata* of choice, and the compulsory *Heian* was *Yondan*. I was then asked to choose between *kumite* (fighting against an adversary/free sparring 組手) or self-defense for the sparring portion of the test. *"Jiyu kumite"*, I said without hesitation. I had to fight three men. Two males with 1st kyu going for Shodan, and a Shodan going for Nidan. I seemed to fly through it on a carpet of pure rage.

Lined up in front of the "Masters" to await judgment, I could hardly believe my ears. I passed! Evidently, some others were experiencing the same hearing problems, as someone kindly came and informed me that Keith had failed again ....

"Norma? She just passed because she slept wi' the boy."

The room palled like Scotch mist. A bleakness descended, and my disbelief turned into disappointment.

Then the voice whispered yet again:

"I should have failed. Why didn't they let me fail?"

"It would have been so much easier."

I stared at the ground so that I would not have to face anyone.

My friend Tim, who did not practice karate and with whom I no longer had a relationship, partly because karate interfered, gave me a big hug. *"Congratulations, Weems (Wee Amos), you did it!"*

A whirling vortex of feelings. I was now a BLACK BELT. I should have been happy, excited, and thrilled.

So, what.

Who cared? No one but me, and I did not want it under circumstances like these.

People started milling around, wondering where the party would be held. Someone suggested my flat because they knew I lived alone and had the space. Suddenly, everyone was getting my address from anyone but me. I just wanted to be alone and try to sort out this squirming conflict inside my head.

About 40 people crowded into my flat, demanding change for earlier payment, beer, drinks, food, glasses, and wanting to pay because they hadn't …… I flipped.

Around the time, someone was saying something particularly nasty because I just wasn't dealing with the trivia fast enough. I lost it. Snapped. I hurled a fistful of banknotes and small change to the ground with all the force of pent-up anger and rage. I screamed at the top of my lungs for all of them to get the hell out of my house because I was losing my mind. The stream of invective that accompanied the outburst had a magical effect.

Sum's wrang wi' wee Norma

Stark, raving mental?

No one knew how to deal with this person, seemingly having either an epileptic fit or a nervous breakdown, I was completely off any scales, yelled everyone to leave because I was definitely out of control.

I sobbed and wailed until I was drained of all excess emotion.

I was completely disillusioned and disappointed.

Karate did not teach morals or ethics, regardless of Dan levels.

Karate did not teach people how to become better human beings.

It did not teach compassion.

There were no samurai.

It was not what I believed in

Karate was only as good as the people in it, and all of them were men.

The rage eventually subsided into cynicism.

I lost respect for karate and all those with anything to do with it. Of course, that included me. I hung up my gi and the black belt Sakunosuke had given me with his name on it and resolved never to go near a *dōjō* or wear a gi ever again.

No more confusing technical ability with ethics, morals, or strength of character.

So much for being the first woman to achieve a Shodan in the JKA in Aberdeen.

Last Months in Aberdeen

By the autumn, I had calmed down sufficiently to consider training again. I went back to John's *dōjō* expecting revilement and rejection, but instead was welcomed with

Well, about time! We wondered how long it would take you to come back!

In 1974, Aberdeen had become populated by Texans, and the city started to change. The prospect of striking it rich in the North Sea oil fields attracted all types of people, some less savory than others. Major oil firms established offices in Aberdeen, and it seemed that there was employment available for everyone, regardless of educational background. We suddenly had massive burgers without onions, fries instead of chips, and Harvey Wallbangers instead of pints. Huge Lincoln Continentals choked our narrow streets, and a variety of cultures and languages began to choke our narrow minds. Middle Eastern men in white djellabah and checkered dishcloths on their heads stepped out of gold custom-built Benz limos; guacamole replaced HP sauce, and tomato sauce became ketchup.

Tiny bucolic Dyce airport became *international,* and flights connected Aberdeen with Amsterdam, Abu Dhabi, and Tehran. Girlfriends married oil barons from Houston or Louisiana and princes from Khartoum and drank cocktails at the Petroleum Club. New service industries sprang up to address every need of the new polyglot industry. Texans seemed wealthy, benevolent, and just as exotic as Arabs due to their unfamiliar speech, strange manners, and clothing. The city accepted them and the changes they wrought with optimism.

I used to attend auctions and buy affordable old furniture to refinish and sell or to add novel decorative touches to bland tenement rooms. Texans were also interested in these items, which they considered antiques. Nothing was antique to us if it was less than 100 years old, but these Texans considered pine chests made only forty years previously worthy of collection. So, my friend Brian and I would buy ratty pine chests, strip and refinish them, and retail them mostly to Texans for a reasonable sum.

It was Brian who introduced me to Talmadge (Tab) N. Foster II from Houston. Brian met him at auctions and started talking to him. Brian liked him and wanted to know him better, so he invited a so-called White Belt Norma, who was different from me, known as Black Belt Norma and Tab, to dinner. Brian had made elaborate preparations, such as marinating the pork in a manner that was supposed to resemble wild boar, and he was excited. Brian was gay, and this was a set-up to provide a comfortable atmosphere because he wasn't sure whether or not Tab was gay.

Tab was not gay and couldn't wait to escape Brian's spooky little apartment, crowded with Clarice Cliff place settings, Tiffany-style lamps, and black silk tablecloths. He offered to drive both Norma and me home.

Norma started training in karate because she had been mugged in Boston. Brian and I sympathized and discussed how dangerous Boston must be while Tab attempted to disabuse us of this notion. We refused to believe that Boston was as safe as Aberdeen.

Ironically, Norma was mugged again within a month or so of that dinner, in the parking lot of the Aberdeen University Rec Centre, while leaving after training to meet us in the pub. Quite a coincidence.

Tab's father was the president of an oil company, so the whole family was expatriated to Aberdeen for an indeterminate period. Tab was also working on a rig, with a two-week on and two-week off schedule. He was the first member of his family ever to make real contact with the Scottish "natives." After two years of living in Aberdeen, he became a popular fixture of the Dutch Mill (pub) crowd. He went to a great deal of trouble convincing me he was not gay—by such means—as loitering outside Marischal College, clutching a bunch of flowers, waiting for me to finish work, and offering to chauffeur me about town. I found the attention acutely embarrassing, but I had to admire his effort. I managed to have him stop it all by agreeing to go out with him. We did for a reasonable amount of time, after which he moved into my Wallfield Crescent flat.

This arrangement worked quite well, as he was still working offshore every two weeks out of four, so I had ample time to enjoy being alone and to enjoy his company. This continued quite smoothly for several months until one day, he came home and told me that his family were being shipped back to Texas and that he had to leave within two weeks. A bit of a shock—to be honest.

He asked me if I wanted to accompany him, and I said yes.

Unfortunately, although entering the US would be easy, staying there and working would not. Since I did not have a degree recognized by Americans, I had no reasonable qualifications for any visa other than tourist or fiancé.

Tab and I both decided that I should go on a fiancé visa. There was much rushing down to the US Air Base at Edzell, having documents notarized and passports updated. A tornado seemed to have entered our lives, the vortex being the realization that I was going to live in the United States of America. It was real. I was going to leave Scotland. I did not have the time to ponder the decision, made so lightly, as within two weeks, papers were in order, and the contents of my flat were already in containers, ready to be floated across the Atlantic. It was reckoned that it would take a while for the company to tow the rig Tab worked on, from Aberdeen to Houston. Also, I was to fly out to Houston within three months, by then, Tab, the rig, and possessions would have arrived. Moreover, this gave him ample time to find us an apartment.

Having emptied my flat of all treasures and conveniences, such as chairs, heaters, and a bed, Tim's parents, Helen and C.B. Pulman, kindly let me stay at their house for the duration.

There was only one thing left to do. Arrange a farewell party. With the help of several friends, including Al Hyland, who printed the tickets on squares of blue denim and played trumpet in the band, I managed to organize a party for 200 at the University Halls of Residence in Old Aberdeen. I sang with the band, played the records, and functioned as the host. I invited everyone I knew to "Norma's Jean Party." The notion of attending a party in denim was unusual in Aberdeen at the time, as people usually dressed up to go out, and most dress codes did not include jeans, a rule enforced by bouncers and managers alike. In fact, many people did not own anything made of denim, and some, like my boss, Colin, had to purchase a pair of jeans, especially for the occasion. The party was attended by an unusual mix of people that included Hamish Keir, the Head of the Department of Biochemistry at Aberdeen, several professors from the department and their wives or partners, a smattering of Americans, the karate clubs of both John Allen and Ronnie Watt and a great deal of the populace that frequented my favorite hang outs. The boys at the Blue Lamp, the patrons of the Dutch Mill, the Earl's Court Hotel, the Star & Garter and Moira

Abercrombie, the wealthy, beautiful and eccentric socialite who owned the granite, turreted mansion Idlewild, as well as a boutique called the Dream Machine across the street from the Star & Garter, held court in the corner of the room. Bejeweled, slightly plump, with a wide, generous smile and masses of auburn hair that set off very attractive, clear green almond-shaped eyes, Moira was at that time in her early forties and an infamous character in the city. She lived her own life and did not care about the opinions of others. She would wear outrageous clothing that showcased her unique taste, and the generosity of her smile was a truly outward indicator of her personality. Moira was very altruistic and opened her home and her heart to everyone. She was not a snob and enjoyed diverse company. She had been particularly kind to me and had allowed me the use of a room at the top of Idlewild, which I could treat like my own. This room was special to me for a number of reasons. One was that it was completely paneled in wood. Floors, walls, and sloping ceiling. Another was its size. It was the smallest room in the house, and it had a tiny arched window that jutted out from the roof. For some reason, I always felt safe and secure in that room, which I loved like no other, and as it was located next to the black bathroom, the only known facility in Aberdeen at the time with gold-plated bath taps, I had the luxury of enjoying showers. The house had 11 or so bedrooms and a kitchen that contained a 15th-century monastic dining table with matching benches. Oil paintings over 200 years old stared down at diners, and huge Satsuma porcelain vases occupied window alcoves. Parties were frequent, and many a New Year had been welcomed in the kitchen at Idlewild. The living room had cathedral ceilings and tall recessed windows. Although the room was vast, it was cozy and friendly, having a huge fire burning in the grate more often than not, and the clutter of antiques, fabrics ornaments, sofas and easy chairs, all of which were in use rather than on display, at once cocooned visitors in the warmth radiated by the lady of the house.

Moira's mother had owned an antique shop, and after she suffered a stroke and was no longer capable of taking care of the store, Moira sold it and everything in it. However, before she did, she gave me a few items from the collection. These included a Chinese lacquered *papier maché* cocktail shaker set. A pair of Japanese lacquered screens and a Japanese China tea set. A small Regency period silver oval box was among the treasures she kindly gave me, and I am happy to say that I still have them all to this day. Moira was like that, not only to me but to several others, who also enjoyed her hospitality, excellent cooking, and unselfish nature. She taught me several lessons, particularly about honesty and truth, for which I remain grateful.

At that time, her eldest daughter Jacqueline practiced karate with me at the University Club and had reached 6th kyu.

The farewell party was still going strong at 1 am, and no one, least of all, myself, wanted it to be over, as I was still coming to grips with the fact that I was about to leave Scotland forever. I would become an immigrant.

Suddenly, I panicked and started to question my sanity. What was I doing by leaving these close and valuable friends, my rediscovered karate?

The day inexorably arrived, and I left in Tim's purple Renault for the railway station to catch the sleeper bound for King's Cross, London. Ronnie Herd and Nicky came to the station to see me off and bought platform tickets so that they could stay until the last moment. Ronnie handed me a bunch of flowers, and Nicky thrust a box of chocolates into my hands just as the train pulled out. I waved to them until they were no longer visible, unwilling to let go of my Scotland—My life.

I stared out of the open window as the train gathered speed towards Stonehaven. Waterfalls of tears accompanied sobs into the wind as the cliffs of the Northeast coast receded into the past. I cried all the way to Dundee, about an hour or so, then told myself that was enough. I had no reason to be crying as though something had been taken away, as everything would always remain as long as I lived and cared to remember. I hadn't lost anything, and I had a whole new adventure to look forward to. Maybe the next twenty years will be much more exciting? At Dundee,

I abruptly stopped crying, opened Nicky's chocolates, and settled down to read a book. I allowed the soporific rhythms of the train to lull me to sleep as it hurtled into the night.

Houston, Texas, USA 1975–77

I alighted first of all onto the tarmac at Miami airport and had a major anxiety attack. I couldn't breathe. I felt as though I had just put my head inside a blast furnace; the air was so hot and dripping with humidity. I had never encountered anything like it. I thought I was going to suffocate. I panicked and wondered if I'd last long enough to make it to Houston, let alone live there. Why didn't someone warn me? Once in the terminal, I discovered Air Conditioning for the first time in my life, and I began to calm down. I arrived in Houston in June 1975 with two suitcases, and Tab met me at the airport. I heaved a sigh of relief and decided everything was going to be just fine. I was looking forward to a new life in a culture not radically different from my own, but more advanced. Women would be more independent; men would be sensitive and understanding. There would be equality and equal opportunity. After all, hadn't there just been revolutions in the US? Bra burning and such? Civil rights? How exciting. Here I was in America! Land of the free!

Except, not in Texas. It was nothing like Scotland, and it was nothing like the USA that I had read about or seen on TV.

Tab's staunchly Baptist grandparents equally feared God and "niggers", a term I thought was obsolete. Women were into big hair, girly voices, dresses, and primping in very fine detail to catch a husband. I came to understand that these Southern white "gals" were a unique species.

I was hugged where a simple "goodbye" would have done just as well. The men drank beer, loved country music, and wore the standard uniform of jeans, checked skirts, and cowboy boots, but everyone was dreadfully insincere. In Aberdeen at the time, no one ever told anyone to have a *nice* day and to come back soon! Maybe that was because nice days were so rare that people had enough of a challenge enjoying them without worrying whether or not someone else had one. We were straight talkers, and everyone was guilty until proven innocent. In Texas, all were innocent until proven guilty! How strange! And all this embracing and other shows of emotion. Quite strange.

Tab worked nights as an electrician and returned home every morning to sleep. We had a reasonably large apartment with facilities I could never have afforded in Scotland. A bathroom, a wet bar, architectural features, a carport, etc., except I didn't have a car.

I could not work because I did not have a work permit. I could not drive because I did not have a driver's license. Here I was in a Houston suburb, alone most of the time, with nothing to do, nowhere to go, no friends, and only Tab's immediate family to try to talk to. They tried so hard to make me feel welcome, but unfortunately, most members of the older Foster generations could not understand a word I said, and there had to be younger members around to translate for them. I could understand everyone except Tab's father, whom I never figured out. Despite this extraordinary inability to communicate, separated by a common language, the family did their best to put me at ease with shows of kindness. However, I was not accustomed to such pampering and felt displaced at meals, garden parties, pool parties, and family events etc. All I understood was independence, and I was not used to being part of a large family. Or any family for that matter. Tab's friends seemed much younger than me, and their interest in swilling beers, shooting animals, playing ball games, and listening to country and Western music was not interesting to me. I had nothing in common with the girlfriends of his friends either, as all they seemed to think about was what kind of ring to get for their engagement and wedding planning. I began to chafe at the bit.

I started to walk around the area alone—exploring, starting to understand it the same way I did the Edinburgh tenements.

Scottish blood must have been very tasty, judging by the merciless onslaught of mosquitoes, chiggers, ants, and no-see' ums (midges in Scotland). I became covered in welts as soon as I stepped outside the door. It was too hot and humid to loll by a pool. Tab understood that my restlessness, frustration, and impatience were partly due to confinement. Wheels are essential for getting around Houston. I didn't even have a bicycle.

As we drove past a lane, Tab noticed a Taekwondo school. I was happy to see that it was within walking distance of our apartment.

A search of the Houston Yellow Pages revealed that there was no listing for Japanese Martial Arts, but there were numerous listings for Taekwondo. Resigned to probably doing this Mickey Mouse karate, I resolved to check it out the very next day.

I walked along the culvert ditches towards the small strip mall where George Minshew's Black Belt Academy was located. It looked closed, but I approached it anyway. A glass door opened at a touch, and I looked in to see a girl wearing denim dungarees, with masses of hip-length auburn hair fanned out all over her back, lying face down, sound asleep on a padded bench. As I entered, she awoke with a start and stood up. She was about the same size and age as me. She looked me straight in the eye, a bright smile already on a pretty, aboriginal-featured face. Jeannie Parker ushered me into the office. She said she was a brown belt and the manager of the school, which immediately impressed me. She explained how the school operated. The franchised $700 brown belt program. Amazing. You could get a bank loan to pay off a brown belt! I came from a country where you paid 50 cents every time you showed up at the *dōjō,* and someone wrote it down in a wee notebook. All this high finance was a brave new world to me, who didn't even have an income. Jeannie figured that this program would not suit me and that maybe if I could pay $30 a month, it would be, OK? It would. I had no idea what this school taught, style, or its attitudes. All I knew was that I instantly liked this person, and that was enough.

When I told her I did nothing all day as I did not have a Green Card, she told me I could bring my gi, and we could work out together just by ourselves, as most of her real work was in the evenings and she only gave a few private lessons a couple of days each week. Wow! She taught people! And she was exactly the same age and height as me!

I brought my gi the following day, and I saw General Choi's Taekwondo for the first time. We did some basics, and then Jeannie suggested we try sparring. The first lesson to be learned was that Taekwondo was not to be spat or scoffed at, and Mickey Mouse could not have been further from my mind as I picked myself up off the floor, bounced off walls, and could not get anywhere near Jeannie to land a technique. I was confused, disillusioned with my karate, and awed at her. Why wouldn't it work?

Jeannie had excellent form and good control, but though she was about the same height and weight as me, she was a wall of solid muscle, and she trained regularly by doing things like stopping a 75-lb bag in mid-swing with a timely side thrust kick, punch, or strike. I had never seen a heavy bag in a *dōjō*, let alone seen a woman work one. I expressed all this to Jeannie, who good naturedly explained that there was nothing wrong with my karate; I had just never really learned how to apply it. And here I was, thinking I was so knowledgeable. A Black Belt, indeed. So much to learn.

I began to go to the *dojang*, as it is called in Korean, and stay there all day, as Jeannie introduced me to some new way of doing things and local culinary high spots such as Dunkin' Donuts, Taco Bell, Wendy's, and McDonalds. We became inseparable friends and would zoom all over Houston on her 250-cc motorcycle. Jeannie personified what I thought women in America were supposed to be. Strong, positive, motivated, intelligent, independent, and compassionate. A great salesperson, fighter, and *hyung* (*kata*) performer. A unique and beautiful girl.

One day, as I was walking along the edge of the culvert ditches on the way to the school, a fellow drove up alongside me in a Honda Civic. He beckoned me to talk to him, and I went, already knowing that I was going to say,

"No, thank you, I don't need a ride. I'm not going far."

Drivers would often stop their cars and ask me if I wanted a lift, mostly on the assumption that my car had broken down. No one walked in suburban Houston, and that explained the lack of proper sidewalks, and these nasty ditches swarmed with encephalitis-carrying mosquitoes. People would kindly offer help, mistaking my daily stroll for a car breakdown.

At the driver's side of the Civic, I immediately said what I had planned to say based on the above assumptions. The male driver looked at me rather intensely and asked if I knew the way to Chimney Rock Road. I said I wasn't sure, but I believed that it was in a particular direction and pointed vaguely towards the left. The man said something else, and I just replied that I was sorry, I didn't know the details about how to get there. Finally, he slowly drove off.

I watched the car pull into an apartment complex parking lot a little further up the street and was somehow relieved. Nevertheless, a vague sense of unease worked its way down my spine as I watched him pull out at the exit of the lot and stop. He watched me approach and pulled up alongside me again. I kept walking, and he kept talking.

Having had enough, I stopped and faced him, saying quite pointedly that I had no idea where he wanted to go or how to get there. He said, "Ma'am" and pointed towards the floor of his car. Finally, I looked where he indicated, only to see that his jeans were open, and he was busily masturbating with his right hand while his left was back on the wheel. I looked up at his face, and as the whole scenario finally sunk in, I just burst out laughing and told him what a silly bugger he was. I guess that wasn't quite the response he was looking for, as he quickly accelerated and disappeared from sight. I continued laughing at my stupidity for a few yards and started to review the situation. The couldas, wouldas, and didnas. I reasoned that he was unlikely to have a gun in the car, besides, as it would be difficult to threaten with it, drive, and masturbate simultaneously. But you never know. It was Texas, after all, and folks were handy with weapons

I arrived at the school and told Jeannie about my latest cultural experience. She was a bit more astute than me and sent some students out to check the immediate surroundings. I saw this individual once again in a supermarket parking lot in the middle of the day. He made eye contact with me, hurriedly entered a different car, and drove off. I got both license numbers, but nothing ever came of it.

Jeannie decided to show me all the other Taekwondo schools, as well as a Shorin Ryū school, which was located on the other side of town. Jeannie was well known because she was a talented competitor. We visited a school where they guaranteed a student would become a black belt in a year. Jeannie and I were instructed to spar with each other for 20 minutes, and then the "instructor" told us that maybe we might earn black belts in his school in about six months. Cool. It is that easy. I stayed with Jeannie's school for a year and met all sorts of interesting people. Skipper Mullins gave a seminar; Raymond McCallum was a frequent visitor from Dallas. I think it was Jack Hwang who owned the *dōjō*, and he would occasionally put in an appearance. Richard McCallum, a Shotokan man from California, also came and gave a seminar. I was ecstatic to see great Shoto form and to hear Japanese terms after so many "*ap chagi*" and "*ha dan maki.*" A whole world was available beyond Shotokan, and I was just beginning to catch a glimpse. However, I did not have a body structure that easily lent itself to spinning face kicks, and six years of equal and opposite reactions were difficult to replace with centrifugal force generation. Furthermore, I had a hard time performing *General Choi's Chon Ji, To San* forms in the manner of a broken string puppet and all the Korean visions of the Japanese *kata*. I couldn't get interested in them. So, Jeannie suggested that I visit Kim Soo's College of Cha Yon Ryū Taekwondo.

By now, I was legally married and had a Green Card; after over thirty interviews, I landed a job as a technician at the University of Texas Health Science Center, passes the driver's test, and purchased my first car, a Honda Civic. After about six months, Tab complained that I spent far too much time with Jeannie. I trained with her daily, carried her equipment for her at tournaments, and attended seminars. For heaven's sake, I was not having an affair. I eventually could not stand the pressure of his expectations that I would settle down, have kids, cook meals, and generally behave like a proper wife. He was still working at night, and I worked during the day. What he meant was that we did not spend time together on weekends because I went to tournaments with Jeannie. We split up after only a year of marriage. Freedom! What a wonderful feeling! We did an amicable do-it-yourself Texas divorce six months later. He moved in with a girl he had known from high school, married her, and they had two daughters. That life was not for me.

Cha Yon Ryū Taekwondo

Good as her word, Jeannie introduced me to this *dojang*. She figured that the instructor, called David Akahane, a Hawaiian, was very good. His original style was *Ryū Son Ryū Shorin Ryū,* so Jeannie thought that I might enjoy studying with him.

She was right. If I had to do Taekwondo, this was a better place for me. Kim Soo had a whole range of *hyung* that differed from those of General Choi. The series were called *Pal Gue,* and seemed to have a closer resemblance to *Heian kata.* The *dojang* was very technical, and instead of honing kicking skills, it was used for another plastic trophy. Furthermore, everyone wore clean, white gi instead of the bicentennial red, white, and blue flags that many of Jeannie's students favored. She considered herself a "traditionalist" and made that statement by wearing a white gi, but it was the exception rather than the rule at Black Belt Academy.

I decided to join Kim Soo's organization and make a commitment. I figured that since these Taekwondo principles radically differed from those of Shotokan, it would be better to start as a white belt and do it properly. Kim Soo said it wasn't necessary, but I persisted. He relented.

I bought a white belt and entered the class. Afterwards, he just said

"Please, Norma, the other class would be far better for you."

Now I believed him, as I found that I really could break boards with my feet and hands – revelation (!) and that I had nothing to learn from that class. It was very basic but included smacking boards for focus practice. I had to put the Black Belt on again. The next day, I joined the "advanced class," where I met John C.

I just saw a blond person, about 5'10", with sharp brown eyes in a black *dobok,* the pants of which swept the floor, and the jacket of which was tied with a thick black belt *at the waist*, not the hip. John was twenty-three, anorexic, and schizophrenic. He had exquisite control over every single muscle, sinew, and joint in his body and could perform any movement in the slowest of slow Motions—awesome! Was there no end to the things these so-called 'Mickey Mouse' *karate* practitioners could do? John also practiced Tai Chi, a hard style of Kung Fu, and was adept with various Chinese weapons. His hero was Bruce Lee, whom he would try to emulate in every detail by memorizing all the fight scenes from Enter the Dragon and other films. John only ate Chinese or Korean food and studied Mandarin. He lived in a River Oaks mansion with his adoptive parents and brother. He did not seem to work or attend college. All he seemed to do was devote himself to his passions, which were martial arts, food, and his physical appearance.

We became an item. His mother hated me and said that I was a gold digger. I never went near their house while she was in it. She drove a brown Cadillac, which John referred to as her broomstick. So, we always knew when the witch was home. Because of this pressure, John moved into my apartment. Since he didn't work, he would cook the most amazing things, like Peking Duck from scratch. We would have parties, and the members of the group, including David Akahane and those from the Rice University Karate Club, would join in. Those parties always seemed to end up with comparative *kata* and *hyung* being demonstrated in the street, interpretations discussed and dissected.

I learned some of the advanced Korean forms and even competed in a closed tournament in New Orleans with a *hyung* called *"Koryo"*. Since there were only about nine competitors, I won first place! I even placed 2nd in sparring. Jeannie's input must have helped. One time, I went to New Orleans and practiced in Takayuki Mikami Sensei's *dōjō*, the All-South Karate Federation. This was the man who tied in the legendary fight with Kanazawa sensei in the 1950s. The *dōjō* in Metairie was very narrow and quite crowded, so training was somewhat disappointing due to the numerous restrictions on movement. However, I met a woman who was a black belt. She was Japanese or of Japanese descent, and I competed against her in Las Vegas eight years later. I believe her name was Miki. Since I had arrived in Houston, she was the first woman with a black belt in Shotokan that I had seen, and she left an impression.

That something was seriously wrong with John over and above mere eccentricity soon became apparent. Jeannie had decided to move to Oklahoma City to work for Jack Hwang, so I couldn't discuss it with her. John denied everything, but it became quite clear that he was so thin because although he appeared to eat more than anyone else at any given mealtime, he would immediately dispose of it all through laxative abuse. This also explained why he couldn't work. It was probably the electrolyte imbalance that caused his whole body to bloat with edema every three days or so, during which he would stay indoors and eat more laxatives to get rid of it. A vicious cycle.

I finally approached his mother and flatly stated that her son needed psychiatric help and that he was way beyond anything I could do for him. I did not have the money to pay someone $60 an hour to talk to him. She broke down in tears and confessed that she knew John needed help and wanted to prevent me from having to find that out. So that explained her previous attitude. She agreed to pay for the treatment on the condition that John didn't know who had paid and that I could persuade him to go.

He went for a few sessions before he learned that I had "betrayed" him by enlisting his mother to help, and he quit. This is how his car happened to drive over my treasured JKA shodan certificate, and my precious red KUGB record book was thrown into a fire. Everything I did, believed, liked, thought, held dear, was a ripe target for attack. The second class, inferior Japanese Shotokan stuff, was just a symbol of martial arts crap and treachery.

I rescued my burned book from the fireplace and dejectedly retrieved my shodan certificate from the parking lot, sporting a new design to complement the pretty Japanese writing: the tread from the radial tires on John's Ford Maverick.

David Akahane finally broke away from Kim Soo, as he had never liked teaching Taekwondo and never felt qualified to do so. He opened a Shorin Ryū school 60 miles away—off the Katy Freeway in Houston, and I immediately joined it. His first students were Randall Stone, who was his *deshi,* and me. David was the first person to teach me Unsu and Gojushiho *kata*. He also tried to teach me some Tai Chi, but it was too slow for me and required more ankle flexibility than I was capable of. Perhaps because David had a kind heart and no interest in running a business, the club folded after only six months as several of his students couldn't afford the *dōjō* fees. He gave up the mainland and returned to live in Hawaii.

Waco, Texas 1978

Watching a tournament one weekend, I noticed a competitor in the men's forms division performing a Shotokan *kata*. I went to speak to him. His name was Luther Duffy. His *dōjō* was the Karate Association of Texas, located in Waco, about four hours' drive Northwest of Houston. He invited me to train there on weekends. He followed Mikami sensei, so I figured that what he taught would be familiar enough.

I made the drive up to Waco in my decrepit convertible Fiat Spyder almost every weekend for the next six months and continued with Kim Soo during the week.

Luther's *dōjō* used to be a service station. A jaundiced yellow carpet covering a concrete floor perfectly complemented a mirrored wall at one end of the room, and a chandelier suspended in the middle of the ceiling reflected yellowish glints. Luther was in his forties, I suppose, no one knew for sure. He seemed to be a benevolent, good ol' farm boy with a bit of a gut. He drove a mobile trash can of a pick-up truck that served as a mobile office and cafeteria; he drank inordinate quantities of beer and imparted the wisdom of a military stationing in Okinawa combined with a childhood in China Springs, Texas, to fascinated karate practitioners and Baylor University students. He could speak some Japanese, which sounded very odd emanating from this country boy in scruffy baggy dungarees. But Luther was a good teacher and the folks in his *dōjō* were friendly, so I became very close, in particular, with Beth from Utah, who was studying at Baylor, and a graduate student from Japan called Atsushi. I looked forward to those Waco weekends when I stayed at Beth's apartment and had loads of fun.

I started to compete in the occasional small local tournament, only in *kata*. I did not have enough experience to fight. Then, when Luther hosted his Heart of Texas Championships in 1977, I had my first experience of being a referee. It was the kind of event where the black belts had a 30-minute meeting before the event started, and Luther would explain the rules. No contact. One-point-two half-point matches. Three times out of the ring—automatic disqualification. Pretty simple. Even for the Taekwondo and Kung Fu people. Endless what-if questions ensured that the event started one hour late, and the judges had to memorize all the what-ifs that passed for rules. Considering the situation, it is amazing that more people were not seriously injured. The only qualification you had to have to be a judge was a black belt in something.

But those weekends made me feel as though I had found another home. Everyone was good-humored, and something was always happening, like a party on the shores of Waco Lake, where I learned to water ski and Luther treated us to barbecued goat.

We laughed a lot and trained hard, with Luther trying his best to erase the Taekwondo from my repertoire. Training was always followed by lots of beer and wine for Norma and close camaraderie. It was in this atmosphere of Texan hospitality that I became closer to Atsushi.

Beth had a crush on Luther. Beth herself thought this was really quite absurd, given the fact that they had nothing in common other than karate. She had just completed a master's degree and had a *bright future*, whereas Luther gave every impression of being totally uneducated and slowly meandering downhill in a dubious lifestyle. He was old enough to be her father, and he was just not her type. She could realize all this intellectually, but seemed emotionally powerless to stop it. The fact is, if he were not her karate instructor, she would not have been attracted to him. Fortunately, she returned to Utah after graduation, which cured her temporary emotional insanity.

Luther's *dōjō* became very quiet in between semesters, as a good part of the garage membership consisted of Baylor students. Everyone started packing up for the summer, and some friends were leaving for good. I was going to miss Atsushi because he was leaving for Fukuoka City, Japan, with no intention of returning to the US. He planned to pursue post-graduate studies at Seinan University and was looking forward to settling down in Japan.

He asked me to visit him, then to stay with his family for a while, as he realized that I didn't have enough money for the airfare, and it would take time to save it. Also, the cost would be too high to consider going for a week or two. So, I wondered how to save the funds and also obtain sufficient time away from work. I wondered throughout July of 1977 and couldn't produce any reasonable plan to finance my way to Fukuoka.

Fate intervened again in the form of the collaborator my boss was working with at Baylor College of Medicine. He and several others had accepted positions at the University of Arkansas for Medical Sciences at Little Rock with a mandate to establish a Cell and Molecular Biology Department. He offered me a job but said that it would not be available until funding came through in January 1978. Perfect. I accepted this timely offer and promptly gave one month's notice to the University of Texas, Department of Urology. I sold everything I had to save, trucking it up to Little Rock in January, and the funds derived from that, plus my last paycheck, went towards the cost of purchasing a ticket to Japan.

However, despite additional funds saved from working part-time at the Marriott Hotel as a hostess, the sum still fell short of a round-trip ticket. A letter from Atsushi stated that I could work as an English teacher to cover the cost of my return portion. All I needed was a one-way fare. I stored my electrically degenerate Spyder in Randall and Janey Stone's garage, and with their blessing, I left for Fukuoka.

How exciting! I envisaged Japan as I might the moon or Mars. It would be alien and beyond my comprehension. How was I going to communicate? Would there be a lot of foreigners? How would Atsushi's parents react? Would they hate me or like me? Could I communicate with them? What would I eat every day? And training! There must be a JKA *dōjō* in Fukuoka. What an adventure.

Fukuoka, Japan 1977–78

It was a long series of flights, with changes of planes in Los Angeles, Honolulu, and *Tōkyō*.

I experienced my first taste of green *zaru soba* (cold buckwheat noodles) on the JAL flight from Hawaii. I thought that if this was representative of the average Japanese meal, I was not going to survive very long.

As the plane approached Japan, I could almost hear a temple bell reverberating off the silver-grey waters, which gently lapped the shoreline. This was IT. I was arriving at the source of karate. Where Funakoshi lived! Everyone was interested in martial arts because they were all descended from samurai and subscribed to the Warrior Code! Where everyone watched Kurosawa movies and lived in homes full of refined spaces, tatami, and high-tech electronics. I knew all about Japan. Luther had given me a book entitled The Hagakure, and I studied it vigorously; presumably, I took it far too seriously. I had also read a great deal of other books about Japan, as well as newspaper and magazine articles, anything I could lay my hands on remotely connected with Japan or martial arts. I had talked with Atsushi at great length about his country and his hometown.

Oh yes, I knew a lot about Japan! Hmm. It's too bad that most of it was a fantasy.

Haneda Airport was a giant ashtray filled with a blue smog of cigarette smoke emanating from the mouths of myriads of small men in navy blue suits rushing about with briefcases. The uniformity was all the more shocking given the immersion in Texas, a land of pastel polyester leisure suits straining to contain large, well-fed men wearing lizard-skin Frye boots and Stetson hats. But then, déjà vu. London. Morning commuter trains, city-bound, stuffed with dark suits, bowler hats, umbrellas, briefcases, and bespoke dark suits reading The Times. How odd, though, that there was hardly a woman in sight.

I had a relatively tight connection to Fukuoka, and I could not determine the gate from which the flight departed. Panic set in due to the absence of English signage. Someone took pity on me and said—in English—that the Information Desk would help me, and that they spoke English there. Before leaving, he pointed in the general direction of Help. But try as I might, I could not find Help in the maze of navy suits. The airport was not well-ventilated and felt more like a dilapidated railway station than an international airport. Tired, jet-lagged, confused, frustrated, lost, sweating with panic, on the verge of just plopping onto the ground and yelling. When I finally identified two females in navy suits as bearing "Help," communication was a fleeting notion, as neither understood any English, and *dōjō* Japanese was obviously irrelevant. Panic rising. No money, no flight back to the USA, I didn't know anyone in *Tōkyō*, and I could have been stranded on an unpopulated desert island for all the good the thousands of men rushing back and forth could do. Just when I really was about to fall over some psychological precipice, another stranger kindly helped me out and pointed me towards the domestic part of the airport. I made the connection with moments to spare. zaru soba

About one and a half hours later, I emerged at Fukuoka Airport, bedraggled, exhausted, and disoriented, having flown in from halfway around the globe with stops in Los Angeles, Honolulu, and *Tōkyō*. I was met by an exuberant welcoming committee with a huge banner that said, "*Noma, welcome.*" I couldn't even see it at first; I was so tired. All I could discern were navy suits and blackheads. Was the entire country dressed as in Mao's China? A body disengaged from the mass and thrust a bouquet of flowers into my arms. I looked at them numbly, uncomprehending. Atsushi materialized from behind the unknown flower boy, and I was so thankful. A lot of introductions and bowing proceeded with much apparent formality, considering the behaviour that appeared to be his norm in Texas. I was bundled into a car with Atsushi and two of his friends, then driven off to his parents' "dream house" in Meinohama. The drive seemed to take forever, and I was less than excited by the chain-smoking friends in the closed car and the driver, who insisted on not upshifting gears in the little Toyota. The rumbling vibration, combined with the suffocating atmosphere, generated nausea. Not a happy thought. Fortunately, we arrived at Meinohama just before I threw up; there, I encountered more people waiting for me to start the party. By the time the rest of the cavalcade arrived, about 20 people were gathered in a beautiful tatami room, the middle of which contained a long, low table covered with sushi and other delicacies. I realized that Atsushi's parents had gone to a lot of trouble for me, and here I was, travel-worn, weary, and ungratefully asking for a shower and maybe a change of clothes. It would maybe revive flagging spirits and induce a party mood. Atsushi told me that all these people had been waiting for me for several hours and that his parents had made a lot of time-consuming arrangements, so I should not be so unappreciative as to want to refresh myself.

"This feast is for your benefit, so you had better look like you are enjoying it and talk to these people," he said.

"I can't talk to them; they don't know any English! I don't know enough Japanese"!

Wasn't my consternation obvious?

"Just smile, and I will translate," He insisted.

However, after everyone had put in their fair share of comments about my hair colour, how old I was, where I was from exactly, and whether or not my parents approved of my being here... Atsushi became tired of translating and laughed and joked in a corner with his friends. I didn't drink beer; everyone kept trying to force-feed me with it. I couldn't drink sake either, so that was equally unhelpful. As the party wore on, I began to feel more isolated and out of control. I couldn't talk with anyone, I couldn't go and shower, sleep, or unpack my suitcase because it was still inside someone's car. First, I felt like an object on display—but was nothing compared to the experience of being lonely in a crowd in Fukuoka.

I could hardly keep my eyes open, as by now I had been awake for well over 36 hours, flying for 15 of them, with an 18-hour jet lag. I felt exhausted and confused that Atsushi was having such a great time with his friends on the other side of the room and ignored me completely. Atsushi's mother noticed that I was nodding off, so she good-naturedly shooed the guests out. Futons materialized from closets, and everything was cleared from the tatami floor. Notable culture shock: Atsushi, his mother, father, and I were all going to sleep in the same room!

After sleeping for nearly 12 straight hours, I awoke to find that mine was the only futon in the room. His parents had left to return to their "everyday house," and Atsushi and I were alone. The sun streamed into the room through floor-to-ceiling glass sliding doors that opened onto a traditional Japanese garden. Strange, pungent smells suddenly gave me a sneezing fit. The air was a heady mixture of brand-new tatami, cedar, and pawlonia-wood kimono chests. When the door to the "western style" room was drawn aside to reveal mismatched doll's house furniture clothed in clear plastic, the air changed again to polyester, synthetic carpet fiber, and polyethylene bags tinged with a slight fungal mustiness. A stereo squatted opposite a doily-covered coffee table and a display cabinet full of Western China. This room had not obviously been used much, and more power-sneezing set in. Atsushi gave me towels and a light cotton *yukata* (informal summer kimono) and showed me where the bathroom was. Heaven! A miniature bathroom perfect for someone 5 feet 2", and I could comfortably sit upright in the tiny *ofuro* (Japanese bath) with my legs stretched out straight in front of me without sinking! Maybe things were to be fine after all. At last, cleansed of travel weariness and much refreshed, I draped the kimono about me and went to sit by the window.

Because it was such a hot and humid day, I said to Atsushi that I would like to change into my bikini and sit in the garden. Er, no. Stupid request. I was berated for being culturally insensitive because no one in Japan wears a bikini in a traditional garden. How could I be so gauche? Furthermore, what would the neighbors think? Well, I couldn't possibly know what they might think, and really did not get the picture at all.

I was then given a story about how much effort Atsushi's parents had made to build this house, how everything in it was the best they could afford, and that they planned on retiring here. I was not to defile it with my peculiarly Western lack of sensibilities.

This was not going well at all. I was a total social klutz already, and I had only been in Japan for 12 hours!

We caught a taxi to Akasaka Mon, where the "everyday house" was located. A first look at Fukuoka in the daylight was not a pretty sight. The entire route that we traveled was under construction, and the buildings all seemed drab, old, and grey. It could have been Glasgow for all I knew. Fukuoka seemed to be consumed with industry, with little or no regard for the environment. Everyone always seemed so busy! Finally, greenery appeared in the form of *Ohori Koen* (park), which was next to *Kuroda Jo* (castle). The taxi turned right, parallel to what may have been the castle moat. Akasaka Mon means red gate, and it was once an entrance to the castle. I learned that people could walk through the castle grounds or visit the park. A huge dog howled and strained at a leash behind a barred compound next to an apartment building facing the park. Oh, this is Zsazsa, a full-grown mastiff that belonged to Atsushi's family, the Otsus. The dog looked frustrated, all cooped up in that little barred concrete jail. If anyone ventured past the building, the dog howled like a Hound of the Baskervilles and managed to keep me awake every night for two months. Since the jail fronted the street, the howls frequently rattled the kitchen windows that also faced the street.

The main living and sleeping area of the ground-floor apartment was a mess. Dust had collected into huge balls on the ledges of opaque windows, which also sported a few deceased insects.

Nothing could have been further removed from the controlled and spotless order of the Meinohama house. The tatami was old, brown, and ripped up in places. Worn-out cushions graced the floor around a scratched, filthy table littered with used teacups, spoons, rice bowls, chopsticks, sticky sauce bottles, and the remains of half-eaten fish, as well as jars of inedible things such as pickled crab ovaries and mackerel intestines. A tabby cat disdainfully picked its way through the debris and then jumped off the table. Nothing new there. The further back one went into the recesses of the room, the more things seemed piled about with nowhere to go. A wardrobe was bursting at the seams; towels were strewn about, women's and men's clothing covered the surface of what might have been a low dresser, the top of a wardrobe, and the far corners of the room. A mirror was covered with a strip of purple silk. Cat and dog hairs covered everything that was not covered in dust or clothing. The room with the washing machine was choc-a-bloc with laundry; the kitchen had a steel sink full of dishes next to an encrusted three-burner gas stove. Dry goods and tins tumbled out of open doors, and clothes, kitchen utensils, and brushes were suspended from bare pipes. A dank, moldy smell mixed with cat urine pervaded the whole chaos, and I couldn't help but compare it with the pure aesthetic of Meinohama. No wonder they called it a "dream house". The other house pet, a pure white, long-haired Maltese called Chalee-pon (little Charley), ran around in frantic circles, squealing and yelping at the slightest human twitch. Upstairs is the room inhabited by Atsushi's eighteen-year-old brother, Takahashi, affectionately called Ta-bo. I had not yet met him as he was away on some kind of school outing. This room indicated an interesting personality. Totally disheveled like the rest of the apartment, but indicating eclectic interests. Stamps, baseball cards, sports, books, tapes, records, and posters made the room feel alive and friendly.

By contrast, outside the house and abutting onto ZsaZsa's jail was a room with its western toilet, a carpet, a desk, a western bed, and a lot of bookshelves filled with English and Japanese tomes suitable for a graduate student of semantics, stacked alongside shelves of manga (comics). This space was the biggest private area in the compound and the most tidy. It was to be my space for the duration of my stay.

Atsushi's father, Hiroshi, was a civil engineer who worked in Kitakyushu, where he left early every morning and returned home late every evening by train. One hour each way. He was a thin, mild-mannered, kindly person who seemed totally at the mercy of his whirlwind wife. Atsuko-san was the mother of two sons, a dynamo of about fifty who never seemed to sleep. She was the caretaker of the apartment complex, which they later bought. She had little concern for housework, and Hiroshi would often come home to find his wife absent because she was at the Ma Jan (Mah Jongg) parlor, where she tended to stay for up to 24 hours at a stretch. On those occasions, Hiroshi would wash a few dishes, make himself a perfunctory supper, and then go and join his wife for a few rounds of the tiles. If it were a Friday, they would both often play until well after sunrise on Saturday morning. Atsushi loved Ma Jan too and spent about as much time as his parents sitting in crowded, smoky rooms eating dried fish, drinking wheat tea, and gambling on what little funds he had earned from tutoring English. I spent so many hours there, watching Atsushi and his friends play, that I taught myself how to play, although I never reached their advanced standards, of course. After about six weeks of this, it became exquisitely boring, and Atsushi would no longer let me actively participate or learn because it would slow down their game. I played Ma Jan against myself in the room. Yeah. *Sozu* (bamboo), *pinzu* (circles), *dora* (bonus tiles), *riichi!* (a developed hand) *kan* (four of the same suit declared before a win), *pon* (three of the same suit declared before a win)! The principle is the same as gin rummy.

The Otsus had lived in Akasaka Mon for a long time, and everyone seemed to know them. People were always dropping in for cups of green tea and chatting with Atsuko-san. Sometimes, if they happened to drop by when she was out, they would just make themselves at home with a cup of green tea and sprawl about the floor. If she didn't return, they would just leave. Atsuko's front door was always welcoming and never locked on the odd occasion that it was closed.

On the first day at Akasaka, I started to feel very tired around 7 pm and wanted to go to sleep. Atsushi told me that I was lazy and that I should be really excited because everything was new and different. Well, I was, but I was also suddenly bone tired. Atsushi didn't believe in jet lag because he claimed not to suffer from it. Therefore, I was just making things up and being selfish. Regardless, I sank into sleep. At about 10 pm, he woke me up and said I had to get dressed because someone really important wanted to meet me, and I'd better look sharp. I said I wasn't up to it, but he wouldn't accept my excuses. This person had gone to the trouble of buying wine for me because he understood that was what I could drink, and Atsushi didn't want to lose face with this individual if I refused to show. Wearily, I dragged myself from sleep, pulled on clothes, and followed Atsushi off in a daze to a smoky pub/restaurant, where the ugliest man I had ever seen was seated alone on a tatami plinth, drinking and staring at a table overflowing with food. Huge ears flapped at the sides of a head that was as big as a melon and sparsely populated by hair. His eyes were all rheumy and resembled a badly poached egg, and were positioned rather oddly. Large warts and skin eruptions decorated much of his face, which was fronted by a generous mouth full of large, discolored, snaggled, and severely bucked teeth. I thought, "Please don't let it be him". Atsushi's face lit up as their eyes met. "*A-chan*" he bellowed, and the entire clientele of the restaurant turned to glance and then stare. Not at him. At me.

He was introduced as Kobayashi sensei, and Atsushi's whole demeanor suddenly underwent another about-face. Whereas with me, he had been patronizing and sarcastic, and in front of this man, he was obsequious and ingratiating. Deferential was an understatement. Did this fellow have no arms? Was he incapable of putting his own food on plates? Did Atsushi really agree with everything he said?

He had brought two bottles of wine, one red and one white, not knowing which I would prefer. He seemed to say a lot of nice things about me, and after the usual wondrous touching of my hair and exclamations about the similarity between mine and that of Chalee-pon were over, I was admonished to eat anything I wanted in the bar/restaurant. The trouble was, I just couldn't face food and my host at the same time. Sleep, sleep, and more sleep was all I craved. Four hours later, we left the company of this Kobayashi sensei, who was very kind despite my abysmal first impression. Exhausted, I asked Atsushi what style of karate our host practiced. Atsushi thought this question hysterically funny. I didn't quite get the joke. The only people I had ever heard referred to as sensei happened to teach karate, so I couldn't see anything peculiar about the question. Kobayashi sensei had been his junior high school math teacher. LOL.

I could have dissolved in a puddle of embarrassment right there. Oh, I said while racking up another faux pas. After a few weeks, Atsushi finally explained to me that once your sensei, always your sensei. And it wouldn't matter if Atsushi had done a PhD in mathematics and was the chairman of the department of mathematics at Tōkyō University, Kobayashi would still be called sensei.

Well, I wished he would have made that and many other things clearer before, instead of after the fact.

Weeks started to fly by, and I needed something to do. I was depressed and insecure. I couldn't speak any Japanese, and Atsushi would not help me. He was always "too busy". His parents, though kind, spoke no English. There were a few other foreigners in the city at that time, and anyway, I had no means of contacting them as I couldn't read the phone book and wouldn't know where else to look. I had no money and no means of transport, so my range of activities was restricted to as far as I could walk. I made myself familiar with the district, explored the castle ruins, visited the park, and even found Mr. Donuts! Nutrition of athletes! I read every English book in Atsushi's room, including the complete works of Shakespeare. Finally, Atsushi came home one day with Japanese language books! He had said that there were few in the city but that he would get me some. My excitement soon turned to dismay as I saw they were for teaching children Japanese. All the verbs had to do with children's activities. Atsushi said, not with a fair amount of condescension, that these were suitable for someone of my level, meaning that I was childish. Nevertheless, I knuckled down and learned the dialogues:

What shall we do today - Eiko chan?

Let's play ball.

What did you do yesterday - Eiko chan?

I played at skipping with Mari chan.

Even after I had plowed my way through the entire book, I still couldn't understand anything because the Fukuoka dialect, Ha*kata*-ben is so thick that I could never match what I heard with anything I learned. No one seemed to speak "standard Japanese".

Further erosion of diminishing self-confidence, as although I was twenty-four, I was still very sensitive to other people's comments and opinions. So, if I liked someone and respected that person who called me an idiot, I would assume they were right, and the word bully would not even enter my mind. Since I had nothing to do all day but analyze a gesture, word, or deed and soul search, I became very adept at reacting negatively to just about everything. Atsushi kept telling me how selfish and boring I was, and that I was not anything like I had been in Texas, where I had been fun and laughing all the time. Here, I was just a burden on his life. I pointed out that he was not quite the same as he was in Texas either, so which one was the real Atsushi? This one, of course! Out poured a litany of complaints about how he had subjugated his true personality to have good relationships with these dumb Americans, how little he thought of them, how he was Japanese, and that was what was important, and that America was just something he had to endure to fulfill his academic ambitions. Japan had a long history and a sensitive culture, whereas America was considered full of shallow, selfish people like me who just missed the point and could not appreciate true beauty and subtlety.

I was flabbergasted. I wasn't sure who this Atsushi was, but then I decided I had the problem, and he was probably right because nothing about Japan was the way I had imagined it would be. I was blind, deaf, and dumb because I could not read, hear, or speak Japanese, and I felt perpetually on the edge of tears. In retrospect, I had no control over anything and was completely dependent on the Otsus and clearly… I was indeed not the person I had been in Texas.

Atsushi's younger brother, Takahashi (Ta-bo), was totally unlike A-chan in every possible way. He was gregarious, active, around 6 feet tall, and had the sculpted muscular build of a serious athlete. He was a *Nidan* in Kyokushinkai karate and spent a lot of time raining blows upon a heavy bag suspended from a washing pole right outside my room. It was his job to take the ZsaZsa out for walks, as he was the only one strong enough to control him. He tried to cheer me up and took me out on his bicycle one day, along with Zsazsa, straining at the leash. I sat on the carrier on the back of the bike while Ta-bo controlled both the bike and dog and delivered a running commentary on the local scenic highlights: *kore wa dog and cat byoin da* (this is the veterinary clinic). He spoke high-school English, which was not much, but he got the message across. He would bicycle around the park, stop at Mister Donuts, and buy a whole bag of donuts. He would eat about half a dozen at once, at any time of the day or night. They never seemed to affect his weight. For some reason, everyone took a dim view of Takahashi trying to cheer me up, and he was scolded by his parents. I was admonished and given a lecture by Atsushi on correct behavior; because I was twenty-four and Takahashi was eighteen, it was most unseemly for me to go gallivanting around the park with him. Lovers went walking there, but it was totally irrelevant to Takahashi, me, the bicycle, and the dog. I thought this was really stupid. Next time I saw Takahashi; he gave me a wry grin. Towards the end of my stay, he gave me a present. It consisted of a one *yen* and a ten *yen* bank note from his collection. I still have them.

One day, I decided to stop feeling sorry for myself and tried to act happy.

I cleaned and tidied the room and the Western toilet; I tried to communicate better with his parents, told myself to eat and enjoy the cornflakes, ham, and eggs they gave me for breakfast while everyone else was eating rice, fish, seaweed, and natto…

It did not work

"Why do you have to wear three rings at once?"

"It makes you look cheap."

"Don't you think that you should wear trousers that are not so tight?"

"It is disgraceful to go out in such trousers."

"No decent woman in Japan would do such a thing."

"Act your age"!

So much for my new attitude, I was so demoralized. Nothing I did or did not do—was right. If I smiled, I showed too many teeth. If I didn't, I should stop scowling. My clothes were wrong; I wore too much jewelry; I was ignorant, insensitive, and stupid. If I tidied up, Atsushi couldn't find anything. If I didn't, I was an untidy sloth. I was selfish and picky. I drank in all the Kool-Aid and started to really lose myself.

I started sleeping in and getting up as late as possible so that I wouldn't have to face the day. Atsuko-san would ask me if I wanted a shower, as she had installed one, especially for my visit. I would invariably say no, just wanting to be left alone and not be chastised for infringing some critically important Japanese sensibility.

But.... a turning point in this personal hell was a small and not terribly funny joke. I learned the Japanese words for today, yesterday, tomorrow, last, this, and next week, month, and year.

When Atsuko-san asked me one day if I wanted a shower, I said, *"No."*

She replied, *"Maybe tomorrow?"*

I responded with my new words: *"No, maybe next week. No, maybe next year!"*

It wasn't much, but she laughed, and it made me feel good. She even told some visitors later in the day what I had said, and they all laughed, too, which cheered me up enormously. It meant that, one day, maybe I could be capable of communicating with these people!

Another fun moment came when I wanted to iron a blouse. I couldn't find the word for "iron" in any dictionary, and I didn't have enough language to describe what I wanted, so I pantomimed the whole show of washing and ironing. Atsuko understood and exclaimed, *"Airon"*. We both fell about laughing as I realized that the Japanese word for iron was, well, iron. Out came the ironing board, which stood 6 inches off the floor. Hmm. Kneel while ironing, and use cushions to iron difficult bits. Another cultural experience.

All this time, I had been asking Atsushi about karate and a *dōjō*, and he always had some excuse for not telling me where it was. It was difficult to find. He would have to go with me the first time, and he was very busy. It was not listed in the phone book. He would have to organize someone to take me because his schedule was so full. Unfortunately, no one was available. Of course, he was not practicing any karate at the time. Finally, he introduced me to his senpai (senior), called Yamazaki, who wanted to have English conversations with me. In return, he would take me to local sites of interest and explain something about local history. Yamazaki had been a polio victim and was a nidan in Wadō Ryū karate, but he hadn't practiced karate for years. How was this going to help my karate, I wondered. Week, he picked me up in his car and drive to a temple, a shrine. One week, we went to Dazaifu, which used to be the seat of government in Kyushu, but my frustration overwhelmed my ability to communicate. Yamazaki then said he would talk to Atsushi and have him take me to a *dōjō*. Here I was, in the birthplace of karate, and I hadn't set foot inside a *dōjō* for six weeks! Japan! The source of karate!

Atsushi relented, but instead of taking me to a Shotokan school, he took me to the *dōjō* where he trained in the basement of the Fukuoka Saiseikai Hospital. Stone floor, institutional green walls, and Mitsui sensei, a kindly dentist. The senior student was called Sakemi, and he was a 3rd Dan. This was my first introduction to Wadō karate, and I found it very strange. An odd warm-up of stretching parts of the body that were never used and dying cockroach exercises, that is, trying to twist spines and raise arms and legs off the floor while lying on the stomach. Weird *kata*, too. Everything was mispronounced, and *Heian* was *Pinan*, *Tekki* was *Naihanchi*, *Nijushiho* was *Niseishi*, *Kanku* was *Kushanku*. They seemed to get *Bassai* and *Jitte* right. Was this *Hakata* ben (dialect)? High, funny-looking stances and odd-looking face blocks. When I asked Atsushi about the mispronounced *kata* names, he came down on me like a guardian of hell.

"You stupid bitch! Don't you understand anything?"

"You ignorant ass! You think you know so much about karate."

"Well you know nothing!"

"Ummm."

"This is original. You stupid Shotokan people took the original kata and changed it to sell karate to the masses and devalue it."

"Pinan, and the others are the original Okinawan names, you idiot," He concluded.

"I'm sorry, I didn't know," I replied.

"Of course not. You are too stupid to understand anything."

I couldn't handle this. The visit to Japan was a big mistake. I couldn't do this karate; it was too different, and no one was going to help me understand anything. Atsushi obviously wanted me out of his sight and regretted his bringing me here; it was all going horribly wrong. He marched out of the room and slammed the door. I cried myself out, then, after I composed myself, I went to the living room, and I found him lying in front of the TV. He behaved as though nothing had happened. It didn't help that I continued going to this *dōjō* and that on Sundays, they trained at another location. The people were different, and they did a lot of free sparring. There were four women with black belts in the *dōjō*, but they wouldn't fight. At first, I thought they were weak little girls, but I later began to think that they were the more sensible. Every time I made any move, I would be hurled into walls and floors with no mercy. It was like being back in Jeannie's Taekwondo realm again, only this time, my opponents were all male, mean, various dan levels, and well-versed in the art of hurling. I was never going to improve in this environment of slippery floors, weird *kata*, and endless pounding on the floor.

At home, the feeling of a step forward with my puny little joke had now been submerged in self-recrimination, introspection, and despondency. Nothing mattered. I was sinking into a morass of blackness, enlivened by counting the days when I could return to the USA. Another two days passed in a blur of oversleeping and depression. Atsushi ignored me. I just wasn't there. I had allowed my entire self to be trampled all over, my karate rubbish, my dreams and goals shredded. I started to have nightmares. In one of them, I was dressed in a formal kimono like a Jion geisha, complete with a Marumage wig decorated with *kanzashi* (Hair ornaments that look like chopsticks) and other ornaments. Other foreign girls were undergoing the same process. I was crying silently, and a person applying makeup admonished me to stop it as the tears were interfering with their ability to apply the makeup. A cruel-looking woman approached me, holding a handful of long pins. They looked like Western hat pins, but longer. She stood in front of me, carefully selected one pin, and started to pierce my lower lip with it. I screamed at the pain as the sharp point emerged through the flesh inside my mouth. She slapped me and told me to look at the other *gaijin* (foreigner). She was having her lip pierced, too, and she wasn't squealing like a pig.

"See? She understands how to be Japanese.

You never will because you are so stupid".

I looked back at the woman as she viciously selected another pin. This time, I produced neither a sound nor a tear as she thrust it through my lower lip with a little more force.

This dream, which was so vivid when I awoke, had a positive effect. I thought, well, I have no wish to be Japanese. I am me. I am Scottish, and I have no reason to ever be anyone other than who I am and what I am. I decided not to have any more dreams like that, and that I was going to assert myself and to hell with everyone. Some of the resilience that I'd had when I was younger began to surface. I tried to look at my situation more objectively and started to fight back. Turn that negative criticism into positive motivation to show them all! I was allowing myself to become crippled by someone else's opinion to the point that it had all but stripped and flattened my identity into dust. I was terribly unhappy, and I didn't like it much.

I asked Yamazaki to look up the phone book, find the JKA *dōjō*, and tell me how to get there. He did. Catch the number 1 bus to Hakozaki Shrine (I had been there!), and the *dōjō* is just behind it. Not so far. With determination and trepidation, I caught the bus to Hakozaki myself and found the *dōjō*. This was what I had been looking for! A free-standing wooden building located behind a six-hundred-year-old Hakozaki shrine. You had to walk through the shrine grounds to reach it and pass under rows of stone torii gates that stretched from the shrine to the shoreline. Pigeons cooed contentedly in the shrine forecourt and beneath a thatched, netted roof. Massive stone lanterns, venerably encrusted with moss, lined the walkway to the front of the shrine. The shrine is dedicated to Hachiman, the god of war. Fitting, I thought. I finally spotted a weary red rising sun at the top of a mottled white moon, half hidden among a crop of trees. This was The Place. Nihon Karate Kyokai is calligraphed over the entrance. Yes. Finally. The building was wonderful and fulfilled all my expectations of what a *dōjō* in Japan was supposed to look like. No modern community center, this or that! No shopping mall, primary school, or hospital basement. It was a *DŌJŌ*. The decrepit wooden shack trembled as I walked shoeless into it. The interior was built entirely of the same dark wood as the outside, right down to the sliding wooden screens that constituted windows. No one seemed to be about, so I took a peek at the inside. It was a long, narrow rectangle, with weights, bags, and benches at one end, a bar on the wall, and a rack of yellowed gi pinpointed with black mold and mildew. One wall served as shomen (front), identified by a small Shinden (small Shinto shrine complete with foxes, sakaki leaves, vases, and a mirror) placed out of reach of kicks and punches. On one side of the shrine, a poster-sized photograph of a bald man in a horse stance wearing black glasses and a karate gi loomed over the floor. Japanese hang traditional pictures on walls at an angle facing towards the ground, rather than vertically, so they are easy to see without glare. A picture of Gichin Funakoshi, the founder of Shotokan karate, hung on the other side of the Shinden. I was so relieved to see something in Japan that seemed familiar, and I smiled. I was about to leave when a man appeared and asked me pleasantly what I was doing there.

I was ushered into the *dōjō* office, which was occupied by a large wooden desk and a massive, overflowing ashtray. A small vase sported a wilting flower amidst sheaves of papers, pens, pencils, envelopes, and a dull lamp. A breeze caused the wooden walls to rattle and the thin glass panes to vibrate. The fellow went behind the desk and sat down in a decrepit swivel chair. Turned out that this was Sakai sensei, 6th Dan, the main man at the *dōjō*. He spoke no English, but he seemed kind, and although he looked a little like Enoeda, the tiger, he did not give any indication of ferocity. Rather, he beamed at me with a warm smile. I tried to explain that I hadn't trained for a while and that I had, once upon a time, been awarded a Shodan but had been training mostly in Taekwondo for the past two years. A fellow called Sasaki appeared. He knew a few words of English, and his small stature and rather simian features simply added to his efforts to pantomime and explain. He was a 4th Dan and the senior senpai at the *dōjō*. It was he who got the point across that Sakai sensei wanted to know if I was the foreigner staying with the Otsu family, with whom Sakai sensei often played Ma Jan. I suddenly flushed with anger. Atsushi knew this man! He probably saw him at least once a week. He knew Sakai sensei was a karate instructor, the location of his *dōjō*... I was almost speechless. But it had to be compartmentalized until later. This was not the time.

Yes, I said. Maybe I wasn't totally responsible for being a problem after all!!! Maybe Atsushi played a part! A revelation! Duh.

Sasaki told me when they trained, which was every day except Wednesday and Sunday, and gave me a *dōjō* membership card. I could hardly believe my eyes. Was it really this easy?

I had brought my gi with me, so I started training that very evening.

Everything I did in the *dōjō* was wrong. A white belt all over again. Fabulous! Sasaki *sempai* often placed me in front of the moldy old mirror to educate me about all my flaws: no hip rotation, weak abdominals, back leg insufficiently bent in back stance, front leg insufficiently bent in front stance, no snap in kicks and punches, no ankle flexibility, no force to blocks, no meaning to *kata*. Every single person in the *dōjō*, and there were about 30 white, brown, and black belts, was faster, sharper, stronger, and more precise than I was. I was totally motivated. There were even two women, Miss Kaneyama, who was a 2nd Dan, and Miss Yamamoto, who was a nineteen-year-old 1st Dan.

Kaneyama *sempai* was very friendly and tried to help me in every way possible. She was just under 5 feet and stocky. She was warm and expressive and told me all about her nasty senpai forcing her to clean a dank, stinking hole in a sloping stone floor that served as the communal *dōjō* toilet. It led to a pit about 15 feet below. Kaneyama senpai cleaned the "toilet" by pouring ammonia into the hole, emptied the ashtray, and changed the flowers on Sakai sensei's desk even though she was the senior woman in the *dōjō*. She indicated that it was a nasty job, that she was not as cruel as her senpai, and that she wouldn't wish this job on anyone, so she did it herself. Quite a character. She introduced me to *okonomiyaki,* food that resembled a pizza married to an omelette and a pancake, and tried her best to make me feel at ease. Interestingly, she was half Korean. Kaneyama was the Japanized pronunciation of the Chinese characters used in the Korean name. What do you mean you are Korean? Were you born there?

No, she was born in Japan, like the 10 generations of her father's family before her, but she was not Japanese. Only half, she said. I couldn't understand this. A double whammy. Korean and female.

Kaneyama senpai had beautiful form, and I would stare jealously at her perfect stances, wishing I could get my body to do what hers found so effortless. But Kaneyama senpai claimed she was rubbish, that her back foot always stuck out at the wrong angle when she performed *Chintei*, for which endless correction had no effect. Looked perfect to me.

An arrogant eighteen-year-old high school boy who wore a brown belt had exquisite timing and directed a fair amount of animosity at me. Every time we studied basics or semi-free sparring, I would have to face him as a partner. Every single time I attacked, he would sweep my front leg, and I would kiss the floor, often rather painfully, and he would nail me with an unnecessarily hard punch in the back once I was down. I began to fear him so much that I would picture him as soon as I boarded the bus to the *dōjō*. I privately called him Ashi Barai Kun (Mr. Foot Sweep). Finally, I had had enough of my cowardice and decided to do something to overcome it. During *jiyu ippon kumite* (semi-free, one-attack sparring), the opponent knows what the single attack and the target area will be, but does not know when it will happen. This exercise was Ashi Barai kun's forte. I started at him grimly, having decided that I didn't care if the whole *dōjō* thought I was out of line; I was going to change something. So, I attacked with a front punch to the face at my usual speed, which was probably very slow, and Ashi Barai kun went for it as usual. But.... instead of me falling in a twisted heap on the floor, he did. I had thrown the punch long before my front foot landed, rather than at the same time, so he mistimed his sweep. I stood there staring at him in a fighting stance, thinking, well, no going back now. Some other breach of etiquette has been perpetrated by the stupid *gaijin*, and this sucker is now going to come back at me with some painful punishment. So, as he hauled himself off the floor, I waited for the expected admonishment and scowl from Ashi Barai kun.

A suppressed giggle from Kaneyama senpai caught my attention. I turned to look at her. She was giving me both thumbs up! Ashi Barai kun, now upright, simply bowed, and from that time on, he never tried that technique on me again. I guess I had passed his test. But I also learned a lesson. Later, Kaneyama senpai said that Sakai sensei had seen the action and was smiling too. Wow. No rules broken. Turned out that everyone in the *dōjō* had fallen prey to Ashi barai kun's favorite technique at one time or another.

I continued training five days a week at the JKA *dōjō*, where various advanced Dan-level individuals whose names began with S would try their best to debrief my mind and body of Taekwondo. I was so inspired and humbled, as everyone from white belts to 5th dans trained in the same line. There was, of course, Sakai sensei and Sasaki, whom I was also to call sensei, and a small, wiry fellow with glasses who was a 6th dan, called Sakuraba. He scared me to death for two reasons. He spoke fluent American-accented English, so I could not hide behind a language barrier in embarrassing situations. He had been a translator during the war, and he still kept up his language studies. But incredibly, it was as if John Allen from Scotland had suddenly beamed himself into Hakozaki! The resemblance was beyond uncanny. Sakuraba sensei was about the same height and weight as John, had similar movements when applied to karate, and even had a similar demeanor and teaching style! I spent more time gazing at Sakuraba sensei in awe, wondering about the genetic code. But he had no Scottish relatives. The bald man with glasses posing in the horse stance on the wall was Miyata sensei, who had trained with Funakoshi and developed his own interpretations of Shotokan. This, explained by Kaneyama senpai, was why the karate in the JKA *dōjō* in Hakozaki differed from that at the JKA *Tōkyō* headquarters. Well, I wouldn't know the difference, but Kaneyama *sempai* claimed that the people in Fukuoka were more compassionate (she said "human") than those in *Tōkyō*. Considering that this was when Masahiko Tanaka was a star competitor, she had a point.

On Tuesdays, there was a *kata* class for *Nidan* and above. I was allowed to join in despite my inadequacies. However, I still knew the sequences of moves to all the so-called "shodan *kata*". This surely was something. We practiced *Gojushiho* (54 steps). I was so excited when Sakai sensei, who was leading the class, stopped in the middle of it, having forgotten the next move in the sequence. Suddenly, everyone was confused and couldn't figure it out. I watched this go on for a while, then couldn't stand it anymore.

Maybe it goes something like this?? I ventured nervously, worried about proffering advice to 6th Dans. But David Akahane had taught me this *kata*, so it was a relatively recent addition to my repertoire, and I knew exactly what the next move in the sequence was.

That's right! Everybody, including Sakai sensei laughed good-naturedly, and we continued with the rest of the *kata*.

We then practiced the *kata Unsu* (cloud hands). This might be considered one of the most flamboyant of Shotokan forms. It is highlighted near the end by a jump that includes a crescent kick that is the initiation for a 360* spin in the air, halfway through which, a back kick is supposed to be executed by what was the supporting leg, followed by a lightly controlled landing on all fours, ready to continue the next move. It is an extremely demanding maneuver and, when executed well, can be truly breathtaking. However, most of us can barely manage the airborne turn, never mind a flawless jump spin double kick with a resounding smack as the sole of your foot contacts your palm. That day, Sakai sensei was no exception. He was in his mid-forties at the time and spent more time playing *Ma Jan* than perfecting *Unsu*. He leaped, twisted in the air, landing awkwardly with a noisy thud, and lost balance. Kaneyama *sempai* giggled. Sakai sensei righted himself, finished the *kata*, and then called an end to the class.

The next day, his right arm was in a bandage. He had broken his wrist when he landed from the jump in *Unsu*. Stoicism.

One November day, the *dōjō* bustled with unusual activity. Strangers sipped tea and smoked in Sakai sensei's office. More arrived, and soon, the *dōjō* had about a dozen middle-aged male spectators milling about, staring at the walls and fingering the woodwork. Kaneyama sempai said that these men were the *dōjō* sponsors and that two things were under discussion. One was the building plans for a new *dōjō*, since this one was a "shack", and the other was the impending visit from the chief instructor of the JKA in *Tōkyō*, Masatoshi Nakayama. I had his book, Dynamic Karate. It was the one with the pictures of Hirokazu Kanazawa, the anatomical model, and Shirai sensei, leaping through black and white strobed images. The main man. The head of the JKA world, my ultimate lord and master! His signature was on my *Dan* certificate, and now I was going to train in a class with him. I was so excited I could hardly sleep.

There was no other fanfare. No extra cost, no name-taking in little books, not many extra shoes in the box outside the *dōjō*, no unusual face training. Just voices coming from Sakai sensei's office.

The great man stepped onto the floor. Good god, he was only about 5 feet 4 and did not do anything exciting, different, or spectacular. Mercilessly, I compared this little aging man; I suppose he was about seventy-something with Kanazawa, Enoeda, and Shirai, the young blood of the JKA, and found him, well, somewhat disappointing. Whereas their teaching had always been invigorating, motivating, and a challenge, this great oracle of all things Shotokan spent almost the entire hour and a half teaching us rising block. I guessed that there must be something really deep and mysterious about the rising block that escaped my shallow Western understanding because surely this class could not be that simple or boring. I couldn't understand all these 6th Dans standing in line, diligently dissecting their own rising blocks! If 6th Dans couldn't get it right, what hope did I have?

After class, everyone in the *dōjō* went to a restaurant, where we were to enjoy a feast presided over by the *dōjō* sponsors. After much shuffling about, I had to sit next to Nakayama sensei, and Sasaki sensei on my right. This was one of my most embarrassing experiences in the whole *dōjō*. Enjoyed watching Sasaki sensei go through a charade of very crude body language, which roughly corresponded to asking me first of all, if what grew under my armpits was the same colour as the stuff on top of my head. I started to feel colour spread over my neck. He then asked if the color that grew on my pubic area, armpits or head was "same-same?" I was mortified! My face burned beet red as I gasped, open-mouthed. I could not believe what he was asking in this situation. I desperately looked around for someone to help me out of this. But no mercy was forthcoming. The whole room was shaking with laughter. Finally, Kaneyama *sempai* berated him and told me to ignore him because he was just a rude country bumpkin, 4th Dan notwithstanding.

I paid rapt attention to the feast to determine what might be edible. The lid of a cup opened to reveal egg custard, at the bottom of which was one ginkgo nut, one mushroom, and maybe a piece of chicken *(chawan mushi)*. Gratefully, I shoveled the whole thing into my mouth while attention was diverted from my body parts and hair colour. Suddenly, not one but two teaspoons appeared. One was given to Nakayama sensei, the other to me. I stared at it dumbly. What was I supposed to do with this? Nakayama sensei tapped the lid of the *chawan mushi* cup, then proceeded to open his own and use the spoon to eat it. All eyes were on the stupid foreigner again. Nakayama sensei gestured once more to the cup, so I lifted the lid off to show that it was empty. He stared at me in surprise. He asked me how I had eaten it. Like this, I showed him. He seemed amazed. In English, he explained that he had never been able to eat *chawan mushi* with anything other than a spoon, and so he was surprised to find that a foreigner had done so with chopsticks.

More good-natured laughter. After dinner, I was informed that I couldn't pay, as the *dōjō* took care of the entertainment and training expenses. People were all over the place, grabbing jackets, gi bags, *kohai, sempai*, chatting, laughing, and then leaving. I could not seem to put myself in the right position at the right time to thank Sakai sensei for the evening, and I went home, feeling somewhat disconcerted.

Arriving at the *dōjō* the following day, the atmosphere seemed tense. Sakai sensei was not teaching that day; it was Sasaki out in front of the class. During training, Sasaki sensei would not look me in the eye, which he usually did, as he was my key communicator in the *dōjō*. After class, Sasaki sensei came up to me and pointed out that I had not thanked Sakai sensei for treating me last night. I could have withered on the spot with remorse and embarrassment. I flushed and stammered; yet another major faux pas. I hung my head and stared at the floor while Sasaki gave me a lecture in Japanese, which seemed to revolve mostly around ingratitude and rudeness. I felt about one-inch-tall and wished I could just slither away to some dark corner where someone could throw salt on me, and that would be the end of it. Just curl up, shrivel, and die.

But I simply left and cried my way through the silent Hakozaki shrine in the moonlight, dragging my feet towards the bus stop. The silhouettes of the *torii* gates at the shrine drew my eyes towards the sea. Out to Korea. Anywhere but here. On the bus, I tortured myself with negative self-criticism, how stupid I am, how insensitive, it's only two words. Thank you. Why is this so difficult? If you thought that was difficult, then there would never be a right time, and you would never be able to apologize for your thoughtless lapse in manners. What words are you going to use? When will be the right time now? You've blown it. They are all going to despise you for trying to take advantage of the *dōjō* ....

In the next class, I knocked on the door of Sakai sensei's office.

Dozo. (Come in) *He ushered me kindly into the office.*

I stepped in, mustering up all the courage I could.

"Ah, Noma chan," he looked at me, smiling benevolently.

Oh god, this is going to be terrible, He is being so nice.

I stammered in the Japanese grammar of a three-year-old playing ball and skipping with her mates, and added two new words I'd carefully selected from among several alternatives in one of Atsushi's dictionaries.

"Ni n-ni-nichi mae, umm, umm, er, watashi wa burei na...umm, gomen nasai. Arigato wasure, eto,..."

"Eh?" He seemed bewildered.

Oh no, he can't understand what I'm trying to say, which was essentially, *"I am sorry I did not thank you for dinner two days ago. I was very rude, I'm sorry".*

I tried again, becoming more hopelessly confused and embarrassed, and thus jumbling up the words even more.

"Eh?" he reiterated.

For heaven's sake, this is turning into death by linguistics! Why doesn't someone just empty a gas can over me right now and toss in a match? Hah. "Foreigner dies in *dōjō* inferno," screams the Japan Times headline.

Scarlet with embarrassment now, sweating and hopping from foot to foot, I fumbled for the dictionary that I had brought along for moral support, and Sakai sensei called for Sasaki *sempai*. Oh no.

I rearranged the words once more, put the dictionary on his desk, and pointed to the keywords. By this time, not only was my face hot with mortification, but my eyes were beginning to tear up, which made any further attempts at communication almost impossible.

Sakai sensei asked Sasaki *sempai* something as if to say, "What is the matter with this daft person?" What is she trying to say?

Ah.

Sasaki *sempai* said, *"Burei na? Eh?"*

"No no… shitsurei na. Shitsurei shimashita. Same - same."

Sakai sensei laughed, not unkindly, and said words to the effect, *"It's OK, Noma Chan, run along"*.

I realized that Sakai sensei had probably not said anything at all to Sasaki and that Sasaki himself had taken upon the responsibility of pointing out my lapse in manners, which Sakai sensei, apparently, was not concerned about.

Crisis over, soul cleansed, I vowed to train twice as hard in the *dōjō* to offset my fuggy manners and justify Sakai sensei's magnanimity.

I didn't know the term *"burei na"* was a medieval term that is no longer commonly used. It was probably like apologizing to someone in a Shakespearian or Chaucerian English. So much for Atsushi's dictionary—I had better gotten mine.

The weather was turning colder. Fall had come and gone, and the bare branches of Ohori Park were not a welcoming sight as I returned home from trying to teach English at a language school for cash under a table in the Nishi Jin area of the city. Some of Atsushi's classmates at Seinan University had arranged for me to get a job teaching at a conversation school that was not overly concerned about details like visas, accents, teaching qualifications, or experience. Being a *native speaker* outweighed any formal requirements. The school paid me directly with an envelope of cash every week, and that is how I earned enough money for my flight back to North America and to buy the occasional donut.

I met these classmates of Atsushi at a lecture on Scottish life and culture that I had presented at Seinan University. The son of the principal, Dr. Murakami, had completed a PhD in Pictish and ancient Scottish history at Edinburgh University. Good god! He was thrilled to learn that I was an authentic Scot, from Edinburgh, no less, so would I mind giving a talk to a class of graduate students who were studying Scottish culture. The attendees were all required to be quite fluent in English to be in the course, so they should have no problem understanding my talk.

I gave a one-hour talk that briefly touched on a range of subjects from the Picts to the present day, highlighting major battles and drawing parallels among famous feuds featuring Japanese families such as the Genji and the Heike and Scottish families such as the Campbells and the McDonalds, internal strife, and personal views about the molding of the Scottish persona. I mentioned the contributions of famous Scots to several aspects of society, which included minor details like the Bank of England, electricity, the telephone, Jardine's, tartan, geography, whisky, antibiotics…

Maybe it was too much, too broad, too deep, too shallow, or narrow. At any rate, during the question-and-answer session at the end, only one hand timidly ventured skyward. I was nervous. After all, these people probably knew far more about my own culture than I did, so what was I going to do if I couldn't answer their questions?

"What do you eat in Scotland?"

I could hardly believe my ears.

"Haggis!" I exclaimed with pride.

It led to another job, though, and more independence. I had six weeks left to earn enough to get back to the USA. Once I started, offers seemed to flood in. I was doing three teaching jobs at one point and was getting paid quite well. What a relief. I hated teaching, but now I had a reason to get up in the morning, somewhere to go. People to communicate with, and something to do

I did a promotion for the first Pizza Hut to open in Fukuoka. A two-day deal, handing out fliers on the street, wearing silly uniforms It paid handsomely.

Confidence and resilience started to reassert themselves in a big way.

I went further afield, discovered new places, and met new people. Karate was going well, and I could almost say the entire *dōjō* kun (motto) without screwing it up. I could keep up with the class and understand everything that was going on.

I was beginning to emerge from being a self-induced emotional wreck. The solitude of walking up and down Nishi Jin, looking at all the traditional wares, and thinking of all the things I'd like to take back to the USA as souvenirs were enjoyable. Ha*kata* dolls, made of clay and hand-painted. All shapes, sizes, and budgets. A *Kuroda bushi*! The samurai who was associated with *Kuroda Jo*, right where I lived, but even the cheapest samurai doll was a bit beyond my budget. I would stare at the crowded windows laden with dolls. All I could afford was a pair of straw flip-flops with cut-up bits of used car tires for soles.

I would go to the Nishitetsu Grand Hotel and buy the Japan Times newspaper, and stroll around the area of Nakasu called Kawabata, looking at more doll shops, or wander by the river. But as the cold set in, and the *kotatsu* (a table with an infra-red heater under it) was rigged in the house, I wandered less and spent more time lying on the tatami floor cozily covered with the quilt that flowed between the heater and the tabletop. The *kotatsu* became the focal point of all activities during the winter months. You would sit down on the floor at the table and gingerly stretch your legs lest a curled-up cat scratch you or a dog nip you for disturbing them. I even began to understand bits of conversations that floated around the table. One discussion revolved around how ugly Kobayashi sensei was. His nickname was Kaba-chan, which I later discovered meant hippopotamus. I made my second feeble attempt at a joke, muttering something about going to the zoo near Ohori Park and seeing some hippos. Atsuko carried it further and said that I must have seen lots of Kaba-Chan's friends because, with the exception of the Otsu family, that is where they all lived. I laughed. A treasured moment in the saga of Norma's stay in Fukuoka.

Bonenkai (year-end party) season was rolling around, and the *dōjō* started making party plans. No choice but to attend all three of them.

Pictures show me arm wrestling with the women from the Saiseikai Byoin *dōjō*, and singing with the band because they demanded I sing a Scottish song. At the Hakozaki *dōjō*, we trained for an hour; then everyone cleaned the *dōjō* while still in our gi, then we changed and set up tables and cushions on the *dōjō* floor. People started carrying in huge vats of oden (a kind of mixed stew), *mentaiko* (spiced cod roe), chicken, pork, rice, a vat of Nagasaki *champon* (chop suey), and raw pigs' ears, some still with hairs sprouting. I gagged. I am NOT eating those. *"NO WAY. NO."*

They were supposed to be dipped in salt and washed down with beer. Yuck. With revulsion, I watched Sasaki sensei do just that, with great glee and much lip-smacking, right in front of me. It was the most ghastly looking food I had seen during my visit. Eels were no problem, and I even liked *natto* (fermented soybean that smells like unwashed socks). The rest of the evening passed uneventfully, and I never let a raw pig ear reach my mouth.

My 25th birthday was spent eating *sashimi* with Atsushi and his friends at a restaurant that consisted of a shallow stone swimming pool flanked by stone, which was covered with tables and cushions. A chef, wearing white and with a towel tied around his head, stood in a wooden, stall-like structure with an awning at the long end of the swimming pool. Atsushi's friends went to the edge of the rectangular pool and pointed at this or that fish swimming happily about. After much discussion, a choice was agreed upon, and a fellow dressed like a chef, wearing rubber boots, netted the fish and quickly transported it to the chef. The Tai (sea bream) appeared in only a few moments, beautifully garnished with shiso leaves and tiny chrysanthemums, on a plinth of shredded daikon radish, a live tribute to the master chef. This fish is associated with celebration in Japan and is often served at weddings. When I saw it, my stomach heaved, and I gagged. The fish looked as if it would be more at home in a pathology lab. Half of it was missing, and the other half clung to life, with a rapidly beating heart and clouding eye staring up at those who had commissioned its slaughter. Through the intact skeleton, blood vessels and organs were clearly pulsating with life; the fish was, of course, convulsively dying. Atsushi saw that I was totally revolted and so touched the fisheye with his fork. The fish spasmed, and I gagged again. The bile would not stop rising into my throat. Clean white slices with reddish edges were set down on small plates in front of us as my fellow lip-smacking diners started mixing *wasabi* mustard and soy sauce with gusto. No way could I raise these slices of live fish to my lips, let alone swallow it. As Atsushi and his friends continued to torture the fish until it mercifully died, I had to leave the table.

When I returned, the carcass had been removed to reappear in soup. That I could force down, as at least the fish was completely dead and thoroughly cooked.

That day ended with another gripe. This dinner was extremely expensive, and Atsushi and his friends had treated me because it was my birthday, but I didn't appreciate their efforts, and I had insulted the chef to boot.

"Did I have no conscience?

Why was I behaving in such an ungrateful manner?

I would never understand how to behave like a Japanese.......Blah blah blah."

But this time, I just tuned him out.

We spent the New Year of 1978 at the Meinohama house, so seeing all the preparations for the New Year was a treat. Fat rice cakes, lobster and seaweed, had pride of place in the *tokonoma* (recess), the focal point of the traditional room. Atsuko prepared mountains of food for at least a week beforehand, and we spent about three days doing nothing but eating it all. We cleaned and aired out the house on the 31st of December, ensuring that no evil spirits were lurking in the corners to bedevil the fortunes for the following year. On New Year's Eve, we went out to throw arrows in huge bonfires and buy new ones at a local Shinto shrine. Money was thrown into collection boxes, and shrine bells were constantly rung by people seeking guarantees for the coming year. Smells of *okonomiyaki* and *takoyaki* (fried octopus balls) filled the air around the bustling shrine. We returned home and drank three ritual sips of sake from shallow cups in the traditional manner, which was the signal for all present to get seriously wasted. Visitors came and went all night through the house, which was made all the more cozy and welcoming by a big *hibachi* in the shape of a log that radiated warmth over the entire room. The next day, special New Year food was eaten, much of which were very sweet, but each of which had a symbolic meaning in terms of prosperity, health, or longevity.

The Otsus held a little party for me before I left soon after the New Year, and all their friends gave me little envelopes full of money! Kobayashi sensei gave me about ¥30,000! I thought he had made a mistake. Everyone laughed. The envelope had *osenbetsu* written on it in Roman letters so that I could read it. *Ōsenbetsu* means parting gift. I was touched and guiltily remembered all the horrible things I had thought about him that were later extended even to include his wife.

Atsuko-san personally escorted me to *Tōkyō* via Hiroshima on the Shinkansen. Upon arrival at *Tōkyō* station, she immediately herded me on a Hato tour bus, and so I enjoyed *Tōkyō* Tower, the Imperial Palace,

Chinese lunch on the 55th floor of the Mitsui building, from where Fujisama (Mount Fuji) was in plain view against a brilliant blue sky.

After the tour, I found myself in Ginza, one of the high-end areas in *Tōkyō*. Atsuko-san would go into shops and point at things and ask me if I liked them. I kept saying no, but she was not to be deterred. She eventually selected a white top with an Utamaro wood block print on it and thrust it into my hands. As I walked along the Ginza sidewalks with Atsuko-san on that last day in Japan, I contemplated the bright sunshine, beaming from a pure expanse of blue, the cosmopolitan feeling of *Tōkyō*, and the view of Mount Fuji; I made myself a promise. I vowed to return to Japan, specifically *Tōkyō*, and I would not come back until I knew I could do so completely on my own terms.

Haneda airport did not seem so intimidating this time around, and I walked through the gate and gave a last wave to Atsuko-san. I could not let her see me cry.

Little Rock, Arkansas, 1978

The flights back to civilization seemed endless, and when I made it to Darlene's room in the dormitory at Rice University, she told me to get into the top bunk and rest for a while. I woke up 18 hours later, completely oblivious to the party that had gone on in the room for at least a third of that time.

I relaxed in Houston for a week and recovered from awful jet lag. I caught up on gossip and learned that John C was now living with a man in Houston, having emerged from the closet he had been in all his life. Surprisingly, everyone had sympathized with me and couldn't understand how I had managed to persevere so long with John. I was sad for him, though, and hoped that he had found some happiness.

The end of January arrived quickly, and it was time to move on. I retrieved my car from Randall and Janey's garage, loaded it up with my meager possessions, and headed North up Interstate 59 for a New Adventure in Little Rock, Arkansas. The drive lasted for 15 hours as a freak blizzard dumped massive amounts of snow on the freeway. Such weather conditions were unprecedented, and after arriving in Little Rock, someone pointed out that none of my tires had any tread left on them and that, in some places, the rubber was so worn that the webbing underneath was exposed! God really does take care of drunks and fools.

Apartments were easy to find, and I eventually ended up downtown on 9th Street. This area had started undergoing some preservation, so some of the grand Victorian homes in the square had been restored, and townhouses had been sectioned. The trees, bare of leaves and frosted with long crystals, sparkled more than even Luther's chandelier against the amazingly blue winter sky and lovely antebellum homes. The air was so clean that each individual shard of ice reflected blinding rainbows like diamonds. The snow is thick and heavy with Atlantic moisture in Northeast Scotland, so it muffles sound and dims light. Here in Little Rock, Arkansas, there was a picture that I had only seen on Christmas cards and felt was a fantasy. Colorful rough trade plied further west on 9th Street. They never bothered me and added color to the downtown of the city, undergoing inevitable gentrification.

The plaque affixed to the wall of the duplex I rented stated that the building had been the home of the first female doctor in Little Rock. It was a handsome Victorian brick building with sash windows and 12-foot-high ceilings. One wall of the downstairs living room consisted of exposed brick, perfect for hanging Chinese swords, and pictures, and a fireplace that was repeated in smaller detail in the master bedroom. The expanse of space on the ground floor and the lack of immediate neighbors would make it a great party house. What a pity, I didn't know anyone… yet.

The job started off very well, as my responsibility was to equip a new lab for tissue culture, receptor chemistry, protein analysis, and genetic engineering. Negotiating with representatives from various equipment and reagent suppliers was great fun, and our lab had the latest technology in the happiest colors. After that, Jim N directed the research activities that Stewart, who had also come up from Houston with his wife, Ronnie, and I, implemented. The atmosphere in the lab was very convivial, as everyone had a great sense of humor, and we had already worked together for about two years.

All I needed to find was a *dōjō*. The yellow pages yielded nothing but Taekwondo, so I phoned some of them up and asked if they knew of a karate school in the city. Fortunately, with their help, I found Doug Chisolm.

I went to the community center where he taught and lucked out in that he was teaching that very night. I introduced myself, and he asked me where I trained. I told him. He then proceeded to spar with me for 20 minutes, which was an exercise in frustration for me and a joke for him. He was in his late forties and was over 6 feet. Long legs fastened onto a peculiarly short body, also adorned with long arms. For the purpose of this exercise in futility, he wore scarlet marshmallows on his hands and mercilessly cuffed me about the head and body like a boxer. Yet he claimed to be Shotokan. I had had enough. I stopped fighting, and all Hakozaki *dōjō* manners out the window, I asked him what the purpose of this nonsense was. He drawled in local good ol'-boy form that he just wanted to see how much I would take. I bowed to him and walked off. Done now. I guess I just failed his test. However, he talked about his best student, a young kid nicknamed Bull, who was so talented that Doug had run out of things to teach him within two years, so he had sent him to Los Angeles to train with Hidetaka Nishiyama. Doug wasn't sure where he was at that moment. I privately considered that if two years was the extent of Doug's knowledge, maybe he wouldn't have too much to offer. Doug much to my horror invited me back to the *dōjō*, where I was not at all comfortable, but at least he did occasionally interrupt his two-hour free sparring rants with a *kata* or two, and he did, after all, have some link to the Shoto vision of karate that I had been having so much difficulty adhering to. I attended his classes intermittently, not terribly inspired. He probably wasn't either.

One day in March, Stewart McLeod, who also worked in the same lab, showed me an ad he had cut out of the local newspaper. A small picture showed five adult men all in white gi, black belts, thuggish facial expressions, and unmistakable Shotokan stances with arms in various interpretations of a downward sweeping block (*gedan barai*). Seemed worth a look.

The *dōjō* was located in North Little Rock, the predominantly black area of town, which lay north of the Arkansas River. A Saturday afternoon adventure easily uncovered it, thanks to a massive rising sun logo outside it.

A glass front door opened into an office with no one in it, and a saloon-style louvered door afforded a view of a spotless new *dōjō* covered in cream linoleum floor tiles. The walls were cream, and a mirror spanned the length of the long wall. A solitary black man at least as tall as Doug, and of indeterminate age, maybe twenties, was putting himself through a series of basic Shotokan exercises. The satin black belt encircling a brilliant white gi said, *"se-du-rikku ro-djaa-zu"* (Japanese *kata kana* for "Cedric Rodgers) in gold embroidered *katakana,* and he had the most amazing Shotokan form I had seen in the southern states. He was very fit, very handsome, and very focused. He did not appear to acknowledge that anyone else was in the building, performed a few exquisitely controlled slow-motion face-high roundhouse kicks, then appeared to just notice me. OK, an ego; well, that kind of physique, face, and skill certainly justified it. He grinned warmly, revealing brilliant white, perfect teeth. He shook my hand, introduced himself, and offered me a seat.

"I'm in! Sign me up!" I thought.

However, I explained why I was there, and that it was not just to watch someone else go through their paces. He had a natural dignity and radiated self-confidence. He asked if I had brought my gi. I had. So, I changed into it and stepped onto the floor, worried. He put me through basic paces that were quite simple, and then I suddenly became exhausted. My lungs had suddenly filled up with sludge, and I couldn't breathe. The *dōjō* was not air-conditioned. We stopped and rested, and I apologized for being such a wimp. We had only worked out for about half an hour. Then, we did some *kata* and some sparring, which was nothing like the workout with Doug Chisolm. He was controlled and kind, and gave me some good advice, allowing me to beat on him to gain some confidence and understand he wasn't going to swat me about the *dōjō*.

Here was someone I could learn from, someone with motivation, who was an excellent teacher and technician.

He said that because the *dōjō* was new, there were not many students at the time. Among those who had signed up, most were children, so I would be quite senior. He stated that most of "his people" had to be taught basic respect, so it was important that they address me in a manner that reflected not only seniority but also etiquette. We discussed Foster sensei. Too pretentious for me. Norma sensei. Too familiar for him. And I was not a sensei, so the title was erroneous. How about *sempai*? They don't really know what *sempai* means. Miz Foster. Too formal. So, I became Miz Nawma to anyone who stepped through the door of that *dōjō*. Surely that was a cotton plantation next door instead of a Chinese takeaway? Mint juleps for Miz Nawma!

The other students who regularly attended training were Cal, a 4th kyu, and Jerry, a brown belt, who was a medical student. I had trained in the *dōjō* about two weeks before I found out that *"se-du-rikku"* was none other than Cedric Rodgers, nicknamed "Bull," whom Doug Chisolm had been so excited about. Good God, I thought, he's only nineteen years old! He had returned from Los Angeles a *nidan*, and Bull's style of teaching was obviously influenced by Mr. Nishiyama, as his native American English turned into Japlish when teaching:

punch *using total bottay,*

tucking in tailbone, and

internal horse

Pearls dropped directly from the mouth of the master. Despite such linguistic giggles from me, he was a great teacher, disciplined, structured, and imaginative.

All was well at the *dōjō*—the members were friendly, we worked together well, and trained seriously. Every weeknight and Saturday afternoons were spent at the *dōjō*, unless we were out campaigning, distributing fliers door-to-door for the *dōjō*, or performing demonstrations in the park, which Bull called free training.

Since Bull had committed himself to karate as a means of financing his life, he also consistently competed in local tournaments. Most of these were so-called non-contact events with trophies as prizes, but they also included three-round, full-contact bouts that offered cash prizes. Bull would enter "traditional" forms, non-contact sparring, weapons forms, full-contact bouts, and win the lot.

He usually returned with a trunk load of trophies for the *dōjō* window and cash to pay its bills. I first attended these rough and tumble events as a cheerleader, mostly attended by Taekwondo practitioners in all colours and fabrics of karate gi or *doboks*, as karate uniforms are called in Korean. Gold satin with black fringes, bicentennial red, white and blue starred and striped gi, V-necked tops that you had to put on over your head, orientalized letters embroidered everywhere, all over the back, up and down sleeves, pants legs... thick black cotton belts with peoples' full names and *dōjō*s and associations embroidered in huge gold block letters. These tournaments were definitely colorful and entertaining. Bull convinced me to enter some of these events, and I did quite well in *kata* divisions. Fighting was another story. I didn't understand fighting and had no interest in it, but why not participate in all of the fun instead of being a bystander? Bull would sit ringside and shout to me what to do and when to do it. *Gyaku! Keri! Tsuki!* Since most of my opponents studied Taekwondo, they were not familiar with Japanese technical terms. This, along with my ringside coach, increased my confidence a bit to the point where I started winning a few trophies as well. Yet, I was never convinced that I could do it by myself and believed that the only reason *kumite* trophies started to be presented to me was that it was really Bull who was fighting through me.

For a while, it seemed that every single weekend was a tournament. Because Little Rock was fairly central, tournaments in six states were reachable by car in a matter of only a few hours. I competed in Memphis, Tennessee; Oklahoma City; New Orleans, Louisiana; St. Louis, Missouri; various places in Texas, as well as Jackson and Clarksdale, Mississippi. One tournament in Clarksdale, Mississippi, was notable.

I had driven there alone in my Fiat Spider and had become quite lost. The road that was supposed to go to a karate tournament progressively narrowed and finally lost any semblance of paving as it led deeper and deeper into dense trees draped with Spanish moss. Around the point where it dwindled to a rough track, it simply dead-ended at the Mississippi River. Actually, almost IN the Mississippi. A panicked stomp on the brakes threw the car into a tailspin that stopped short inches from the water. Shuddering despite the oppressively humid 95°F swelter, a moment was spent reflecting on narrowly missed possibilities … gators! Chomp! Totally lost, sitting in the little red car that was now dangerously low on gas, with no sign of civilization, with cicadas, crickets, bullfrogs, and god knows what all else—started to send me into major panic. My map had no indication of this road. Oh god, how was I going to make the tournament - this was the Deep South, and Chain Saw Massacres and Klansmen might be lurking right around the next mangrove. I had been warned:

"Y'all should lock y'alls does when y'all is draaivin' over thaya in norf li'l rawk."

"Some of dem niggers maight tray ta git yew."

"Hah! I drive a convertible! Mostly.… with the top down!" The only time I had ever been accosted was by a white homeless man who tried to climb onto my car while I was waiting at a red light in North Little Rock. He had failed to sell me a miniature Bible for a quarter. I thought him harmless and wished I'd had a quarter. Squash the rising panic, stay cool.… think rationally, where was the missed turn or sign? Backtracking eventually led to a main road in time to put the "E" light on the gas gauge.

Clarksdale seemed dull, drab, and dirty, and the tournament was located in the most dreich and dirty end of it. Amazingly, I arrived before the tournament started and astutely noticed that the full bustling gym contained only one white person. Me. Bull was nowhere in sight. The gym was not air conditioned, and the mercury was hovering around 100°F. I signed in and changed into my gi. Thank god, Bull arrived soon after with some black students, and I walked over to the gym entrance to say "hi", and express relief. However, just before I reached him, a black female competitor, wearing a white *dobok* with a red, white, and blue striped edge, very red lips, and very fluorescent blue eye shadow, ran up and threw her arms around Bull, and exclaimed, loud enough for all to hear,

"*Bull, ah goan kiyll yo' black bel.*" (Bull, I am going to kill your black belt) Good God! I should just leave while I still have all my parts. "Brown Sugar" (huge red letters on the back of the dobok jacket) clarified that she was indeed referring to *ME!* Did I survive alligators and chainsaws just to make it here in time for slaughter and sacrifice in the name of civil rights? Well, this is going to be a great triumph for humanity when 140 lb of mean streak annihilates me within a two-minute fight. Bull disengaged himself from her clutches and told her just to do her best. A vision of Kali, killer grin, girdle of hands, and necklace of skulls. Brown Sugar was planning to bring *Attitude* into the ring along with centuries of wrongs supported by a roomful of fans because every single participant, spectator, and official in this tournament was black …except me. She had *Rights!*

Then Luther appeared from Waco. Now there were two white people in the room. He was going to be a *kumite* referee. I hadn't seen him since the pre-Fukuoka days, so we spent pleasant moments reminiscing about the previous summer. For a moment, I went water-skiing on Lake Waco and ate barbecued goat again. Anywhere but here. Turned out that Bull knew him too, so a comfort zone started to form.

But not for long.

The women's "traditional forms" division was called up, and I went and stood in line. Brown Sugar was also entered and five of her daughters, all black belts, ranging in age from about seven to fourteen, wearing corn braids, red lipstick and blouses with frilly collars under their *doboks*, all sat ringside to cheer for mama. Scary stuff.

I performed *Unsu* and the Taekwondo judges liked it a lot better than anyone else's *hyung* and gave me first place. Brown Sugar smacked me on the shoulder and demanded to know what was wrong with her form and why didn't *she* win first place. I said that I didn't know anything about Taekwondo form and that perhaps she should ask the Taekwondo judges.

For *kumite* competition in such tournaments, the draw was a simple, time-saving process involving straws. I started off OK, and won my matches, but the fates were against me. I had to fight Brown Sugar for first place. I went to the bathroom so often that I had memorized all the graffiti in the stalls with no locks. The moment came, and it had to be endured. Bull sat by the edge of the ring, and Luther was the referee. The one-point match started with Brown Sugar beating me about the jaw, left and right, with a wild series of haymakers. Luther stopped the match and admonished her to use control, as this was supposed to be a non-contact match. Cheering poured forth from the bleachers. She argued with him. Luther scowled at her and directed her to stand on the line. She scowled at me. She then tried to do exactly the same thing again, but Bull shouted at me to execute a *gyakuzuki* to her stomach. I did. POINT called Luther and gave it the score. Brown Sugar glared at Luther and yelled:

"Hell! that aint no goddam point. I didn't feel sheeit."

Boos floated around in the humid air.

Luther gave her a warning for her attitude. She rained more blows upon my head, and Luther stopped the match to give her a warning for more contact. She was wearing quite large gloves, but they didn't seem to cushion anything. She came at me again with a series of punches that I managed to avoid, then she drove me clean out of the ring with the force of an uppercut to the diaphragm. POINT to red, gesticulated Luther. Wild noises from the stands. Now we were even. Somewhere in a haze of pain and humiliation, I understood that I was trying to score points, but she was out for a kill. She grinned malevolently and shouted at me:

"I gotcha now, bitch!"

I agreed with her. I was no match for her rage. Luther gave her another warning for contempt, and I looked at Bull with an air of resignation. The audience was becoming extremely agitated.

"You can do it, Miz Nawma."

If he believed it, well, what the hell, maybe I could too. Only a few more seconds, surely. Quiet from the stands.

The time bell went, and the corner judges crossed their flags. Luther announced a draw. Loud booing from the audience. Just give her the decision. Trophies had never been important to me, and my jaw was far more important than any piece of plastic and paint.

Sudden death overtime. Oh Lord, spare me from this torture and just give me a sudden death. By this time, moving my head, jaw, or mouth was not an option, and I couldn't even *kiai* (shout). An eye started to swell up. Wearily, I faced Brown Sugar and tried to avoid her wild attacks that were all aimed at my head. She unleashed a kick. A mistake, because she was quite slow, and the kick was easy to pre-empt. I reverse punched her in the stomach upon Bull's advice, but the judges would not agree with Luther that it scored. She smiled. I was becoming exhausted and demoralized. She came at me one last time, and I never knew what hit me. My head was slammed backward by an uppercut, and I heard the words.

"POINT to the red"

roared by Luther.

"Red wins."

Music to her ears. I went forward to shake her hand (!) and she grabbed me tight to her and said close in my ear:

"We know who really won that first match bitch. If we wiz alone in a field y'all KNOW no overtime ain't needed!"

She was right. You name the pain, I had it. I was so severely beaten that my head felt like a football, my ears rang, my jaw wouldn't move, and I was on the verge of fainting. Brown Sugar smirked. Bull gave me a big hug and kept me vertical. After the floor stopped heaving and rolling and the white *doboks* looked white again instead of ultraviolet, I left the floor and sat high up in the stands, well away from the action. I closed my eyes, held my head in my hands, and reflected that I was alive, and what could I expect from a tournament in the poorest part of a poor Mississippi river town? Look what I represented. It wasn't Norma Foster who was having the stuffing knocked out of her; it was just a white person in the wrong place at the wrong time doing the wrong thing. I tried to rationalize and make some sense of the situation.

A concerned, honeyed Mississippi twang startled me out of this trance.

"Honey, y'all got a mouth guard?"

What? I opened my eyes and turned my whole body to face the speaker due to not being able to turn my head. A black lady, maybe in her early thirties, with a huge Afro, looked at me with great concern.

"Me?" I said.

"Uhuh

No."

"Hun, y'all sho' should git y'all wun, y'all haiyuv such purddy teeth. We waz so worried 'bout y'all cuz that thayuh Brown Sugah is some kaine uh naiyusty wumen".

I stared in astonishment and attempted a wan smile. Wow! Someone in the audience was worried about *me*. Suddenly, my spirits soared; not everyone in the gym supported Brown Sugar, and skin color and integrity were not as connected as I thought. The crowd had been cheering for *me* and not Brown Sugar! The kind lady told me that and lifted my spirits. Oh my god! What a lesson. I relaxed to watch the rest of the tournament. The woman's kind comment made me cry. And then, horror of horrors, Brown Sugar, along with the tournament director, were scanning the stands. She saw me and pointed. The tournament director signaled to me to come down. Oh please, please, what now?

It seemed that I was in the unfortunate position of having won first place in forms and second place in sparring, whereas Brown Sugar had placed first in sparring and second in forms. So, we were equal contenders for what they called the Grand Champion trophy. She made it quite clear that she wanted this trophy; the only problem was how to get it. She pointed out that if we had a fight off in forms, I would beat her, so she wanted to compete in sparring. I mumbled without moving my lips much that I wasn't interested in doing either, and to just please give her the trophy since it was so important to her. Brown Sugar thought this was a fine idea, but the tournament director thought otherwise. He announced over the microphone that there would be no women's grand champion trophy awarded at that event. I sighed with relief.

Later, Brown Sugar's instructor directly apologized to me for the behaviour of his student. She was subsequently banned from competing in Mississippi and from practicing in his *dōjō* due to her attitude being contrary to the spirit of martial arts.

Stunned, I thanked him and said not to worry.

I collected my trophies at the awards ceremony and removed the commemorative metallic strips from them. On the way to my car, I tossed the trophies into a dumpster and vowed that I would never fight again in competition. I had nothing to prove; I wasn't interested in amassing tasteless trophies, which implies that I was never going to make a Vogue cover, I liked my face the way it was before Brown Sugar had her way with it.

Eventually, the black eye faded to misty violet, and my head again turned from left to right, but I never did fight again in competition in the Southern states.

As fall arrived and the city turned all the classical shades, my boss started showing an unreciprocated and undesirable interest in me over and above the call of cell culture. He showed up uninvited outside my home on Saturday mornings with donuts, requesting for coffee. He commented on my clothes and summoned me to his office for "research discussions", where he would try to grab me, hug me, or pin me against the wall. He harangued me with questions such as:

"Don't you like me? Why did you choose to work for me if you don't love me"?

I patiently explained more than once that I thought he was a bright and motivated researcher, that I enjoyed his professional style, I was working with Stewart, and that I liked my job. This would not be a sufficient explanation.

Eventually, he poured all his unrequited love into five sheets of paper replete with poetry and literary quotations and express-mailed it to me. It was too much. I reflected upon this situation, trying to decide the best course of action. I didn't want to make an issue of it, as I felt that my boss had not really intended to harass me; he was just being stupid and not thinking straight. I thought about it for a week during which I acted as though all was normal and sane, and then walked into his office to hand him a letter of my own. As he read it, his face dropped.

Why? he asked, consternation written all over his features. He really didn't get it. I told him that I didn't like the quality of the unsolicited mail I had received lately and asked him how his wife was likely to react if she knew about his sudden interest in donuts and the literature of love.

The letter said that though I enjoyed my job and living in Little Rock, I would miss Stewart and his wife, Ronnie (Veronica), when I left his lab 30 days later.

Karate-wise, Bull had decided to return to Los Angeles to study again with Mr. Hidetaka Nishiyama, and no one else was quite like him in the city.

I held a party and a garage sale and wondered what to do and where to go. Little Rock had exhausted its possibilities.

Aberdeen and London, UK, 1979

Well, being November, with Christmas looming, the only place I thought I could go was back to the UK. Ride with the tide and see what happens.

I stayed with Helen and Clement-Barker (C.B.) Pulman, Tim's mum and dad. Helen smothered me with roast beef, Yorkshire puddings, and roast potatoes. C.B. looked exactly like Sir Alec Guinness in Star Wars, and indeed, had been a Shakespearean actor before World War II. He was interested in everything: botany, astronomy, genetic engineering, pen and ink sketches, linocuts, watercolors, and he had had a few books of poetry published. He was a self-confessed snob in the tradition of enjoying tea and cucumber sandwiches with the Earl of Mar, or beers and rolls on the docks with the stevedores, and ignoring the rest of the population as being uppity mediocrity, with dull little lives and nothing to contribute to society or culture. He spoke with a carefully cultivated upper-class English accent that had nothing to do with his native Bradford, and he was a master of timely putdown I loved CB. He was so eccentric. Helen was raised on a farm around Colchester. She was so totally unlike CB, being warm, natural, earthy, and unaffected. She had been drawn to the theater in her youth and had the distinction of dating Trevor Howard, who later became famous in the movie "Mutiny on the Bounty". However, instead of Trevor Howard, she married CB and ended up in Aberdeen. She ran the three-storey household in clockwork fashion, producing scones and tea at precisely 4 pm on Sunday afternoons, lunch at precisely noon, and tea at precisely 6 pm on weekdays. Breakfasts were always formal sit-downs with butter knives and poached eggs. Their terraced granite house was situated opposite a park; which Helen would often paint in watercolors on an easel in her airy bedroom.

I lived in the guest room for three months before I originally left the UK for Houston, and although the relationship between Tim and me had been over even then for about four years, we were still friends, and I was quite close to his parents. While I had been gone, CB and Helen had kept up a faithful correspondence with me. CB even wrote to me from Foresterhill Hospital, where he spent his last days.

CB had died earlier in the year, and Helen was still quite devastated and depressed. Tim thought it might be good for her if I stayed at the house, as he had a flat of his own and Helen was all alone, with nothing but CB's ornery Cairn terrier, Haar, for company. Helen agreed, and so I stayed once more in Argyll Place, where I enjoyed "my room" and cocooned myself in Helen's unconditional love manifested as poached eggs, roast beef, and nips of sherry.

However, I had a need to finance this pleasant downtime. Tim's girlfriend Barbara, was the manager of a boutique on the main street of Aberdeen. She offered me a part-time job as a sales assistant in the shop. It was perfect. I just wanted to relax and do something to earn a little money to survive.

I had no plan, no apparent future, few possessions, and no emotional strings. I was open to suggestions, if and when any came.

I started training with Ronnie again and followed up on John Allen. He had retired from teaching, had been married for about the 6th time, was unemployed, and seemed quite ancient. We had a pleasant chat about old times, during which he explained why he had originally refused to have me in the *dōjō*. It was because when he first met me, I had long fingernails covered in scarlet nail polish. He figured that anyone with that sort of vanity would never survive in karate. We laughed as he examined the current shade of nail polish. He said he could never figure out how I could do knuckle push-ups with long fingernails. I assured him that in no way was karate training going to be allowed to interfere with vanity, or, for that matter, vice versa.

Ronnie now had a fairly large organization that seemed to grow daily.

He had a class of about 40 black belts, a great deal of whom were women. I was pleased to see that he had been so successful, but his teaching style did not really align with what I needed. Ronnie could generate a great deal of spirited enthusiasm, but I knew that I needed something to be enthusiastic about, and it just wasn't there.

A seminar with Kato had been planned in several towns and cities in Scotland, so I decided to join in the fun. I would go down to Edinburgh with Ronnie and see my old friend from Boroughmuir School, Susan Ireland Gerrard, who was now a nidan in Ronnie's organization. Thereafter, I would return to Aberdeen and then attend the series of seminars in the North of Scotland, which started in Inverness and would be repeated in Banff, Buckie, Peterhead, and Huntly, centers of martial arts excellence in the North of Scotland.

Kato was in fine form and gave a seminar typical of those I recalled from six years past. Lots of quirky combinations, *kata* interpretations, advanced *kata*, and sparring techniques. I was immediately inspired to train, so I looked forward to the following week, packed with action and knowledge.

A bunch of us went up to Inverness and checked into a hotel. Kato was staying as the guest of a family, of whom three members practiced karate. Father and two daughters. They considered themselves privileged to host Kato and treated him with the utmost respect and deference. As soon as rooms were assigned and luggage disposed of, we all went out to meet Kato at a restaurant and then headed towards the gym. I met Ronnie and Dolina Ross, who had started training around the time I had left. They said they remembered me teaching some class up in Inverness when they were white belts. I was the first woman they had seen wearing a black belt, so the image had stuck in their minds. Now they were both nidans, whereas I remained a shodan. Vaguely familiar faces seemed to fill the gym.

"Norma! You remember me, don't you"? Honestly, I didn't. Much to my embarrassment.

Kato was now part of Kanazawa's organization, Shotokan Karate International (SKI). Kanazawa had indeed split from the JKA in 1974, and Kato had followed him. Shotokan karate had boomed in the north of Scotland, mostly thanks to Ronnie's efforts, and though he was in the SKI, Kato was a frequent visitor to all the little towns no one else cared to visit. So, there were not really too many demarcations among associations headed by various Japanese, because people were all too grateful to be visited by any High Dan-Level instructor with a Japanese face.

During the class, among several demonstrations with partners, he used a young girl who had recently passed junior shodan. That meant she was under sixteen. In fact, she was fourteen, although she looked quite mature for her age, being tall and having a reserved, mature manner.

After training, I went straight to the pub in the typical unhealthy Scottish style, for several hours of pint quaffing. Margaret, the junior also joined us. This was not unusual in Scotland, because as soon as you looked old enough to pass for eighteen, the legal drinking age, you went to the pub. So, girls learned fairly early how to behave in adult company, smoke cigarettes, drink martinis and lemonade, and not draw attention to themselves with inappropriate childish behaviour.

A wry reflection.

The party wore on. I noticed that Margaret was wearing a real sapphire and diamond ring on her left wedding ring finger, and mentioned it to Ronnie Ross.

"Aye, that's Kato's latest present to her. Smitten he is."

He also told me that Kato was staying in her parents' house and that they seemed to endorse his showering their daughter with jewelry from Amsterdam. He told me that the ring was just the latest in a series of pricey gifts bestowed upon the girl.

I considered that Kato was now around forty. Was he now pursuing younger and younger girls? Many of his comments during social gatherings centered on how fit he was, how healthy, and how young he looked. The more I pondered the subject, the more I thought that Kato was sick. However, if her parents encouraged such attention, there was nothing for me to say.

The evening came to a close, and the last I saw of Kato was him piling into Margaret's father's car to chauffeur him to their home.

We all meandered back to the hotel and kicked around Kato's latest perverted penchant for young girls. We laughed about it and, having talked it out, went off to our rooms to recuperate in time for the next class scheduled 12 hours later.

The next morning, we met for breakfast in the hotel restaurant, and I received a page. It was Ronnie Ross. There would be no class today, or any other day. Please inform everyone to go home, as the rest of the seminar was cancelled. Kato had been arrested and was currently in jail. Well, it had to happen.

Margaret's parents had caught Kato in flagrante *delicto* with their eldest daughter. However, although this surely might have been a rather unpleasant surprise rather than a total shock, the mother hit the roof when she found her youngest daughter, aged eight, in the same bed. The police were immediately called, Kato was hauled away in handcuffs, and charges were brought. A fine abuse of hospitality. The newspapers reported the incident as "physical education teacher", Kato S, jailed for child abuse. He managed to get them to omit any references to karate.

We returned to Aberdeen with various opinions. Some of the men, who had a long history of affairs with girls of indeterminate ages, simply thought Kato was a fool to allow himself to be caught. Others wondered what the eight-year-old was doing in situ. *Probably trying to get some sleep* I ventured, not without a fair degree of cynicism.

The upshot was that Kato spent three days as a guest of the Inverness constabulary, later appeared in court, and was simply fined a very token sum. Men were still men, and sheep remained nervous in the North of Scotland, and I am sure that there were many who considered that sleeping with young girls was a perfectly fine, macho thing to do. No one in the Scottish justice system seemed to consider the effects of abuse of power, which Kato was found guilty of, or that this was not a momentary aberration. He was quite likely to repeat the behaviour. Kanazawa sensei, however, removed Kato from his organization immediately, and it was a long time before Kato showed his face again in Scotland. Because of Kanazawa sensei's reaction, it occurred to me that Kato's offer of a threesome on the night before my shodan exam might not have been made with Kanazawa's knowledge after all. I therefore chose to regard Mr. Kanazawa as innocent.

Christmas approached, and old friends started to return to the city. One of these was Brian, my gay friend who had introduced me to my ex-husband, Tab. Brian was doing a post-doc at Simon Fraser University in Vancouver. We had stayed connected, and he had even visited Houston. Brian's research interests were changing from plant physiology to plant receptor biochemistry, and since hormone receptors were the focus of my work in Houston and Little Rock, he suggested that I should consider coming to Vancouver for a couple of months to help him set up the lab and teach him the techniques involved in receptor binding studies. Well, this would make a change from breast cancer, prostate hypertrophy, and testicular abnormalities. Brian studied cucumbers. My least favorite vegetable. In fact, the smell of cucumbers, as well as melons, makes me quite nauseated. However, Brian assured me that I would have no problem because I would be working with seedlings and shoots. He convinced me that it would be great fun, and having obtained my commitment to go, said he would arrange for Lalit Srivastava, his boss, to pay me an honorarium and that I could stay in Brian's apartment. He was so sure that I would love Vancouver, and that he would have all the details arranged by the spring of 1980. Sounded perfect. Just the opportunity I had been waiting for. So, Brian and I celebrated this new plan at Gerrard's restaurant. Oh yes. Aberdeen now had a French restaurant. We had become very cosmopolitan since the Texans had been and gone. The oil boom had busted, as it became evident that the cost of extracting North Sea Oil was so high that profits were insufficient, and most of the major oil companies had retreated, leaving only skeletal offices. There was a bit of a ghost town feel to the office blocks and private properties with For Sale or Lease signs in windows. However, Aberdeen was in the process of transitioning back to its traditional industries, including paper, fishing, agriculture, and tourism.

Another returnee to the city was Eddie Stainer, another old friend, who now lived in Madeira and London. He said that if I wanted to go to London, I could stay at his flat in Maida Vale, as he would be gone for four months, working on oil rigs in the Middle East and living in Madeira on his weeks off. He would appreciate someone living in the flat in his absence.

Things were beginning to take shape, so I considered living in London for a few months.

Barbara's company had several shops in London, and she found out that the Oxford Street shop needed help. If I were interested, she would recommend me, although there was no guarantee that I would get the job. She also said that this shop was used as an outlet for all the others, so morale in the shop was not high. There was suspicion of embezzlement, and that overall, the working environment would not exactly be as well-ordered and friendly as the Aberdeen branch. I didn't mind. It would only be temporary anyway, so I figured I was up to the challenge for a few months.

Everything fell into place perfectly. I had free accommodation and a job in London to keep me in chocolate digestive biscuits and sightseeing money, while I saved for the plane ticket to Vancouver in the spring. I was happy; there was a now and a future.

During this interlude, I had not visited my mother or contacted my father's relatives. Those who lived in Aberdeen, who were most of my father's side of the family, were quite confused when they opened up the special pull-out TV section of the New Year's edition of the Evening Express newspaper. Occupying the entire black and white cover of the section was a girl reclining on a table holding a glass of bubbly. An open bottle of champagne sat on a nearby table, and party streamers were all around. The blond girl with long hair, laughing at the camera, wearing a party dress, looked a lot like me. However, family riots and arguments lasted for a week as some said it was me and others said it couldn't be because everyone knew I was buried somewhere in hillbilly America, somewhere with a rock in its name.

It was me. I decided that after that bit of publicity, I would have to conform to some sort of familial obligation and visit them.

Barbara was supposed to have been the model, but she had double-booked herself. Since this job did not require height, as it was only a photographic session, she figured I could do it. I was even paid for the work. What a life! I imagined what it would be like to be paid simply for existing. Look this way, walk over there, tilt here, wear this dress, accept this payment. It could only happen in Aberdeen. At 5'2", being a model is not a career option, and my face was certainly not cosmetic counter material. I had horrible hands from years of karate abuse and from throwing boiling concentrated sulphuric acid over them in an accident in the school chemistry class. My feet were too small to make me money as a foot model, and here I was, this imperfect specimen of humanity, gracing the tables of a quarter of a million homes for a week—what a joke.

Sure enough, the minute I sat down on Aunt Grace's floral sofa, her husband Alan said

"*I told you it was her!*"

Much rattling of the China cabinet doors to reveal China that only became exposed on special occasions. Alan and Grace started a good-natured fight based on whether or not the China was appropriate for me since I was "just family". They went on like this as though I wasn't there, then as though they just remembered what the squabble was about, they asked me if I had seen *her*—referring of course to my mother. A long interlude followed over the tea and shortbread biscuits, where

Grace and Alan discussed my mother and how it was truly amazing that Norma to all intents and purposes as far as their eye could see, had *turned out fine* despite that alcoholic slut. I resented their attitude and said so, as mother or not, they were certainly not terribly helpful when I was fourteen and rejected by all of my father's well-to-do sisters. Yes, it was truly amazing, wasn't it, that Norma, unlike Cousin William, was not a registered alcoholic, a drug addict, or psychotic. Yes. Quite remarkable. I wondered if I had disappointed them. After shifting them from this subject, because I felt forced to defend my mother, I discovered details of my Aunt Margaret's wedding. She had worked in the same engineering firm as a secretary since the war. She looked after my grandfather until he died rather inconveniently for her at the age of ninety-two. She had remained the spinster of the family, the maiden aunt. However, when retirement rolled around, she married Jim Bryson and moved to Haddington, which, incidentally, was where my grandfather had spent his youth. I learned that the youngest of the Amos sisters, Linda, had taken up Taekwondo at the age of forty-nine. Apparently, my cousin Lindsey, Linda, and Gordon's son, was secretary of the Scottish Tukido Association and was a purple belt. I was impressed. One aunt embarks on an uncharted new life, and another begins studying a martial art. There was some kind of spirit in these women that I didn't know existed. I finally learned to respect them and to feel a kinship with them, which I had little reason to feel before. I visited them all, including Aunt Betty, who lived in Ellon with her husband, Tommy, and their son, William, a legally registered alcoholic. His sister, Lorraine, had married Ron Milne and, as far as I knew, was happily reproducing herself in Preston, England. I was shocked to see William, my father's namesake, emerge from a filthy, dank, shaded room to answer the front door. He was just as shocked to see me and hurriedly closed the door to his room, not before I had caught a glimpse of the closed curtains, dirty bedding, and the rank smell of unwashed, alcoholic fumes that had wafted into the hallway. His face, so like my father's was uncanny, was puffy, and colored grey. His eyes, once Mediterranean blue on a sparkling clear white background, were bloodied custard, and the blue had faded.

He was overweight and somehow lumpy, and he struggled to put on a filthy olive drab sweater with stains down the front. This appalling vision was my handsome cousin William, whose trim and healthy form I had last seen about ten years ago in the Star and Garter, sporting a European tan that made his eyes positively glow with visions of Mediterranean summers and shimmering white sailboats. He explained that as a registered alcoholic, he didn't have to work, and he received a government pension that fed his habit. Nice life. Sponge off your seventy-year-old parents and drink yourself to death. William fussed about, obviously ill at ease, and tried to make me feel at home, but he wasn't sure where the tea things were. On the other hand, Tommy was out bowling, and Betty was meeting some cronies, and he wasn't sure when they would be back, but I was welcome to wait. I put him out of his misery by leaving.

I was seventeen and had not seen my mother for three years. I had been working at the Department of Lipid Biochemistry in the Rowett Research Institute for a year, and I was visiting Edinburgh with Tim on a shopping spree. I had taken some time out to visit my mother and found a dreadful metamorphosis in the flat. Mother was sober when she answered the door, and tears filled her eyes as she brought me through to the living room. I wandered through the flat, looking at the thick layer of dust on top of all the furniture, noticing the lack of a phone, the threadbare carpets, and the worn, exhausted look on Mother's face. My minuscule bedroom was exactly as I had left it when I fled to Aberdeen with her sister, Isobel. Bottles of caked calligraphy ink, my stamp collection, books, my hockey stick and ball, and my black tracksuit—all enshrined. Mother was on the dole, receiving a minuscule benefit from the government. Since she had been stabbed by one of her pickups, and it had punctured her lung, she hadn't been able to work much. Somehow, she didn't seem threatening, and she was too frail to hurt anyone. She only used two rooms of the enormous flat, and the rest was closed and silent, covered in cobwebs in some places. I immediately felt sorry for her and proposed that I come back and live there, pay her rent, install a phone, clean up the place, and help her get a life. She agreed, so I quit my job in Aberdeen and started working as a technician in the Immunology Department at the Royal (Dick) School of Veterinary Studies (known locally as the Dick Vet).

I transferred college credits to Napier Institute of Technology, named after the Scot who invented logarithms, and settled down to sleeping once again in my bedroom, where the single bed touched three walls.

Mother soon began to regain some pride and spirit. She smartened up her appearance and started to enjoy wearing clothes that had not left the wardrobe and its mothballs for years. She started a full-time job, and we cleaned all the rooms. However, after the initial burst of focused energy, it did not take long for her to start the whole downward spiral again, and she started to come home later and later—smelling of alcohol. She started to inflict the same mind games, and I started suffering the same migraines. When she came home one night wasted and accompanied by a man, I screamed at him to leave, and I called her an irresponsible tramp who would throw away her daughter for a bottle. I screamed some really dreadful things at her that incited her to act. Which, of course, was the point. She grabbed an arm to sink her manicured nails into my flesh, but as the blood started to seep out of the four parallel cuts, I told her that I would not tolerate such abuse. Of course, I was a lot stronger than her, even after only about a year of karate training, and I twisted her arm, turned myself around, and grabbed her other arm, which I twisted such that she lost her grip (was this an application from Heian Shodan?), and I pushed her hard. She staggered across the room, lost balance hopelessly, and came to a stop by falling into a spindly table with rickety legs that supported a massive 1950s EKCO TV that crashed down and partially pinned her to the ground. I checked to see that she had not suffered any injury, but felt no remorse. When she realized that all was well, she started cursing me at the top of her lungs and yelling that she was going to get the police to move me out of there because I had attacked her using karate.

"I will save you the phone call."

She struggled to her feet and started pushing me about. I went into my room to try to gather up a few things, and she started throwing things at me. Take this. And this. It was 1 a.m., and I had no money for a hotel room and nowhere else to go. Mother started hurling my meager possessions that had been preserved over the banister into the darkness of the basement, four stories below. She took a large steamer trunk, threw everything she could conveniently grab into it, closed it, and personally bumped it down 30 stairs into the garbage pile waiting to be collected later in the morning.

This is how I lost my extensive collection of British stamps dating from Victoria to Elizabeth, a Regency period book with maps of various countries on pages interspersed with tissues, the field-hockey stick, and its bag. Tragic. I stood outside the street door with its polished plates and stared mutely at the pile of trash containing my history. My mother's head appeared at the front room window, then the sash was thrown up, and more of my belongings came hurtling down into the street. I was devastated, angry, and standing there in the street wearing everything I owned. I held my head up and walked smartly to the corner of the street, where I just stopped and crumpled in a flood of tears, where she couldn't see or hear me. Tollcross, 2.00 am.

I ended up walking for an hour to reach the basement flat of two heroin addicts from Aberdeen that I knew. They let me spend the night and gave me the train fare to return to Aberdeen to start all over again.

All of this was vividly recycled in my brain as I trudged up the 30 stairs to face the door of my mother's flat on the top floor. Although the above events were now about a decade in the past and I had not seen my mother once during that time, the familiar, sickening feeling in the pit of my stomach tried to reach my throat as I mustered up the courage to press the doorbell. She had installed a magnifying eye on the door so that she could identify visitors without their seeing her. The violence that had so often climbed the stairs to explode at this door was obvious in crude plywood reinforcements nailed to the door and a series of dents where the paint was peeling indifferently.

Mother had aged considerably. Her hair was a rude mixture of crimson red and silver roots, and it hung to her waist like tangled rusted barbed wire. Her face was puffy and deeply lined. I supposed that her lifestyle had destroyed her. Was it just a trick of the light that made her look exactly like my memories of her psychotic mother? She was quite pathetic and also quite intoxicated… in the middle of the day. She tried to collect herself for my unexpected presence but failed miserably. Soon, the vicious hatred that she spewed forth when inebriated surfaced and overcame any attempts on my part at perfunctory politeness. After about 30 minutes of listening to a tirade about my worthless father, the wicked Amos sisters, sarcastic remarks about my personal appearance, a diatribe about men, in general (all "weak good-for-nothing arse holes"), and a series of belittling remarks all intended to "put me in my place", I could feel an emerging desire to take a serious swipe at her head and just stop her. I had survived Brown Sugar. This little bundle of hatred and venom would not take long to subdue. As she ranted on, I started to fantasize what it would be like to beat her senseless, tie her to a chair, stuff her mouth full of socks, wake her up with a snort of ammonia, and force her to listen to another side of her story. I guess that the image fooled my brain into thinking I had actually done it, as it calmed me somewhat, and I stood up to go.

"Not good enough for you, Miss High and Mighty. Look at you! Lady Muck! Who the hell do you think you are just "dropping in?"

Take yourself out the door right now… F***ing Amos. That is what you are. Call yourself Foster? You are just another one of them. An arse hole …AMOS!!!……

Gosh, here was me thinking that my middle name was Anne all this time.

Well. No need to visit any more relatives for a while. The status was never going to change. My father's family treated me like a curiosity that had somehow endured a life that resembled the Garden of Earthly Delights yet had not fallen by the wayside and disgraced them. My mother saw me as a reflection of her failed marriage to a weak man, and therefore could not communicate in any other terms but spite and poison. I decided to identify with my father's talented and deceased elder brother, Alex, the family hero who went down with the HMS Kelly during World War II. From the little I knew of Alex, I liked him and decided that he would not have held these attitudes and that I was his reincarnation. Somewhat macabre, the stuff of soap operas, but it gave me a sense of belonging to a family, whether they (or I) liked it or not. He was dead, and I was a misfit. Perfect.

All relationships reconfirmed, farewell parties attended, and teddy bear presents given by Barbara and her staff, I left Aberdeen yet again on the King's Cross sleeper bound for London. This time, without tears. Scotland held nothing for me. No future, no job, no dreams. I understood implicitly that my friends were of far more value to me than my family. Although Helen is my mother's name, it was Tim's mother, also called Helen, to whom I felt closer. Heroin addicts had helped me and sheltered me; Ronnie Watt's parents had allowed me to stay in their cramped two-roomed flat when I returned to Aberdeen previously. Ronnie Herd gave me the odd piece of pork and a constant supply of vegetables from the butcher shop, and Robert Turnbull would often slip me some haddock wrapped in newspaper. These people sustained me when I had nothing. No job, no future, and £10 to last me the rest of my life. None were my relatives; they were my friends.

London, 1980

I started working in Oxford Street, right around the corner from Foyle's, the bookstore. Yes! There was a large section of books about oriental subjects and things in Japanese in particular, so I picked up a useful chart that showed all the hiragana and *katakana* alphabets and their *kanji* sources, and quite a few books about Japan.

I visited Keinosuke Enoeda's *dōjō* at the top of Marshall Street baths, with all intentions of knuckling down and making the most of the opportunity to train with the Tiger, who was now a 7th Dan or so. After trudging up several flights of stairs, all the while inhaling the chlorine vapors from the pool below, I reached the top of the building, gasping for air and sweating profusely. A woman appeared wearing a gi and a brown belt, and she positioned herself inside a kind of booth. She looked at me disdainfully. If I were in that state after simply climbing the stairs, I obviously was in the wrong place. I said that I wanted to train, so would she give me the schedules and costs? There was a class that night that started in an hour, but Enoeda sensei wasn't there. I could pay the £2 visitor fee and train with whoever was teaching the class. I did. The *dōjō* was long and narrow, with white adobe-looking walls lit by small windows placed very high, almost at the ceiling. A Japanese flag and a British flag were crossed at *shomen* (the front where a Shinto shrine might be placed) and there was a mirror at the short end. The *dōjō* itself would have had a pleasant ambiance if there had been no one in it and no chlorine smell. Arrogance pervaded the *dōjō* and extended its way into the changing rooms. The class was fine, though the British instructor seemed to think he was a reincarnation of Enoeda sensei, emulating the body language and Japlish bellowed by the absent master. I figured that training with Enoeda did not make you Enoeda, or even a tiger, and it did not mean that you were technically superior. And… what was the point of training there if you only saw the main man once every couple of weeks, if you were lucky? I decided not to join this club, the headquarters of the KUGB. The following day, I went to Earls Court to search out the *dōjō* taught by Masao Kawazoe, who had been sent to the UK as Enoeda's sidekick. Kawazoe sensei had split from him, forming his own clique of admirers, which eventually grew into an association. His *dōjō* was in a scruffy church hall, the floor of which was rubbed slick from the shoes of several generations of the faithful. He trained barefoot in an ice-skating rink, and most of the class was spent just trying to keep upright. The hall was huge, and the interior of the Protestant church was covered in somber dark wood with nothing to lighten the shadows. Several women trained with Kawazoe sensei, and that day, they actually outnumbered the men. I should have felt good about this, but there was a strange mixture of tension, condescension, and favoritism in the air. Kawazoe was a good technical image that

I would like to emulate, but his teaching style, the attitudes of those women, and the state of the floor did not appeal to me, and even his training fees which were considerably less than those of Enoeda could not bribe me to return.

What was I looking for? I didn't know exactly. It was not enough to simply stand in a class run by an oriental face. Something had to reach me. If I could only identify it.

I gave it no further thought, and considering that the only Japanese karate I really knew was Shotokan, it never occurred to me to seek out other styles. As far as I knew, there were only two *dōjō*s for me in London, and I didn't care for either of them.

So, I dealt with it by quitting karate altogether for the entire six months that I lived in London.

This decision freed up time to discover the city. The nights were becoming longer and longer, and I walked all over the place, Whitechapel, where Jack the Ripper had committed his infamous crimes against women in another era, the Tower of London, the jail of many an imprisoned monarch, Tyburn Hill, where common people were hanged, the market at Petticoat Lane, Portobello Road, Harrods. I really enjoyed London, and I had fun recreating its turbulent and fascinating history on weekend rambles.

I was never lonely while I lived in Eddie's spacious, empty apartment and knew no one other than the shop girls who were living in a different world from me. I viewed it as an opportunity to relax, shed unnecessary baggage, not think too deeply, read books, and get to know my way around London. Maybe I would come back someday, maybe with a visitor who didn't know the city, and I would be able to help make their stay enjoyable. (I did later). I was quite content, and within three months, I found myself as the assistant manager of a struggling retail shop.

By the time I left, I had managed to earn the respect of everyone in the store, stopped sales assistants from chewing gum at the front of the shop, glaring at any customers who dared enter the premises, sourced and stopped the embezzlement that had indeed been happening, and lowered the incidence of petty theft by staff and customers. The girls were even coming in on time and asking permission to have tea breaks or leave at the end of the day. I was quite amazed because the staff of 10 ranged in age from seventeen to fifty-three, with an absent manager, and a shop that was located on two floors. No management training had been offered, of course, so everything that was done was led by my gut. I was lucky. The shop struggled on, and I enjoyed the insights into the lives of these shop girls, who left school at fifteen, had boyfriends who were into all kinds of rackets, including drugs and grand theft, and lived with one adult relative or a boyfriend. They were no different from me at the same age, although they were a lot more street-smart and, despite the petty theft and embezzlement, had a peculiar streak of honesty based on trust and boundaries. They did not respect the manager, who could not cope and made herself ill, but they respected me. Much to my surprise.

A letter arrived for me from Brian, saying that Lalit had agreed to his proposal that I help redesign the lab for biochemical investigations into cucumber (!) receptors, and everything was ready for me to come to Vancouver. I gave notice to my employers, and the girls held a farewell party for me in a bistro around the corner from the shop. They kept me well entertained, mimicking my behaviour when I first came to the shop and the day, I decided I had had enough of their disregard for every retailing rule. One girl in particular, Jo, did such a superb job of copying every gesture and nuance that I had and exaggerating my Edinburgh accent, no mean feat for a Cockney, and the whole group soon became so convulsed in hysterical laughter that every customer in the bistro became infected with it. One of the girls gave me a deep red leather manicure case complete with all the essentials as a going-away present. It was quite extravagant, and she confided that it had accidentally fallen off the back of a lorry (stolen). Her boyfriend had given her a box of them to sell. What could I say? I left London with many fond memories, and the manicure case, complete with all its tools, remains one of my fondest treasures.

Vancouver, BC, Canada 1979–1981

The Canadian Pacific aircraft circled around Vancouver from the east, allowing a stunning view of rugged mountains sweeping down towards calm waters in the west. A massive harbor and trees and trees and trees. A delta separated into convoluted sandbars as a greyish river emptied into the Georgia Straits. It was mid-June, and the sun in a clear sky caused gentle ripples on the blue water that sparkled invitingly. Even before the 747 touched down, Vancouver seemed welcoming and full of promise.

Brian was bubbling over with enthusiasm at the airport. He couldn't stop talking about the lab, his apartment, his friends, lovers, and the city. His verbal momentum carried us throughout a 30-minute taxi ride to the West End of the city, where he lived on the 8th floor of a 14-storey high-rise. Although that section of Vancouver is densely populated, with block after block of residential high-rises punctuated by the occasional Victorian family home, there was no hint that anyone actually lived there on the day I arrived. In retrospect, they were probably all at the beach located at the bottom of the street!! Lush trees were so full of leaves that they formed a canopy for the entire length of several streets. The overall effect was amazingly peaceful, broken only by an occasional car lazily meandering towards Stanley Park. Brian said I would enjoy a comfortable combination of the best of Britain and America without the nastier aspects of either. There were no guns in Vancouver (Nuclear Free Zone!) as there were across the border, and no class distinctions based upon accent—which was important to Brian, as he had assiduously cultivated an upper-class British accent to hide a Yorkshire brogue and survive undergraduate years at Oxford. Even more dear to Brian's heart was the fact that the West End harbored a large gay population in which he was totally at ease for the first time in his life. Aberdeen was not very sympathetic towards those with Brian's inclinations, and he had suffered the occasional beating for simply walking down the main street of Aberdeen and looking like a "poofter". Vancouver had none of that.

Brian bought a car because he reckoned, I had become used to such conveniences in Houston. Although he had a driver's license, he was too nervous to drive and traveled everywhere in Vancouver by the inefficient electric bus service, or by taxi. Of course, he could not buy a simple Toyota or Ford. The car would need to have either aesthetic appeal or historical value, or both. He finally decided upon a red 1964 Buick Electra 225 convertible,

with five ways to change the station on the A.M. radio, two enormous leather bench seats, a gas-guzzling engine, and it was precisely the same length as the Ford 12-seater van alongside which it was parked when we picked it up. It cost him all of $700, and it was only a matter of weeks before that much had been spent again feeding it gasoline and fluids and having brakes and tires reinstalled. It was very distinctive, and Brian referred to it lovingly as his jalopy.

Transportation assured, Brian and I went endlessly sightseeing in the jalopy: West Vancouver, North Vancouver, Steveston, Stanley Park, Whistler, Deep Cove, and Horseshoe Bay. A short stroll to the bottom of Barclay Street in the early evening for a cappuccino at an outdoor cafe rewarded one with memorable sunsets over English Bay almost daily. A cruise up Cypress Mountain beheld a view that spanned the mountains on Vancouver Island, one hour and forty minutes away by ferry to snowcapped Mount Baker, hovering mysteriously in the air in

Washington State to the Southeast. The Coastal mountains prevented further views east up Indian Arm, but a fjord or two was hinted at where Burnaby Mountain falls into the water between Burnaby and Port Moody to the east. Brian pointed out the buildings on the top of Burnaby Mountain and as being the University where I would work. A university on the top of a mountain? Wow! He then showed me another crop of four or five high-rises at the far western edge of the city, looking out to sea, and identified them as the dorms at the University of British Columbia, which was why Simon Fraser University was located where it was: as far away as possible from UBC.

We went to Harrison Hot Springs to bathe by the lake and in pools of spring water, and to peculiarly British Victoria, the provincial capital on Vancouver Island, which is about the size of England. The scale of things! Everything was clean, bright, and seemed full of happy people. Tourists, perhaps, but then again, perhaps just locals enjoying this fabulously vibrant land. He introduced me every day to a new restaurant and delighted in ordering some new kind of ethnic food I couldn't pronounce and didn't know existed. Chinatown for red bean shaved ice and ethnic bakeries, where English was not the lingua franca. Every night, a different club, cuisine, cinema, or café. The choices were endless, and the variety staggering. What a change from Little Rock! Aberdeen!

Thus acclimated, I started to work for Lalit Srivastava in the Bioscience Department at Simon Fraser University (SFU), ostensibly for a period of two months. After about a month, it was actually possible to find the lab unaided, as the department in the concrete multilevel rabbit warren designed by Arthur Erikson apparently moved every time I tried to locate it. The first time cruising up Burnaby Mountain was a drive through a dense forest of pine trees. The road banked alarmingly, then sharply spiraled in amongst trees that suddenly parted to reveal a concrete construction site with a glass top supported by scaffolding and covered in polythene (due to leaks). Oops. Silly me in my ignorance. It was not a construction site; it was Architectural Art. Based on an Inca or Aztec temple? Tiers of cracked concrete steps, wide open spaces, and a glass roof over more space formed a pyramid that was topped by a quadrangle and grass with a reflective pond, stream, and bridge that clearly said "Art". It was said that when it rains, which is a lot of the year, it is possible to go from one end of the campus to the other under cover, but I didn't believe it. The student body seemed to be entirely Chinese, unlike Aberdeen, or for that matter, Texas or Arkansas. I settled down to organizing the lab and ordering supplies for Brian's venture into cucumber receptor chemistry. When the two months ended, the experiments had not, so Lalit and Brian asked me to stay for another four months. A stay of execution. Living at Brian's apartment as his roommate was fine, and he would be out of town for a few more months anyway.

OK. Time to look for a *dōjō*.

The Yellow Pages yielded lots of ads describing the merits of several karate schools, and far more karate was represented than taekwondo. One ad described a "*Shoto Ryū*" school that was located downtown. Sadly, the phone number had been disconnected. I went to the address listed in the ad and saw no sign of a karate school, so I phoned up a *Shitō Ryū* school and talked to someone who identified himself as "Sato". He told me that the *Shoto Ryū* instructor was called Hidetada (Hide) Narumi, the *dōjō* had moved, and that he didn't know where. Maybe on 61st Street. He asked me if I might want to join Shito Ryū. I declined and said I wanted to find a Shotokan school because that is what I had studied. Pretty similar conversations followed with all other listed numbers called. *Dōjō*s could be located in all sorts of places and would not necessarily be listed in the Yellow Pages, but how do I find them? I drove down 61st Street but never found the elusive Shoto Ryū *dōjō*.

I had not trained for several months, and it was time to get back in shape.

I played racquetball with Brian at the West End Community Center, where he also studied Tai Chi. One day, we were off to play a game when someone wearing a white karate gi with a green belt rushed past me. The jacket had a Shotokan tiger on the back! This particular cartoonish tiger was used as a symbol by Funakoshi Gichin to identify his style, and it supposedly originated in a Japanese children's book, so it was quite distinctive.

I asked the green belt what style of karate he studied, just to confirm.

Shotokan, he called as he ran into the gym.

I watched some of the class. The gym had a perfect, sprung wooden floor, mirrors at the front, a bar, and an abundance of natural light from huge windows all along the long end of the gym. The boughs of a massive tree gently swayed in the summer breeze and tapped the window occasionally. The *dōjō* contained about 40 people, about 15 of whom were women! The Chinese instructor was about the same age as me, and the amazing thing was that—so was everyone in the room. The instructor seemed technically proficient, and his teaching style did not consist of barked orders and insults. People even occasionally laughed during the class! Unheard of in my experience. However, all the students worked very hard.

However, it was not Shotokan, although it seemed Japanese, definitely not Korean or Chinese. I left and asked at the front desk which days the group practiced: Sunday, Monday, Wednesday, and Friday. What is the instructor's name: *Yuwa Wong*. What style is it? *Karate*. How much is it? *$25 per month*.

Brian then trounced me at racquetball.

The *dōjō* was located six blocks from Brian's apartment and was affordable. I could walk to class—amazing!

I brought my gi for the next class and introduced myself to the instructor. He was very friendly and told me to change and join in.

Soon, I was learning *Naha Te* according to George Sakai of Hawaii as interpreted by Yuwa Wong, a graduate student of philosophy at SFU and a whiz kid of several martial arts. He had studied this vision of Naha Te in Hawaii, then, while attending Trent University in Peterborough, discovered Shotokan. He also studied Chinese martial arts, including Tai Chi. He communicated clearly and succinctly and had the technical expertise to demonstrate everything he wanted done. He was a very smart and accomplished person.

So, I learned another version of five *Pinan kata, Chinto, and Seishan,* while also practicing five *Heians kata, Gankaku,* and *Hangetsu.* I learned some new *kata*: Sanchin, Tensho, and Geiryu, which resembled the first half of *Seienchin,* then stopped, as though someone had forgotten the rest. Yuwa said that the founder of his style of Naha Te was Choki Motobu, also known as Kwan, and according to Yuwa, this person was a bit of a renegade and lout. So, he was never allowed to participate in regular "Te" classes taught to allegedly royal siblings. This Kwan thus spied on various schools in Naha and developed his interpretations of what he saw. Considering he was often caught before a *kata* was completed, it was inevitable that he would either invent something new or practice as much as he knew of a *kata*. I don't know if any of this had any basis in fact, but the point where this "Geiryu" *kata* stopped was definitely suspicious. The *Tensho* and *Sanchin kata* are, of course, fundamental pillars of *Gōjū Ryū* with distinct emphasis on different types of breathing. The Chinto *kata* was performed entirely at a 45-degree angle to the start line, similar to some Shorin Ryū versions, but for some reason, it was difficult to wrap my head around this.

After about a year in Yuwa's club, I competed in a tournament attended by many Chinese martial arts practitioners. My rough and ready *Unsu* was no match for the precise, entertaining acrobatics of Kung Fu and Wu Shu entrants, and besides, I didn't feel that great about entering a tournament with no proper preparation.

As the class was about to begin, one sultry Friday evening, a strange apparition appeared at the *dōjō* door. As people turned to look, they erupted in gales of laughter, pointed, made some rude comments, and then fell about. Soon, the entire *dōjō* was falling about, writhing on the floor, holding their sides, and laughing to the point of tears. What could cause such commotion? Stepping into the room with a sheepish grin and an afro was an oriental fellow I had never seen before, with a nose that could actually support glasses without them falling off. Obviously, everyone knew this person, and his Tokaido heavyweight gi top and brown belt were in flagrant competition with royal blue boxing shorts exposing wiry, muscly legs. This person seemed quite at ease with himself, and the evoked responses explained that he had forgotten his gi pants. Folks just laughed all the more and pointed out that the lack of gi pants was temporary, whereas what was on the top of his head would have to be endured for a bit longer. He had evidently had a perm.

Unfazed, he scanned the room, spotted me, and horror of horrors, came straight towards me with an outstretched hand,

"Hi. My name is Kikuma, but you can call me Kick."

Obviously, he was Japanese as confirmed by the characters for Yamaguchi embroidered on his gi jacket. Does Kikuma mean chrysanthemum horse? What a strange name. But Kick! A great name for a karate man? How to handle this confident introduction? I shook his hand, bowed, and said I was pleased to meet him, my name was Norma, with as much aloofness as possible to discourage this buffoon. To further exacerbate matters, he stood himself on my left, indicating that he was senior to me in this group, brown belt notwithstanding. He tried to talk to me during the class, but I did my best to ignore him.

I later discovered that I just happened to be standing in his usual spot and that his positioning had more to do with habit than hierarchy. The spot had an unobstructed view not only of Yuwa, the teacher, but of the tree and the sunset, for those moments of wandering attention. I had never met anyone quite like him.

After becoming comfortable with his terrifying friendliness and his over-the-top hairdo which had become tempered by repeated visits to various barbers, he did indeed show up to class properly dressed, and I began to appreciate him as much as everyone else in the *dōjō*.

Before long, I joined Kikuma, Philippe (bottom half French-Canadian, upper half Filipino), and Yuwa in eating and partying with gusto. A restaurant would be selected after training, and the others had to determine their key virtues: good dessert (Yuwa), inexpensive (Yuwa), pretty waitresses (Philippe), quantity (Kikuma), different (Norma) ambiance (all)? Kikuma, Philippe, and Yuwa were good cooks, and so when we had exhausted all the choices that we could find within our respective budgets, they all started to cook at home. Thus, was established the multicultural Buta Kyokai-Pig Association.

One day, Philippe noted that one among the group of pigs ate as much as everyone else but never cooked at home. Eventually, I had to succumb to pressure and overcome my *Fear of Cooking*.

Mother had drunk herself into such a stupor late one usual Saturday evening of rock and roll, Jim Reeves, squeaky springs, and heavy breathing, that when the late Sunday morning sun brightened her nasty disheveled bedclothes, she was still far from sober. However, she was alert enough to remember a lunch guest, Flora, who was due to arrive at 1 pm. She ordered me to *"get the lunch ready"*. I was nine years old and had never learned any cooking skills, other than peeling potatoes and opening cans of processed peas and spam tins. But this lunch demanded gravy, tenderizing cheap mince (hamburger meat), and actually boiling potatoes. Dumplings were beyond hope. Mother barked what to do with great sarcasm directly from her chamber (of horrors) while demanding more drink and the occasional sandwich.

Flora arrived at precisely 1 pm to find me in a state of terror and her hostess with a balance problem. Flora had brought a quarter bottle of brandy, which would further exacerbate Mother's condition, and a bar of chocolate for me, which Mother swiped because...

"You don't deserve this."

Flora quickly became uncomfortable, then clearly agitated. Dismay arrived when undercooked potatoes, overcooked mincemeat, runny gravy, and canned peas were ladled onto Willow-patterned dinner plates.

Mother took one look at this depressing effort, picked up her plate, and hurled it at my face, accompanied by a stream of profanity. Flora blanched with shock as she tried to reason with Mother and comfort me, who was by now screaming, with embarrassment, humiliation, and fear, lunch running down my face. My yellow, black, and white t-shirt and yellow shorts became a murk of brown, green, cream, and tears. Flora could not exit the house fast enough. I don't think she ever came back, and Mother never apologized for her behaviour, neither to me…

"Your fault. You are useless, you can't even cook potatoes!"

nor to Flora

"What her business, did she have telling me how to talk to such an incompetent idiot?"?

I vowed never to cook anything. Ever.

I held true to that vow objective until the day the Pig Association explained its new rule: You only have to cook once Norma, and even if it is really awful, they would eat it anyway because they would respect my efforts and besides, they really could eat anything. I had seen them all eat chicken feet and dim sum (dim yuck) with my own eyes.

"I don't know how to cook anything." I replied.

"No problem, Norma, just cook something Scottish!

"I don't know how to cook anything Scottish!"

Bowing to such pressure interfered with sleep for a week before the appointed day of death by haggis.

I took a day off work to purchase all the ingredients of a traditional Scottish meal that the Pigs had requested and bought a Scottish cookbook. Started preparing the base for Scotch broth from a lamb neck the night before the dinner party, and slept badly. I even dreamt of a restaurant painted by Bosch, patronized by demonic hordes cackling and spluttering over ladles of fat, dripping from a spit-turned lamb, screaming in agony because it was being cooked alive.

The next morning, a wicked tension headache worsened as the day wore on. I bustled about a galley kitchen completing Scotch broth, haggis, neeps (turnips), tatties (potatoes), and a trifle soaked in sherry. The dinner was to be washed down with French wines, Glen Morangie single malt Scotch whisky, and Drambuie. I figured that maybe if they drank enough, no one would notice the awful food.

The doorbell rang exactly on time, and the starving Pigs descended upon the formally set dining table, bright-eyed with anticipation. My headache achieved blinding intensity, and nausea joined in. After downing more ineffective aspirins, I ladled soup from a cauldron into bowls, and they all sat down. I couldn't eat.

In stunned amazement, I watched them consume all the broth and then demand seconds. I thought they were just being polite, and then Philippe asked me what stock I had used for the soup.

"Stock? What's that?"

Philippe was now stunned and explained about the stock. He was a gourmet cook, you see, and had studied at Vancouver Community College, another reason why I should not cook for him. He understood that I had made the soup from scratch, exactly like a Scottish farmer's wife might have done.

The haggis, neeps, and tatties were very simple, but prepared with large amounts of high-cholesterol dairy products to enrich the flavors. Again, each one of the three Pigs ate seconds. The trifle disappeared quickly, along with butter shortbread.

Roommate Bill and a friend arrived in the middle of this Caledonian feast and polished off all the remains, so absolutely nothing was left except the sounds of smacking lips and pounding in my ears. The Pigs accused me of lying to them, and that I was just being lazy because I undoubtedly had hidden these culinary skills from them for so long! Soup without stock. Indeed!

Well, all day Sunday was spent recovering from the ordeal, and by

Monday morning, the headache had run its course. I learned a lesson. It was possible for me to cook, but the emotional cost was still too high. So, about another five years or so had to pass before I could volunteer to cook, and now I do so routinely and will try to cook anything. If you don't like it, don't eat it... and everyone has allergies to something...

These wonderful Vancouver friends had a very positive impact on my life.

The West End, Vancouver

I returned to the 8th floor of the high-rise I now shared with Bill, as Brian had decided to stay in the UK for another six months while I continued his project at SFU! A secure income well into 1980 and receding career concerns. Kikuma lived in a West-facing apartment on the 10th floor of the neighboring concrete high-rise, and so he was the last person to whom I said "good night" one balmy summer evening after dinner with the other Pigs.

Around midnight, I climbed into the single bed in the tiny pine-floored bedroom and settled down to read a few lines of a James Clavell book. Around 40 minutes later, I started to smell smoke. Nothing unusual in the Vancouver West End, as Victorian homes were frequently torched to make room for developers and profits.

The smell became stronger, so I looked out of my westerly window but nestled back down among cozy blankets to continue reading about the Battle of Sekigahara since no signs of action were evident.

The smoke nevertheless became more pervasive, and I was not altogether surprised when Bill knocked on my door in a panic, quivering in his striped jammies, unlit cigarette in shaking fingers, mumbling and breathless.

He had smelled the smoke. He had gone to the front door and opened it onto a wall of smoke. He ran into the stairwell entrance next to our door. A thicker wall of smoke. The building was on fire!

I repeated Bill's actions and confirmed the reasons for his rising panic.

There was no escape from the apartment other than by jumping out of the window. I closed the front door and told Bill to get dressed and go to the balcony. I returned to my room, found some comfortable clothes, put my passport and diaries into a bag, threw it diagonally over my shoulder, and then, having secured my most important possessions, tested the phone. It worked, so I called Kikuma and delivered the wry message at 12.50 am that:

If I don't meet Yuwa for dinner tomorrow, please tell him it was because I couldn't jump out of a window.

Kikuma thought I was joking.

I reiterated the message, saying I wasn't joking, and that if he would please put on some clothes and go down into the street, he would see that I was deadly serious and trapped on the 8th floor of the building adjacent to his. Furthermore, if he would kindly tell me which floor was actually on fire and what was happening, I would like to go to my grave knowing the circumstances of my demise.

Kikuma still thought I was joking and humored me by saying he would call Yuwa.

I joined Bill chain-smoking on the balcony. "Appropriate behaviour in a fire," I pointed out.

By this time, smoke was swirling around the building, and people had gathered in the street to ogle at the catastrophe and hamper the efforts of the Vancouver Fire Department to control a rapidly spreading inferno.

The street was a mass of flashing lights, wormy high-pressure water hoses, oxygen tanks, ladders, and yellow helmets.

The phone rang. It was Kikuma, losing his marbles.

"Your building is on fire!" Duh. Still think I am joking?

"But...your building really is on fire!"

"Did you imagine that I would phone you at 1 am to tell you a bad joke?"

He told me that the 5th floor on the north side was an inferno, but the firefighters seemed to have it under control. This was a bit disappointing, as I had actually envisioned leaping onto sheets or being carried down ladders on the shoulders of handsome firefighters while exuding exemplary bravery and control.

Fortunately for me and my imaginary bravado, as well as Bill and his cigarettes, it never came to that. We read on the front page of the Vancouver Sun newspaper the next day that three people had died in the blaze, including a firefighter who was caught in an elevator that opened inadvertently on the 5th floor, a resident who suffered a heart attack while trying to escape to the roof and the person who started the fire by means of falling asleep with a lighted cigarette. The entire 5th floor was gutted, and the building required a facelift to erase the effects of the smoke.

It made for a good dinner story, as Kikuma had phoned Yuwa around 1.30 am to tell him all about it, so he had a scoop on the news the following morning.

Chinatown

After training, we often went to a particular restaurant in Chinatown that was famed for delicious and inexpensive gyoza (dumplings). One evening, Philippe, Yasmin (who had earned a green belt), and I piled into Kikuma's car (Jeep-san) to meet Yuwa and some others at the restaurant. Once in Chinatown, Kikuma slowed down to look for a parking place, which was difficult to find on a Friday evening. A car behind us started showing signs of impatience as headlights belligerently flashed on and off, and then a horn blared. Philippe, with a mischievous grin, asked in his Quebecois accent if he should perhaps shoot them ....

"Ze finguerr?"

"Yeah, yeah Philippe, be a daredevil." Show them the bird.

We continued to badger him, and he raised the middle finger of his right hand precisely in the middle of the back window. We all laughed at his audacity. Kikuma decided he was bored looking for free parking and decided to pull into a pay parking lot. Still laughing, Philippe jumped out of the passenger side of Jeep-san. Yasmin was next, and then when I jumped out, I crashed into her as she was rigidly standing upright behind Philippe, who was facing two overweight Chinese thugs wielding nunchaku. Their gold Mercedes 450SL was parked at right angles to Jeep-san, blocking any chance of a reversal. Kikuma, still laughing and talking, locked the door and came round the other side of Jeep-san. He stopped laughing immediately and assessed the situation. Here was Philippe, staring down the thugs who looked like they were playing bit parts in a bad movie, with their threatening *nunchaku*, chewing gum, and demanding to know....

"Which one of you assholes shoot the bird?"

Philippe told us girls to get back inside Jeep-san, and Yasmin sensibly did so. But I wanted to see this.

Kikuma (easy confidence of the privileged) stepped forward, arms akimbo as in a gracious welcome, which also served to confirm a lack of weapons. Kikuma showed not the slightest trace of fear and was in every way in command of the situation.

"Shooting the bird? Very sorry about that. Not sure about a bird, but maybe one of us accidentally raised a hand and maybe it could have been confused for a bird, but no, well, maybe it was just a finger and let's be friends and let's not do anything that might cause a night in hospital or jail or such a beautiful car as that Benz to get scratched...."

Amazing. Not a common reaction to a potential fight.

The Chinese men continued to threaten and posture, but eventually realized that a fight was not going to materialize. With continued threats and slander, they retreated into their golden Benz and drove off. Incident averted by Yamaguchi sama! Where did he learn such a skill? Was he born that way?

Now that the coast was clear, I advised Kikuma to move Jeep-san, as these chaps struck me as being the type that would come back and slash tires or inflict some other grievous bodily harm while we innocently downed dumplings.

Philippe decided to accompany him while Yasmin and I walked to the restaurant. Yuwa and the others were waiting for us and immediately wanted to find the thugs and exact revenge on them. It was too late, but Yuwa went to take a look anyway.

After what seemed a very long time, Kikuma and Philippe arrived at the restaurant.

They had pulled out of the parking lot, gone around the block, and come back to find the same Mercedes in the parking lot. They took off again and met them in an alley, nose to nose. They then moved again to a parking space on the edge of Chinatown and looked for trouble all the way to Main Street, where the restaurant was located.

We consumed more dumplings while reiterating with great excitement the look on Philippe's face when he scrambled out of Jeep-san and came to a sudden stop, and Kikuma's calming effects on the would-be attackers using only words and non-threatening body language.

This is karate, I thought to myself. Here is someone who understands how it works, and all is hidden behind this exterior of buffoonery that didn't seem to take anything seriously, including being Japanese. Kikuma earned a lot of respect that night.

Women in the Naha Te *Dōjō*

The Naha Te *dōjō* at the West End Community Center was the first karate class I had ever seen that consisted of about 30% women. Most of them were not born and raised in Vancouver; they had traveled to and lived in all sorts of exotic places.

Colleen, whose Indian, Slavic, Scottish/Irish genes conspired to bestow her with high, prominent cheekbones, a firm square jaw, and arresting pale green almond-shaped eyes. A perfectly even tan made a toothpaste commercial of her dazzling smile. She was an emergency nurse, highly skilled in cardiac care, intelligent, sharp, and witty. She had traveled extensively in the Orient, Eastern Europe, and even Scotland, and had studied Tai Chi. Colleen had a sharper tongue than even I, no doubt a product of her lack of height, about which I would razz her often, as she was an inch shorter than I.

Suzanne was married to Branch, involved in Tai Chi, and, like the others, had quite recently started karate. Loads of self-confidence, an easygoing, friendly demeanor, and thick, curly black hair, jailed in a waist-length braid a la Joan Baez. Suzanne was positive, humorous, and very kind. Her compassionate green eyes held a warmth, intellect, and action that was directed towards high-risk youth. She had left school and home at fourteen and financed herself through university in Montreal, from which she graduated at the age of eighteen.

She had written a proposal to the provincial government to provide funding for a halfway house for patients who were being released in droves from closing mental institutions in the Lower Mainland, called The Kettle. Soon, it became an extremely successful enterprise, blossoming from its initial two rooms to populate the entire building, then moved to a specially commissioned building in the same area in the 21st Century.

Suzanne remains interested in the plight of abused children and in helping First Nations children overcome the effects of living in a hostile environment, be it their own home or mainstream society. She has worked with prostitutes, alcoholics, and abused children and is now trying hard to change how the law deals with perpetrators of these crimes against the most helpless of humanity. She wrote a book about bullying, and I am privileged to still have such a remarkable person among my closest friends. Today, with her rolled-up sleeves, elbow-deep in the scuffed, scarred, and terrifying lives of East End humanity, she, unmarried and remarried, became the mother of twins, who are as remarkable as Suzanne… known as "Mimi" to her three grandsons.

Suzanne attained Shodan in *"Naha Te"* karate, then studied other styles of karate, *Wu Shu,* aikido, and finally *hapkido,* which she quit after being slammed onto the ground by a male twice her size and splitting her spleen. She returned to Karate—much safer.

Yasmin spoke with a delightful French accent when I came to the *Naha Te* school. I thought she was French. She could beat me at sparring any day due to an enviable sense of timing and a long reach. She was so charming and self-effacing that it took me a long time to discover that she was an excellent skier and golfer and a student in kinesiology at SFU, where I still worked.

Born in the Belgian Congo and into a Gujarati family, her father had discovered how to make soap and made a reasonable living selling it to Africans. The family hurriedly escaped to Belgium to avoid the revolution in the 1950s that birthed Zaire (now DR Congo). She was sent to school in Switzerland, followed by a French lycée in London. Her peripatetic parents moved from Belgium to the UK, spent time in Sardinia, then moved to Montreal, and finally, North Vancouver. Yasmin recalled living in huts with dirt floors, where the family chickens strutted. She also recalled garden parties at their Sardinia home and the regional Gujarati dialect of her parents. Because Yasmin was attending SFU, we became close friends as we saw each other almost every day, as well as in karate class.

Yasmin eventually left to live in Los Angeles, where she remains, having given up karate after two years of study with Hidetaka Nishiyama. During that period, she achieved a brown belt in Shotokan, along with bursitis, tendonitis, and every other possible shoulder-itis. After a couple of years of massive doses of aspirin and severe pain, she finally succumbed to surgery, which cured all her problems in a single slash. She then focused more on golf, a sport in which she has always excelled. More about that later.

Joan had a few years of Tai Chi tucked under her karate white belt. Married at that time to a musician who did so many drugs that he eventually died of the natural causes associated with rock stars. She was a quintessential earth mother from the '60s with flowing ankle-length clothes, shawls, and large silver hoops in her ears. Her daughter, Jenny, was adopted in Laos, where Joan lived for a couple of years. She had had a son, who had perished in a fire in Australia at the age of two. This tragedy scarred far more deeply than the fall from a second-story window she suffered soon after, which caused her to be immobilized for several months.

Yet here was Joan, in her late 30s, having overcome such terrible catastrophes, always pleasant, always positive, learning a new martial art. Gentle, kind, and warm, with only good words for everyone, Joan eventually achieved shodan, married Michael, also from the *Naha Te dōjō,* and had a daughter called Rachel.

The other peer at the *Naha Te* school was Christine, a beautiful, blue-eyed blonde model from Australia who had lived in London, been photographed by David Bailey, and had traveled the globe, occasionally accompanied by a husband or two, or maybe more. Her most recent jaunt had been to South America, where she and her current husband, Rick, had reputedly indulged in many natural and synthetic substances. Rick also indulged in a great deal of firewater and, when having reached a level of saturation, would become violent and aggressive. They had a son called Galen, as beautiful, blonde, and blue-eyed as his mother. One of six children, Christine had left her home in Sydney, Australia, at the age of fourteen. Her mother had committed suicide during a night when Christine happened to disobey her parents and sneak out of the house to a dance. Christine was still living with the notion that she had caused her mother's death by her behaviour, when in fact, it was the behaviour of her abusive father that had caused her mother to take her own life. Christine was a serious and diligent student, writing down things about karate at every opportunity in a notebook, discussing and questioning everything. I wish I had done such things!

Christine was very talented and so overcame the absence of a formal education by developing an amazing range of skills. She could grow any kind of plant, motivate children, cook numerous delicious ethnic meals, design and sew clothing, model, cut hair, and make up other people's faces. She could make things out of nothing. Bits of string became macrame, bits of paper became fridge art, and scrap metal became jewelry... She also came of age in the 60s, matured beyond her years by being the homemaker for her siblings after her mother's death, and then by extensive travels. Christine was a survivor with whom I could identify. We became close friends for a long time, though we eventually grew apart in the early 1990s.

All of these women possessed rich life experiences, intelligence, and common sense; they loved life and looked for more. They had such drive and motivation, and right now, they were all driven and motivated by Karate. I was thrilled that they accepted me so easily and warmly into their lives and homes. They, along with the Pigs, particularly Kikuma, were instrumental in helping me believe in myself and that I could do anything if I chose to apply myself. They supported me in reaching some later goals and collectively helped me change some attitudes forever and for the better.

This was a golden time for me. I suddenly had all these male and female peers for the first time since I had left Aberdeen. It was so comfortable, this group of world travelers who were from somewhere else. Yuwa is an ethnic Chinese, thrown out of Indonesia, brought up in Hawaii, and educated in Toronto and Vancouver. Kikuma, a Japanese, educated in *Tōkyō*, Lake Tahoe, Denver, and the Banff Springs Hotel. And Philippe from Montreal, who studied culinary arts and worked until he retired from the CBC in Vancouver, were added to the mix. I was afloat in a warm, balmy cocoon of humanity, humor, and understanding – and in such a city as Vancouver! More interestingly, we lived within walking distance of each other and all practiced karate! Some kind of heaven.

I worked with Lalit Srivastava on Brian's behalf for a year studying plant hormones. Unfortunately for me, the plants being studied were cucumber, which I loathe. Karoun Nair then asked me to work for him studying vitellogenesis in desert locusts. The thought of working for Karoun gave me goosebumps on two accounts. One was a phobia of insects, despite the wildlife I had shared my apartments with in Houston, and the other was that my balding boss with rheumy eyes bore an uncanny resemblance to the insects he was famous for investigating, and had a dubious reputation concerning female staff. However, he was determined that I should work for him for a year, and I needed a job, so I explained my phobia and said that if he agreed, I would work for three months in his lab to see if I could cope with the job and that if we were both satisfied, then I would stay for another nine months. He agreed, and in fact, I worked for Karoun until the summer of 1981, when I changed careers altogether.

I eventually moved into Kikuma's apartment after Bill moved to Toronto and Brian decided to stay in London indefinitely.

Cypress Bowl, West Vancouver

Kikuma had been a ski instructor at Naeba, in Japan, and had been motivated by skiing to attend university in Colorado and then to gain hands-on knowledge of the hotel industry in the middle of the Canadian Rockies. When winter rolled around, he encouraged me to learn to ski, as he thought I would enjoy it. Everyone in the Naha Te *dōjō* could ski except Christine and me, and I stubbornly resisted Kikuma's persuasions for at least one season, imagining that skiing was like going shopping in the bleak, wet-frozen, windy winters of the north of Scotland. I could not understand how joy was to be obtained from snow.

Kikuma persisted, and eventually, at the age of thirty, I relented and found myself on Cyprus mountain wearing Kikuma's ski pants, sweater, and gloves, outdated boots from Yuwa (all of which were a bit too large for me), and short Rossignol "Chicken Little" skis donated by Colleen. Kikuma's designer poles completed my chic appearance, and off I went to the bottom of the hill with Kikuma and Yuwa feeling a bit silly. The pristine snow on Cyprus mountain glittered and squeaked in the early spring against my big red boots. Tall pine trees glistened emerald and crystal, and smiling people milled, buying tickets for a perfect day on the mountain. I had never believed such landscapes existed except on Christmas cards. Snow had never been so clean, so pure, so white that it appeared blue!

Kikuma started a warm-up and stretch. Preparations completed to his satisfaction, he bolted on his skis and threw away the poles.

"OK Nom, hangetsu dachi" (half-moon stance in Karate)

Angle your feet like this and push out with your heels. This is how you stop. Practice it 20 times". I did and worked up a sweat in no time.

Next…..the rope tow.

Position your skis like this, and as you grab the rope like this, tense your lats and stay that way until you reach the top of the hill, where you do what I do.

No problem. I was hooked. Yuwa was already impatient and disappeared up the chair lift. After I was sure I could handle the bunny hill and the rope tow, I told Kikuma to ski with Yuwa, as he would know where to find me.

I spent the time bombing straight down the hill and going up and down repeatedly. By the time Kikuma reappeared, I was ready to show off my new skills. I took off, straight down the hill. At the bottom, I came to a perfect skid stop, remembering how to do them based on weekly ice-skating jaunts at Murrayfield ice rink in Edinburgh at about the age of thirteen. Kikuma did not know I could stop like that and was horrified when he saw me take off, as he was already too late to catch up with me to stop the increasing momentum. He breathed a deep sigh of relief as I proudly turned around to face him.

"EEE, no? (Good …. right)"

"That's great, Nom, but there is more to skiing than hurtling down hills. You have to learn how to turn."

Yuwa just shook his head.

The next three seasons were spent learning how to turn and ski with control. Every skiing day was a lesson opportunity with exercises and challenges. Winter holidays in Kamloops, as guests of Jean Cimon of CP Hotels and Derek Campbell McDonald, meant weeks of uninterrupted ski lessons with Kikuma at Tod Mountain (Sun Peaks), which rapidly improved my skiing. This improvement warranted new skis and ski clothes that fit. Kikuma stressed and supervised the technical aspects of skiing, such as boots, bindings, settings, ski length, pliability, edge, and pole height, while I focused on the sartorial aspects of ski suits colours, fit, sunglasses, hats, and gloves vs. mitts. I loved skiing, much to my amazement, and Kikuma showed admirable restraint in not saying too many "I told you so's".

Kikuma also tried to interest me in golf, with much less success. Although golf is also fashionable and technical, it did not elicit the same effects as skiing. Perhaps the casual hole-in-one on the par three course I inadvertently scored at the age of seven coloured my attitude to golf.

"Duh. If it is that easy, why bother? What a load of rubbish, etc., etc".

I reluctantly played a few rounds of golf with Kikuma and Yasmin (who was a great golfer) and practiced at the driving range. He even bought me a set of clubs. However, not even this generous gesture and the fact that just about everyone in the Naha Te *dōjō* skied and played golf could motivate me to love the game. However, I put it on the back burner for further investigation in the future. Indeed, my attitude toward golf started to improve when golf attire started to resemble that of Zumba rather than Sherlock Holmes hats, tweed jackets, brown plus-four trousers, woolly socks and leather brogues, and woolly socks. Also, Yasmin had moved to Los Angeles and really started to pressure me into visiting her there and…. playing golf.

All Canada Karate Association (ACKA)

A couple of Japanese individuals visited the Naha Te *dōjō* one Wednesday evening in late 1979. It turned out that they were Toshiaki Kanamaru, who lived in Ashcroft and taught Sho-Sho Ryū, and Takeshi Uchiage from Steveston, who was a Gōjū instructor. They wanted to bring the Naha Te *dōjō* into their association. They claimed that the mainstream organization governing karate in British Columbia (BC) was run by a bunch of drunken louts, headed by a fellow called Hidetada Narumi, who was corrupted by power, alcohol, and drugs, like several of his Canadian students. Their group was called Shiseikai, and Hidetada Narumi was its chief instructor. The Shiseikai, according to the Gōjū people, controlled karate in the province of BC, along with a few Shito and Chito Ryū folks, and were bitter enemies of all Gōjū practitioners in the vicinity. Yuwa was never exactly mainstream and had no interest in joining any kind of larger organization, as he could see no benefit in it. He was just happy teaching his extremely successful *dōjō* and believed they would want to control him. Nevertheless, the ACKA people seemed to have a point but were woefully lacking in terms of organization. Yuwa finally relented and supported them for a while. Because of this decision, we were exposed to Tomoaki Koyabu, who taught Shorei Kan Gōjū Ryū, headed by Seikichi Toguchi, Sho Shō Ryū, taught by Hideaki Kanamaru, which was similar to Shotokan, FAJKO Gōjū Kai, headed by Takeshi Uchiage, and included Isao Yabunaka, and two others, Patrick McCarthy, the dark, dangerous, and dubious Irish Canadian who had a Shorin Ryū *dōjō* on Kingsway and who was a reputed fount of martial arts lore, was also on the fringes of this group. He demonstrated *kobudo* at a lower-level amateurish tournament that was hosted by the West End Community Center and swore to help find a way to approach the government to break the insidious monopoly on funding held by the wastrel Narumi and his untamed supporters. Patrick was a tad more cynical than most of us and decided to remain on the fringes.

Seikichi Toguchi *kanchō* (head of the house), visited Koyabu sensei for the 10-year anniversary of his *dōjō* in Vancouver, and a big production was staged to showcase what Koyabu sensei had achieved in Vancouver. Since it was around Halloween, Toguchi kanchō and his wife ended up wearing fancy dress at a party Kikuma and I threw at Yasmin's parents' house, where we lived for a while. And this is how I learned that the kata Yuwa called "GeRyū" was actually only about half of *Seienchin*. This was the first indicator that the Naha Te style of karate might not, in fact, exist beyond the West End Community Centre. Mind you, Toguchi kanchō also announced that Shotokan was just gymnastics for schoolchildren in answer to a question specifically designed to wind me up. Not that I felt qualified to defend the style to a ~70-odd-year-old delightful gentleman who had practiced Okinawan Gōjū for almost all of his life. He was very sociable and had a good sense of humor. He was about 5'0" and could do strange and wondrous things with limbs and joints that we would never achieve. He was also a kind and patient teacher. I just laughed. Besides, for the past six months, I had been practicing once a week at Koyabu sensei's *dōjō*, preparing for this showcase production, so I was beginning to understand that Shotokan might just be in the first stages of adolescence in comparison with older, extant forms of Okinawan Gōjū.

After the euphoria of Toguchi kancho's visit faded away, the *dōjō* resettled into its close fraternity of kicks, punches, failed marriages, and new relationships. Yuwa, the PhD candidate, Yuwa the philosopher, the economist, the tight-fisted, Yuwa the *sensei*, started to become distracted and direct his attention towards completing his Ph.D. and making money, which caused massive unrest among his students. The brown belt members were beginning to exert pressure on him to give out black belts and back them up with some kind of certification. Perhaps the style was so haphazard because it consisted of personal interpretations and experiences with various Japanese/Okinawan karate styles, as well as Chinese Kung Fu and Tai Chi Chuan. There was no clear sense of direction and no black belt certificates on the horizon. The class started to fall apart when Yuwa was absent, which became more frequent. People started looking for structure, a syllabus, *dan* certificates, and credibility, but Yuwa was already on a different path.

Yuwa went to Hawaii, where he had originally studied with George Sakai, and returned bearing simple Dan certificates that stated, *"Nisei*

Karate-Do" (Second-generation Karate Way) and were signed by George Sakai. This was timely, since George Sakai died a few months thereafter.

And so, Philippe, Kikuma, Joan, Suzanne, Colleen, Christine, and several others all received black belts, mostly accompanied by certificates from Yuwa Wong, PhD, who was later described as master of the Wong Way. Yuwa gave me an honorary Nisei Karate-Do 1st Dan. It meant nothing to me in terms of credibility, but it remains a souvenir of golden summer Sunday mornings, training in backyards, brunches on patios, and falling about when Kikuma would proffer advice such as pulling back your "foot thumbs" when practicing side thrust kicks. Everyone was healthy, passionate, and full of fun and joy in Lotus land.

Attacked in Hawaii

Kikuma was the first to introduce me to the concept of going on a holiday for two weeks to lie on a beach, soak up sunshine and Piňa coladas, spend money, and be a tourist.

I had never been able to do this before, since two-week holidays generally required more money than I ever had to pay for it. My concept of a holiday was to go somewhere for two months and work, then see what would happen.

I saved up the requisite $700, and Kikuma took off early to fly to Honolulu. His task was to assess and book hotels for the following year's inbound tours from Japan, organized by a travel agency that he managed. He met Christine and me at Honolulu airport, already chocolate brown, wearing a straw hat, a lei of flowers, and a huge grin: *"See! Look at my arms! Building already!"*

The floral smells and the perfect temperature were not going to go the way of golf. We stayed at the Sheraton Moana before the restoration, so I could easily envisage Victorian Englishmen in summer whites, Panama hats, and Malacca canes, writing world classics under the banyan tree in the Moana courtyard. Yes. Somerset Maugham! Robert Louis Stevenson! Norma's diary and photo album! Our room had a lazy fan that circulated the sea breezes around the Victorian furnishings. The bed was situated on a plinth that overlooked the Pacific sunset, lulling the visitor into sleep with the gentle swishing of palm fronds and the rhythmic flow of the tides. Kikuma showed us everything. Not a single tourist activity was neglected. Pictures were taken, as well as professionally posed photos, cartoons were drawn, silly clothes worn, Hawaiian shirts purchased, pineapples consumed, beautiful sunsets and sunrises consistently watched, and surfing attempted. Kikuma became so dark that his hair bleached reddish, so that people would mistake him for a native, which sometimes got him into trouble. Mind you, he always seemed to bounce right out of trouble with a few new friends, an enviable skill.

I fell in love with Hawaii and all its Polynesian tourist lures. However, there was still time to think about karate, and I managed to contact David Akahane, who had left Houston and was now back in his homeland. So, I convinced him to introduce me to his Shorin Ryū sensei, Mr. Murasaki, who was also a Buddhist priest. He managed to overcome his gatekeeper instinct and took me along to meet the man, who happened to be in the midst of a cleansing ceremony to purify a Japanese sword that had just been acquired by one of his acolytes. Murasaki *sensei* was also a priest. He was another Japanese Doppelganger for John Allan, or Sakuraba *sensei* from Fukuoka, with the same slight build and intense eyes that made you feel that your soul was stripped naked. I trained in his class, but Kikuma felt uncomfortable showing his Wong Way and declined to get on the floor. I had no shame, and anyway, here was a chance to learn from the teacher of someone I respected. Murasaki sensei was no ordinary teacher. The class included 6th dans, and I thoroughly enjoyed the session.

After training, we all went out to a coffee shop, and Murasaki sensei told me that the next time I came to Hawaii, he would perform *Kushanku* kata on a *goban,* a board on top of a small table for playing Japanese chess (called Go), that measures 14.61 × 14.61 × 0.04 inches. I was thrilled at this offer and vowed to return for that purpose. David also introduced me to Ed Fujiwara, the JKA instructor, who was teaching at the University of Hawaii. I didn't train with him then, but promised to practice with him on my next visit, as Kikuma had behaved rather oddly at Murasaki sensei's *dōjō*.

Christine was in the doldrums after splitting from her abusive husband and a failed emotional fling with one of the Pigs. Kikuma thought it would be good to cheer her up. Thus, two nights after we arrived, the three of us walked along Kapiolani Boulevard, the main thoroughfare in Waikiki, inhaling floral air, enjoying the perfect temperature, and focusing on which restaurant we would visit.

We paid no attention to anyone but ourselves, so when I felt pressure at the back of my knees that caused them to buckle, I stumbled. I turned around to look into the face of an angry Aboriginal couple who both cursed me roundly for being a tourist, for walking too slowly, and for generally being scum. I replied that I was sorry I did not have eyes in the back of my head; otherwise, I might have been able to get out of the way.

The pair passed us, shouting verbal abuse. Incident over, we continued where we had left off. Kikuma decided he needed a bio break and disappeared inside a restaurant to ask if he could use their facilities. The restaurant was jam-packed with diners, and tables for two were positioned up against floor-to-ceiling glass windows that faced the boulevard. Christine and I opted to wait for him outside, as the night air was so much more pleasant than the smoke-filled atmosphere inside the restaurant.

At ~ 8 o'clock at night, patrons enjoyed a clear view of the street. A cashier and the Maître'd' were situated near the restaurant door. A uniformed African American equipped with two holstered pistols guarded a closed door on a building adjacent to the restaurant.

Christine and I caught up on some girl talk. Suddenly, I became aware that the same couple that had made me stumble had backtracked and were walking back toward us, looking for a fight. The looks on their faces indicated that they planned to spoil someone's vacation.

Mine.

The woman came up to me, planted herself about 6 inches from my face, and while spitting the question, "Why the f*** couldn't you get out of the f***in way", she launched a haymaker that landed squarely on the right side of my chin.

My face bounced back to its previous angle on the top of my neck, and I just stared at the woman. The following events occurred so rapidly that taking the time to write about them would be a disservice. It was a pure moment of *"Ichi byō shi,"* a Japanese homily that means "in a heartbeat".

While she continued to swear and challenge, Christine stepped forward and asked what the hell was going on, which caused the man to step towards her. Since he was larger than her and showed all signs of perpetrating violence upon her, Christine wisely put up her hands and said, OK, no worries, mate, I'm just a casual observer here, and backed off.

Within a heartbeat, I assessed three choices and their possible consequences: if I attacked the woman, the man would attack Christine; trying to reason with her, she would use it as another reason to attack me again, and Christine would be vulnerable; if I attacked her, Christine would become a victim. If I did nothing, she would become bored with the lack of response and go away.

I was also aware that the security guard stared straight ahead. The cashier, the Maître d' stared, the diners stopped dining, and a crowd gathered in a time warp of milliseconds. I reasoned that neither a hospital nor a jail cell would be my idea of a holiday.

So. I adjusted my stance to distribute the weight 50:50 on my feet and let my arms fall naturally at my sides. I exhaled slowly and forced myself to relax, saying nothing, all the while never removing eye contact from the woman, who continued to yell, no doubt for the benefit of the restaurant audience.

She finally reached a point where she realized that I was not rising to the bait, and if she attacked me again, she would have negative consequences according to the law.

Do not blink. I did not blink. Maintain a neutral facial expression. Perhaps my attacker also became aware of the increasing number of witnesses. She and her partner backed off, slowly turned around, and completely disappeared from sight. Suddenly, all onlookers started to disengage themselves as if from a trance. Knives and forks started slicing and dicing. Food morsels were delivered to mouths, and conversations and wine started to flow again. The Maître'd and the cashier at the restaurant door fell over themselves to tell me what an amazing thing they had just witnessed and asked what they could do to help. It was a bit late for that, I thought, but I asked them to use their bathroom so that I could check my face. After all, what's the point of having an evenly tanned bruise? I asked Christine to say nothing to Kikuma. I need not have bothered. He emerged from the bathroom before me, and Christine blurted out that I had been slugged by an Aboriginal person. He wanted to go searching for them

I emerged from the bathroom, having confirmed no marks on my face, and calmed Kikuma down. It is over, finished, and no harm done. We still had a holiday to enjoy.

We were still discussing it when we rounded a corner and stumbled into a crowd, staring at something on the ground. An unconscious Caucasian man was sprawled half on the sidewalk and half on the road with blood pouring out of his nose, mouth, and ears. "Beaten up by a native", someone said.

We were lucky. But… I was disappointed. I really wanted to smack her. I had been training for ~12 years in karate to do nothing. I finally reconciled with myself that nothing was exactly the right choice.

Possible Dreams

I began to feel dissatisfied with the Naha Te *dōjō* as the classes were being run by people who had been practicing for only a few years and lacked the depth of understanding that comes with many years of experience. The ACKA offered nothing in terms of technical learning or development, and in fact, having failed in their aim to convince the provincial government to recognize their claim to public funding, the organization soon disbanded.

Two ideas started to simultaneously germinate at the back of my mind. I couldn't even bring myself to voice them for a few months until I had formulated a suitable strategy with which to realize them and suitable words with which to describe them.

My goal was to represent Canada in international karate competitions, and I wanted to leave the laboratory and find a way to return to Japan under my own terms.

The first notion was absurd from at least three perspectives. I was not in a *dōjō* that belonged to the provincial sport's governing body. I was not part of a system that engaged in a selection process. I was not even particularly adept, as my claims to be a Shotokan practitioner had been diluted by two years of Naha Te. I was not a Canadian citizen or even a landed immigrant; I was still on a work permit.

Professionally, I was becoming rather bored with pursuing science in its deep and narrow dimensions and was no longer comfortable with locusts, despite running experiments with hundreds of them over the year. I started to search for a job that would provide more challenges, Canadian citizenship, and possibly a chance to go to Japan.

While I was going through this life reassessment, Kikuma was undergoing some extremely difficult emotional pressure, as his father was critically ill with cancer in Japan. He, too, was in a life stage where one tide was starting to ebb and another was flowing. He had quit his job as manager of the successful tour company branch, he had set up on behalf of a Japanese operator and started his own business, which would do almost anything legal to make money. It was an amazingly confusing and unstable time for both of us, and compounded for him by the death of his father and my hospitalization for a cone biopsy, a simple piece of surgery designed to prevent cervical dysplasia from developing into cervical cancer.

Kikuma could not differentiate between my condition and that of his father and deliberately stayed away from the hospital, which hurt me deeply. Colleen brought me a green stuffed dragon to keep me company because I was born in the year of it and reputedly acted like one! Well, I certainly did not breathe fire during that hospital stay, but rather doused a great deal of smoldering resentment and guilt with floods of unstoppable tears. Those were long, depressed nights, spent alone, mostly upright and perpetually awake due to the indescribable discomfort of three feet of packed cotton wadding pressing insistently on the bladder wall. And when the tears stopped, I berated myself for all my sins, real and imagined, and wasted no time in charting the next course of my life.

Vancouver 1981-1988

I accepted a job as a representative for a biotechnology company that sold radioactive isotopes to the research and medical environment, and the territory encompassed BC, Alberta, and Saskatchewan. The head office was just outside London, the Canadian head office was in Toronto, the North American Office was in Chicago, and the Japanese office was located in *Tōkyō*. Sales meetings were usually held at Florida resorts, and none of this thrilled Kikuma. I had accepted the job against his wishes, as he wanted me to stay in Vancouver, where I would be under his control every minute of the day. Although I had given him good reason to express this opinion, it nevertheless conflicted with the support that he gave me—that screamed, *"Yeah! Go for it! You can do it!"*

So, we split up. This was not an easy decision, as I still loved and respected him for many reasons, not the least of which was his belief in me. However, I could now devote myself to the job and getting on with my dream without worrying about someone else's opinions or concerns. This job was important because I firmly believed that no amount of hard work in the laboratory would lead to me becoming chairman of the department, whereas a good sales result could theoretically pave the way to becoming chairman of a company. With this particular company, I could, in principle, work in each country where I already had or could acquire the right documentation. I did not know if I really could sell anything, so there lay a challenge in itself.

The Shiseikai

I found the Shiseikai instructor Takayuki Sameshima, in White Rock, about an hour's drive from Vancouver, so I went there intending to join his club, as I thought it belonged to the association that I needed to be in to realize my aims.

The class was run in a school cafeteria after the club members had moved all the benches and tables to the side of the room. The concrete floor, covered with plastic, was slippery, gritty, and grimy with the offload from hundreds of middle school sneakers. I hated the floor and felt doubly awkward as my Shotokan was rusty around the edges, and I could hardly maintain a stance on that foul floor. I enjoyed Sameshima sensei's classes, though, and decided to tolerate the venue and get on with relearning Shotokan.

However, after about the 3rd class, I went to the *dōjō* and found Sameshima sensei in street clothes. He asked me to teach his class because he had to go to the airport to meet Masami Tsuruoka from Toronto, who was arriving to conduct a referee and judging seminar on the following weekend. I was mortified and declined, pleading with him to have one of his brown belts teach, as I was in no position to do so. I mentioned to Sameshima sensei that all his brown belts, including the talented Ezaki brothers, were far more technically skilled than I, and

I had no right to suddenly go out there and teach them anything. Tak insisted, and so I ended up doing it. I felt like a total fraud in front of these sincere students, who kindly did everything I asked them with a good attitude and their usual 100% effort. This just made me feel worse, and so I changed my vow. I couldn't be teaching, as I needed to learn and improve, and if I was going to be put in this position, maybe this was not the right place for me after all. My dream started to recede, but I decided to attend the weekend referee seminar because I had never been to one, and I should learn the competition rules anyway. Sameshima sensei told me to phone someone called James, who informed me of the details. The seminar was scheduled to take place at a *dōjō* located at 61st and Nanaimo Street in Vancouver. I had attempted to find this *dōjō* before and failed, and it wasn't until then that I learned I'd been looking for the wrong street.

I arrived at the seminar, knees shaking with apprehension. I didn't know anyone! I walked in and paid my dues to a Japanese-Canadian woman called Dulcie and passed by the office of this beautiful *dōjō*. A quick look inside, revealed three men: one older Japanese who I assumed was Tsuruoka, a swarthy-looking individual smoking a noxious, unmistakable French brand of cigarettes, and an African American fellow sprawled across a swivel chair. His eyes inadvertently caught mine, and I wasn't sure I liked how he looked me up and down.

We lined up, and the seminar started. Horrors. I was in a den of thieves, drunkards, and fearsome people. The African American fellow was none other than the soft-spoken James Johnson, whose voice on the phone gave no indication that he was at all as bad as rumor had it. Bino Felix who owned the *dōjō* was Portuguese, and they, together with Sameshima sensei and Dulcie Oikawa, who was a nidan of their group, Howard Hewitt from Banchory (just outside Aberdeen, Scotland!) and Bill Thorpe, comprised the heart and soul of the Shiseikai, a rumored bastion of alcoholism, drugs and everything that is wrong and corrupt. I suppose that a reputation for flagrant womanizing, fast living, and fast-driving E-Type Jaguars had as much to do with jealousy as some of these individuals tended to win competitions, and James was the current Canadian national kumite champion.

Well, compared with all the perceptions and rumors, the Shiseikai seemed to be full of normal people after all. Sameshima sensei had been extremely kind, everyone at the seminar had been friendly and welcoming, and they introduced themselves with a smile and a handshake. I began to wonder where I had been for the past three years. Brian Wilson and Kevin Kelly kindly helped me with the written portion of the referee test, as I was totally lost, having never seen a rule book for over 10 years. Participants from at least three other styles of karate attended the seminar, all proudly displaying their *dōjō*/style logos. I finally noticed that one had a rising sun patch on his gi top. The red sun on a white background was the logo of the JKA, so I went and introduced myself. I discovered that Mike Scales was a JKA 3rd Dan and that he ran a *dōjō* in the BC Telephone building, a mere 20 minutes' drive from my apartment!

Mike was from the Northeast of England and held Andy Sherry, Steve Cattle, Terry O'Neill, and Keinosuke Enoeda in high regard. While still in England, he had passed a brown belt exam during the same Kanazawa sweep through the country in which I had passed that fateful Shodan, so I was, in fact, his *senpai* if you cared to look at things that way. It was a cause for many jokes, as Mike would take great pleasure in incredulously pointing this out.

This *dōjō* was run on terms that I understood from Scotland, with a fairly demanding structure, a clear beginning, middle, and end. I enjoyed practicing familiar combinations that had been supplanted by spinning back kicks and exotic routines, and I was happy and comfortable. Kata were practiced on a regular basis, and input was given even into advanced kata, which I had not practiced properly since I lived in Little Rock. Mike was a member of the JKA, of which Hidetaka Nishiyama was a founding member. Canadian members included John Hanratty *dōjō* in Calgary, Alberta, Rick Jorgensen in Regina, and Jerry Mar in Winnipeg. There were more in Quebec and Ontario, but I did not know them.

I found myself a member of the JKA International of Canada and Karate BC, the allegedly evil junta run by the *deshi* of Hidetada Narumi in the Shiseikai. Mike had been a part of the Shiseikai himself when he first arrived from Southport, UK, but interpreted the kata differently and wanted to do things his way, following the KUGB JKA in England. So, he started his own club based upon what he had learned at the famous Red Triangle club, where his icons trained.

I became secretary of the JKA in Canada, but I resigned soon after I realized the extent of mishandling and misappropriation of funds, which was tacitly supported by the directors and met with resistance to changing the status quo. I had no respect for a 4th Dan who creatively disposed of member funds and could not bring myself to support such activities by being on the board. However, I continued to pay this organization's annual dues as Mike's club was a member.

Mike was quite competitive, so when the 1981 BC Spring Provincial tournament rolled around, he encouraged me to enter. I was excited about this, as clearly there were rules that referees learned and applied, and everyone was a Japanese stylist, so there would be no Kung or Taekwondo throwing haymaker punches and centrifugal kicks. The kumite event was non-contact and had round-robin matches, so there was ample opportunity to learn. Kata was a three-round event, with the scores from the second and final rounds being cumulative. How inspiring! A tournament consisting solely of karate practitioners and with enough women for divisions in sparring and kata.

Well, there were only five women in black belt kumite: Dulcie, Molly from Fort St. John, Luba from Kitimat, Jeananne Duncan from Prince Rupert, and me.

I was trounced! I won only one fight, and that was against Jeananne, who was about ten years older than me.

Her *kata* wasn't much better. There were brown belts included in the division to expand it, and, no doubt, to shorten the day. I placed 6th out of a total of nine competitors.

This was a great start, as I learned something about my competition, what the judges were looking for, and all the areas that needed working.

Mr. Akira Sato of the Shito-Ryū Itosu Kai demonstrated Sanchin by bashing two-by-four planks against his slight frame, and Mike later introduced me to him. He surprised me by remembering that I had phoned him up looking for a Shotokan school a while back. I figured it was my Scottish accent, but in fact, it was the lack of women looking for a *dōjō*.

Yaz Yamamoto of the Itosu Kai reigned supreme in male kata, whereas James and Bino were among the top three in kumite. The atmosphere at this tournament was friendly, and all the women introduced themselves genially. Dulcie did a lot to make sure that I was welcomed and that I knew what was going on, and through her kind guidance, I learned that at this tournament, the BC provincial team was selected by Mr. Sato, Mr. David Akutagawa of the Chitokai, and Sameshima sensei, who was also the BC provincial coach. I vowed to do better in the next tournament, which would take place in the fall, located in some other part of the province. The provincial team was selected based on the accumulation of points for placings in spring and fall provincial events, as well as the BC Winter Games. If a selectee was also a member of the provincial team the previous year, then performance in the Western Canadian Championships and the Nationals would also be taken into consideration.

In the fall provincials, I failed to make the medal rounds, but I inched my position upward. These Chito and Shito kata would certainly require some serious effort to overcome!

I sensed that although Mike's training was very good, and he had some good up-and-coming women in his *dōjō*, the kata training was not quite right for me, and I knew that excessively heavy breathing, sometimes more akin to barking, stomping every move, did not impress the Shito Ryū and Chito Ryū judges. They interpreted their kata as riddled with fake power and wanted to see more feeling, interpretation, grace, elegance, and sensitivity, particularly in the female kata. At least, that was my gut feeling at the time.

By 1982, Mike started to talk about his *kohai* visiting him from the UK. Andy Holmes was from the same *dōjō* as Mike and had passed his yellow belt when Mike became a brown belt. He was a JKA 2nd Dan in the KUGB, and in Shotokan Karate International (SKI), headed by Kanazawa sensei.

Andy was casual, single, compassionate, and highly talented. Since Bull, I had not seen a non-Japanese person have such control over all his limbs or perform the entire repertoire of Shotokan techniques in such a relaxed and fluid way. Andy had been a policeman in Liverpool and, among other achievements, had received a medal to commend him for bravery when he hurled himself into the freezing cold depths of the sluggish, noxious effluent called the Mersey River to save a drowning woman's life. Andy was congenial, ready for laughs and jokes washed down with many pints after training, and was paradoxically naive and wise beyond his years. His understanding and interpretation of Shotokan karate were also quite different from that of Mike, and I instinctively knew that I could learn from him and improve. Time was of the essence, as I would have a thirtieth birthday later that year, and I was never going to represent Canada unless I got a move on. As it happened, Andy's objective was to emigrate to Canada and teach karate. It couldn't happen fast enough for me.

Miz Nawma Resurfaces 1982

Andy left Vancouver to study with Nishiyama sensei in Los Angeles for a few months. We were sad to see him go, having impressed many people with his personality and technical teaching ability, but he vowed to return soon, subject to immigration. During that visit, Nishiyama sensei's key student, Toru (Kellam) Shimoji, a Japanese man from Okinawa who had been raised in Hawaii, asked Andy where he was from. Upon understanding his connection with Vancouver, he asked

Andy if he knew Miss Nawma. Andy was astonished at this question. Do you mean Norma Foster? Get out of here! He did. Toru had trained with Luther Duffy in Waco, Texas, and also knew Bull, and I had, of course, trained with them. I knew Toru from Nishiyama sensei's *dōjō*. Too funny. The coincidence was magnified further as Bull showed up to train with Nishiyama sensei and asked Andy the same question. Andy returned to Vancouver, probably a bit bemused.

He started teaching with Mike's blessing, and I was one of the first to sign up and train with him at Champlain Heights Community Center and then at Simon Fraser University, which allowed me to train six days a week. Sometimes, I still showed up at the Naha Te *dōjō*, so I was consistently training six or seven days a week, and by the time the Spring Provincials rolled around, I was far more prepared. Andy had improved my confidence in sparring and did a great deal in tuning up *Bassai Dai* and *Unsu* kata to make them presentable in competition.

But this time, the competition would be tougher. A newcomer, Ingrid Bischoff, was training at the YMCA JKA *dōjō* downtown Vancouver, which had been established by Hirō Yamashiro sensei in the early 60s. Ingrid had been a junior national kata champion in Germany, where she had lived until deciding to attend the University of British Columbia (UBC). Ingrid was an excellent kata athlete poured straight from the mold created by Hideo Ochi, the JKA instructor in Germany. Barely touching 5 feet, Ingrid could deliver a masterful presentation of the kata Sōchin (Tranquil force/energetic calm) which calls for a great deal of rooted strength and stability, not commonly seen in Canadian women at the time. I could not understand why Ingrid trained there, as not many members of that club participated in the competition. And although that *dōjō* was not often involved in competitions.

Another woman emerged after a break from karate and was highly competitive. Sarah Sato was 25% Japanese, and if you knew that, you could see the effects of those diluted genes despite her blue eyes and auburn hair. Sarah had been a member of the Canadian Junior National Ski team and was currently a 2nd-degree black belt with the Shiseikai, vacillating between the Shiseikai and the JKA versions of Shotokan. A student at SFU, Sarah had been on the Canadian National Karate Team before and had withdrawn from karate for personal reasons. However, Sarah excelled in anything she chose, whether academics or sports. A gifted athlete with a body structure that lent itself well to karate, Sarah was equally talented in kata and kumite. Because she trained with Mike frequently towards 1983, I began to know her quite well and respected her seriousness and application to karate after her return to karate.

I entered the 1982 spring and fall provincial competitions, again not making the medal rounds but becoming a familiar contender on the edge of a turnaround.

Being a perpetual loser was a positive experience for me. I was happy to compete, leave the ring with all parts functioning, meet people, enjoy watching some excellent karate, shout and cheer for my friends, and generally be caught up in the spirit of the event. The fall provincials provided an excuse to visit a new city and meet new people who rarely visited Vancouver.

My job was progressing well, and I was learning a wide range of new professional skills through practical and corporate training programs. Through the company, I visited Florida Resorts, Chicago, Seattle, Toronto, and, of course, the major cities in the three Western provinces of Canada. Every time I went to a new location, I visited a *dōjō*, made new friends, and maintained training even on the road. Thus, I practiced with John Hanratty (Shotokan) and Peter Brown (Gōjū) in Calgary, Rick Jorgensen (Shotokan) in Regina, and at the YMCA in Edmonton. I even bought a car through the company and drove it from Toronto to Vancouver, stopping at *dōjō* across the country. That way, the five-day drive (12 hours/day) through a blinding December snowscape from became less boring as it was interspersed with *kihon* (basics), kumite (sparring), and *kata* (form).

Provincial Championships 1983

I approached the provincial event in the spring of 1983 full of motivation and fired up with the belief that I was doing The Right Thing. The company had obtained landed immigrant status for me. I was generating loads of new business and I was obsessed with training. Every spare minute revolved around training, reading, discussing, and thinking about karate. My office was in my Kitsilano apartment, which, of course, was decorated with as many oriental touches as my budget would allow. Such single-mindedness did not allow for any meaningful relationships with lads, but I did not feel at all lonely and reveled in my aloneness and control over my life. I had close friends, including Kikuma, whom I still saw quite frequently, but on a purely platonic basis. The women from the Naha Te *dōjō*, some of whom were now also training with Andy, were another step in their life quests to find the best instructor for their needs.

I had reflected on my experiences competing in BC over the past year or so. The women's *kumite* event was not being taken seriously enough by the tournament organizers, referees, or the audience. It was certainly true that the quality of women's *kumite* was far lower than that of the men, and sometimes attempts to score would disintegrate into catfights with no scorable techniques. The women's final was invariably relegated to a far corner of the room while some mundane male elimination event was taking place to distract the audience from the female medal rounds.

I figured that this was partly because we were given the most inexperienced or incompetent judges, as no one wanted to referee the women. In fact, Robert Sheng, a senior Shito Ryū practitioner, was usually the center referee of the women's matches. He was a very nice person who practiced Tai Chi and Chi Gong in addition to karate. However, he had a glass eye. Although many defended Robert's ability as a judge, I campaigned vigorously to have him removed from refereeing our matches, not because he lacked knowledge or sincerity, but because anyone with one eye lacked depth perception. These were still days when a hard, well-timed punch to a woman's stomach was just as likely to get a penalty as a point, and since Robert had this potential for misperception, he was likely to ignore a punch that did not hit, then give a warning for one that did. So, I had a reasonable justification for my complaint. Some of the other female competitors agreed, so I voiced this to the BC Referee Council. They agreed to my request for a referee with at least two eyes at the 1983 Spring Provincial tournament.

I also campaigned for the women's' final to be showcased either immediately before or immediately after the men's *kumite* final and not hidden in a dark corner of the basketball gym. However, the Referee Council decided to run it at the same time as the men, starting in the spring.

Thus satisfied, I then polled all the women I knew with black belts, regardless of membership in the association, and told them that I wanted to improve my level of sparring. Would they be interested in helping me do this? I explained that many of us had been training in different styles of karate for several years and surely had some experiences to share with the rest of us that would be fun, motivational, and perhaps improve some aspects of our sparring. I also reasoned that while most of us were trained in *dōjō*, which consisted mostly of men, it was difficult to suddenly switch and fight someone more your own height, weight, and physiognomy in a tournament.

For example, most of us would not attempt a foot sweep with a sparring partner who outweighed us by 30 kg, but might be inclined to do so with an opponent similar in terms of weight. Likewise, most male heads were considerably higher than ours, so face kicks in a tournament were rare because they were infrequently practiced.

About 15 of us agreed to meet once a week to practice *kumite* techniques. Each week, a different individual would be responsible for creating a class outline and conducting the practice. The women who were not part of Karate BC agreed to join a *dōjō* that was a member of the association and sign up to compete in the Spring Provincial Championships.

We studied tournament kumite every Sunday for nine months, in addition to our regular practice, so I trained every day of the week. I was determined that all of us would improve and that the karate world in British Columbia would recognize that women would no longer be content with being second-class citizens in provincial karate, but would be taken as seriously as the men.

This time, I placed 3rd in kata to Wendy Fong's 1st and Ingrid's 2nd.

When the women's kumite eliminations rolled around, we no longer had Robert as our referee, and the size of the division was sufficient for a murmur to rustle around the room. Sixteen of us instead of six! YEAH!!

There were some amusing moments when Suzanne, who had a scrappy, street-smart, fight-to-the-death style, attempted a whole range of techniques never seen before or since in a karate match. They were accompanied by endless wild *kiai* and avalanches of blows that failed to score. Nevertheless, she continued undaunted for the entire two minutes, and her spirited enthusiasm also caught the undivided the audience's attention!

The medal round, as promised, proceeded in parallel with that of the men. I was thrilled to see that we had all improved ourselves so much due to our own efforts and the experienced eyes of David Akutagawa, our center referee. In fact, the audience had difficulty deciding whether to direct their attention to the male or the female finals. I was riding the crest of a wave that day when, at the post-tournament party, I waited with the real contenders to discover who would be selected to represent the province in the Canadian National Championships in Vancouver just two months later.

I could hardly believe my ears and almost collapsed into Jello when I was included among the selected! I had to reconfirm to make sure. But there was no mistake. I was to compete in the Nationals!!!

Sarah was not selected, despite her results being quite similar to mine, having a 4th in *kata* and a 3rd in *kumite*. She asked me to ask Sameshima sensei why she was not selected. Since I was the bearer of bad news, I was blamed for her not being on the roster, and from that day on, her attitude towards me distinctly changed. She and Ingrid had become close friends, perhaps partially because Ingrid was technically superior to Sarah in *kata* and vice versa for *kumite*. I, on the other hand, was inferior to both, so why was I selected for the team? I understand that this question might have occupied a few of your waking moments.

Canadian National Championships 1983

This event was a turning point in the school of my karate life. I understood the need for motivation, self-confidence, and total commitment to the goal.

I had trained like a maniac, and I was well aware of my deficiencies. I had no natural talent. I had stiff joints. There was (and still is) no Shotokan stance that I could perform precisely, so I always felt unstable, and my performance closely depended on my state of mind, the texture of the floor, and the room temperature. A slight hint of a slippery floor distracted me from concentrating on presenting a kata. A great deal of focus would be directed somewhere around my ankles, berating their stiffness, or my feet, for not being flat and graced with a web-like arrangement of toes designed for vacuum suction.

Fortunately, the floor at the British Columbia Institute of Technology (BCIT) gym was quite user-friendly, so I could abolish that worry from my list of competitive concerns.

I also had an opportunity to train with my fellow teammates, some of whom were very experienced, having represented Canada in international events! Such an illustrious company somehow also gave me some added confidence.

The women included Ingrid, Molly, Luba, Diana, and me. A picture shows us in royal blue shiny polyester tracksuits, after a weekend of

Sameshima sensei's team training, delivered in his inimitable style.

Andy and I would immediately lock eyes, which indicated a wealth of disrespectful interpretations for this particular command and indicated to other teammates, especially those of the Shiseikai. However, we both liked and respected Sameshima sensei, but from a UK point of view, irreverence is a sign that you do such respect that both Andy and I suffered from, along with several other expats Brits, and I don't believe that either of us would willingly forego it on account of someone else's interpretation of the *sensei-seito* (teacher-pupil) relationship.

"Take head and fook, sensei?

"Hai sensei! Take head and fook."

Many members of the team were a bit dumbfounded by this command, but Andy and I both knew precisely what he meant:

Sen no sen. Take the initiative before an opponent starts an attack using a foot sweep.

This translation made Andy make a noise like a horse with its nose in a feedbag, which gave way to more silliness since it meant that we should perhaps also use some *intaanaru hawssu* (internal force), a quality much prized by Nishiyama sensei. Despite such moments of team giggling, we trained seriously, liking Sameshima sensei all the more for his ability to twitch the corners of his mouth as though he were suppressing some huge joke and tolerating the irreverent Brits under his care with an imperturbable grace.

Come the tournament, I was excited and ready. After almost two years of walking on this dream path, I was about to pass a milestone.

The women's *kata* elimination was the first event of the morning, which was not a great thrill, as training in the evening naturally made me feel more alive and awake. Anyway, I was never a morning person.

Nonetheless, I made it through the first round into the next. Wow! And here I was, competing against women from all over the country. I could hardly believe the scores. However, I had just scraped into the second round with the lowest score.

The next round confirmed that the likely winners would be from BC, but the others would probably score higher than I. I felt confident about my kata, though, and believed it to be far better than the judges were giving me credit for, and that I was suffering from the bane of newcomers. An unknown face equals an automatic low score. Whether or not this was a deliberate strategy on the part of the judges, I wouldn't know, but that is how it felt. Furthermore, there was a system whereby kata competitors lined up for the next round according to scores in the previous round, such that the person with the lowest score had to perform first, thus biasing the judges in favor of a winner from before the start of the second round. The scores could be guaranteed to creep up towards the highest, with little or no variation, as competitor names were called into the ring.

I performed Bassai Dai and achieved a score that would squeeze me into the final medal round, to be held later in the day. Ingrid was running in third place but only about 0.2 behind the gold medal contender, and everyone knew her Sōchin would wow the judges into making up the difference that would result in the gold instead. Our scores would be carried into the final round and added to the numbers awarded in that event, to determine the medal placings.

To go into the final with the lowest score was a guaranteed failure, an 8th place, which was no place at all, even in the National Championships. This had been applied forever at the Canadian National championships, but I was going to ignore that and show everyone in the room, including myself, that this was no excuse for being 8th. Many friends came to watch the tournament in the afternoon; even Kikuma showed up and yelled support along with the others.

Jan from the Shoreikan Gōjū Ryū Karate, run by Tomoaki Koyabu, sat at the ring with her camera to bolster me up.

I had just given myself a pep-talk. It included everything I wanted to fight against or made me angry. I thought about my mother and her rejection. I thought about being sad and alone in the hospital; I thought about the emotional toll karate had exacted from my private life. I even thought about the attitudes of some of my fellow competitors, some of whom were arrogant and unapproachable. Well, I would show them! I would conjure up every personal demon, large and small, real and imagined, and triumph over them all for a minute and a half through the medium of Unsu! I was ready. Physically and mentally prepared for battle.

I was first to be called in the round, my low score no doubt firmly branded into the brains of each and every judge, all of whom differed from the previous rounds.

Ossu!

I responded to the roll call and stepped forward to the edge of the ring, feeling confident and energized. I bowed slowly and reverently and stepped into the ring. Another bow to the chief referee, a deep breath, then I consolidated thirty-one years of calamity into one word.

Unsu!

I assumed the attention stance of the *kata*, with my feet together and arms at 45° angles to the floor, while exhaling in time to the arm movements. I collected myself into a fully synchronized machine, ready to fight myself and emerge victorious.

I launched myself into the *kata* and vanquished demons north, south, east, and west. Fall on the floor; take that and that! Roundhouse kicks to invisible devil groins. Up, slowly from the floor into a horse stance. Dispel fears with dynamic tension, north and south, then kill goblins with a flurry of blocks, knife hand strikes, and feints topped with a reverse punch. Cloud hands weaving about in a confusion of bear paws, chicken heads, and vertical knives. Stop for breath with a *kamae* position at 45°. Look out! Demons from behind, grab that troll, and kick it! Right. More trouble from behind the southside! Block down. Another one. Block up. Repeat sequence. Grand finale, a slow turn into *fudō dachi*, to prepare for the 360° airborne kick, down for ground gorgons, up to twist a writhing Medusa head a couple of times, then finish this performance against multiple imaginary self-imposed ghouls with a meaningful reverse punch delivered right between the eyes of the seated chief judge.

It was over. I couldn't see the score, and I couldn't hear it for the blood pounding in my ears. No matter the score, this was the most vital and alive *kata* I had ever performed, and I knew it. I had taken that list of hateful things and transformed them into positive energy that was directly manifested through the *kata*. It was almost as though an alter ego had actually performed the kata, not me. So, when I sat down and saw Jan signing me with a circle made from her thumb and index finger with the other fingers raised, I figured she liked it too. But there was no discernible reaction from the crowd, so I guessed that my score was going to guarantee an 8th place after all.

Content nevertheless with my first performance as a provincial representative, I mentally relaxed and prepared to enjoy watching the other seven kata in the round.

The next competitor was called, and when she had completed her kata, Jan gave me the same symbol and a grin. Well, I thought Jan did *Gōjū Ryū*, so she must have liked this *kata* too, as she might not have seen it before.

This went on until the top three performed their *kata*, after which Jan changed her sign to thumbs up. I was horrified, as Ingrid had also chosen to perform *Unsu*, and I wondered how foolish I had been to choose *Unsu* when she had chosen the same *kata* and was better at it than I was. The contestants stood up, and there was the usual time lag as the scores were added up, checked, and delivered to the announcer's table.

"In third place, in the Canadian National Championships, from British Columbia."

Bob Howlett's smooth deejay tones filled the gym

"Norma Foster"

I thought there had been a mistake. But Jan was jumping up and down, clapping and shouting unintelligible things.

There had been no mistake. What I had done was to achieve the highest score in the round, beating out all the other competitors, and to reach a cumulative total that would earn me the bronze medal. In other words, I had broken the taboo of the lowest score and overcame this bias to win against all odds. I was gold medal material! I knew it. I felt it. I believed it.

Vancouver 1983

During the reception after the 1983 National Championships, in which James at the relatively advanced competitive age of thirty-nine, became the men's Canadian National champion for the fourth and last time in his career, tension mounted as the National squad was announced.

I did not believe I could feel any more content that year, as I was so thrilled with how everything had turned out. I was with friends; we were pacesetters, achievers. We in BC had exposed wrongs and made them right! Achieved the impossible! Beaten the system! Changed the system! Become a part of the system! I was proud to be a member of the provincial team, happy to train hard and party with my teammates. The women waited with increasing trepidation as the men were announced.

"..... and for the women, Ingrid, Luba, Wendy, and Norma Foster"!

I had been named to the National Squad!

However, there was still a minor detail that needed to be taken care of. I was not yet a Canadian.

No matter what, Canada had a rule that a person had to be a resident in the country for five years before one could apply for citizenship, and time spent in the country before obtaining immigrant status was considered valid. I studied for the citizenship exam and became a Canadian in 1984.

Of course, I could not have been selected to represent Canada at the International Amateur Karate Federation (IAKF) championships in Cairo, Egypt. Ingrid and Luba were awarded that particular honour. I could not be disappointed, as there was nothing to be done about it. However, I had always wanted to visit Cairo, having learned about ancient Egyptian history and legends, and having lined up for three hours outside the British Museum in London to view the Tutankhamun exhibition. Visions of the Nile, snakes in baskets, pyramids, and camels faded as quickly from my imagination as they had arrived. It was just not possible, so that was that.

The banquet after the championship was catered by Bino, who was involved in the restaurant industry, and once all the food had been snapped up by starving competitors still on a high from the day's events, the lights dimmed, and disco had everyone releasing yet more energy long into the night.

It seemed that my star was indeed in the ascendant, as all kinds of people suddenly had things to tell me. Dancing to some of my favorite music was suspended as a Japanese fellow, about the same size as myself, introduced himself as Suenori Tominaga. He was one of the judges at the tournament and lived in Toronto. He heard that I had trained in the Fukuoka *dōjō* from Sasaki sensei, on a visit to Fukuoka during the past year, and so he decided to do some bonding. Doubtless, the glue contained a high proportion of alcohol, but he told me about the last days of Miyata *sensei*, whose picture graced a wall of the Hakozaki *dōjō*. He had died of cancer, some say due to alcohol consumption, and Tominaga *sensei* waxed lyrical about his relationship with this *sensei* and all those that I knew in Fukuoka until his eyes filled with tears. I was on the verge of tears myself, having become caught up in this intensely emotional, personal story. It was kind of Mr. Tominaga to share those times with me, and since the subject revolved a great deal around death, it was easy to forget the noisy party and become immersed in the transient nature of life and the pursuit of gold medals. A bleak picture of forgotten ashes threatened to completely remove all my euphoria from just a few moments ago. I felt a sudden burst of clarity, an understanding that tournaments are just a comma, a pause in a life story, and shuddered at the thought of mortality. I gave Mr. Tominaga a hug and thanked him for seeking me out to tell me all this, and ushered him back into the lively, raucous atmosphere of the disco before it became impossible for me to return.

Next to appear was Mr. Okuyama, also from Toronto. Turns out that he had graduated from Takudai, where he started learning karate, and his roommate was none other than Sakunosuke The world had started to compress. Since Mr. Okuyama's personality was rather different from that of Mr. Tominaga, I began to feel cheered again and plunged into the spirit of the party.

I believe that both of these instructors were highly ranked in Tak Kubota's organization and had become successful in teaching karate.

As with all of my teammates, I gave James a wide berth. I did not feel comfortable around him and felt very ambivalent about what I felt when he looked at me. When he talked to me, there was usually a kind of challenging edge to a question or a joke that had a double entendre. I understood that he had been involved in the Civil Rights movement in the US. He smoked. He drank gin martinis straight up, with an olive. He was close friends with Bino, whose marital status did not prevent him from filling the passenger seat of the E-Type and sipping from a bottle of vodka for the road. Bino was talented, wealthy, and self-destructive. French cigarette smoke preceded him by about 50 yards and hung about him like a wraith. He liked vodka martinis, straight up, with a twist of lemon. He reputedly did drugs. I could never fathom how Bino and Jamese managed to combine all this activity with training, competing, and winning. Lifestyles of Canadian champions. I felt rather cold and clammy when James walked up a corridor to where I was standing up against a wall, shrouded in cigarette smoke, and said something to the effect that I was on his list. Babe, I shuddered for the second time that evening and left the corridor—where a few of us had taken a breather from dancing—feeling quite disconcerted. I had to show respect to this person, a senior member of the national team. All I understood about James from hearsay just slotted perfectly in place. I concluded that everyone was right and that he and his Shiseikai friends were to be avoided.

What a typhoon of emotions, thoughts, and feelings I was caught up in that night! Here was Dulcie saying how much she respected me, which I found hard to believe. Didn't she understand that it was the other way around? Dulcie remembered the Japanese internment camp located between Hell's Gate and Purgatory on the Thompson River, where she spent the first six years or so of her life. She was a devout Christian, and when she was raped in Toronto and found she was pregnant, she kept the baby. Her son was about fourteen years old at this point. She was firm and assertive but in a very soft-spoken, non-threatening way. Her self-possession and deep commitment to karate were being put to use as the only woman on the Karate BC Executive. She functioned as Director at Large, then as Tournament Director.

She expressed a desire to start a women's karate club, and that at the age of 39 years, she felt that it was time for her to retire from competition, in which she was not particularly interested anyway. I appreciated her seriousness, dedication, and ability to overcome such devastating trauma with her belief in God intact. This woman was on a different plane from me altogether.

I could not reconcile how this compassionate Christian belonged to the Shiseikai and respected the likes of James and Bino?

Carnegie Recreation Center, Vancouver 1983

In early 1983, Andy was very successful in teaching at Champlain Heights Community Center in suburban Vancouver, but that only accounted for two evenings and one morning each week. He also wanted another location. The opportunity was presented to rent a space in the Carnegie Recreation Center at the corner of Main and Hastings in the east end of downtown Vancouver, on the edges of Chinatown and Japantown.

The community center was once a library, and the landmark building had recently emerged from major surgery and a facelift to provide survival, social, and recreational services to the downtown Eastside of Vancouver. Homeless people, drug addicts, and alcoholics loitered outside the Recreation Center. Syringes in gutters, bottles on doorsteps, people huddling around the Centre for free orange juice and donuts served by volunteers, and free meals provided by various charitable organizations

The Centre, in an effort to provide distractions for those sober or straight enough, offered organized games of chess, darts, and ping pong, and wanted to include more recreational activities. Andy agreed to run a karate program for one year. However, the clientele around Hastings and Main had little use for the perfect, rubber-floored gymnasium on the third floor.

In the UK, the *dōjō*s with the best reputations were often located in dubious areas, and people would choose to train there because of the quality of instruction. The situation was quite different in Vancouver. People wanted convenience, safety, and security, and among those who thoroughly enjoyed training with Andy, few ventured to that part of the city for an hour and a half of karate because they felt threatened.

A few of us supported Andy in his effort to establish a viable group at Carnegie, but the club never expanded beyond that. It was too bad, I thought, that people considered the downtown Eastside so dangerous. After all, the city did not have a gun issue like Seattle, and though those loitering in the area appeared intimidating, I knew they were usually harmless due to being sedated, high, or drunk. Strangely, in the year that we religiously attended workouts at Carnegie, not one of us was attacked or threatened. But then, maybe our group itself appeared intimidating.

There was Randy, who was loud, brash, and frequently offensive to unsuspecting individuals, particularly women. He lived close to a frantic edge with a highly unstable sense of reality, and Andy spent a lot of time pulling him back from the brink of some terrible personal pit. It was as though Randy had never learned the rules for living in society, and the discipline of his karate training seemed to hold him together for reasonable periods. He could be taught where boundaries lay, and he tended to keep within them once he knew where they were. A locksmith by trade, he ran a lucrative mobile business that I had to make use of at least once, having locked myself out of my own house. Randy had achieved a 1st-degree black belt, was in excellent physical condition, and thrived on committing himself 100% with no thought for life or limb, whether it was fighting an opponent or throwing himself down forbidden ski slopes with hysterical laughter that made all who heard it just keep out of his way. The fact that his electric blue eyes perceived the world with a hyperthyroid intensity sometimes made him look quite manic, but underneath it all was a kind and hopelessly confused individual.

Randy's tall, willowy girlfriend Daria was as languorous as a Savannah summer. At 24 years of age, she was making a reputation as a stripper, and she danced at various clubs around the city's suburbs. It wouldn't have mattered how Daria danced, with her flawless skin—a smooth, unblemished shade of iced *cafe au lait* from top to exquisite toe, perfect figure, and dancer legs. Drooling patrons paid simply to become mesmerized could not care less about choreography. Daria was untouchable by those who paid to see her and devoted herself to Randy, who undoubtedly kept her adequately supplied with whatever she needed to dance through the night.

Daria stayed straight for long enough to earn 6th kyu (green belt) during that year in Carnegie.

Alain had once trained in the Wong Way and was now a 3rd year student at SFU, where he played football. After leaving the Naha Te *dōjō*, he sought other karate instructors and was involved in kickboxing for a while. He was very strong and flexible and had lost all vestiges of technique control by training in full-contact martial arts. Alain was quite shy and awkward with the his size, which was quite intimidating. He was close friends with a Sikh who had also left the Naha Te (with the reputation of having the most hirsute posterior in the JKA, a dubious honour). Raj and Alain were graded as Shotokan 6th kyu, but they both had several years of training in other martial arts.

Elizabeth was a loyal student of Andy, who followed him anywhere, including places he preferred she didn't. She idolized him and was consumed by a passion for karate that was unhealthily fanatical. She was the only female among four male siblings and was raised by a submissive mother who was tyrannized by an alcoholic husband. Elizabeth was often the butt of her Dad's sarcasm and grew up trying to win his affection, but never succeeded. She became a driven overachiever who excelled academically and in sports. She was a chemistry undergraduate at SFU, en route to a PhD that she eventually also achieved.

Karate-wise, her behaviour was translated into doing at least twice as much as everyone else. If the count was for 30 sit-ups, she would do them 60; she would find a harder way to do something just to prove she was trying harder than everyone else in the room. After class, she would ask endless analytical questions, demand corrections, or continue training by herself until Andy gave her some earnestly desired input. It seemed as though Andy had really become a kind of surrogate father, and it was understood that a great deal of Elizabeth's efforts were to achieve Andy's approval. With this kind of drive, she could not help but progress rapidly, and she became the first of Andy's female students to achieve *Shodan* a couple of years later.

Me included, we constituted the odd group of die-hards that braved the east end of Vancouver twice weekly to reward ourselves with pints of beer and glasses of Okanagan red wine at the Mar Bar, a strip joint, a block or two north of Hastings, on the verge of Japantown. Andy had become friends with Wayne, the muscular bouncer of this strip joint, partly on account of Wayne's being the provincial coach of a wrestling team and a dedicated powerlifter. Wayne would clear people out of choice seats so that we could have views of the girls that only a doctor or a lover should see. It was some kind of experience for me being the only girl in a strip joint wearing clothes. I became quite friendly with some of the girls and asked them why they chose to work like this. I found that some were paying for college, children, a drug habit, rent. Some were clearly bored by their acts and stared at themselves in the mirrors lining the walls while listlessly moving about the stage, occasionally paying attention to the music. Others would show imaginative, original choreography or perfectly controlled gymnastics.

Kikuma, along with Andy and his core group, once invited a Japanese visitor named Tsutada to the Mar Bar after he had expressed a desire to see such activities. First of all, we wined and dined him at a buffet-style seafood restaurant. Tsutada san consumed two plates of assorted raw and marinated fish, followed by three plates piled high with raw oysters. He also sampled about 10 of the desserts on display and washed down the feast with liberal amounts of straight Scotch whisky. Even though Tsutada san was a fairly large, broad-shouldered ex-judo practitioner with ample capacity to accommodate this excess, he was a tad unsteady on his feet by the time we reached the Mar Pub. Ever ready to enhance intercultural exchange, Wayne sat Tsutada san at the edge of the raised floor, where a clean-shaven apparition just happened to yawn invitingly on the stage about one foot from his chair. Tsutada san blinked. A double whisky on the house materialized in front of him, courtesy of Wayne, along with a glass of the dreadful house red for me and juice for Kikuma.

The naked dancer played performed her best repertoire for the apparently important guest for 20 minutes. This involved up-close and personal views of genitalia mere inches from Tsutada san's face, which started to turn an unhealthy shade of green. Sweat began to pour in a torrent down his face, and soon the jumbo handkerchief that graced the breast pocket of his gray silk suit was sopping. About the time another double arrived, Tsutada san had experienced enough of the dancer and leaped up from his seat, gagging, muttering the words,

"Kaki, aahh, kaki aahh oh nn", while trying to find his way to the rest room.

Kikuma was falling about laughing with no mercy, and the girl who had given a sterling performance was not thrilled to find that she had caused this guest to empty his stomach contents into the women's toilet.

I berated Kikuma for his lack of compassion, but when he told me that *kaki* is the Japanese word for oyster, I had to laugh too.

Free fighting was a frequent part of Andy's training regime, and Andy used to spar with all of us, regardless of level or ability. I always enjoyed fighting with him, as he never had an ego that needed satisfying by showing off how much he knew. He could be counted on to spar with complete control, using a range of techniques without condescension so that you never felt frustrated, afraid, or incompetent. Free sparring was usually practiced in the final portion of the class, and so, when Alain let loose a totally uncontrolled spinning hook kick to Andy's face, the class ended just a little earlier than usual, but with bows and a short meditation led by Andy. Only this time, Andy did not go to the Mar Bar but to St Paul's Hospital, where his cheek and jawbones underwent rewiring to put his face back in its original arrangement. Alain had unintentionally shattered a few bones in one side of his instructor's face, a kick which Andy gave him all due credit, as, uncontrolled though it was, he had failed to anticipate it with a block or defensive move, and such was the cost.

"One hell of an ippon" (a score of one point in a karate match), said Andy.

Alain felt terrible and was filled with such remorse that we had to make tactless jokes about how improved Andy's face was going to be, how handsome and what a favor Alain had done him. Even Andy would have smiled if he could.

Per the contract, karate classes at Carnegie closed after one year, as convincing people to train there was impossible.

He then started teaching extra-mural karate at Simon Fraser University (SFU), which, of course, was an obvious source of young fit, and healthy students just waiting to learn Shotokan karate. This club expanded rapidly and soon developed a large core group that stayed well beyond their graduation. Every year, the *dōjō* would start off with about 60 students, and the following year, about 80% of them returned, so there was always a long line of rainbow belts lining up to pay obeisance to the imaginary *shinden* (shrine) in the long end of the basketball gym in the new SFU sports and recreation facility.

Inspired not only by the success of the Spring Provincial and Canadian championships, but also by Andy's enthusiasm and consistent training, I entered the 1983 BC Fall Provincial tournament and left Duncan, BC, with a gold medal in *kata* and a bronze for team kata.

Having addressed the status of women's individual kumite in the province, I immediately launched straight into changing the prevailing climate regarding women's team kata. No teams in the province consisted entirely of women in 1983. A division was simply called "team kata," which contained one or two women. Barbara McLean, for example, competed on behalf of Mike Scales' *dōjō*, with two brown belt men.

I figured that convincing Ingrid and Sarah, who had become close friends, to join me in a team, regardless of what they thought about me, might be a reasonable proposition. We all knew the same kata and had trained essentially with the same people, so there should not be major adjustments in interpretation but rather issues of timing and presentation. To my surprise, they both agreed, so we met once or twice weekly for several months to practice the kata Unsu, Kanku Sho, and *Gojūshiho Sho* (54 steps, small) By the Fall Provincials, we were ready to show the results of our efforts, and among seven teams, we placed third, beating out Andy's and Mike's teams. We were pleased with this result, as the two teams ahead of us both contained siblings who trained in Chito-Ryū with the same instructor for their entire karate careers. At this point, I was satisfied as I had something to campaign for. See what we could do? It was a sign for all the women practicing karate in the province to get involved in a team and establish a women's team kata division at the provincial level, at the very least. The idea carried all the way to the Nationals.

In the Western Canadian Championships in Winnipeg, I earned a gold medal for kata and a silver medal for individual kumite. This performance was repeated in the BC Winter Games in Fort St. John. Consistency!!

Hidetaka Nishiyama sensei, San Diego 1983

Nishiyama sensei, 8th dan JKA, ran a summer camp in San Diego every year, and I found out about this in late 1982. Around the spring of 1983, it was pointed out to me that I had been a 1st-degree black belt for nine years, and that no one was going to come and tell me I was sufficiently accomplished to attempt 2nd Dan. I suffered from the illusion that your instructor informed you when you were ready to challenge the dan examinations, and that it was a conceit for a student to assume that they were ready. Kikuma pointed out that no instructor was going to tell me any such thing, so I should consider flying to San Diego and attempt the 2nd Dan with Nishiyama sensei. I rather liked this idea, but could not afford the time off work to attend the whole week of camp. Kikuma assured me that Nishiyama sensei would nevertheless approve of the effort I would make by going to San Diego at all. I finally allowed myself to be convinced and flew down to UC San Diego. I registered for the test, and the first thing that Nishiyama sensei (he looked just as sparrow-like as he did in the book!) said to me was,

"You not training summer camp whole week?"

"Well, no, sensei." I replied.

I immediately understood that I was wasting my time and should just return home. Of course, I did it anyway. Nishiyama sensei's test required that everyone memorize the entire grading exam and then perform it in the correct order, starting with basic combinations repeated five times, followed by kata decided by the examiners. I had not memorized the order. Had I been at camp the whole week, I would have known this. I moved on to the next table of stone-faced examiners.

"Compulsory kata, Jion" said. Shirai sensei and I panicked.

Does it have *kagi zuki* (key-shaped punch), *mizunagare no kamae* (water flowing posture), and *morotezuki* (both hands punch) in the 17th and 19th movements? I checked with John Hanratty. Unfortunately, I followed his advice.

By no means was the *kagezuki* the only reason for failing *the 2nd* Dan test in the JKA International of America, but I was not thrilled to have it added to all my other lapses in the practical understanding of Shotokan at the required level.

I was angry. Kikuma was wrong; Nishiyama sensei had already labeled me a failure for not attending the seminar all week. I was angry at myself for not knowing the kata sufficiently in the first place. Thus motivated, I decided that I would try again with Nishiyama sensei another day and that I would not fail.

Mother, Vancouver 1984

I was quite successful career-wise, earning good commissions from building up new businesses in the three Western Provinces, and I had gained a fair amount of self-confidence. Kikuma suggested that I was now perhaps secure enough to invite my mother to visit Vancouver and try to reconcile with her. I fought this notion for some time, but Kikuma was also very stubborn, and I finally capitulated and sent her an air ticket valid for a two-week stay.

A telephone conversation with Mother revealed that she was quite sober and loved the idea. She did not have a passport, so I suggested that she obtain the application forms from the post office. She felt that the forms were to be found at the Social Security (SS) office. Since it was the middle of a freezing, wet Scottish winter, I suggested she telephone first instead of aggravating her arthritis by walking in the slush and snow to the SS office, only to find that she would have to go to the post office.

Her voice, after a pause, became a thick, iced wall of sarcasm.

"Who the hell do you think you are? Just pick up the phone, says she. I am quite capable of walking on my two, perfectly adequate legs and asking for the forms personally, thank you".

Silly me. I had forgotten that you are charged for local calls from private telephones in the UK, and that was what she was really pointing out. However, the manner in which her response was delivered suggested that the whole exercise of bringing her over to Vancouver would be a horrible mistake.

Kikuma was insistent. I should not call it off. I had only one mother. I should try to help her. After all, wasn't she now approaching sixty years of age? Were there not mitigating factors beyond her control that caused her to behave the way she did?

"Yes. Her genes. I have at least half the same set, and there are a lot fewer bats in my belfry than in hers, 'dammit.'"

Kikuma was unfazed.

I mobilized all my friends and asked for their support. There was to be dinner at Christine's, and tea at Joan's. Kikuma would take her sightseeing, and if the going became too rough, I could rely totally on him. I only went through with this because I knew I could still depend on Kikuma.

Mother arrived at Vancouver International Airport on a perfect late-spring day in a blue coat that buttoned up the front, accompanied by a matching turban and a rather petite blue suitcase.

"How small and fragile she seemed." Said Kikuma.

"Do not be fooled, Kikuma; this woman has wreaked havoc upon the lives of her family and countless others. She is not harmless."

With trepidation, I greeted her.

She was not totally sober, but it was a long flight, with plenty of opportunity for indulgence, so I was touched to see that she had exercised a fair amount of self-control to avoid having to be escorted into the country.

It was her first time on a plane, and she loved it. She was not afraid,

"The seats were so comfortable, and the girls in the uniforms were very nice, Norma."

She had sat next to an agreeable woman, and they had enjoyed nine hours of continuous conversation punctuated by lovely meals and a nice film.

Kikuma drove us to my apartment and then left. She was very excited and wanted to go outside, so I took her on a short drive to enjoy some nearby sites. She was almost speechless, intoxicated by the beauty of a pristine spring in Vancouver. Pink and white cherry blossoms carpeted the streets, and people smiled in a relaxed, friendly manner. She loved it. She also liked my apartment, which had a sweeping view of downtown Vancouver, Stanley Park, and English Bay. She was enthused about everything. She could not express enough gratitude for this wonderful opportunity.

I had to perform a demonstration of the *kata Unsu* at a small tournament Andy was hosting, and Mother came along to watch. After 15 minutes of watching the event from the head table, where Andy graciously permitted her to sit, she commented,

"I'm sure karate is all very interesting, Norma, but if you are not interested in it, karate is quite boring."

Quite true—but her remark stung because she had made a similar comment when she had watched me for the last half hour of swimming training twenty-three years previously. Sport of any sort never interested her.

I could see that the visit would not be beneficial.

Mother had brought a bottle of whisky with her, which she kept hidden from me. She attempted to drink it in the bedroom while I was making dinner on the second night of her stay, so she sat at a desk in the bedroom and conversed with me through a door and a short corridor separating it from the living room and kitchen. I started to sense something was not quite right and went into the bedroom, announcing it as I went. There was no obvious drinking glass, but the smell of whisky was quite distinctive, and I saw the top of a whisky bottle covered by a brown paper bag under the desk. I asked her why she felt she had to hide it. Why not sit here in the living room and drink, where I didn't have to shout?

"I am not drinking," she said.

"Well, how much whisky do you suppose is in the bottle, conveniently located at your feet? You never used to drink whisky," I replied.

"None of your business. Where is my dinner?" she asked.

"Your dinner is in the living room should you care to eat it," I responded sternly.

"I will eat when I am ready."

"Why not now, when it is still hot?" I asked

"What did you cook anyway?" she asked with apparent lack of interest.

"Spaghetti with pesto sauce."

"I'm not eating that tripe. Make me a decent meal," she demanded.

"Oh no Mother, I don't think so."

She came through to the living room and to the dining room, looked at the setting for two, and sneered again that she wanted a decent meal.

So, I pointed out that this meal was perfectly edible and that if she didn't want to eat it, I would simply throw it in the garbage. I did, and she returned to the bedroom to take slugs of straight Scotch.

I left the apartment, having provided her with a key but no Canadian money. I phoned Kikuma and confessed that I didn't think I had the strength to continue with this experiment. After all, she had only been here two days, and already she was trying to control me as though I were fourteen years' old all over again.

Kikuma said he would take her out for dinner the next day, so I returned home to find Mother sound asleep.

The next day started with her asking what we were going to do, like an eager child promised a day at the beach. It ended with her saying some pretty nasty things due to a few more furtive swigs of the grain, but fortunately, she did so in front of Kikuma. He offered to drive her in his Mazda RX7 to the restaurant. She liked that idea, as she had instantly taken to Kikuma and always enjoyed cars, and loved driving.

We arrived at an unpretentious, unlicensed Japanese restaurant that was full of noisy oriental families having dinner. Mother's face arranged itself into a scowl. When Kikuma went to the bathroom, she hissed, looking disdainfully around at nothing in particular.

"Fucking ugly monkeys, these japs."

What did you say?

"I said nothing."

"What kind of a restaurant is this? When I go out to a restaurant, I expect decent food and a nice atmosphere, not these howling, disgusting brats."

So, she stood up, sniffed, and walked out of the restaurant.

Kikuma returned to find me on the verge of tears and the seat vacated by Mother. He went outside and talked to her, pointed out that he had personally selected the restaurant, as it would perhaps be an easy introduction to Japanese food, which he knew she had never eaten, and coaxed her back inside long enough for her to actually try the food and discover that she liked some of it.

He drove her home, too, and took good care to extol the virtues and accomplishments of her daughter and how she must be really proud of me because everyone else was. He refused to listen to any of the put-downs Mother tried to voice. By the time she arrived at the apartment, she was, at least, approachable.

Kikuma left, having seen both of us safely home.

Oh, horror of horrors—back to the bedroom and the furtive whisky indulgence. I had had enough and told her to come into the living room and relax.

"What are you doing in there," I called from the living room.

"Just getting ready," she said, so I crept up to the door and strode into the room, catching her in mid-gulp from a shot glass.

I had had enough. I snatched the glass from her hand, took the bottle, which was only about a quarter full, and poured all its contents down a sink. Bottle and glass made a satisfying crash as they simultaneously hit the bottom of the trash can. Mother assumed her most frigid expression, glared at me, then came into the living room to sit, straight-backed, on the edge of the sofa.

I busied myself while cleaning spilled contents from the glass and washing dishes.

"Open that window," came the imperial edict.

"Well, I am not terribly warm, so I think I'd prefer to leave it closed."

"I am suffocating in here."

"You seem to be breathing just fine to me. However, if you want the window opened, please feel free to open it."

I could feel a rising tide of something not very nice. Suddenly, a vengeful fantasy in my head was interrupted with....

"You open this fucking window, bitch!"

I stopped washing dishes. I held the dragon at bay. I controlled the beast that threatened to consume all my remaining logic and make me act unreasonably.

I dried my hands, collected myself, and approached where she sat with no intent of opening the window. I dropped to face her and delivered the following information in a relatively controlled voice.

"First of all, you must understand that this is my home, and you are a guest in it. There are some basic rules that every guest should understand, and one of them is

that you do not command your host to do any goddamned thing. So, if you want the window open, go ahead and do so, or ask politely."

"I don't know how to do it."

"Well, Mother, you are not stupid, and the lock is not terribly complex. I am sure that if you looked at it for a moment, you could figure it out."

"You bitch! I am suffocating in here. The air stinks. The food stinks".

"Well, Mother, if life is so difficult for you here, I will gladly rearrange your flight back to Scotland as soon as possible."

"My ticket is for two weeks!" Mother replied.

"Don't worry, Mother, I can fix that."

"Fine. I want to go home," Mother demanded.

"Good! Give me your air ticket."

"I don't know where it is," Mother said.

"Oh, I think you do."

"You find it since you want rid of me."

"No Mother, you are going to find it, since you have expressed a desire to leave," I insisted.

She showed no signs of moving, so I grabbed her by the wrist and forced her to stand up. How light and frail! My invincible mother. Probably no more than 90 lb of skin and bone.

She grabbed my arm with her free hand and tried to implement her favorite self-defense move, sinking her well-manicured talons into the flesh of my forearm. Mistake. I was definitely not 14 anymore and was considerably stronger than her, so it was an absurdly easy matter to use her grip on my arm so that she contorted herself in such a way that she found her arm rather painfully twisted halfway up her back.

The ticket, Mother.

Still, she refused to get it.

I walked her through to the bedroom and forced her head down almost into her suitcase and asked her in the most controlled tones to kindly produce the ticket.

She did so while swearing roundly and screaming that I was using karate on her.

Hardly.

Pocketing the ticket, I left the house and walked across the street to retrieve the laundry I had left in a commercial dryer. Barely in control of my emotions and legs, I tried to think of what to do next. I folded the laundry, put it in the car, and called Kikuma. I broke down completely and in floods of tears in the telephone box, cried because I couldn't do it. I had failed. I nearly lost all my self-control and knew I could not live for two more minutes with my mother, let alone two weeks. This was only the 4th day of her visit! I shivered uncontrollably.

Kikuma consoled me and told me to come to his place, where I stayed overnight, knowing I would have to deal with the situation in the morning.

Apparently, she phoned Kikuma during the night, but he did not tell her my whereabouts, although he reassured her that I was probably just fine, that I had many friends in the city, and not to worry because I would soon show up.

I called the travel agent and arranged for her to depart, not on the available flight the next day, but the day after, which would perhaps give her some time to reflect, think, or whatever. She had not seen much of Vancouver. Slowly, I collected myself and prepared my mind for the confrontation that would surely ensue when I arrived home. Good God, I told myself, I had dealt with this so much better as a child! I hadn't seemed to have learned much since then!

With trepidation, I let myself into my apartment to find Mother polishing her nails on the sofa. Neither of us said anything, and she would not look me straight in the eye. Before, she had been wearing my clothes, which fitted her quite well, but now she was wearing only her own, and the remainder were packed back in her blue suitcase (without wheels).

"There is some mail for you, Norma."

"Thank you."

(How civilized).

"When am I going back?"

"Day after tomorrow."

"Oh."

She stopped painting her nails, stood up, and walked into the bedroom. I busied myself for a few moments, then paid close attention to what was happening. It couldn't be whisky because she had no money to buy any.

Sniffing and snuffling noises crept under the door.

I entered the bedroom, and she immediately turned away. Such pride, my mother.

Crying confirmed, I pretended not to see it and went into the walk-in closet to retrieve a hand-knitted, wool Cowichan Indian sweater.

"By the way, Mother, Kikuma bought this for you. He wants you to have it as a souvenir, and besides, he thought it would be useful because the winter in Scotland is so cold, and he was worried about your arthritis."

She looked at the sweater with eyes brimming with tears.

"For me?"

"Yes, mother, for you."

"Oh, I can't accept it!"

"Why not? It is for you."

With that, she could control herself no longer, and the tears spilled over the edges of her eyes, taking rivers of Max Factor brown block mascara along with them.

"Because-... because ...he has been so kind and, and.... - I don't deserve it! I don't deserve the vase he gave me either! It is so-so beautiful and I am horrible."

The dam burst, and she covered her face with her hands as she released a wail that seemed to release all the anguish of her entire life.

I sat down on the bed and hugged her. When she had stopped sobbing hysterically and had regained some composure, I said,

"You are right, Mother; you certainly don't deserve it. All my friends and I have gone to a great deal of trouble to make you feel welcome and comfortable, and you have really behaved dreadfully. You know, Mother, when you are sober, you are a very neat lady. I like you. You are intelligent and sociable, and you can be warm, charming, witty, and lots of fun. But when you drink, you seem to be so hateful and spiteful; it is very difficult to like you."

Another sob.

"Sometimes, I hate myself so much I can't imagine why anyone should like me."

I was impressed with this revelation and jumped at the chance.

"Why do you hate yourself, Mother?"

And finally, I understood why she seemed so normal when sober, but another person at the slightest whiff of alcohol. I also understood why I would never be like her, no matter how much wine I consumed! Her life was based upon guilt that was medicated by alcohol.

She said that she felt responsible for her sister Isobel, being "in the nuthouse", because she was a coward.

My mother.

A coward?

Mother, Seaton, Aberdeen 1936

The little girl skipped over the rise of the hill at the top of Seaton Place East and sauntered down the street, eating a penny lollipop. Tiny and fragile, the probably undernourished eight-year-old Helen with the cheeky freckled face and straight auburn hair was accompanied by her elder sister Isobel, who at eleven had similar features and coloring but a stocky build. They lived with their father and two brothers in the flat just a few yards further down the street. The younger girl suddenly dropped her lollipop treat, frozen with terror, and screamed at the sight of a psychotic, violent harridan storming up the street from the beach with a hessian bag full of metal bits and parts that she had scavenged to sell to Scrappy Ross the recycler up the Chanonry.

Isobel said not to worry, that she was not afraid of this witch and would face her. She was not going to run away. So, Helen took refuge behind her big sister's voluminous skirts and remained there, paralyzed with fear.

Sure enough, the witch faced the two children, spewed a verbal salad of abuse, and set the heavy sack of scrap metal on the ground. Isobel stood up to her mother and, true to her word, held her ground.

A tactical error.

Isobel regained consciousness in the hospital quite a bit later, having been gouged on the side of her head with a heavy iron horseshoe that was selected from the bag of miscellaneous washed-up armaments. Helen, of course, was physically unscathed, but there were deep psychological wounds that no one saw because they only became obvious to Helen herself after Isobel came home from the hospital. Of course, she couldn't tell anyone about how she didn't help Isobel because she was such a coward, and now Isobel was hurt. the years passed, Isobel became depressed and then permanently institutionalized. The grown-up takes on the little girl's fears, magnified and festered, becoming an awesome burden of self-loathing. She believed that she alone was responsible for her sister's condition, and so her life followed a course hemmed in by bitter self-recrimination, shame, and guilt.

I thanked Mother for sharing this story and said that I was glad she had told me, as it clarified so many things. I also decided to show her some eight-year-olds.

She had never even considered that there just might be a genetic predisposition or an organic reason for Isobel's later condition or that an eight-year-old would be powerless in the face of an enraged adult. What a burden to carry for a lifetime.

In that atmosphere of soul-cleansing and mother-daughter bonding, I insisted that she try on the sweater Kikuma got for her. It fit her perfectly, rightly measuring her long arms and all, and she was thrilled.

Meanwhile back in Kitsilano…

"Go on, woman, wash your face. You look such a sight with all those brown rivulets running down your face.

Tell you what. Let's get you some clothes and we'll go sightseeing and have some lunch."

"But I've packed them all."

Here, mum, wear this, and that, and these shoes, and this jacket. Yes. it all looks perfect on you."

She exhibited her alcohol-free side as we went on a personalized tour of the city. Photographs show her at Wylie (her maiden name) Street, at Famous Amos (her married surname), where she was given free cookies because she was an Amos. A beautiful day, with more conventional sites en route and a pleasant lunch at Salmon House on the Hill, from where the perfect panorama provided just as big a feast for Mother's eyes as the excellent seafood did for her stomach.

The following day, I drove her to the airport. As we waited in line for her to go through the X-ray check, the people behind us in the line were definitely a little shocked, judging by the sharp intake of breath held as they eavesdropped on our conversation.

"Norma, I am really sorry I screwed up. I want to come back another time."

"That's great, Mother, and you will be most welcome. But you must understand that as soon as you get on the plane to Vancouver and for the entire duration of your next visit, you do not touch a single drop of alcohol."

"Yes, Norma, I fully understand. It is such a marvelous city, and everyone has been so kind I will not let them down again."

Suddenly, she changed tack and exclaimed,

"Oh! Norma! It must have cost you a lot of money to rearrange my ticket so that I could go home early."

"Not really."

"Tell me. How much was it?" Mother asked.

"$200."

"TWO --- HUNDRED --- DOLLARS??!"

"Yes."

"That's really expensive."

"Yes, mother. But you know,...... it was worth EVERY penny."

She paused, looked at me directly in both eyes.

(A group who were behind us suddenly stopped chatting, breathing, and pretended not to stare. No blinking. No breathing).

She laughed and laughed until she was almost crying again.

The people behind us started breathing and chatting again.

"I'll behave myself next time, I promise." Mother said.

"Great stuff. Bye mum, just try to like yourself a bit."

William Amos Jr, Aberdeen 1984

Later that year, my father died. It was difficult for me to feel anything, since I had very rarely seen him throughout my life, and the last time was around fifteen years before he arrived at my apartment unannounced and drunk. He left the imprint of his fist on the wall of the furnished apartment that I rented to demonstrate how much karate he had learned from a book. Nothing, evidently.

Throughout my childhood, my father had shown an insecurity that I didn't understand. Everything I did, he had done it better. When he learned that I was earnestly training in swimming, he said how he had taught himself to swim in the River Dee.

"Diving? When I was your age, I used to dive off the Chain Bridge (over the River Dee).

Karate? I know all about it. I studied from a Teach Yourself book".

Great, Dad.

Although I received the news about a week after his passing, I flew back to Scotland anyway, as it would be a good opportunity to see if I still felt the same way about the Amos sisters and their attitudes, and to learn more about my father. I had missed the funeral, but Mother, however, had not. She arrived at the funeral parlor, fortified by about half a bottle of whisky, and reminded the Amos sisters plainly that she had never divorced their wastrel brother and was still his legal wife. I can imagine the bitter sarcasm with which she would have spat this at these rather conservative and constantly sober women. The Amos sisters had no qualms in describing Mother's deplorable behaviour, and I was obliged to defend her. I knew that she could not face them sober, as she believes that they think she is inferior, and she also knows that she is.

My father's ashes were scattered to the winds at the funeral home, so I went there and stared into the clear October day and tried to summon some filial emotion. However, only regret was identifiable. He was on this earth for six decades, and all he left behind was a digital watch, a raincoat, two books of my grandfather's, and £1,000. He had been an intelligent, talented, handsome, doomed man. He could play the piano and drums; he could sing, dance, swim, dive, fix marine engines, cook mysterious meals, and play soccer. Someone who should have thrived.

What happened to it all?

I learned that he did indeed have a huge inferiority complex. The Amos sisters fought over whether or not they should tell me the scandalous stories about my father. I encouraged them to do so. Scandals are interesting, especially when they are close to the bone.

William was the youngest boy and the second youngest child in a family of seven siblings. He was his mother's favorite, which annoyed his stern, Victorian father. He was afraid that young William would grow into a sissy, so he sent him to school in a dress to teach him a lesson. That experience scarred my father for life, ensuring that he would develop a relationship with his father based on hate, fear, and public and private humiliation. This was the first of several psychological punishments applied to young William. Another was sending him to school barefoot to stop him from kicking cans and stones to perfect his soccer technique. More humiliation. I began to understand my father's attitudes and the reason for his behaviour.

My father smoked hand-rolled cigarettes, endlessly, it seemed—brown stained fingers told the tale—and he was very fond of whisky and rum. Over the years, his career in the Merchant Navy spiraled down from 2nd engineer and occasionally chief engineer in the Merchant Navy (presents from exotic destinations!), down, down until he would accept the most menial job on any bucket floating in the Clyde estuary until no one would hire him at all. By then, it was a matter of hanging out in dockside bars in declining Scottish ports for as long as whatever money he had earned was poured down his throat. Then, he would have to find another job. That vicious circle had been going round for a decade until one day, while in Aberdeen, he had difficulty swallowing and had to visit a doctor. After a cursory examination, the doctor sent him directly to

Woodend Hospital for immediate surgery. No time to go home. The operation to remove a malignant esophageal tumor was successful. However, he now had a hole in his throat.

That evening, his sister Margaret went to visit him, and he asked her to bring his pajamas as he was wearing a hospital gown. By the time Margaret returned, he had chosen to die. She speculated that my father simply lost the desire to live since he understood that half his throat was gone and that rollup cigarettes, whisky, and the taste of food were no longer an option. Perhaps she was right. He did not seem to have much to live for. No aims, no future beyond the next drink, the next rollup.

She also said that he had always enjoyed an easy life, never really taking responsibility for anything or anyone, and that the surgery, in a sense, gave him one last chance to be accountable. He finally took responsibility for something....

I returned to Vancouver with my father's digital watch and the two books that had belonged to Granda. The cost of the flight was just covered by his scant legacy. Quite pathetic, really. So, there I was, the last of that branch of lowland Amoses. Time to take responsibility for my own future.

JKA instruction, Vancouver, 1984

Around 1983, we became aware of a JKA instructor living in Montreal. He seemed to be having a hard time making a go of teaching karate professionally, and his progress was supposedly being interfered with by the vociferous president of the Quebec Karate Federation.

He had been in Montreal for about three years on a work permit and was in despair of ever obtaining immigrant status in that environment.

Yasuyuki sensei was a graduate of Komazawa University, and Hiroshi Shirai sensei and Oishi sensei were his *senpai* (seniors). Coming from Shizuoka, another senior in his hierarchy was Toru Yamaguchi sensei, a suspected member of the Japanese underworld (Yakuza). The fact that Yasuyuki sensei had only a single joint of one little finger incited much gossip, but the story was time-making. Anyway, it was his karate and ability to teach and communicate that concerned us. We were all enthralled by his teaching style, in the manner of Shirai sensei, and his technical ability.

He wore his gi in the style of a competitive schoolboy, no doubt a throwback to his university days, when he finished in the top 8 of an All Japan JKA Championship. He could make the heavyweight, custom-tailored gi snap crisply with clean, sharp techniques that made his Shotokan look natural and effortless. We invited him to BC for a series of seminars, as he was a refreshing change from Nishiyama sensei, who tended to talk endlessly, spraying saliva through rapidly disappearing teeth, and had people practice reverse punch for hours. Undoubtedly, what he was trying to teach us had fundamental merit, but Yasuyuki sensei would challenge minds and bodies with imaginative combinations, and he seemed sensitive to the physical and mental well-being of everyone in the *dōjō*. He could coax that little extra out of a person who thought he was on his last legs and motivate individuals who were training for recreational purposes while challenging athletes who participated in his seminars. He also seemed personable and was willing to communicate with all of us and to work within the framework of the National Association. A key issue was that, although his English vocabulary was perhaps not as extensive as that of Nishiyama sensei, he could pronounce it more clearly, so everyone could understand him, regardless of how long they had trained in karate.

When he asked Andy, Mike, and me for help in obtaining immigrant status, we willingly did so. We pulled out all the stops we knew. Letters describing his unique qualifications to teach Shotokan karate in British Columbia were written, and a rationale for bringing him to Vancouver was developed. Andy and Mike worked out a teaching schedule that would guarantee him a basic income and introduce him to all the outlying *dōjō* province-wide. Andy stepped down from his teaching positions at SFU and Champlain Heights, handing over two successful clubs to Yasuyuki sensei. Private lessons were arranged as a source of extra income. Several people pitched in to help, offering all kinds of goods, services, and anything they could do to ensure that this person could be brought and that he would become successful and stay. Randy gave him a Volkswagen Beetle that once belonged to Andy. We were thrilled to have our own technically competent Shotokan instructor, a figurehead for the organization, who would increase our level of understanding of karate, be a friend, and a sensei.

Sure enough, members of our group excelled over the next couple of years. How much of it was directly due to Yasuyuki sensei is, of course, difficult to say. However, I know that at the National Championships in Calgary in 1984, I won a gold medal in kata and a gold medal in kumite. I did not achieve the kumite medal on my own. The kumite medal— Yasuyuki sensei was in the audience and gave me some tips on what to do in the final medal round. I followed his instructions and became the first woman to win the Canadian National Championships in both kata and kumite.

He gave private lessons to Shawna Escher, who collected drawers full of medals as a junior and then also became the National Women's champion.

We successfully obtained Yasuyuki sensei's immigration status and made an effort to make him feel welcome and included as part of the group. Perhaps we approached it the wrong way, for it soon became obvious that now that he was a legal immigrant, he began to detach himself from all his students, and would talk about maintaining the correct distance from them because he didn't want anyone to relate closely to him. The Volkswagen did not suit his image; he had to live in a particular part of town. He had no friends, only people he would ask to do things for him. As soon as the usefulness was finished, the relationship was over. He lived with a woman who had come out to join him from Montreal. Like at least one of his previous relationships, she was also one of his students. Both she and Yasuyuki sensei worried about people "taking advantage" of them and isolated themselves. They never joined in the camaraderie of drinks at the bar after class, rarely went to any social function presented by group members, and gave the impression that they had descended from the heavens if they graced your *dōjō* Christmas Party. Yasuyuki sensei complained more and more about things he did not like. For example, he was offended that he was not allowed to referee without taking an exam. All other instructors in the province who wished to referee had done so, regardless of their nationality. The Karate BC Executive was perhaps unaware of what a gem they had sparkling in their midst, and it became obvious that he considered himself superior to the other Japanese instructors in the province.

After about three years, his feelings must have begun to manifest themselves indirectly as the membership of the various *dōjōs* started to dwindle. He would not perform demonstrations. He would not communicate with his students. I finally asked him what it was he thought he had to hide. No answer was forthcoming.

He had a peculiar view of women when the surface was scratched. His current partner notwithstanding, a favorite come-on line to women was to the effect that no one understood him except whoever was listening at the time. He felt lonely, had trouble communicating with Canadian males, and had no friends because teaching karate is such a lonely job.

So sensitive. Several people lost respect for Yasuyuki sensei at one of Nishiyama sensei's summer camps. Shirai sensei used him to demonstrate a technique that involved a punch, toppling Yasuyuki sensei off balance, throwing him, but holding him just above the floor as he explained a key feature of what he had just done, then dropping Yasuyuki sensei on the floor. Every time Shirai even faked a technique, Yasuyuki sensei, well, winced.

The entire attendance at summer camp, about 300 individuals, had ample opportunity to witness this spectacle of a JKA 5th Dan shriveling every time his sempai as much as blinked in his direction! Perhaps we understood that being punched by Shirai sensei would not be a picnic, but Yasuyuki sensei knew his sempai, and should have been prepared to endure such treatment. We, his students, were put in a position of having to defend his behavior on the floor, which was particularly difficult, since he would avoid talking with any of us.

We should have seen the signs. He wanted to be part of the National Karate Association of Canada (later renamed Karate Canada), but without contributing anything beyond membership fees. This was rather unusual for a senior technical representative of a large style group. All the other instructors pitched in by helping out at tournaments and occasionally giving demonstrations, and no one liked the imposition on their personal time any more than he did.

Suddenly, Yamaguchi sensei was his enemy.

He did not want to have to go through Nishiyama sensei to conduct Dan tests; he wanted to do them himself.

He had little respect for Yutaka Katsumata, who was now the JKA instructor in Montreal.

As the number of these "enemies" increased, so did his dissatisfaction with his lifestyle.

He would talk about his ham radio setup in Japan, his wife, from whom he was not yet divorced, his daughters, how he couldn't pay for their piano lessons, and how they were beginning to forget him. All this sadness, this melancholy....

Andy's nose had been broken a few times, and though it did not look particularly pretty, he had never thought of cosmetically rearranging it. After all, it might be broken again. However, a cosmetic surgeon said that Andy had breathing problems that could be fixed by nose surgery and that it would be paid for by provincial medical insurance. Andy decided to undergo the surgery.

Soon after that, Yasuyuki sensei decided he wanted his nose fixed, too. Nothing was wrong with his nose. He then went to see the same surgeon whom Andy had complained about breathing problems. Around this time, Yasuyuki sensei had indicated that he wanted to become involved in movies, and claimed that fixing his nose might lead to good parts. At any rate, he, too, underwent rhinoplasty, but unlike Andy, he emerged with a nose he didn't like. He then demanded that it be broken and reset to a more aesthetically appealing contour. Thus beautified, he did indeed perform in a movie about a small-time Japanese crook who gets killed early in the story.

He said that he used to be fat and ugly throughout his school life. This statement explains his concern with the right attire, the car, the haircut, the right nose, and the film star hopes. He lusted after one particular girl who never took the slightest notice of him for several years. She was beautiful, perfect, and untouchable. Many years later, after he had become slim and presumably more attractive, he saw her on the street and declared how he had loved her for years and that he was, indeed, the new Yasuyuki sensei, svelte and streamlined. After recovering from shock, she told him that she had been married for a couple of years now.

Who knows whether or not any of this is true, but it all adds up to a rather unusual individual, easily revealed by scratching the surface. Maybe that is why he put ever-increasing distances between his students and himself. Maybe he didn't want anyone to discover that what lay under the surface was at odds with what seemed to lie on the top.

When the SFU *dōjō* dwindled to a mere handful of loyal followers, the SFU recreation office issued an ultimatum to the club secretary. The club would no longer be allowed its prime-time basketball gym slots unless there was a dramatic increase in attendance. Yasuyuki sensei took this as a personal affront and refused to do anything about it. The desperate secretary figured out that the only way to save the club from an ignominious death would be to have Andy return—but this time, in the front of the line. Andy agreed, since he didn't want to see this club wither away to nothing after it had been so successful at the start. He tried to discuss it with Yasuyuki sensei and tried to work out a way for him to continue teaching. Sadly, that was not going to happen. Andy was now one of his enemies.

One reason for Yasuo's attitude might have been that the SFU club did not generate enough income, though it required attendance three times each week. Thus, it was probably easy for Yasuyuki sensei to give it up, as the other *dōjō*, which were also dwindling, were a direct source of income.

Though well qualified, his girlfriend failed to obtain a suitable job in Vancouver and left the country. Yasuyuki sensei eventually returned to Japan for a while, then resurfaced in Vancouver around 1994, expressing a willingness to work within defined frameworks and asking for the executive director's help in finding a low-rent location for his second coming.

He now has a thriving organization in B.C. and is recognized by one of the JKA organizations as one of its representatives in Canada.

The Top, 1984-85

I had proven to myself and the National Karate Association of Canada, without an iota of doubt, that I was gold medal material. I had lost frequently over the past three years, and neither cried with regret nor blamed anyone other than myself for failure. I tried to overcome my personal limitations, perceived and real, and learn from my failures. When successful, I tried not to be too excited about it because I felt it insulted and hurt the opponent. Also, I felt that many people were indirectly or directly involved in such success, such as coaches, instructors, and companions. Win or lose, I believed that maintaining a sense of balance is an important aspect of self-control, so it was important to leave the tournament ring with dignity, having respected my opponent.

I was frankly puzzled by some individuals who claimed that I didn't *deserve* to win and wondered who did. Or maybe I *deserved* to lose? Why does one deserve or not deserve it? I started to analyze what I really felt. I was hurt by the fact that some teammates whispered behind hotel room doors. They did not want to talk to me simply because I had won that day. Would this mean that I would be more acceptable if I lost? I had to try to put their feelings in perspective as well as my own, and finally concluded that they felt disappointed. It was a kind of negative pressure that distracted me from being too pleased with myself, but after a while, it did start to depress me. I thought everybody liked winners, but I discovered they didn't. There is resentment, jealousy, disappointment, and anger that losers' direct outwards. The referee is blind. The judges are asleep or don't understand the *kata*. The level of competition is low; the home team always wins, and it is a fluke. Such things to say within the hearing of a winner is an attempt to lower the value of their success. I wanted to believe that the referee saw. The judges were not asleep, and they did understand the *kata*. And that they selected the correct winner. We were all winners. We were all selected from among the best. The best in our provinces in that association and the best Canada had to offer on the day. All we could do was go out there and give our best on the day. And if it was not as good as some other person's best, how could you, the most subjective of all judges, dare to imagine that your best was better than anyone else's when you lost? I could not understand the point of being angry and upset over losing a fight, as so many factors are beyond the control of the competitor: where you are placed in a draw, whether your randomly selected opponent in the draw is experienced or inexperienced, the referee supervising the match has one eye, or the chief *kata* judge has no idea about your style; a slippery floor or a sticky floor, the temperature of the venue, and more... Furthermore, karate competition is an artificial microcosm with little meaning in the real world. That is to say, winning a *kata* or *kumite* match does not translate to the street.

After considering these issues for several months and asking others about their thoughts on the subject, I let it go and accepted that there is nothing wrong with being a winner. It is reasonable to be proud of your achievements as long as the baseline is common sense. On top of all this soul-searching, the thought kept popping up that I came from a culture that downplayed success and personal achievement and that a winner would usually minimize an achievement by just the right amount of self-deprecation.

After about a year, I concluded that losing with grace was also a kind of winning and began to feel comfortable with the North American view that everyone is a winner. Having come to grips with these rather frivolous concerns, I decided that the bottom line was that I rather liked winning, but I really didn't mind losing, because that's when you learn.

Fort St. John 1984

After experiencing my first Winter Games, I decided never to go again as a competitor.

The government would pay for hundreds of athletes, coaches, and officials to travel to and stay for a weekend in sleepy communities in isolated regions of British Columbia that could cope with an event. A typical example was Fort St. John. It was a gold panning and mining town at mile 1 of the Alaska Highway. With a very small population, the town did not need an airport with a runway long enough to accommodate aircraft the size of a Boeing 747.

As the giant CP charter (filled to bursting with happy teenagers on their way to a weekend without parental supervision) approached the shed that served as the airport, the plane shuddered enough to subdue the raucous laughter that had circulated in the completely full interior for an hour. A glance outside revealed several locals, warmly bundled against the chilling 18 °C temperatures, seemingly glued to a fence around the perimeter of the sole runway in the minuscule airport.

"Why are they doing that?"

"They are waiting for the crash."

"What crash?"

"Us."

"Huh?"

"The runway is not long enough for the plane to land."

"Brilliant."

(Norma Foster carbonized with teammates from Zone 5 in a Boeing funeral pyre. Promising career as martial artist ended at frozen airport).

Much to the disappointment of the thrill seekers, we landed beautifully to a mass of loud cheering and enthusiastic clapping.

James and I had been communicating in a rather offhand way. He was involved in the games as some sort of official. Positions and responsibilities were quite interchangeable at any given moment in terms of participating in provincial tournaments. One was likely to be a competitor one moment and a referee or coach the next. Being from the same zone in the province, he was on the same plane as me, but in the smoking section. At one point, he had walked down the aisle of the 747, ostensibly to talk with someone else who just happened to be seated near me.

We filed out into the frozen wastes of BC tundra and marveled at the masses of bags and equipment that emerged from the bowels of the 747. No automation here. All luggage was unloaded totally by hand. I used to think that a karate gi was a hassle, but the sight of all those tons of ice hockey equipment made me grateful. We piled into massive tour buses and alighted in front of a primary school. Our home for the weekend.

We were accommodated in classrooms, whereas the officials were billeted in hotels as befitted their lofty status.

The community at the provincial taxpayers' expense and with the help of sponsors and volunteers who fed, housed, and transported hundreds of individuals representing several winter sports such as karate (a winter sport). Hence, the athletes bedded down on foldaway cots, 20 to a classroom, with a 9 pm curfew and a sponsored care package consisting of a piece of fruit, one carton each of juice and milk, and a candy bar. An envelope contained all the information you would ever need to last the weekend, a nylon Windbreaker from the Milk Board that was colored according to sport, and a commemorative enamel pin with the name of the town on it in case you got lost or forgot why you were there.

We were marshaled in an ice rink wearing our freshly minted purple milk jackets to the sound of an echoing brass band. The frozen rink was covered in cardboard, so before long, around 2,000 athletes were stamping about in a futile effort to keep warm as local politicians spoke for about an hour about the features and benefits of their city and why we should all come back for holidays and boost the town's economy.

Back to the classroom for sleep and talks on the rules of the weekend and the dire consequences of breaking them—someone always would, of course, and they would be sent home at their parent's expense and an example made to all. Court martialed, all that shame and hanging heads. I suppose that since most of the athletes were minors, it behooved the provincial government to take care of them so that their parents would not sue for negligence.

I was glad to have experienced this once, as it must be similar to life after an earthquake. Communally, and at the mercy of volunteers, charitable individuals, corporations, and, of course, politicians.

It was uncomfortable, disturbing, and always noisy. Schedules were tight, and adherence was strictly enforced. Not finished your event? Too bad. The bus leaves at 6. I was jealous of the officials being billeted in hotels and decided there and then that I would participate the next time, not as an athlete but...

Not even the official letter from the Premier that arrived soon after congratulating me on my gold medal would incite me to compete in this tournament again. Karate was one of the few, if not the only sport, that included adult competitors, and having noted this, I wondered if perhaps it wouldn't be better for karate to also consider only including juniors, as it struck me as being a fun weekend for a fourteen-year-old. In fact, that is what later came about.

However, there was only a consciousness of a gnawing pit of hunger, a stiff neck and tiredness from restless nights spent trying to sleep on lumpy cots, and freezing waits outside in sub-Arctic temperatures for people, buses, and school doors to open.

Repeat Nidan Exam, 1984

Hidetaka Nishiyama sensei visited Vancouver to teach another weekend of *"intaanaaru hawse", "heepussu phyburayshyon"*, and *"connec- shion wissu fro-ah"*.

Amazing! Something clicked! A moment of clarity was swiftly gone. About 200 people in a basketball gym had been standing in the same spot for an hour and a half, trying to wiggle their hips in a most ungainly manner, as though wearing invisible hula hoops of various diameters. The key issues seemed as follows: to keep the back straight, the shoulders relaxed, and to slightly rotate the hips in a barely perceptible right-left-right squiggle parallel to the ground while keeping legs not locked but straight and the body mass evenly distributed between both feet. We had to then add the equal and opposite reaction mechanism of a front punch towards the stomach, so that all the joints and muscles that could be involved were maximized from a stable base and to breathe naturally. When performed correctly, this would generate the maximal impact force at the point furthest away from the central pivoting axis, namely the front two knuckles of the outgoing punch.

In Nishiyama-speak, it came out something like this:

"Using tottarru botteh, making conneku shion wiss phroah, squeezing roah bottei, keeping back storaito, making heeppussu dohtaishiyon."

Having checked to see that we were all still enthralled by this explanation, he would again stare into the beyond as if concentrating on his English and continue with much spittle flying through the remains of his teeth and accumulating at the corners of his mouth:

"Wiss letoroaction and intaanaaru horse, good powah making."

Fortunately, all this was delivered with demonstrations by the master and a great deal of body language. At any rate, after about another 30 minutes of this, I made a punch that seemed as though it had been shot from the barrel of a gun. It all magically made sense! All that Nishiyama sensei had been trying to say coalesced into a front punch that hit only air! However, I couldn't repeat it even when I tried. Still, something changed—a flash of intuitive understanding that the technique was somehow right.

After a few attempts, it came together again. I smiled—and did it again! By now, I was grinning like a Cheshire cat as I reproduced this one punch repeatedly. Nishiyama sensei caught the look on my face. How could he not? I was the only white suit in the entire class, wearing an idiot grin. He looked a bit longer, and then he smiled, too, in that toothless, birdlike manner he had.

When the exam rolled around, I was ready. No way was I going to fail on *Jion* or any *Shodan kata* this time.

Four candidates were going to challenge *Nidan*, and we were called up two by two.

I was called up with Perry Foster from Fort St John, who had flown down to Vancouver for the seminar and examination. Perry, like me, had also received his *Shodan* from Hirokazu Kanazawa in 1974, so the two of us joked about trying 3rd dan in 1994 if we passed *nidan* this time, just to maintain order in our coincidental decades between certified advancement.

Perry stood on my right as we faced the examining table, headed by Nishiyama sensei, who shuffled some papers about in an imperious manner, looked up, and said the fateful words:

"Which one, Noma Hostaa?"

He could not have asked any better of me. Watch Doris Day in the 1953 Technicolor version of Calamity Jane.

[Thinks: I'll show you *which one, Norma Foster,* you stupid horrible man!

Norma Foster is the one you *failed* for *Nidan* last year.

Norma Foster is the one who will *not* fail this year.

Norma Foster is the one who collected you at the airport two days ago and drove you to your hotel.

Norma Foster is the one who sat and ate lunch with you and another Japanese person. I will clarify beyond any reasonable doubt which one is not Perry Foster.

I angrily raised my hand: **I am Norma Foster!**

My state of mind must have been written all over by my face as a sudden loud audible silence descended among the other examinees and spectators, followed by a loud "phew" and maybe a suppressed giggle or two.

I had memorized the syllabus. No catching me out in basics. Reasonable demonstration of key Shotokan principles referred to as "hip vibration" by Nishiyama sensei, rotation, relaxed upper body, *kime* in every technique due to correct breathing, hips square to the front for punches, and to an unnatural 45-degree angle for blocks. I added a meaningful kiai at the end of every sequence. Now, I was fighting Nishiyama sensei with every block, punch, strike, or kick. Compulsory kata? Jion. Hah! I laughed inside my head.

Shitei kata Unsu. Pure vengeance.

Applications? Try me. No further questions.

Free sparring? A whirling dervish.

I fought with Perry, then John Hanratty from Calgary, who was attempting 3rd Dan that day. I battered him mercilessly backward into a wall. He had no time to complete a single technique, and I refused to let up. I didn't care because, as far as I was concerned, I was fighting Nishiyama sensei, manifesting as John Hanratty.

Both Perry and I passed 2nd Dan that day, which was 10 years after passing 1st Dan. After paying for the certificate twice (the second sent by registered mail and waiting for one year), I received a fresh JKA certificate in a creamy washi paper cover.

The wait was not a problem. After all, I still had my little red KUGB book, and I had Nishiyama sensei sign and date it. Only one more space to go, and the book would be full. All I needed to complete the book was to pass 3rd Dan, which suddenly did not seem out of the question.

Osoyoos-Oliver, 1985

I drove to this twin town in the BC interior, about four or five hours from Vancouver, to participate in the 1985 Winter Games as an official, true to my vow.

I remember nothing about the event and much about the party afterwards.

First of all, the venue was well disposed to the high jinks that proceeded in its normally subdued lounge. The karate officials were housed in two small hotels, some distance apart. Ours was the more fun of the two, and the young owner was a good sport, his tolerance level perhaps augmented by the amount of dollars that disappeared over the bar counter in return for an endless supply of brimming glasses that enhanced the party spirit.

Here was Jim Hamilton, a 5th Dan in Wadō Ryū, who lived in Prince George and who was the senior exponent of Wadō in the province. He was devoutly and doggedly religious, in a somewhat Scottish Presbyterian, fanatical sort of way. He was quite thin, with very blonde, straight hair and a blonde beard that bespoke some Viking ancestry. His finely chiseled features were almost totally obliterated by thick, heavy-framed, black spectacles, through which his pale blue eyes would peer myopically as he poured forth great chunks of fluent New Testament rhetoric. A reincarnation of John Knox, I mused upon finding out that Jim hailed from Edinburgh. Not only that, but by the standards of the assorted Japanese instructors joining in the fun, he truly was my *sempai*, as he had been to Boroughmuir School! The same school as me! What a world! He had trained with Hamish Adam in Lothian Road, just down the street from Tollcross, and here he was, responsible for introducing Wadō to B.C. Upon realizing this, he began to reminisce about the Auld Country and recite many verses of Robert Burns with as much passion as he had when reciting biblical texts. He refused to drink anything alcoholic and seemed to be having trouble resisting the admonitions of James and Bino to stop pretending that he was pure and free from sin, when everyone remembered quite well that he used to enjoy more than an occasional dram of Uisge Beatha (water of life; Scotch whisky). People kept buying him drinks so that he was torn between the sin of rudeness in not drinking them, or weakness in the eyes of God for doing so. He finally broke down and had a few sips of a very dilute, well-carbonated cocktail. And he was off! Suddenly, he was singing bawdy songs of Scotland like the 200 verses of the rugby-related Ball of Kirriemuir at maximal volume. The whole room was reduced to uncontrollable laughter. We soon degenerated into a duet about Hairy Mary, a famous Scottish street song about a lady of the night which silenced the entire bar until the punch line was reached, when everyone erupted into gales of hilarity all over again. Jokes were endless. Tak Sameshima was forced to overcome any pretense of dignity in front of his fellow Japanese and act The Bottle Song for the last time. This is typical of Japanese bawdy songs, which revolve around a series of comical gestures with a prop, in this case, a large bottle, which substitutes for a portion of the male anatomy. Of course, none of us understood the words, but the actions spoke for themselves, and so language was never an obstacle to understanding. The group pressure to perform, recite, tell a joke, sing, or do something outrageous. Next thing I knew, I was located on *sempai* Hamilton's knee, as he fondled my arms from elbow to wrist, muttering with a kind of hypnotic, unfocused stare and a pronounced lowland Scottish burr.

"The arrrums. Aye! The Arrrums....."

He said he was going to pray for me so that I would cast out the devil, repent, and thus be saved. I responded that I was beyond salvation and not to waste his time on an ungrateful soul like me, which set him off again.

The Soul! Aye. The Soul. (Pity there wasn't a pulpit in the bar).

He told me not to use profane language (I'd told him he was *"spikkin' shite"*), which incited a cacophony of profanity from everyone around poor Jim as he desperately tried to save us all from doom and destruction at the gates of hell, for where we sinners all were definitely destined.

We all became increasingly boisterous, though in a high-spirited, humored way, such that people joined in the fun who weren't even part of our group.

The next thing I knew was Dulcie, spread-eagled, face down on the carpeted floor, being ministered to by Jim the Baptist. A double-take! A massage. Ah well, in full view of about 30 people plus God, it had to be fairly innocent.

That night was the last philosophical torment of our very own Holy Willie, as he withdrew from karate upon receiving direct divine instructions from God, who told him that karate interfered with his true purpose in life: saving souls. It was not a good start for his career.

Jim had a very difficult life. He told me the following morning that he had emigrated to Canada to start a new life, which initially prospered. He settled in Prince George and opened a printing business and a karate school. He married a Canadian, and they had a son. The town suffered an economic downturn, and in the late 70s, his business started to struggle, and his marriage began to show signs of strain. His wife left him and found solace in a fundamentalist Christian group. Worries and tension conspired to slow him down and forced him to reevaluate his life. Then he collapsed in the middle of a karate demonstration. He figured he had a nervous breakdown.

His wife suggested he join the group that she had recently joined as a means of therapy. He did so, and the marriage was renewed. He immersed himself in the teachings of the group, declared bankruptcy, and announced his intention to become a missionary and to bring God to heathens. Before he did this, he mailed me a few poems and exhortations to let Jesus into my life in a style that bespoke his six years at Boroughmuir.

However, not long thereafter, his twenty-year-old son died in a freakish boating accident on a BC lake, and the last I heard, his wife was so overwhelmed with grief, she lost all zeal for saving heathen souls and parted from Jim. Rumor has it that he visited Japan to save people, but it is unconfirmed. He returned to East Vancouver, aiming to preach to the godless and anyone associated with his previous life, should paths accidentally cross.

But in 1985, Jim had yet to face the torment his God had in store for him, and there was no way that my soul was going to be redeemed. I had no room for Jesus but plenty of room for others.

Guernsey, Channel Islands, 1985

My winning streak continued throughout 1985, as I collected more gold and silver medals at each of the Provincial tournaments, the Western Canadian Championships in Regina, Saskatchewan, a Shito Ryū Itosukai invitational hosted by Fumio Demura in California, and another gold for *kata* in the Nationals, along with a silver in *kumite*. Despite failing to repeat the performance of the previous year, I was still the National champion for two years running in *kata*, and there was no doubt that I would again be named to the National squad.

My dream of representing Canada in an international match materialized when I was selected as a member of the team to go to the Channel Islands and compete in the 2nd Commonwealth Karate Championships.

Luba and I were the only women representing Canada, and she competed in *kata* and middleweight *kumite*, whereas I competed in *kata* and lightweight *kumite*.

It was November, and although the climate of Guernsey is usually considerably milder than that of the UK, which is a bailiwick, the gods did not favor us with the sunlight that I hoped for. Rather, the wind whipped off the Straits of Dover and blasted frozen, wet needles through our woefully inadequate white, polyester tracksuits with CANADA emblazoned across our hunched and huddled backs. The Royal Hotel was situated right on the coast, and to go outdoors, there was always the prospect of battling freezing drizzle and howling winds. The hotel was Fawlty Towers, which was rewritten by Agatha Christie. Clocks ticked in the upholstered sitting room, replete with antique loo tables and tapestry easy chairs. The Times and the Observer rustled gently as pages were turned. No tabloids here! Regency stripes and furniture, gleaming with the patina of decades of loving care rendered unconditionally by generations of the family who still ran the hotel. Framed oil paintings, over 200 years old, were not permanently affixed to the walls! The private rooms were heated by radiators that bubbled and gurgled with boiling water, and when the huge aluminum "H" bath tap was turned clockwise, sputtering, boiling lava exploded in all directions into an immense, claw-foot porcelain tub. After much dilution from the "C" tap, I reveled in this ancient, elegant, understated British hotel, complete with a long-term resident, a batty colonel who relived his wars daily.

"I say old sock, where do you hail from?

Canada? Canada; I say! Yes! Once knew a chap from Canada, Vancouver, actually. Good gracious, wonder if you might know him?"

Breakfast often did not sit well with some teammates, being, of course, totally English and consisting, therefore, of cold white toast, runny boiled eggs served in the shell in small egg-shaped cups, marmalade, kippers, sausages, fried tomatoes, black (oxblood) pudding and tepid tea in larger China cups with handles apparently too dainty for Canadian hands. (Come to think of it, not so different from what you get in a Japanese ryokan!) Cultural differences were accentuated between us Canadians and our breakfast, as several members of the team stared at the eggs and wondered how to break the shells without throwing bits of them and egg yolks all over the pristine white tablecloth. So, I explained about toast soldiers (strips of buttered toast cut about 1-inch-wide by 2 inches long that get dipped into eggs - things I had forgotten). How North American I had become, without noticing it. What? No non-fat milk? Corn flakes? You call that cereal? Must be joking. Can't eat all that fried stuff.

Despite these culinary worries, we somehow made it to the venue without any of us becoming frostbitten.

Male kata was before our events, so Luba and I watched Peter Brown from Alberta perform the Gōjū kata Seienchin. The judges, particularly Tommy Morris, frowned upon this, as his son, Steve Morris, had also made the same choice. Peter scored quite low relative to Steve, despite James Johnson's score for the latter being perhaps more honest than any of the other judges'. He made an enemy of Tommy Morris that day, but then, Tommy might have also made an enemy of him. After all, James was just an unknown Canadian corner judge.

Yaz Yamamoto won the men's kata for Canada, with Steve Morris forced to accept 2nd. In the women's division, I made it to the final, where *Seipai*, performed by British athlete Helen Rahe, outdid my *Unsu*. I was impressed that she could perform kata from two different styles with such ease. I congratulated her and her coach, Ticky Donovan.

Ticky pointed out Hamish Adam to me, so I introduced myself to him. He was most agreeable and asked me if I knew Jim Hamilton, who had turned into a bit of a "Holy Willie?" I laughed and we amiably chatted about Jim spreading the gospel.

The men of the British team spent a great deal of time lying on floors, eyes closed and ears plugged with "Walkmans" (obsolete portable tape players you could strap on an arm), but that belied their performance. The British team did indeed consist of *"big ugly Sooties and nasty little Scots"* to quote an Englishman, and I had never seen such skill and dexterity, a whirlwind of spectacular techniques. Many of us in Canada were still struggling to overcome the effects of *ippon* (one point; sudden death) *kumite* according to the rules of the JKA, which had not been seriously amended since the late 1950s. In contrast, the British team had been fighting under World Union of Karate Organizations (WUKO) rules of sanbon (3-point match) *kumite* for years. They were experienced, talented, and coached by a pro.

Luba gained a bronze medal for her Chito Ryū *kata* and a silver medal for *kumite*. I also managed to win a silver medal in *kumite*, after being trounced by a British girl. The skill gap between 2nd and 3rd place was not too large, but that between the winner and I was huge. How do you learn to fight like that?

At the presentations, I was rather perturbed when Barney Whelan and or Tommy Morris insisted upon adding at the podium:

"**…and second place goes to Norma Foster from Canada** …… *but really from Scotland.*

Hell, Scotland never gave me the kind of opportunities in karate that Canada did…."

I bristled as I accepted unwieldy trophies. The absence of any Scottish women in the British team indicated that it would be a while before the Scots would wonder why women were absent from such opportunities.

I ditched the twin towers of plastic and metallic paint in the hotel garbage bin and retained only the commemorative strip. My teammates were aghast, but I had no room for such baggage, and anyway, I knew the important information. I had finally represented Canada in an international event, but it felt disappointing. Maybe I was perturbed by people not perceiving me as representing Canada. Come off it, folks, aren't we all pals in the "Commonwealth"?

James Johnson 1985

He ran his landscaping business and taught *Gima Ha Shoto Ryū* at Cameron Recreation Center. He was a loyal *deshi* (disciple) of Hidetada Narumi sensei, who had returned to his native Kushiro in Hokkaido in 1979, just when I arrived in Vancouver.

James had just started training in Los Angeles with Nishiyama sensei when he decided to flee for his life to Canada. He was involved in the Civil Rights movement of the 60's and established a branch of the Civil Rights movement at LA City College. I was surprised to learn that he was so committed to human rights that he ended up staring down the barrel of a shotgun during a scuffle between civil rights activists and police. His face and name ended up on a wanted list for daring to challenge the government on behalf of the discriminated, oppressed, and poor. It is not difficult to imagine his consternation when, attired in baggy overalls, a scruffy T-shirt, and his face obscured by his Afro hair and beard, he learned from a psychological test that his most ideal job was that of a bureaucrat. I can almost hear how he would have expressed his disgust in the language of the day.

A tour of duty in the US military sent him to Thailand during the Vietnam War, and soon after, he married the proverbial high school sweetheart. After many months, he returned home to find that she was the mother of a baby boy who was not his.

He then remarried, this time a quintessential California blonde, and they both came up to Vancouver and settled in the Kitsilano area.

There were very few black people in Vancouver in the early 70s, so there was no need to categorize this group as poor or oppressed. However, James channeled his interest in human rights into helping youth who were suffering from poverty, homelessness, family abuse, and drug and alcohol addiction.

Soon after, He and his second wife went their separate ways.

When he arrived in Vancouver, he visited a few *dōjōs*, but did not find what he was looking for until he met Narumi sensei, who emanated white light as far as James was concerned. Initially, having been initiated into the Japan Karate Association's version of Shotokan for six months, he sought a replica of Nishiyama sensei. When he saw Narumi sensei, he knew that his karate needs would be fulfilled, and they were until 1979. James says that when Narumi sensei first laid eyes on his awkward stances and uncoordinated movements, he shook his head and wondered what he would do with such an unlikely creature.

Nevertheless, in his university-style teaching manner, Narumi sensei managed to extract nothing but the best from his students, among whom was James' senpai, a green belt called Bino. The group became tightly knit and close to their sensei, head of the Shiseikai (Association of the Heart/Spirit/Mind) in BC. They would consume sake after training in the downtown east side Firehall and soon became after-dark fixtures in various restaurants in Japan town, tumbling out late at night to stagger into various cars and drive home.

One fall evening, around 1978, timed to coincide with the Shiseikai training session at the Firehall on Cordova Street, a group of individuals appeared wearing karate gi and wooden geta, looking extremely angry and seeking trouble. Here was the Gōjū mafia, headed by Takamasa Uchimura sensei, accompanied by a fellow called Tanaka, who wanted to relive some version of Okinawan history by entering another *dōjō* and challenging them to a "fight to the death". The rationale for this behaviour might have been due to the notion that Uchimura sensei, Tomoaki Koyabu sensei, and Ike Yabunaka sensei, and several other Gōjū members of the fledgling Karate BC were convinced that Narumi sensei was stealing money from the association he had established. They also suspected that the association was paying for his nightly post-training forays and were demanding blood. Others have said that it was because Uchimura sensei objected to challenging Karate BC referee exams. Whatever the true motivation, Uchimura sensei apparently had a reputation for being rather aggressive. He had worked as a taxi driver in Edmonton, Alberta, where he allegedly had some run-ins with the local constabulary, so he returned to BC.

One practitioner who was there that night recalls that Tak Sameshima was also in the *dōjō* that day, and he gathered students of the *dōjō* who together and made them all go upstairs to avoid a scene. Some of them were itching to fight, but Tak firmly refused to allow it. Seeing these men outside the *dōjō* spoiling for a fight brought a vision of a Spaghetti Western to Mike Scales, who was practicing that night. The members wanted to fight.

But it was not to be. Tak Sameshima called the police, who removed the Gōjū crew due to their trespassing in the Firehall, which was a temporary shrine dedicated to Makoto Gima sensei, the founder of the Shiseikai.

Stress test, 1987

I was Vice President of Karate BC and was involved in setting up a goodwill match and the travel arrangements for a visit requested by the Japanese National Team. I arranged the hotel reservation and logistics, selected the restaurants, created the itinerary, and took care of all the details that needed attention for a 20-person visit to a foreign country. I was to represent Canada at the goodwill match and was under severe pressure from the JKA International of Canada not to do so, or they would kick me out of the association. The visiting group was headed by Fusajiro Takagi sensei, Secretary General of WUKO and arch-enemy of Nishiyama sensei. Therefore, he was supposed to be my enemy by default. I chose to represent my country, not my style, in the goodwill match, despite portents of expulsion from the JKA.

Due to the demands of my job, I travelled a lot, and I had spent one week each in six parts of North America, interspersed by alternate weeks in Vancouver.

In any event, without noticing it, I had become totally exhausted due to the demands of my job, karate administration, competition, politics, and my emotional involvement.

I collapsed while leading a fairly aerobic warm-up in a cold room (13°C) for a karate class during the fall of 1987. I was sparring with Yasuyuki sensei, and suddenly, my bronchus spasmed shut. No air in. No air out. Panic in the *dōjō*. I could not breathe air in or out or speak because an invisible demon had just placed an invisible pillow on my face and sat on it.

Auto asphyxiation; self-offense.

The entire class came to a standstill, then people rushed over and stared in shock. No one had ever seen me in such a state of helplessness. Yasuyuki sensei thought that this was the result of him kicking me, but he hadn't. It just happened out of nowhere. I collapsed against the wall of the gym and tried to stem the tide of internal panic while calming the students who were only adding to the horror.

"So, this is what suffocation feels like."

Yasuyuki dealt with it and encouraged everybody to continue fighting again, away from where I was now lying on the floor.

I closed my eyes and concentrated on what was going wrong with my body. I innately understood that the smooth muscle of the bronchus had gone into spasm. I did not know why, but that could be dealt with later. Reciting the names of inflammatory mediators and smooth muscle relaxants over and over inside my head like a mantra. Maybe if I willed smooth muscle relaxants into my airways, they would open up. Mercifully, the bronchus began to relax, and I gingerly tested my ability to inhale through my nose. Slowly, I could feel the tension dissipate as precious, sweet air began to flow freely in and out of my lungs. I cautiously ventured to breathe more deeply and found that I could do it. I stood up on rubber legs, then joined the line at the end of the class.

Yasuyuki finished the sparring as soon as he saw I was vertical and initiated a cool-down.

"Time to visit the doctor, Art Hister."

He said I was stressed; what I had was cold-induced bronchospasm from doing aerobic exercise in an environment with cold air. The temperature in the *dōjō* was 13°C. He gave me an inhaler just in case and a bee sting kit so that if this ever happened again, someone was supposed to give me an intramuscular shot of anti-bee-venom, which would relax the spasm. He also prescribed a holiday, and a battery of tests, spots and all, which revealed only high cholesterol levels. However, I was diagnosed with cholinergic urticaria, which means that I am pathologically allergic to cold.

I decided to withdraw from everything stressful. That meant simplifying my life down to a keyring with one key and changing my lifestyle.

I went to a party where I met someone. I had known Michael from Andy's class and had trained with him for about four years. Despite being the salesperson of the Year, Canada 1984 and salesperson of the Year, North America, 1985, I quit my job—I had had enough. Six years of sales and business travel had definitely added their share of stress to the pie.

I also withdrew from karate competitions and daily training. I decided to practice karate purely for exercise, maybe once or twice a week.

I moved out of my townhouse and rented it. I signed up for unemployment insurance and then went to Hawaii for two weeks, followed by two weeks of skiing in Switzerland.

Anything and everybody that caused me stress was removed from my life. No responsibilities, no bills, keys, or commitments. I lay on the beach all summer and concentrated on rest and rehabilitation. I learned how to say "No".

James was now the Executive Director for Karate BC, the sport governing body for karate approved by the government, and we worked very well together. Under the vision of Karate BC President, Mark Stacey, we achieved numerous objectives for karate in the province in 1987. For example, I believe that we three were responsible for any goodwill that developed between Japan and Western Canada during the visit of the delegation headed by Fusajiro Takagi sensei. We were also not afraid to stare down threats from the IAKF faction in Canada, whose zeal for Nishiyama sensei's visions began to approach that of a cult. It was a time of sincere soul-searching for me, and I realized at the age of thirty-five that I was not yet adept at handling a particular level of responsibility and that I still had some growing to do. The thought also occurred to me that I was like my father in that respect, so I should find the level of optimal responsibility that suited my life and live it to the fullest.

I understood that James was an excellent conceptualist who could see all sides of an issue as well as the pros and cons of subsequent actions. An instinctive grasp of human nature combined with his willingness to lay his life on the line for a principle that he believed in made him a powerful opponent in a debate or discussion and a very difficult person to hide from. He was intelligent, quick, and articulate. I trusted him implicitly.

Las Vegas, 1985

James and I went to Las Vegas in January 1985 to participate in a series of seminars and a tournament hosted by Osamu Ozawa sensei.

I wasn't quite sure what to expect, but I knew that the event drew many participants from all over the USA, and several from elsewhere, too.

At the first sight of Ozawa sensei, a wave of *deja vu* enveloped me. Despite being Japanese, he looked remarkably similar to my father. After I returned from the Twilight Zone and stopped staring at him, I decided to introduce myself and tell him that. He was in his late 50s at that time, and in every way, he was a congenial host, behaving as though this were one huge party and not a gathering of relatively traditional karate people.

Thousands of people milled about Bally's hotel, where the tournament and all its accompanying seminars and parties were held. There was a welcome party where people seemed a little ill at ease, and a farewell party that developed into a "we all love each other" kind of spirit, softened by endless amounts of alcohol. Then came the *nijikai* (2nd meeting) at Ozawa sensei's Japanese restaurant.

Technical seminars taught by the following sensei: Yoshiaki Ajari (Wadō Ryū), Minobu Miki (Shito), Takayuki Mikami and Hirokazu Kanazawa (Shotokan), Morio Higaonna (Gōjū). This interested me as I had not seen him since 1974 and wondered how he had changed. He was gracious and taught the kata Kanku Dai.

I attended all the seminars and tried to retain some of what I learned. What a great concept—Tournament and seminars—something for everyone.

Over 1,000 athletes competed in 12 rings of elimination rounds marked out on the red-carpeted floor of Bally's conference center. There were divisions for everyone, young and old, from white belt to black belt. The kumite competition was *Shobu ippon,* and there would be two rounds of kata. All eliminations were finished on a Saturday, and the finals were showcased—the following day—on a wooden stage on a Sunday. Mr. Ozawa had an eye for drama because he had worked in the television industry in Japan before coming to North America. His involvement in the gambling and hospitality industry also seemed to have taught him a few things about marketing and management, as this huge undertaking, complete with participation certificates for all, proceeded smoothly from start to finish.

Turned out that Ozawa sensei, 8th Degree Black belt in the International Martial Arts Federation, was originally a JKA Shotokan practitioner and senpai of both Mr. Kanazawa and Mr. Mikami. This explained why he kept referring to them as "these young boys."

I emerged from the elimination rounds of both kata and kumite in the top eight and had to perform again on the following day!

On the Sunday, the ballroom did not look anything like it had the previous day. A huge, elevated stage was set up and seats fanned out around it in a huge semicircle like silent soldiers awaiting orders.

The show started when the room was almost full, with a slow dimming of the lights. The animated audience suddenly hushed, and the whole room became swathed in darkness. Drums started pulsating, at first barely audible, building to a deafening crescendo, then fading away to a distant rumble and again becoming silent. The audience was entranced.

An eerie light slowly appeared at the wings of the stage, and spotlights suddenly focused on two individuals clad in theatrical Japanese garments, one at each side of the stage. In unison, they lifted conch shells to their lips and heralded the approaching dawn. A solitary taiko drum started again, but this time, the beats were of equal volume and at equal intervals. An eerie whistle, a shakuhachi? A flute? Filled the room with a plaintive, Japanese melody. Slowly, as the black of the stage became inky blue, the ink became navy, and the navy became royal. Then, the sun started to rise and bathe the stage in warm radiance, dissipating the blue tones to final colorless clarity and highlighting twenty silhouettes performing the *Kanku Dai* (Look at the sun). The sun completed its morning ascent, having banished the darkness, at exactly the same moment as the evocative melody and the kata stopped, and the silhouetted shapes assumed human form.

Quite breathtaking, when seen for the first time.

This was followed by a series of demonstrations by various masters, including Fumio Demura sensei, who showcased his well-choreographed defense against multiple opponents; Yamazaki sensei, who demonstrated the ability to cleave various objects in half with a katana; and Miki sensei, who performed the kata Seipai with its applications.

I wanted to sit back and enjoy this most entertaining show, but I was tense because the final had yet to start, and I was a part of it.

The top eight women and the top eight men for *kata* were called to the stage and introduced.

I performed an *Unsu* and gained a silver medal. Well, I was quite pleased with that result, as I was no match for the winning Kanku Dai, performed by one of Mr. Mikami's students from Louisiana, the same woman I'd met in the late 70s.

After team kata, the top four men and the top four women were called onto the stage for the kumite finals.

The first fight was for the men, followed by the first fight-off for the four women. Two of the five judges alternated in being the chief referee.

I won my first fight. This meant that I would fight the winner of the next fight for the gold. The men's fight for the same decision came and went.

Kanazawa sensei was the center referee for that fight, and I was thrilled to win!

Now, I felt that I was on a platform floating well above the one I was physically standing on! It had been over 10 years since the experience before my Shodan test threatened to kill my interest in karate forever, yet here I was, having overcome it and triumphed in front of the man whom I partially blamed for those events so long ago!

At the post-competition party, I just had to talk with Kanazawa sensei and see if he remembered anything about that time. Well, of course, there wasn't. After all, that was when he left the JKA and had taught seminars and held dan examinations all over the world that year and every other year thereafter. It was totally unreasonable to imagine that he would remember anything specific about a dan examination that was only one among hundreds in which he had participated.

However, I do believe that the light in his eye sharpened almost imperceptibly when I asked him directly if he remembered Sakunosuke.

I instantly knew that Kanazawa sensei was innocent of those events.

Sydney, Australia 1986

At the age of thirty-four, I represented Canada for the first and last time as an athlete in an international event, the 9th WUKO World Championships. The most exciting part of this event was that they were being held in Sydney, Australia. The team, including Wendy Fong and Karen Antrakidis from Quebec, flew *via* Hawaii and Fiji to arrive in Australia, bedraggled and severely jet-lagged after 22 hours of flying and interminable waits in airport lounges for connections.

We were billeted in a hotel on Parramatta Road in Sydney along with the USA team, who were already recovered from jet lag, having arrived several days before us. I met the elegant Katherine Jones and the Tang sisters from Seattle in the lobby on their way to a waiting taxi. I said "hello," and smiled, and received a frosty response. Oh well, I thought. Some people are like that before a tournament, and may be quite different after. My experience in Guernsey had taught me that much, at least. Unfortunately, in terms of sports psychology, we received very little of it in BC. Our national coach, who just happened to hail from Newfoundland, seemed to consider himself an expert on the subject and seemed to use the team as guinea pigs upon which to test his recently discovered knowledge. Well, since most of us had little respect for the poor man at the best of times, this was rather difficult for him, and furthermore, most of us felt that it was a little late in the day for implementing his personal brand of pseudo-psychology. So, his efforts had little effect. Our manager was Rick from Saskatchewan, *deshi* (disciple) of Nishiyama sensei, and allegedly virulently anti-WUKO on account of his being a deshi of Nishiyama sensei, but who nevertheless did not refuse to accompany us on this trip at government expense.

Manuel Monzon won a bronze medal for Canada at this event, and the rest of us went home empty-handed. However, I was not displeased with my performance in the -53 kg kumite against Yumi Yanagisawa from Japan. I lost to her 6-5, and she went on to win the silver medal. She was fourteen years younger than me.

In kata, I placed 18th, which was exactly in the middle of the 36 competitors. This showed me where my level was on the world scale. Average. This was no revelation. I enjoyed the exquisitely controlled performance of Mie Nakayama, whose gold medal was a clear and unequivocal win. I had seen her on a video and was amazed at the control she exercised over every muscle in her entire body. To have seen her perform in person was a great thrill as she retired thereafter. I also enjoyed Katherine Jones' kata, and though she placed 5th. I was impressed with her performance and presentation, and wondered if it would be possible to train with her to observe how she taught, what she taught, and how she practiced, in order to learn more about this style of Hayashi Ha Shito Ryū. After all, Seattle was not so far away from Vancouver.

However, the timing of this tournament was not optimal for me.

For the past year, I had felt an unidentifiable pain in my right knee. Because it couldn't be touched, seen, or even precisely located, I had ignored it. However, it started to interfere with my range of motion, and I could no longer perform a snap kick, a back stance, or kneel down. Pivoting was excruciating. Training before this world championship, my dream, was therefore rather intermittent. But I wanted to go as there might never be another chance. Finally, I went to Alex McKechnie, a Scottish physiotherapist in Vancouver who dealt only with national-level athletes. For six weeks, I did everything he told me to no avail.

My fight with Yumi had not been distinguished by even one kick.

So much for the stuff of dreams. I stayed for an extra three days in Sydney as a guest of Christine's brother, who kindly escorted me sightseeing and also showed me where she used to live and get into all sorts of trouble. I ate Vegemite and jaffles and visited an opal mine and King's Cross. Overall, it was a memorable visit despite the lack of karate success.

Earlier that same year, I passed 3rd Dan with Nishiyama sensei on the first attempt, thus completing all the spaces in the little red book. By this time, he knew exactly …..

"Which one was, Norma Foster."

It was merely coincidental that, like me, he is a Libran dragon, though his birthday fell exactly seven days before mine and his birth year was exactly the same as my mother's. A stubborn sort of chap.

Later that year, orthopedic surgeon Bill McConkey removed most of the meniscus from my right knee, which eradicated the pain. It was not my imagination after all. Six weeks later, in January 1987, I competed in Las Vegas again and once more emerged with gold and silver medals. However, I was not doing so well at home. The emergence of Rassamee Ling, followed by her equally talented sisters, Tanya, Lisa, and Mee Lain from Chito Ryū, ended the reign of Shotokan over Canadian Women's competition. My teammates Ingrid and Sara were approaching thirty and thirty-three, respectively, and I would be thirty-five that year. The Ling girls came into the senior division from a strong background of personal training throughout childhood, supervised by their father, Dr. Chee Ling, an alderman, general practitioner, and 4th Dan in Chito Ryū karate and practiced Iaidō. The family lived in Kitimat, a small town in Northern B.C. All four girls were strictly disciplined in all their endeavors and became most accomplished at anything to which they directed their efforts. From the moment each of these girls stepped onto the competition court, you could almost hear the tolling of bells for us Shotokan. All the Ling sisters became National Champions and remained there only until other interests channeled their energies elsewhere. Rassamee, serious and intensely focused; Tanya, strong and resolute; Lisa, talented; and Mee Lain, determined to outdo her elder sisters in everything, have all represented Canada in the WUKO world competition, with both Lisa and Rassamee making the top eight in -60 kg kumite and kata, respectively.

Since they all entered adult competition as soon as they were old enough, they could look forward to a long competitive life.

Their only problem was that WUKO did not accept Chito Ryū kata as an elimination kata, so the Ling sisters were obliged to learn those of Shito Ryū, which they did with considerable success.

Obviously, my short window of competitive opportunity was rapidly closing, and it was time to explore other aspects of karate.

Reflections, 1988

After about six months of loafing, during which the Canadian government and Michael supported me, I received a phone call from the company where I had worked, asking me if I might be interested in working in the marketing department in Chicago. The president of the Canadian company said that after a short stint in our American office, the opportunity would arise for me to go to Japan. I was by then totally fit and healthy, free of migraines and rashes, and bored. The prescribed inhaler and bee sting kit remained untouched. I was ready to re-enter the workforce. I had learned lessons about myself. I understood that a specific level of control is essential to my physical well-being and that when I start to lose it, I become ill. The migraines are the result of a sleep disorder. Ping Pong! Satori and instant enlightenment! This explained the increased probability of getting migraines after flying distances with time differences of as little as three hours. Other things fell into place, such as not being able to smoke marijuana or drink lots of alcohol (relatively speaking!) without becoming extremely ill. This physical reaction to a loss of control only occurs when one is conscious. For example, anesthesia is not an issue, and succumbing to that kind of loss of control, is usually, after all, a choice. It was quite a revelation, but with this understanding, it became easier to recognize when to step back and not let events overwhelm me to the point of interfering with my quality of life.

The timing of this summons was perfect, and I was delighted to learn that my desire to return to Japan was being taken seriously!

Chicago, IL, USA 1988

I moved to Arlington Heights, a suburb in the north of Chicago. Naturally, as soon as I was settled into my new apartment opposite the company and provided with a car, I went off in search of *dōjō*.

Firstly, I visited the *dōjō* of Shojro Sugiyama sensei, a JKA instructor, who had a reasonably sized ad in the Yellow Pages.

He had me fill in a form and asked me what university I graduated from. I thought this was a rather strange question, so I answered that I didn't think he would be familiar with the college I attended in Aberdeen, and therefore there was no point in telling him. I gave only my name and address.

I found his training rather unusual.

Mr. Sugiyama said he was a deshi of Nishiyama sensei and that his classes were exactly according to the teaching of this master, who, of course, was in California, quite a distance from Chicago. Sugiyama sensei would make us kiai on the last of a series of techniques, and hold our tongues out like panting dogs throughout a kiai ("spirit" shout), for several seconds after the moment of impact.

Ei-i-i-i-i-i-i-i-i-iya-a-a-a-a-a-ahhhhhh!

It seemed that he had taken some of Nishiyama sensei's ideas about how to differentiate his "traditional" karate from WUKO "sport" karate and extrapolated them well beyond their original application. My understanding was that his organization, the International Amateur Karate Federation (IAKF), had evolved into the International Traditional Karate Federation (ITKF), which was intended to retain the Shobu Ippon (one-point scoring system). However, this prolonged kiai was intended to demonstrate zanshin, a state of alert concentration directed at an opponent after achieving a waza-ari (half point) or ippon (one point) victory. However, to stand on the spot for five seconds or so, emptying your lungs seemed ridiculous. After all, what happens if your punch is missed and you are standing there, posing, with your technique still extended along with your tongue?

Sugiyama sensei was very sarcastic in his classes and would say things to his students such as

"Look at you. Huh! Master's degree in history and you can't even follow simple orders.

Call yourself a PhD? You cannot even punch."

So, he was a bully. I was glad I had been close-mouthed, and wondered if Sugiyama sensei had ever attended an institution of higher learning. I never went back to that *dōjō*, but I discovered much later that, indeed, Mr. Sugiyama had never graduated from a university or college.

I then contacted the Illinois Shotokan Karate Association (ISKA), run by John DiPasquale. This organization had several *dōjō*s, a few of which were pretty near where I lived, which was a real stroke of luck. I went off to visit the ISKA. John D., as he was called, was a voluble Italian American who had been very successful marketing his *dōjō* and building up a huge booster club to support it. He said he was a 4th *dan* and had started with Sugiyama sensei. He ran his *dōjō* empire in a way that was halfway between a cult and a franchise, but I liked his students and the way that he taught. He had the spirit of his convictions and dispersed them accordingly. He was also a master marketer and salesman. I decided to stay in this group and promptly became a member of the Amateur Athletic Association, which was in contrast to the group in the USA that was currently affiliated with WUKO.

Through John D., I learned about some of the other karate instructors in the Chicago area. I drove an hour and a quarter on the freeway to the diametrically opposite Southwest side of town and visited John Nanay's *dōjō*, because it was Shito Ryū and a part of the USA Karate Federation, the WUKO group. So, on Fridays, I would go and train with John N. and the rest of the week with John D., which, for the time being, covered two style bases.

I soon became involved in local competitions, either as a competitor or a judge, driving to Indiana and Springfield, Illinois, the birthplace of Abraham Lincoln. There were few female black belts in the area, it seemed, and the *kata* competition was often against men. I didn't mind because I no longer seriously considered myself a competitor, but it seemed that little had progressed in the way of women's karate, given the size of the urban center that is Chicago. Where were all the women? John D had a few and lots of girls in his children's classes, but there were few adult women, even at the brown belt level.

I rapidly became close friends with Sharon, who passed Shodan that year. She really helped make me feel comfortable, and being about the same age, we had quite a lot in common. She did her best to introduce me to all sorts of places and people, and her job at an art gallery reignited my interest in things like Art Deco.

Chicago was beginning to feel quite secure as I found my way around the city and enjoyed roaming about downtown, where Sharon would never go because it was "too dangerous". I spent my days selling and marketing image analysis equipment and my evenings practicing Shotokan or Shito Ryū.

One day, a registered letter arrived from Winnipeg, Manitoba.

It was a letter from Jerry Mar, President of JKA International of Canada (JKAIC), explaining that I was being expelled from this organization because my principles were clearly contradictory to those of Nishiyama sensei and his ITKF. This was because I had dared to represent Canada in the informal goodwill match against the Japanese national team when they visited Canada the previous year and had participated in the accompanying seminars given by 7th Dan Wadō-ryū master Kazuo Tanizawa from Hokkaido, and Goshi Yamaguchi of Gōjū-ryū.

I had a few concerns about this letter. Firstly, I had not been a member of the JKA International of Canada for at least a year and had paid no fees to that organization for that period. This indicated that their organization was in disarray if they could not identify their members.

I also found a conflict with the apparent JKAIC policy that one should be loyal to a Japanese citizen who resided in the USA rather than to anyone Canadian. If this were a war, wouldn't such an attitude be considered treason?

Since one of the decision-makers in this process was Rick Jorgensen, who had managed the WUKO team in Sydney, I felt that by their own criteria, he should have been expelled from the JKAIC organization in 1986!

Finally, this farce seemed even more absurd from the JKA viewpoint. Canadian students of Nishiyama sensei and Canadian students of Teruyuki Okazaki sensei all had the same dan certificates. The JKA in Japan was and remains a member of the Japan Karate Federation, the national sport governing body for karate in Japan, equivalent to the Karate Canada. The JKF runs tournaments in Japan from which the national squad is selected to compete in WUKO tournaments. The JKA in Japan saw no violation of their principles to have their students aspire to be members of the national team and, in fact, to have some of its members be coaches of it. (Katsunori Tsuyama sensei was a fine example). So why were Mike Scales, Andy Holmes, and I being banished? Really, these questions were merely theoretical issues to be pondered and discussed at leisure, as I had no intention of following some vision that was diametrically opposite to mine. Surely, I could think independently and develop my strategy instead of blindly following some 8th Dan simply because he had a Japanese face? It is funny because I often hear about how Mr. Nishiyama's wrath was going to come down on my head, and I was going to suffer. However, I never once heard such threats from Nishiyama sensei himself. Only from these followers, especially when their power base was being threatened, either in reality or perception.

I sent the letter back to Jerry Mar, thanking him for the notification and taking the opportunity to inform him that I had not paid annual fees to his association for the previous or current year and was, therefore, not a member. Therefore, it was impossible to expel me from his organization. I also informed him that I had been living in the USA for the past six months.

The division for which I was a product manager in the company was shelved, and the staff spread throughout other divisions of the company. As the Canadian president had predicted, within three months, I was scheduled to transfer to Amersham Japan in *Tōkyō*.

International competition as an official New Orleans 1988

In 1988, I attended a Pan-American referee seminar in New Orleans, where I passed the examinations that qualified me as a kata and kumite judge at the Pan-American Karate Do Organization (PUKO) level within WUKO. Mr. Kiyoshi Yamazaki from Los Angeles was my ring controller during the tournament, which meant that he was responsible for ensuring the ring ran smoothly, that the available referees, judges, and arbitrators were effectively rotated, and that no one made too many erroneous judgments that would negatively affect any competitor. He gave me as fair a chance as anyone else to show my judging capabilities under pressure. At that time, the mirror system was in vogue for refereeing kumite, which meant that the referee and judge faced each other throughout matches while moving around the tatami in synch with the actions of the athletes while remaining alert to techniques that scored, were off target, or fouls such as contact to the head had occurred. All this running around was stressful and tiring, particularly when the competitors were very tactical. In addition, some of the older referees probably spent more time wining and dining than training and soon became tired. It was not the most elegant sight…

About two hours into the event, a migraine attacked. It started with a flickering jagged light shaped like the letter C in the bottom left corner of both eyes. This expanded over a period of 20 minutes and obliterated my vision. It is like being up close and personal with a giant disco ball, although peripheral vision was not affected. This meant that I could not see the results of most actions that resulted in awarding points and penalties. I endeavored not to panic. How could I tell anyone? I could just imagine the response.

"She had a headache.

Had to quit in the middle of the tournament.

Couldn't take the pressure.

Just goes to show you, women can't judge."

If I didn't tell Mr. Yamazaki and get some serious painkillers, I would not be able to do the job on that day. If left untreated, it lasts for 24 hours. I would fail the test, not be able to referee, and would suffer pain so intense (think skull being crushed in a metal vice while being pounded by a hammer along with every heartbeat for the rest of the day and the night. However, I can state that part of the classical migraine if I take the highest dose of over-the-counter painkillers within 20 minutes of when the hallucination disintegrates. But… I had no such medication with me.

If I told him, I would have to take a break to find some analgesics, and that would look bad because none of the men had taken a break. I would be seen to be weak and incompetent.

I decided that it was a lose-lose situation, so I decided to tell Mr. Yamazaki and save wiping 24 hours off the calendar. I explained the problem and asked for a 20-minute respite as well as permission to obtain some painkillers from the tournament doctor.

Mr. Yamazaki agreed, and after taking a hefty dose of codeine, I pronounced myself fit to see action. Back on the floor, with a dull ache for the next seven hours, the activities in my ring proceeded smoothly, and I passed the judging exam.

First Fukuoka Women's World Cup 1990

By 1990, I was living in *Tōkyō*, and the First Fukuoka Women's World Cup was scheduled for July. I obtained the consent of the National Karate Association of Canada to attend the referee course, try the exam to gain experience and learn what to expect from the WUKO world.

Molly Hand from Canada also attended this tournament. We participated in two kata seminars, one Goju and one Shito, as well as a kumite judging seminar. The latter was a tense affair, with several judges and referees dressed in navy blazers with crests, gray pants, white shirts, signature neckties and lapel badges, going through the motions of refereeing with volunteer athletes. If the referee council found what they were looking for in a candidate, that person was asked to perform again for a second look to see how they did with different athletes.

Mr. Arakawa had schooled me in posture and form for several weeks before the seminar, so I felt confident that even if I made mistakes, they would not be without dignity.

Molly and I both attempted the written test. I was now having a good time, the reason being that, as I was so young on this circuit, there was no chance of my passing the exam. Therefore, I approached the written test with a rather insouciant attitude.

To pass (or fail) this particular screening, the entire referee council for this event, consisting of Tommy Morris (Scotland; WKF Referee Committee [RC] Chair, Julius Thiry (USA) and Katsumi Hakoishi (Japan), had to agree unanimously. I listened to this without much interest, as it had no relevance to me.

In contrast to my opinion, it certainly was of relevance; I passed. I was awarded a "Judge" certificate. I was horrified, pleased, nervous, and surprised all at once. The outcomes of the tests were not published until after the event, so tension started bubbling in my gut like a hot spring.

I could hardly sleep that night for worrying about making major errors in judgment in front of the gathered representatives from over 25 countries and a few hundred spectators. Molly did not pass, which meant that there was only one female among the referees, so I knew that everything I did —every score or foul I flagged —would be carefully scrutinized. After all, no one in WUKO had ever seen a female judge at an international event.

The first day of the 1st Fukuoka Women's World Cup dawned far too quickly, and I realized while fumbling a Windsor knot in my meaningful tie that I was more nervous than I had ever been as a competitor.

What if I couldn't see anything?

What if I had another migraine?

What if I failed?

What if. What if. What if.

Bottom line? If I failed, I would probably be responsible for blocking the path of other women who might have similar aspirations, at least in the present environment. The day of the tournament started for me with a very light breakfast that was rapidly eliminated.

At the venue, I was assigned to a ring with several other unfamiliar judges and referees. They were all from European countries, did not speak English, and were very experienced. I felt way out of my depth. Sure enough, I was to mirror judge the very first match of the day, with Raphael Ortega from France as the referee.

Moments before I was due to step onto the dazzling white and blue rubber competition mats, one member of the referee council came over to me and said in distinctive Hungarian-accented English,

"We all voted for you, Norma. Don't make any mistakes out there."

This was the best thing that could have happened. I became so angry I forgot to be nervous. What kind of encouragement was that? Did he not imagine the extra burden that it contained? Was I supposed to be perfect in an imperfect world? Was I supposed to be intimidated? Did he want me to fail? Did all the male officials in the room make consistently perfect decisions? Did they receive such an admonition? I doubted it. This only confirmed that the RC would definitely scrutinize me, so I replaced my self-induced terror (What the hell am I doing here?) with defiance. That was a pivotal moment; I decided to fight for the right to be evaluated on individual merit and not on the fact that my balls are located where everyone can see them because they were eyeballs. Just like every male official. This was 1990, and if karate wanted to enter the Olympics, how could it run a women's tournament and have women only as competitors, tea ladies, or "attractions"? Where were the female administrators, guests, judges, referees, VIPs? Well, the buck started here.

I politely replied with control, given that I was furious:

"I can only do my best.

Nothing more.

Nothing less. It is up to you to decide whether or not my best is acceptable, or whether you made an error in judgment."

With that, I almost marched onto the mat, determined to take on this world, for better or worse.

Raphael Ortega from France was a very experienced referee. Although I did not speak much French, I felt confident that I could communicate with him sufficiently through eye contact, gestures associated with the process, and the "O" level French I had learned in secondary school. It so happened that I was on the ball that day, and most of my judgments were in agreement with those of Monsieur Ortega.

As the day wore on, I worked with several experienced referees from Japan, Mexico, Australia and Italy, but I was mostly paired with Mr. Ortega. This was no coincidence, as it is routine to place an inexperienced newcomer with an old hand. Nevertheless, Mr. Ortega gave me the confidence to proceed, assuring me that I was capable and could do the job.

The RC evidently thought so too, as at the end of the tournament, I received my returned record book, officially stamped with the words WUKO Judge, Fukuoka, 1990. This reflected well on Canada, being the first country to present a female official to a WUKO-sanctioned world event and achieve certification. I happily submitted a report for publication in the Karate BC newsletter later that month.

Tōkyō 1989

The company flew me out to *Tōkyō* to select a place to live. I hoped to live near the company, as joining the typical one–to–three-hour commute of *Tōkyō* office workers on trains packed to 130% capacity did not seem an ideal way to start or end a day. The company was located in Hakusan, in Bunkyo Ku.

Hakusan can also be read as *"shiroyama"* and both readings mean the same thing: white mountain. It is a question of whether the reading is *kunyomi* (Japanese) or *onyomi* (Chinese), respectively. Some places in Japan are called *"Shiroyama"*. The area still boasts over 15 temples and shrines, that are all within walking distance of each other. It is refreshing to stumble across a fox shrine, hidden away at the back of a grocer's shop, accessed by a narrow pathway between a polished Granite bank branch and a new curry shop, or a Buddhist temple dedicated to Kannon, complete with a minuscule Zen Garden. Our office used to be in the fashionable and expensive Ginza, so when the company moved to Hakusan, the staff were bitterly disappointed with the new, less expensive but more spacious lodgings.

didn't

I was taken to view some Japanese-style apartments, the rental costs of which would be subsidized, in part, by the company. I had been asked if I wanted to *live like a foreigner* or *like a Japanese* when I came to *Tōkyō*. I expressed the desire to live like neither. I didn't see the point in living in a costly western-style apartment when I could live in a more inexpensive, interesting Japanese "mansion" (condominium). On the other hand, I did not want to live in a six-*tatami* room rabbit hutch of 100 square feet. The company was sensitive to this and respected my wish to live near, but not on top of, the office.

I was taken to a mansion that was under construction in Nishi Sugamo, which was three stops up the Mita subway line from Hakusan. If I stayed there, it would only take 15 minutes to travel to and from work. What luxury. As the orange/red building was incomplete, I wandered into all the apartments and immediately fell in love with a three-room corner unit that occupied a floor space of 54 m². One of the rooms was a traditional six-*tatami* mat room (approximately 100 sq. ft.) with sliding doors leading to a futon closet, white walls, and pine trimmings. I loved the layout. A bedroom was separated from the living and tatami rooms, as well as the toilet and bath/laundry room, by a glass door and a small hallway with a tiny *genkan* (entrance). Both ends of the apartment were graced by balconies so fresh air could circulate and washing could hang out to dry (as in Scotland). Japanese balconies are often used to hang out laundry, and Japanese women frequently use parasols in the summer. But I could already envision plants on the balconies, reclining chairs, and cool summer drinks. Sugamo Beach! I visualized antique *tansu* (chests) and *hibachi* in the *tatami* room. I was totally enthralled with the 5th-floor miniature penthouse at the intersection of Meiji Dori, which encircles Tōkyō, and Naka Sen Do, a major north-south trunk road. Facing south, it overlooked a branch of the Mitsubishi Bank, Teikyo University, a fire hall, and a construction site and south view.

However, I didn't let anyone know what I thought and asked to compare some other properties. After satisfying myself that Taihō (Great Treasure) Mansion was indeed the best value for the Yen, with an optimal layout and the most convenient distance from the office, I moved into the penthouse three months later.

I set about acclimating myself to the company, my role, and the sundry details of life in a country where you can't speak the language: how to open a bank account, decipher bills, set up automatic deductions from the salary on payday, how and where to buy groceries, knee high socks, buttons, picture hangers. For three months, I did nothing other than go to work and return home exhausted, only to wake up in the wee hours, sweating, with an irregular heartbeat pounding in my chest. I understood what was happening to me. Culture shock. I knew that I just had to ride out the frustrations, allow the complete lack of control, and not worry about the pounding arrhythmia that refused to let me sleep beyond 4 am. Culture shock in Japan made me feel like a three-year-old dressed in adult clothing. I felt awkward and embarrassed. I feared contact with people and avoided them because I would not understand anything they said. This cocoon persisted until I obtained a bicycle, which expanded my knowledge of the neighbourhood. I was mentally exhausted most of the time due to a perpetual assault upon all senses and the pressure of not being mentally at ease. *Tōkyō* was awake 24/7, 365 days a year. Nonstop fire engines, cars, and motorbikes revving at the intersection at 3 am, ambulances, music, questions, announcements, indecipherable graphics, loudspeakers assaulting the ears, traffic, whistles, horns, and translations. Indecipherable Chinese characters (Kanji) everywhere. *Katakana, hiragana*, adulterated English (Japlish) that made no sense. Procedures with no apparent logic. A total lack of control over the simplest daily tasks. Personal questions.

"Can you use chopsticks?

Can you eat natto?

Can you drink Japanese tea?

I understand you have two passports."

"That is correct, Suzuki san, I have a Canadian passport and British passport."

I cannot imagine having two passports.

Hmm. *"You are married, aren't you, Suzuki san?"*

"Of course."

"You have children?"

"Of course".

"How many children do you have?"

"Two."

"I cannot imagine having two children....."

Upon being given permission to use the only English DOS-equipped computer in the entire company, I was told it was "not impossible" to move it onto my desk. Another "impossible" issue was my driving to Tsukuba University three days a week to develop a new product in collaboration with a professor in the Department of Medical Genetics.

I had been in Japan for about six months before I acquired (another) Honda Civic from Claude destined for the scrap heap. It was puke yellow, perfect in every detail, but it was ten years old, which marked it for disposal.

If I traveled by bus to Tsukuba, I had to catch two trains to reach a long-distance bus stop at *Tōkyō* Station, sit on the bus for up to 2½ hours depending on traffic, and then catch a local bus to the university. Total travel time: 2½ - 3 hours one way. Since I lived on the north side of the city, with easy access to the Joban expressway to Tsuchiura, I could make it from door to door in just over one hour if I drove. So, I did.

After I had been doing this for about six months, my boss suddenly realized that the expense receipts I was submitting, and which he was signing off with his stamp, were for gasoline charges and road tolls, not hotel stays.

He said:

"It is not possible for you to drive to Tsuchiura."

"But Ohrui san, I've been driving there for six months, so it must be possible," I said.

"Not possible. You must take the train or the bus."

"Why?" I asked.

"Very dangerous."

"Hmm. No accident for six months," I said.

"What car you drive?" He asked.

"My own." I replied.

"Aah! Aah! Not possible."

"Why not?" I asked.

"You don't understand Japanese."

"What does that have to do with driving on the freeway?" I questioned.

"You can't read the signs."

"Ohrui san, most signs are in Roman letters as well as Japanese. Anyway, after six months, I now understand all the road signs."

"Aah! Oh!"

"But you don't have a driving license." He added.

"Of course, I do."

"But Canadian."

"Yes, and Japanese."

"International?"

"No. Japanese."

"Impossible. You cannot have a Japanese drivers' license." He said.

"Here. I'll show it to you."

"(Looking at it) Aah! Not possible."

What he was really saying was that he didn't believe that I could drive in Japan because I was not only a foreigner but a female foreigner, and that, furthermore, if you drive on company business, you must have appropriate insurance, which was more to the point. You see, if you are involved in an accident and another party sues, it is not the driver of the car that will be sued but the company that employs the driver.

I was then forced to drive a rental car every week instead of using my own, which was a significant improvement, as my car tended to have expensive temper tantrums on the freeway that required costly attention from unwilling Honda dealers in small bedroom communities in northwest *Tōkyō*.

This type of intractability was new to me. This type of thinking definitely gave a novel insight into the minds of the seniors in the company.

I received another dose of it from a researcher at Jichi Medical University on another collaboration.

"I hear you were a salesman in Canada."

"I sold products for the company, 'Yes.'" I replied.

"Canada is a big country, no?"

"Yes, but I only looked after the western part of it."

"How did you visit customers."

"Well, by car if in Vancouver or Victoria and by plane if anywhere else." I replied.

"Didn't you hesitate to get on a plane?"

"Hesitate?"

"Yes, most ladies hesitate to fly."

"Hesitate to fly"? I repeated for a second time.

"Yes. They don't like flying."

Good god! What was the matter with these people?

Compare it with a section manager's comment that he

"........ could not get on a plane because they were all full of young ladies."

This, of course, was due to the hesitant ladies receiving their biannual bonuses thanks to corporate success and overcoming their fear of flying.

I wondered how long I could survive this, and heaved a sigh of relief, recalling that I had only promised to stay for one year in case I found the whole experience beyond my ability to cope.

Nevertheless, the sense of paranoia and isolation slowly ebbed, and I reached a comfortable level of function. I managed to tune out the loudspeakers in the subway:

The Mita bound train is approaching platform 1, so step back behind the white line and wait.

The doors are about to close; be careful. The next stop will be Sugamo; the doors will open on the right.

This stop is Sugamo.

Sugamo.

Change here for the JR Yamanote line.

Don't forget anything, especially not your umbrella, don't drop anything...

I ignored all the posters that I had tried so hard to decipher: labels, shop names, announcements, food wrappings, books, newspapers, and magazines, which were alien territory, and started to feel less drained by sensory overload. I started to have the energy to stay awake until late in the evening, so it seemed about the right time to knuckle down to the luxury of studying karate.

Training in Japan, 1989

Before I came to Japan, I had informed David Akutagawa of the Chito Kai in BC that I wanted to study refereeing and asked him to convey this desire to Fusajiro Takagi, who was still the President of the Japan Karate Federation (JKF) and Secretary General of WUKO. Now it was my turn to make contact, so I sent a fax to the JKF, saying that I was there and asked Mr. Takagi to kindly advise me where I should train.

Within a day, he replied, saying that he would introduce me to a non-JKA Shotokan instructor with a *dōjō* in the southeast side of *Tōkyō*. I was given instructions to meet Mr. Takagi the following Monday at 7:00

p.m. on the platform at Tōyōchō Station to board the eastbound Tozai subway line.

When I arrived, he was already there. He ushered me up the stairs and out of the subway. I found myself in a small cul-de-sac at the intersection of Eitai Dori, a major thoroughfare in Taitō City. A narrow, quiet street consisted of new buildings and construction sites that dead-ended in a massive danchi (apartment block), nestling up against a shiny sterilized YMCA building. It looked as though it had just been completed the previous week.

The glistening interior and silent elevator added to the image.

I asked Mr. Takagi why he had chosen this particular instructor, and he replied that, "Some people like him".

Hmm.

Words were passed at a reception desk while I shuffled about, having exchanged outdoor shoes for the ubiquitous green plastic slippers, three sizes too big, that await visitors to Japanese public buildings. Another flight of stairs and the smell of a swimming pool made me sneeze. More stairs and gleaming handball courts, surrounded by glass, gave way to aerobics gyms. All with beautiful wooden floors and mirrors.

Another flight of interminable stairs, trying to keep slippers on my feet with little success, led to a perfect dance studio with mirrors at one end, windows at the other, a bar, mats, and loads of space. A few people were standing about in karate gi, waiting for an aerobics class to finish. A rotund man with a priest-like shaved head that rested on a thick, folding neck and a broad smile that revealed rows of blackened, snaggle-toothed teeth decorated with at least two colors of metalwork detached himself from the crowd and came running towards us on incongruously dainty little feet. The man could have been Attila the Hun, Genghis Khan or some Mongolian chieftain. I would not have been surprised if I had been told that he lived in a yurt.

Here was Mitsuji Ichimura, JKF member and instructor at the YMCA *dōjō*. Mr. Takagi introduced me to this odd person, and a woman in a gi appeared to show me where to change. Lockers. Sinks. Hairdryers. Showers. Weigh scales.

All very comforting.

I changed into my gi, and when I returned, Mr. Takagi had disappeared. I worked out in the class under a senpai and waited for the master to do something. Mr. Ichimura's feet seemed to reflect the true essence of his body, as, despite his ungainly bulk and rough technique, he was amazingly lithe, fast, and could execute movements with almost delicate precision. There was no doubt, however, that if he chose to do grievous bodily harm, it would, indeed, be very painful. He had a loud, booming voice and talked a lot about practical applications and samurai. I knew instantly that I would not last long in this *dōjō*, and again wondered why Mr. Takagi had really recommended him.

Ichimura sensei was extremely kind and insisted on taking me to eat sushi at a restaurant in Misakichō, near Jinbōchō, which was on the Mita Line that led to Hakusan and Nishi-Sugamo subway station, located in front of Taihō Mansion.

Misakichō is also not far from the Imperial Palace and within the bounds of the area called Shitamachi, the downtown of old Edo. Mr. Ichimura lived there and thus called himself an Edo-ko, a true child of *Tōkyō*, in between uttering self-deprecating references to himself as a Mongol. The *dōjō* members all came to this restaurant too, and I promptly forgot all their names, except for Torigoe, who was a cartoonist and handball player. He wanted to draw me for a cartoon magazine. Mr. Ichimura kept up his loud bluster and ruled the restaurant with clipped commands. Upon discovering that I could not drink sake but could drink wine, he immediately sent someone out for a bottle or two of red Tokachi wine, which appeared in an ice bucket. This continued for the next two years. Train, drive with Mr. Ichimura and his daughter, Asano, a priest who trained with him, or whoever was planning to come for dinner to Misakichō and eat sushi or steak accompanied by liberal quantities of the Tokachi wine. I really didn't know how to deal with this excess of spoiling, which was extended to any individual I brought to the YMCA. I was never allowed to pay for training or dinner, and I never saw him pay for anything. Sometimes, I had to leave before him; sometimes, not. I was given a free membership to the YMCA, a benefit that was also extended to any friends or visitors I brought to train. So, for a while, every Tuesday and Friday, I would wake up with a hangover. For a while, I joined in everything that his members did. Entered the tournaments presented by the *Jitsu Gyo Dan* Karate Association (Workers Karate Association), attended the funeral of Mr. Ichimura's father, a man I had never met, and participated in *bonenkai* (year-end parties) and *shinenkai* (new year parties).

Mr. Ichimura supported me in several ways. This was not, of course, due to any outstanding qualities on my part but to the fact that he obviously held Fusajiro Takagi in high regard or owed him something.

Technically, Mr. Ichimura was less than what I was looking for in a land presumably overpopulated with karate experts. Some of his explanations or rationales did not make much sense to me, and his method of imparting knowledge seemed to rely more heavily on his senior senpai, whose teaching style consisted of staring at the ground and barking out commands to no one in particular. I became quite frustrated and guilty for feeling that way, because Mr. Ichimura was truly the epitome of kindness.

The Japan Karate Association, Ebisu, *Tōkyō* 1989

A visit to the JKA *honbu* (headquarters) in Ebisu in late 1989 indicated that this institution was on a downward spiral, with a psychotic 6th *dan* sitting in the corner of a black-ice-slippery *dōjō* floor, totally engrossed in picking his feet while verbally abusing those who were "training" on the floor. The class was understandably tense, and of the one hour that I watched, 15 minutes were spent wasting time running around the floor, 5 minutes on a warmup, 15 minutes on *gyakuzuki* (reverse punch), 15 minutes on *mae geri* (front kick), 5 minutes on *Heian Shodan* (the most basic *kata* of the style) and 5 minutes on a cool down. For this "advanced class" of about 20 participating black belts, the drop-in fee was 2,000 yen (about $20).

I decided that Mr. Ichimura was not so bad after all, just inconveniently located, and I felt an obligation to accept his kindness. In the current JKA environment, you could die, and you'd probably be ridiculed for not correctly bowing to some so-called reverence. It was a dangerous environment, with bullies in positions of authority. The cigarette butts burning in overflowing ashtrays in the front office, the dust and filth that clung to horizontal surfaces, rust on the metal cabinets, the disdain from people sprawling about in gi in the office as the front door opened, the rank smell of soiled moldy gi hanging in the foul changing room and the palpable tension of the practitioners worshipping at the shrine of Funakoshi under the baleful, nonchalant stare of sadistic instructors, all convinced me I did not have to be there.

I understood why Mr. Takagi had not suggested that I attend this *dōjō* in the first place. It had the reputation of being somewhere foreigners could go to get beaten up by xenophobic new graduates of the JKA Instructor program. Few of the staff spoke even rudimentary English and did not like dealing with innocent foreigners who found their way to Ebisu daily, having dreamed, saved money, and sacrificed to come here. To be battered and used as fodder for people who demanded to be addressed as sensei was not attractive to me. The behaviour and attitudes mocked the *dōjō kun* (motto) that hung from the front wall and was yelled with great enthusiasm by kneeling practitioners at the end of each class.

A long way from my fond remembrance of the Hakozaki *Dōjō* in Fukuoka. Had the JKA changed? Or had I?

Since I had no intention of returning to this *dōjō*, I was most upset to receive a telephone call from Mike Scales in Vancouver, asking me if I could help retrieve some missing Dan certificates from the JKA. I did not wish to be involved in this issue, but I felt compelled to do so on principle, as I was on-site, so to speak.

Several Canadians had passed various *dan* exams under Mr. Nishiyama throughout the 1980s and had given money directly in anticipation of receiving a calligraphed JKA Dan certificate. After several months, no certificates were forthcoming, and Mr. Nishiyama explained that the JKA honbu (head office) had made an error and that they would be forthcoming soon. More time passed, and Mr. Nishiyama stated that the money had been lost due to a paperwork error, so if everyone paid again, it would help expedite the matter. Some paid again in cash. Ears up, I knew this was unusual, as students of Teruo Okazaki at the other side of the USA had no trouble receiving Dan certificates within a week of passing exams. Mr. Nishiyama explained that Mr. Okazaki had a stack of unsigned JKA certificates, whereas he did not, and so it was easy for Mr. Okazaki to issue them. I suggested Mr. Nishiyama do the same as Mr. Okazaki. I also suggested to those awaiting certificates that if money were to be given again to Mr. Nishiyama, a bank draft should be made out to JKA International of America and sent to him by registered mail. I had done this, and coincidentally, never had a problem obtaining Dan certificates from Mr. Nishiyama. Cash, however, disappeared into a vacuum.

So, the years passed, and several Dan certificates refused to show up

Students progressed to 2nd, 3rd, and 4th Dan with no certification to prove it.

By 1989, there were approximately nine certificates still to be issued since 1981, some of which had been paid for multiple times. Among these, approximately six had proof of payment in the form of travelers' cheques, bank drafts, or copies of personal cheques. I reasoned that I could do nothing about three of them, but with some evidence of payment, I could approach the JKA and ask the questions.

I hated to climb those metal stairs to the dilapidated, second-floor front office of the Ebisu *honbu dōjō* (headquarters) and try to get my point across to the lone teaboy indolently lounging on a tattered green chair, head down on one of the 12 gunmetal gray desks shoved together in Japanese office style. My Japanese was rudimentary, and his English was non-existent. Furthermore, he was a lackey with no authority to deal with this. However, I kept pestering him by showing up to his miserable office day after day, politely looking for results.

After a few weeks, the lackey informed me that there was nothing to be done. There was no evidence to show that Mr. Nishiyama had ever paid the JKA *honbu,* so there was no reason for them to issue certificates.

I refused to accept this line of reasoning. I confirmed in horribly fractured Japanese, helped with a dictionary, that Mr. Nishiyama was still recognized as a founding member of the JKA, then pointed out that whether or not Mr. Nishiyama had paid them was of no concern to the six Canadian individuals who had paid him in the belief that they were paying the JKA. Therefore, they should not be penalized for their good faith in believing in their instructor.

I also added that the JKA had the ultimate responsibility for Mr. Nishiyama's actions, and they were aware that he still had the authority to represent them in the USA.

The lackey, whose name was Honjo, said he would speak with someone in authority for a little while, but that there was nothing he could do, because all the cabinets in the *honbu* (HQ) were locked and he couldn't open them.

Which authority?

Mikio Yahara.

Fine. I asked him when Mr. Yahara would be present, and he said he would check back.

After a few days, which was ample time for Honjo *san* to discuss the issue with Mr. Yahara, I trudged up the stairs once more to the *dōjō.*

I met a woman wearing a brown belt, whom I had seen only once before, when I trained with Hiroko Abe (the first woman to graduate from the JKA Instructor Class). She asked me what I was doing there. I told her that I was going to speak with Mr. Yahara.

She told me that it was impossible, that he was teaching, and that he would not speak to me unless I had an appointment...

I repeated that I had come to speak with Mr. Yahara, and there he was; I was not leaving the premises until I had spoken with him. I settled down on the spectators' bench to watch the class. It was definitely different from the class led by the psychopathic 6th Dan, and had a beginning, a middle, and an end, after which I corralled him as he stepped off the floor.

He listened to what I had to say, and since his English was quite good, I was able to communicate the issue more succinctly. He gave me his card and promised to do something. I suggested a time frame of a week. He agreed.

One week later, I caught the Yamanote line train to the Southwest side of the city, 40 minutes from my home, and wearily dragged my feet up the metal stairs to the JKA honbu once again.

However, this time, Konjo san had a pleasant surprise waiting for me. A pile of Dan certificates! All documents are correctly signed and stamped, with the names of the current JKA board listed as signatories. Most of these certificates should have been issued before Masatoshi Nakayama passed away, so the JKA simply issued new certificates that did not reflect the dates when the Dan tests were passed. But hey! Mission accomplished because the certificates were authentic.

Mike was thrilled with this. I was thrilled as I no longer needed to visit that seedy place. I later learned some of the JKF board members were responsible for locking the cabinets. This was part of the fallout of bitter infighting that became public knowledge after Nakayama sensei passed away. It was a classic symbol of what happens in karate organizations when a leader passes. The students start to fight over who should replace him, and this inevitably leads to fragmentation.

The JKA split into two factions and won a series of vicious lawsuits in the *Tōkyō* Local Court, the *Tōkyō* High Court, and ultimately, the Japan Supreme Court in 1999. The legal executive register was reinstated to its previous status before the uproar, and the now-legal JKF was not only restored but also strengthened, thanks to powerful internal solidarity. The association soldiered on and moved its headquarters to a better location, and JKA Shotokan still thrives[1].

Buddhism and Yamanashi; JKA 1990

Claude, who lived in Kofu, which is halfway between *Tōkyō* and Osaka, invited me to spend a weekend at a 300-year-old temple in the mountains of Yamanashi, the fruit-growing region of Japan. She advised me to bring my gi as we would train with the priest on Saturday and Sunday.

After a two-hour ride on the Tokyu (rapid) train, it arrived at Ohtsuki station, where Claude was waiting. We then caught a local train to Tsuru Shi; a small village scattered about rice fields and tiny curving roads with deep ditches and no protection on the edges. Upon arrival at the station, Claude called the temple and informed whoever answered that we had arrived. Within a few moments, a van swung into view, driven by the priest's wife, *Hideko*. We stepped into the van, and Hideko performed some skillful manipulation that caused the van to ricochet from one side of the road to the other, without its wheels somehow disappearing into the 3-foot-deep irrigation ditches on either side of the mountain hairpin roads, which were not much wider than the van. We suddenly pulled into a wide gravel driveway and screeched to a stop in a cloud of dust and a crunch of pebbles. The temple was situated halfway up a hill, and on its side was a graveyard, replete with weeds, old sake bottles, dead flowers, and the occasional new, shiny granite tomb. The deceased had an excellent view of the surrounding steep, ragged, conical hills thickly forested with dark green velvet. A polluted, greyish river meandered through the bottom of the valley, looking as though it had seen better days. The gray color was due to the effluent of a

---

1. https://www.jka.or.jp/en/about-jka/history/

concrete-making factory situated on its dwindling banks. It was visible from every vantage point around it.... except the cemetery.

A large bell hung in front of what appeared to be a large shed, but was in fact, the *dōjō*.

I entered the living quarters of the Fuku Gen in temple. A stone floor gave way to the *genkan* (entrance), where outdoor shoes were removed. A hike of about 2 feet led to an ancient *tatami* (straw mats) floor graced by a massive tortuous tree root, sculpted by the elements. The air was thick with mold, aging tatami and *Pawlonia tomentosa* trees (deciduous hardwood tree native to China and Korea). The *hon kan* (main temple building was on the left, and the living area on the right of it was divided by *shoji* (screens) covered in torn and scratched paper. The right *shoji* slid by to reveal the chaos that many Japanese families live in regardless of their station in life or the size of their living areas.

Taido (his Buddhist name), the priestly head of the temple, also ran a household comprising his wife, one son, daughter, dog, and at least two white cats. The family embraced the entire village and weekend visitors such as Claude and me. Another temple in an adjacent valley had recently been reconstructed, where Taido's mother, the daughter of a priest, continued her deceased husband's duties, who had also been a priest.

It was already ordained that his son (Taido) would attend Komazawa University to study to become a priest and that their daughter would marry a priest. Thus would make the wheel continue to turn. We called his wife Hideko sensei, because she taught things like calligraphy and was the local leader of the Girl Guides. Taido was out doing "priest work" and would be home soon. Claude said that we would know when he returned, and it wasn't only because Yuki (snow), the white temple dog, would bark and Tenbu (one of the cats) and her offspring would leap through the holes they had clawed in the shoji.

I awaited our host with great trepidation because Claude refused to elaborate.

As training time rolled around, and Taido had not yet appeared, so we changed into karate gi and sandals to cross the gravel divide to the *dōjō*. Since the windows to the *dōjō* were wide open, and since the *dōjō* was located in the middle of the untamed countryside, the room was a cloud of several insect species. Many of them were airborne piranhas that flocked to me, then flew off, satiated, while my skin immediately erupted in angry welts. Battalions of low fliers and scuttling crawlers inserted themselves in spaces between pants and legs, sleeves and arms to enjoy more tender morsels of *gaijin* (foreigner) flesh and blood. Increasing numbers of children made short work of removing dust, as well as most airborne and grounded beasties to reveal an uneven plastic floor with curling edges covered in plastic made to look like wood Hideko sensei said that she was currently fighting with her husband because she wanted a western style convenience to replace the stinking hole in the center of a stone floor at the back of the temple that served as the household privy, cobwebs, wasps and all. In contrast, Taido wanted to replace the floor in the *dōjō*. So far, an agreement had not been reached, obviously attested to by the ammoniacal aroma that swirled round the kitchen any time the door to the outdoor latrine was opened. The trickle of small humans wearing gi became a flood, and all of them bowed to Claude. The group of ~30 children having cleared the *dōjō* started running, jumping, chasing each other, shrieking, and yelling like they ought to. Just as the noise reached deafening proportions, all movement stopped as a one-year-old boy about 4'6" wearing a black belt (I referred to him as Counting boy) yelled:

Kiyotsuke! Taido sensei ni rei! (Attention! Bow to Taido teacher!) as Taido emerged from the entrance, all students in heavyweight *Tokaido* gi bowed simultaneously, then magically formed themselves into two straight lines.

Claude introduced me to Taido, who was definitely impressive, being over 6 feet tall, with a shaved pate (of course) and was a doppelgänger for Yul Brynner in the movie The King and I. His gi might have fitted him a few years earlier, as the side ties stretched to breakpoint against his sides. His belt was barely tied below a heft usually associated with consuming large quantities of beer. In a loud, commanding voice, he signaled Claude and me to sit with him in front of the lines of students as they knelt down in seiza (a formal posture seated on heels, back straight, and balls of feet tidily crossed) at the beginning of class.

Then, the (junior) senior *sempai* announced:

Shomen ni rei! (Pay respects to the Shinto spirits enclosed within a small shrine at the front of the *dōjō*. Everyone bows.)

Funakoshi sensei ni rei! (Everyone bows to the spirit of the founder of Shotokan.)

Taido sensei ni rei! (Everyone bows to Taido sensei.)

Kurodo sensei ni rei! (Everyone bows to Claude.)

Then he looked at me. After a momentary hesitation, when a shadow of confusion flitted across his face, it then changed into a barely subdued cheeky grin, he yelled....

Gaijin sensei ni rei! (a few muffled giggles as some students start to bow, then stop) when Taido had a fit and mercilessly scolded the boy:

"Baka! Kanojo no namae wa gaijin de wa nai… baka!" Kanojo no namae wa *NOMA desu!* (Idiot. That person's name is NOT 'gaijin'. Her name is Norma)

No-o-ma sensei ni rei! (Everyone bows to Norma) Claude scowled at Counting Boy

Little rascal! I smiled at him, and the whole room grinned, including Taido sensei.

Not yet finished with all the formalities, Counting Boy recited each line of the *dōjō kun* that is usually heard at the start of Shotokan classes, which is echoed by all in the room.

Then…*Tate!* (Stand up!)

Claude led the *junbi taiso* (preparation; warm-up exercises). She said that their warm-up was perfunctory at best, and furthermore, most of the children could do things like the splits any which way without warming up. They could all kneel with their butts on the floor and feet splayed out at 90° behind them. These were things that neither Claude nor I could ever do, and the class suppressed giggles watching these stiff old gaijin trying their best just to sit.

After junbi taiso, Counting Boy barked out at the top of his lungs

Gedan barai. Kamae! (Lower level block. Ready!)

Oizuki. Ichi. ni. san...... (Front punch. One, two, three...)

Halfway through the first round of block and punch basics, Taido picked up a dried yellow gourd, tied it onto his belt, and started to hit it with a stick. It made loud hollow clunks that could be heard anywhere in the *dōjō*. Counting boy stopped counting as Taido gave him a sharp smack on the butt with his stick as he directed a short inspirational lecture to the rest of the class. Brows furrowed, eyes alight with Buddhist demons, Taido scowled at the room, pretending to look angry. Come to think of it, he had perfected a scowl that Daruma (Bodhidharma, founder of Zen Buddhism) himself would have approved....

Baka. (Idiot) You call that a punch? I thought I taught you all how to punch three years ago! Who taught you to punch like that?

His gaze settled on Counting Boy.

He smacked him on the butt with his stick, to which Counting Boy responded loudly and with a great deal of enthusiasm:

Arigato gozaimashita (Thank you very much!).

The class giggled, not the least fazed by Taido's righteous indignation.

An electrical storm suddenly caused all the lights in the *dōjō* and the temple to go out. The entire class immediately stopped what they were doing and sat down on the floor without panic or noise. Such discipline was exemplary compared with what one might have thought before the class. Taido left to switch on a generator, so we enjoyed listening to the rain lashing against the roof and breathing in lungfuls of damp, earthly air. When Taido returned, the class continued, with a gourd and stick doing the count. He would start off loudly, with a predictable rhythm, then would vary the intervals between thwacks, then hit the gourd with a lighter and lighter touch until he virtually stroked it with the stick.

The purpose of this was to ensure all the children paid attention, as they had to be quiet and listen for ever-diminishing thwacks and immediately execute the technique of the moment. This also took care of their reaction timing as they would all race each other not to be the last; otherwise, they would be subjected to another saintly smack on the butt.

Arigato gozaimashita.

Another loud attack on an 11-year-old posterior, followed by another, *"Arigatou gozaimashita"* and a broad grin that immediately belied all sincerity.

The class went through its paces, which included everything from some devastating one-attack sparring routines to some *ho hum Heian kata*, and some inspired advanced *kata*. The energy of the children and the good humor with which they all submitted to Taido's whimsical commands and demands made for an entertaining, enjoyable experience. Taido would cajole, expostulate, demonstrate, clown, correct, coax and encourage. He employed an impressive range of facial expressions, complemented by expansive gestures, and gave the distinct impression that he was acting the part of a fearsome Kabuki actor in a play about warrior priests. After class was over, the group lined up, knelt down, closed their eyes, and held their hands about 9 inches in front of their chins, palms together in a prayerful attitude, with their forearms parallel to the floor. Counting boy took up the gourd bell and stick and started chanting Buddhist sutras. All the children joined in, and Taido walked about, adjusting postures and ensuring everyone stayed alert. Now, the *dōjō* hummed and throbbed with impassioned hypnotic monotones as the children were well-schooled in monotonal Buddhist sutras for about five or six minutes:

"......... *run run go hyaku sei sho ren shi ro...*" or something like that.

This was followed by shouting the *dōjō* kun again as fast and as loud as possible, as though with the same energy but a different spirit.

"*Jin kaku kansei nitsutomeru koto...*" (Seek to perfect your character...)

This was followed by a series of bows.

To Noma *sensei*, Kuraudo sensei, Taido sensei, Funakoshi sensei, the Shintō Kami sama and the founder of the Soto Zen sect, which we were currently immersed in. A few extra bows to the Emperor and maybe even the Crown Prince might have been included. At any rate, a lot of bases were covered.

Just as we were about to leave the *dōjō*, Taido asked me to check Counting Boy's performance of the kata *Enpi* (flying swallow) and *Gankaku* (crane on a rock), which he intended to compete with at a junior tournament the following week. Anything I could do for this boy's *kata* was beyond me. I hadn't even practiced it myself for about a year. I tried to tell Taido sensei this, but he would have none of it.

Instead of doing this in the *dōjō*, which he locked up, Taido led the way through the pounding rain into the honkan. Counting Boy performed his *kata* a few times on the worn *tatami* in front of the altar while Taido went off to exchange his wet gi for freshly laundered gray lounging monk pajamas, and Claude went off to enjoy the *ofuro* (bath). A cavalier attitude to an altar. Taido returned and asked me if I had seen a Buddhist altar before. I said I had, but not this close-up. He then explained everything to me about it and showed me a burnt fragment that looked like wood, but which might have been bone. Another relic of Buddha, I surmised, or maybe at least *Takuan*. I suggested to Taido that Takuan was always in a pickle, which was a feeble attempt at a joke, as *Takuan* is also the name of a pickled daikon radish. Taido roared loudly with delight. *Ha ha ha! A pickle! Oh, hahaha-a-a-ah!!* I appreciated his response to my rather irreverent joke. Counting Boy diligently practiced *Enpi* and when Taido and I emerged from the other side of the altar, me having now made the acquaintance of several Buddhist deities whose names I promptly forgot, he put on an inspired performance. This child was a mass of lean, taut muscle, sinew, bone and sweat. Taido had him repeat the leap in the air at the end of Enpi a few times, each time higher than before. The boy clearly could jump all night. Fortunately, after a few positive comments from me, Taido seemed satisfied that new input had been given and received and told us to come and join the party in the temple banquet room.

First of all, I had to clean myself up as my damp gi had become a stiff mixture of sweat and rain. After all, the ambient temperature was ~ 100° F accompanied by 100% humidity. Claude showed me to the bathroom, where the ofuro was full of near-boiling water. The temple had a 300-year-old air conditioning system, which is to say, a natural breeze was promoted by exquisitely carved *ranma* (lintels) strategically placed above the shoji. I poured buckets of hot water all over myself and tried to ignore the acrid night's oil vapors emanating from the 300-year-old latrine.

A quick towel down and clean, dry clothes that were hastily thrown on immediately became damp by the time (about 10 seconds) we entered the banquet room.

It was the Japanese village equivalent of a PTA meeting, with parents, karate teachers, and seniors all gathered around a long, low table covered in bottles of beer, whisky, and a variety of food, including meats of several sorts, and the ubiquitous, overflowing ashtrays that accompany such social events. Taido was a very popular and practical priest.

The electrical storm ramped up again overhead, with impressive bursts of thunder in the distance and sheets of rain over the temple forecourt. Soon, angry lightning struck, and one particularly bright, ferocious flash was followed by a deafening boom. The temple swayed on its foundations for a fleeting instant; then, suddenly, the electricity was cut again. Taido muttered something unpriestly, stubbed out his cigarette, and went out of the room. He soon reappeared, clutching several tall candlesticks from the altar that he lit with his cigarette lighter, reacquainted himself to his beer, and lit another cigarette from a priestly candle. and continued to enjoy the fun with everyone else. About five minutes later, the electricity was revived, and Taido tucked into a plate of pork and noodles. I said that I understood that Buddhists were vegetarians.

Me. Anything eat!

He announced with pride.

He then announced that:

Me anything drink!

Me Scotch whisky like! Me fine correction Scotch have, you like see?

"*Sure,*" I said.

Surely, Scots would all ditch the Presbyterian Protestant church for Buddhism if Taido established a temple in the Auld Country.

At around 11.30 pm, the party was pronounced over, and tables were cleared away to make room for our futons. Three-hundred-year-old pictures of Kannon and Daruma benignly glared at us and indecipherable scrolls of sutras occupied pride of place in the *tokonoma* (alcove). I drifted off to sleep, cocooned in a slightly damp, slightly moldy futon and mercifully still and quiet darkness.

Seven hours later, at 6.30 am, Claude and I were awakened by purrs and meows from her imperial majesty, Tenbu, the real ruler of the household, reincarnation of Dōgen (Source of the Way; Japanese teacher and philosopher, founder of Soto Zen Buddhism) and mother of equally perfect, totally white nameless offspring, called *Son obu* (sons of) Tenbu. All felines were perched inches from my face. One on the *tatami* and one on my futon, loudly functioned as alarm clocks. They were the advance guard, because 10 minutes later, 120 kg of gray-clad Taido entered the room, wielding old, torn kimono strips attached to a bamboo stick, and started noisily whisking dust out of the corners and singing with gusto.

We dragged ourselves up, stuffed folded futons into cabinets recessed into the walls, rearranged tables, and helped to sweep the tatami. The cats found this all rather funny. So did Taido.

no No NO! Hold the broom like THIS! Laughter.

Household chores over, he sat down to calligraph *kaimyo* (names given to Buddhists after death) onto grave markers. Taido has monk business today. He must preside over a funeral.

"*No like,*" he says, the edges of his mouth turning down.

"*Many money. Many money.*" Grins and mimics secreting away stacks of 10,000-yen notes into the folds of his voluminous formal vestments. Then his expression changes again.

"*....but, no like.*" *Rueful smile.*

He disappeared for a few moments and returned, wielding a large bag (presumably containing a lot of loot) and various folded garments.

He grinned and put on a show of Monk Dressing for A Funeral. A one-act play with a one-person audience. With a flourish, he produced a piece of cloth from the bag, displayed it like a merchant, explained what it was and why, then he donned black silk priestly robes with elaborate patterns woven or silk-screened sutras on the inside, close to his heart. The priesthood should be happy, healthy and wealthy, but humble. He strode off in a billowing flurry, squeezed himself somehow in the space between the steering wheel and the front seat of his sparkling clean, new Nissan, and exited with a scrunch of jamming gears and a tailspin on the gravel. He returned a few hours later with an envelope about one inch thick. It was full of 10,000 yen notes (about $100 each), tax-free payment for priestly services.

Despite his frown, I'm sure it helped pay for the new *dōjō* floor that appeared a couple of weeks later, swiftly followed by a gleaming white ceramic western toilet.

Next step on the Way

Mr. Takagi had also promised to introduce me to another instructor, and sure enough, a fax arrived with details about how to meet Toru Arakawa sensei in front of Tokyu Plaza in Shibuya one Tuesday evening. I was told that Mr. Arakawa practiced on Tuesdays and Thursdays, whereas Mr. Ichimura taught on Mondays and Thursdays. O dear… overlap.

I spoke to Mr. Takagi on the phone and thanked him for kindly making all these arrangements.

"By the way, sensei, what style does Mr. Arakawa teach?"

"Wadō Ryū," he said.

"Wadō ?????" I reiterated.

How disappointing. I had been hoping he would have recommended Shito, or maybe Goju, with Goshi Yamaguchi, who also taught in *Tōkyō* and was part of the group that came to Vancouver in 1986.

Yes. Wadō. The material that Jim Hamilton taught, which seemed unusual at a clinic I attended in 1984, was presided over by Tatsuo Suzuki. Fortunately, one small experience of Wadō *kata* had removed a bit of the edge of the strangeness when Yumi Yanagisawa of the Japan national team demonstrated Seishan at the *kata* seminar in Vancouver during their goodwill visit. Mr. Tanizawa had taught Chinto, and I found that these versions of both kata made sense.

But still, I thought maybe there had to be a reason for introducing me to a Wadō instructor that I don't yet understand.

Among the four styles officially recognized by WUKO at the time, Wadō Ryū had to be the oddest and the most obscure in terms of *kata* competition. In Canada, Wadō practitioners rarely reached the podium in *kata* competitions, and I discovered the same pattern elsewhere in the world. The *kata* looked weak and was not particularly interesting to watch. Where was the grace, elegance, and power? Such was my perception of Wadō, so I was surprised that Fusajiro Takagi thought

I should study a style in which the *kata* was rarely seen in international competition.

It was true that the British team, coached by Ticky Donovan, contained several Wadō practitioners and had won the team kumite at the WUKO world championships for a decade. I had the opportunity to attend a three-day seminar in Chicago given by Jeff Thompson, a member of the British team. Jeff was a fighter, and I'm not sure if he ever bothered studying *kata*, but his seminars were a lot of fun. The training was Wadō in principle, but it was applied to winning medals. Therefore, I respected Wadō practical fighting, but overall, I really didn't know much about it and tried to be enthusiastic about the imminent meeting with Mr. Arakawa.

Arakawa *Dōjō*

I waited at the front of Tokyu Plaza department store in busy Shibuya on a Tuesday evening and watched the sheer density of humanity rushing to and from JR Shibuya station, the comings and goings of several busses, taxis, bicycles, hundreds of red, amber, green stoplights changing, and the perpetual fashion chaos of tidy female bodies in tidy clothes with immaculate hair and appropriate accessories that resembled flight attendants or people going out first dates! Young boys and girls were dressed in school uniforms, and male office workers wore grey business suits accompanied by leather accessories. I wondered how I was going to recognize Mr. Arakawa.

It was not difficult. A taxi stopped almost in front of me, and a thin, unobtrusive gentleman with gray, pomaded hair stepped out wearing a tweed jacket over a white gi and dress slip-on shoes without socks.

Arakawa sensei?

No-ma?

Jackpot.

I entered the taxi, and was off to Sarugaku Sho Gakko (Sarugaku

Primary School) gym to start training in Wadō. Mr. Arakawa seemed rather reserved and didn't say much. Part of this might have been due to his level of English and my level of Japanese, but I sensed that it was also his nature. His back was ramrod straight, and his head seemed to swivel on an axis.

I tried to ask questions in Japanese.

"How many people are there in the dōjō?"

"Hm. Not many," he replied.

"Is it far from here?" I asked.

"Not much," he replied.

Ok, no more questions.

The taxi recklessly careened around a maze of narrow, curved streets and alleys as images of white slavery sneaked into my mind. The silent taxi finally reached Sarugaku Sho Gakko (Sarugaku Primary School). I was shown the dungeon where a woman might change, a stone-floored, filthy storage area under the stage of the school gym, where cockroaches scuttled among disused props. Planks of wood and rusting or broken chairs left tracks in a thick layer of gray dust that covered everything, including the floor.

The men changed upstairs on the stage.

I emerged from this fusty old cave with trepidation and faced about 20 male black belts. I wished that I were anywhere else but here. Maybe I should just leave now. But I owed Fusajiro Takagi and … of course, myself. So, I bowed and walked straight to the one end of the room, where I thought was the low end of Dan ranks. The class had not yet started, and no one spoke to me or to each other. Everyone was immersed in stretching or fixing some personal technical flaw. I performed some perfunctory stretches and waited for something to happen.

Mr. Arakawa went over to one of the three open doors along one side of the *dōjō* and sat on a stoop. He produced a cigarette from inside his gi and proceeded to light up and have a smoke. This wasn't quite what I had envisaged either.

However, soon after his nicotine fix, an order was called, and everyone formed into a large circle. Someone called Hori led the warm-up. So far, so good. This was a good warm-up that lasted approximately 30 minutes, incorporating aerobic, stretching, and strengthening components. All good so far.

The warm-up then continued with stationary basics, and Mr. Arakawa spent a lot of time fixing me. Input!

After about 20 minutes of this, the class took a very short break and then lined up in seiza, with Arakawa *sensei* at the front. The side of the line where I should I sit was luckily defined by the arrival of a student wearing a brown belt. I sat on his left, indicating that I was lower than him in the Wadō hierarchy because I knew nothing about it.

Opening ceremonies completed, moving basics began. *Jun zuki* down the length of the floor. *Jun zuki* with *maegeri* back again. *Jun zuki no tsukomi,* the strange-looking punch where everyone looks as though they are going to fall over their front leg. Same with a kick. *Gyaku zuki,* same with a kick. *Gyakuzuki no tsukomi,* another peculiar-looking punch where the upper body leans forward, the front knee is bent way over the ball of the foot; the weight is shifted sideways towards the supporting leg, and the body is torqued to generate impact force for the punch and avoid an attack. Same again with an added front kick. *Tobikomi zuki* and *nagashi tobikomizuki,* also features of Wadō, completed the moving basics.

Everything I did was wrong! Mr. Arakawa had a field day dissecting every movement, but did so kindly. Shock! What he was teaching actually made sense. His explanations gelled. Wadō suddenly looked normal and made sense right from that very first night. There was no huffing and puffing in the *dōjō*. People did not bark from their throats or stamp their feet when they executed forward techniques in an effort to make them appear "strong". All this acting to fool kata judges was absent. I felt invisible to the now 30 practitioners or maybe some kind of joke. But it didn't care. I had been introduced to a real *teacher*.

I remained in the Wadō Kai from then on and slowly began to understand what was and who was. I discovered that Mr. Arakawa had another *dōjō* on Saturdays, so I started training with him on Tuesdays, Thursdays and Saturdays, and with Mr. Ichimura only on Mondays. Also, I still visited Taido's temple about twice a month on the weekends.

Mr. Arakawa was well in his fifties and had a very dry, pithy sense of humor. He was not a big man, quite unnoticeable in a crowd, except perhaps for his perfect posture. His hair never became disheveled, and he always came to class with perfectly creased pants, usually a shirt and tie. He always wore a jacket except at the height of midsummer. After class on Thursdays, many of the *dōjō* members would accompany him to a local restaurant full of cigarette smoke and beer. Mr. Arakawa would chain smoke and drink constantly, starting with beer and ending up, more often than not, with sake. He never seemed to eat much, saying that he preferred to drink.

I eventually met the only woman who practiced at the *dōjō*, Chizuko Sato. She lived near me in Ikebukuro, with her mother, who was very ill. She was a couple of years older than me, and although she wore a white belt, she had been training with Mr. Arakawa for four years and also held a shodan in Shito Ryū, which she had earned during her university days. Sato-san was very kind and always took responsibility for ordering all the food for the boys and ensuring I was furnished with an ice bucket containing a bottle of Sapporo wine.

Slowly, all my Heian *kata* metamorphosed into *Pinan*, then *Chinto, Seishan, Kushanku,* and *Naihanchi* respectively replaced *Gankaku, Hangetsu, Kanku Dai, and Tekki shodan.* This did not cause any real conflict because the *kata Jion Wanshu (Enpi), Jitte*, Bassai, and *Niseishi (Nijushiho)* were rarely practiced in Mr. Arakawa's *dōjō*, whereas the only advanced *kata* that Mr. Ichimura ever announced were Jion and Bassai Dai. I settled into the business of learning Wadō.

Referee Clinic, in Nagoya 1989

I received a fax from Mr. Takagi's secretary, Hiroko Noguchi, inquiring whether I was interested in attending a referee clinic. I eagerly replied *"Yes."*

So, she sent me another fax pointing out that the clinic would be in Nagoya, so was it still possible for me to go? I quickly figured out the cost of the *shinkansen* (bullet train) to Nagoya, with two nights' hotel, as well as the unknown cost of attending the seminar, and thought it was going to be pretty expensive. However, since I had expressed a desire to study how to referee *kumite* and judge *kata*, this opportunity had to be accepted. I fired off another fax reconfirming my intent and inquired about the cost of the seminar.

A day or so later, another fax arrived with details. These included the time, train station, and where on which platform I would meet Mr. Takagi on a Saturday morning. The *shinkansen* tickets were already purchased for me, and I was to spend the weekend as a guest of the Japan Karate Federation. Good heavens. What on earth did that mean?

I met Mr. Takagi exactly at the appointed time and place at *Tōkyō* station on a muggy mercurial vapor day in July. He was tall and smoked endless cigarettes with a naturally elegant, laissez-faire demeanor that belied his age of over 70. Imagine my surprise to find myself in a Green Car (first class) seat.

Imagine my horror to find it was a hermetically sealed, high-speed ashtray that would have to be endured for 2 hours. Hardly in a position to mention this, I settled down to the business of inhaling the output of the 20 or so first-class chain smokers and enjoying a conversation with Mr. Takagi through a blue haze.

I asked him whether the beautifully tailored jacket he was wearing, which was a vivid royal blue Thai silk with some kind of regimental gold buttons, was custom-made. Whereupon he displayed the label inside the pocket. Mitsukoshi, it said, is a prestigious department store with a reputation for catering to wealthy, elite, and conservative customers. I expressed surprise that Mitsukoshi was the tailor rather than a Thai establishment.

Mr. Takagi explained that perhaps he adhered to a Japanese notion that a label on finished goods is essential to understanding quality. Without a label, how would he be able to judge it?

This started a lively exchange, which ended with him drawing my attention to the buttons on his blue silk blazer. Keio University buttons. His alma mater. He said the date on the buttons was the founding date of the institution.

Gosh sensei, I thought it was your date of birth!

(Oh for gods' sake, Norma, to whom do you think you are speaking? Stop it at once. Tone it down. You have surely offended the President of the JKF).

But he laughed.

After a silence punctuated only by repeated clicks of a cigarette lighter, he asked the following question, fraught with traps.

"*What do you think about budo?*"

"*Budo sensei?*"

"*Yes. Budo.*"

He twirled his cigarette and languidly looked at me who screamed *"appraisal"*. The only problem was that I didn't know what was being tested. After all, here was the man whose motto graces the front of the Japan Karate Federation diaries, of which this is a rough translation:

"*That, is a cultural (novel) creation that evolved from karate-do.*

That, is sport karate."

I carefully considered my answer.

"*Grapes sensei.*"

He chuckled at that, and I seemed to have passed the test.

The Japanese words for martial arts (武道) and grapes (葡萄) are both pronounced *budō,* but the Chinese characters differ… and the Japanese words for wine are *budō shu* (ぶどう酒).

So, we continued along those lines for three hours, during which he told me that *budō* (武道) is not unique to Japan. Mr. Takagi was radical, and it was easy to understand why he was an "enemy" of Hidetaka Nishiyama, given that Shotokan karate was popular at Keio University. What either of them had to say did not fundamentally differ, despite one ranting on a "traditional" platform and the other on a "sport" platform. His view was that tradition and sport are intertwined. Sport has become a new tradition in the short history of karate. He poses the questions of what causes a tradition to start? When does a repeated activity become a tradition?

Mr. Nishiyama had "traditional" held summer camps annually since the late 1960s. A goodwill tournament at the end of the camp each year that consisted of kata and *(jiyu* freestyle) kumite became a tradition. However, it has to be recognized as a sport because it has rules and is not directly related to life and death.

And so, I pondered as the bullet train hurtled through Kansai at hundreds of km/hours.

When we reached Nagoya, my navy-blue referee blazer was saturated with recirculated cigarette smoke twice, and the creases in my gray referee pants had somewhat flattened from the three-hour journey. I felt comfortable with Mr. Takagi, but totally uncomfortable in my clothes. Too bad, as we would go straight to the seminar from the train.

At the venue, Mr. Takagi decided to have tea, and insisted that I join him. After a while, a person appeared and sat down to discuss something with Mr. Takagi. I was introduced and sat quietly as they chatted amiably for a while.

After about 30 minutes of tea, I was taken to the referee seminar, which was already underway and full of Japanese males. I attended a monotone presentation which I did not understand. After that, the group split into two, and I was sent to work with one of them to referee matches. Everything I did was wrong. Fortunately, it seemed that everyone was at least as bad as I, so I supposed that I had been put with the more incompetent of the two groups.

I had to center referee with a mirror judge who refused to acknowledge that I was even in the ring. So, when I asked him to give an opinion, he refused, and repeated this twice. Soon after, I gestured for him to come towards me, which he didn't, so I became annoyed, and of course, it showed on my face. I was immediately advised about how to arrange my face and how to call the judge. I could not defend myself, as I did not have enough language, so I tried to put on a mask devoid of animation.

Next, we split into *kata* groups and had to put on karate gi to perform kata. Who knows, Shito Bassai? The group separated into those that did and those that did not know this kata. I went into the former, thanks to part-time studies in Chicago with John Nanay. I received a lot of positive criticism from a rather friendly fellow called Katsumi Hakoishi, who spoke quite a bit of English and was obviously senior in terms of running the seminar. I assumed that he was a *Shito Ryū* stylist.

The kata seminar concluded when everyone in the room was able to perform the entire kata and had covered several applications. Back in my smoky uniform, I was taken to a restaurant and introduced to the assembled 20 or so instructors who had attended the clinic, and I quickly forgot their names, except for two.

Mr. Hakoishi told me with a little giggle that his name was easy to remember because it meant "box-stone" in English, which was similar to the names of Firestone and Bridgestone tires. I did not catch the name of a *Goju* instructor who asked me if I knew Mr. Uchimura in Vancouver. Yes, I know Mr. Uchimura. He had tried to start a fight with the Shiseikai group at the Firehall *Dōjō* in Vancouver all those years ago. He, who failed to establish an alternate group, had applied for membership in mainstream Karate BC while I was Vice President. I had campaigned to allow him back into Karate BC against serious opposition from all those who remembered his prior actions. Although Mr. Uchimura allowed his contempt for me to show publicly in terms of low *kata* and kumite competition scores, Karate BC needed a competent Goju instructor, as the organization was dominated by Chito-Ryū and Shotokan practitioners. So, I fought against the prevailing memories.

Anyway, the nameless Goju instructor in Nagoya developed a severe allergy to me that was immediately evident, despite his limited English. Whether or not his attitude had anything to do with his relationship with Mr. Uchimura, I will never know. However, I speculated that it also had something to do with his dislike of Fusajiro Takagi.

The dinner wound down to a thankful close in a blue haze of second-hand smoke mixed with Scotch whisky vapors.

Now what.

Mr. Takagi said the men were all going to *nijikai* (second meeting) to continue partying. He said he was tired and wouldn't be attending, so I didn't need to either. Fine with me, but what was I supposed to do next?

A taxi was hailed for Mr. Takagi and me, and he was ushered into the back seat (important people typically sit in the back seats of cars in Japan) as the assembled diners bowed respectfully. I entered the taxi and tried to imagine what would happen next.

The car stopped in front of the Nagoya Castle Hotel. An "international" hotel, as opposed to a traditional *ryokan* (inn). Mr. Takagi said he preferred this kind of hotel sometimes. He checked us both in, and the clerk handed me a key to a room on the 10th floor. Mr. Takagi said that he wished to go to his room, change his clothes, and relax, and that he wanted to meet me in the lobby for tea within 15 minutes.

We traveled up in the same elevator.

I was absolutely astonished when I opened the door to a spacious, luxurious room in darkness, because the majestic, floodlit Nagoya

Castle occupied almost the entire opposite wall. An unexpected and truly glorious surprise. I just stared, transfixed. I began to understand why Mr. Takagi had decided to meet me for tea in 10–15 minutes. Sure enough, his first question between sips of *hōjicha* (roasted green tea) was whether I was satisfied with my room.

I could not enthuse enough about it. It was the most spectacular vista I had ever seen from a hotel window in my life. I hope he was satisfied with that.

The following day, Mr. Takagi said he was leaving early but that Dr. Hakoishi, whom I learned was an orthopedic surgeon, would ensure that I was taxied to the railway station for my return to *Tōkyō*.

After the seminar, another meal was arranged, where the Goju sensei spared no time in directing a malicious verbal attack on me, and I had no defense because Mr. Takagi had gone. Had this nameless sensei contacted or phoned Mr. Uchimura in BC? Unfortunately, he demanded that what he said be translated, so poor Dr. Hakoishi was put in an unenviable position. He was very apologetic as he repeated the words.

Who do you think you are?

Here you are in Japan, and you are being treated like a queen.

And what are you?

You are nothing.

I replied that he was absolutely right, that I fully understood that I was staying in a fine hotel in a city 2 hours from *Tōkyō* and that I was only able to attend this educational seminar purely thanks to Mr. Takagi. Furthermore, I did not ask Mr. Takagi or the JKF for such treatment; certainly, did not expect it; and therefore, if he was not pleased with my situation, he shouldn't hesitate to contact Mr. Takagi directly instead of attacking me. Dr. Hakoishi translated my response, which resulted in a lot of words from this person that were not translated. Dr. Hakoishi changed the subject.

Everyone was leaving after the lunch meal, and about five participants, including myself, were trying to get taxis. I ended up in one with the nasty Goju sensei who was also going to the station.

What train are you catching? Let me see your ticket.

I showed him my ticket, which was for a 1st-class reserved seat on the 4:10 p.m. train. It was presently 3 pm.

"First class, eh? You don't need to catch the 4.10 train. You can catch any train. In fact, why don't you catch this train; you don't need to sit in first class."

I profusely thanked him for helping me and allowed him to watch me get on the train in the second-class compartment. I even sat in a non-reserved seat, smiled and waved at him. He saw that I was safely on the cheap seats and alighted from a train waiting at the opposite platform, which left before the *Tōkyō* -bound train.

Once he was safely out of sight, I stepped off the slow train (not a bullet train) and avoided stopping at every single station between Nagoya and *Tōkyō* . I was in no hurry; I had not yet bought any souvenirs for the staff in the office, so I found some at the kiosk and then sat down to relax, read a book, and wait for the 4:10 train. That way, I could enjoy the full benefits of the first-class ticket on the fastest *shinkansen* that the JKF had so kindly provided me.

Later in the year, Mr. Takagi retired from his positions as Chairman of the JKF and Secretary General of WUKO. I was appalled to discover that a rumor had surfaced East of the Pacific that claimed I had indulged in biblical relations with Mr. Takagi. Strangely enough, the route was via a Goju source, although, to be fair, the rumors on the East Coast of the Pacific implied that Mr. Takagi had a history of such behaviour, which is why he withdrew from his positions in two karate organizations. Because of his love for quality, I later gave him my lapis lazuli-and-gold Dunhill lighter, which I no longer used, and he gave me a copy of his autobiography, which I wish could be translated. All of that was complete rubbish. He resigned from these responsibilities because he had been diagnosed with cancer. His attitude and behaviour towards me were beyond reproach, and organized karate lost a remarkable, intelligent analytical thinker with a deep knowledge of history and a vision of the future. This was not how most Japanese who replaced him might have thought...

Kaiseki ryōri (Japanese seasonal delicacies) somewhat like Haute cuisine Mount Takao 1992

Competition in Japan

The first tournament I was encouraged to enter was the Higashi Nihon Jitsu Gyo *Dan* Senshu Ken Taikai (East Japan Workers Karate Federation Championships), which were held at Nissan Plaza in Aomono Yokocho, on the southwest side of *Tōkyō*. Because Mr. Ichimura was a member of this federation, his students had entered this tournament every year.

I placed 2nd in *kata* and was disqualified from contact in *kumite*, but I made it into the top eight. This was significant, as the "best eight" from all the divisions would compete in the All Japan Jitsu Gyo Dan Championships, which were to be held in Osaka. I was excited as I had never been to Osaka, and the trip would be financed by the Jitsu Gyo *Dan* (JGD). I was also the only representative of the YMCA *dōjō* that placed. Mr. Ichimura was happy, and the party after the tournament was quite lively.

For several weeks thereafter, I concentrated on kumite techniques and three *kata*.

One hot, sticky Monday, I walked into the *dōjō*, and one of the women said that she was sorry to hear that I wouldn't be going to Osaka. I thought I heard her wrong. I tried to say that I was definitely going, as I had made plans, etc. She tried to get the message across, but I really did not understand it until Mr. Ichimura appeared, looking quite dejected.

He told me that the board of directors of the JGD had decided that I was forbidden to compete in the national competition because I was not Japanese. Mr. Ichimura was furious, but there was to be no changing of minds. The whole *dōjō* was very apologetic, and everyone tried to express some kind of sympathy and the accursed JGD Directorate, which apparently comprised right-wing sexist jingoists from Osaka. I carefully pondered how to deal with this. First of all, I tried to hide my disappointment and, with more difficulty and anger. So much for the "age of internationalization," as the Japanese were so fond of saying.

Since I was banned from competing, that left spaces in the *kata* and *kumite* divisions for the competitor who had placed 9th to be included in the qualifying "best eight." That person for *kumite* happened to be Takeda san from the YMCA, so they would still have a representative after all, and the members planned to go to Osaka to cheer for her.

I asked one of the group members to obtain for me a copy of the program for the tournament so that I could find out the names of all of the JGD directors.

Upon receiving this, I sent a letter to the entire board and copied it to magazine editors in the UK, the USA and Germany. The letter essentially pointed out that such discrimination was contrary to the spirit of internationalization and karate-do. That many foreigners make incredible efforts and sacrifices to study karate in Japan, and that if this kind of attitude was typical among Japan's highest-ranked personnel, then it would reflect very negatively on karate, the Jitsu Guo Dan association, and Japan.

I also mentioned that my personal disappointment was nothing compared to the feelings of my instructor, who was saddled with the burden of telling me this in the first place.

Nothing happened. The world did not stop turning, and karate in Japan continued as usual.

Terry O'Neill (from the Red Triangle club in England) published my letter in Fighting Arts magazine; however, Black Belt in the USA did not, and Dierk Hickmann deemed it too controversial to publish it in the German karate magazine that he edited. However, Dierk gave a copy of the letter to Fritz Wendland, who brought it to the attention of Nagatomo Yamaoka, a lawyer and current Chairman of the JKF, who was a member of the *Wadō Kai*. Mr. Yamaoka introduced himself to me several months later at a party and said that he would ensure that such a thing would never happen within the JKF again and that he was deeply ashamed to learn how I had been treated by the JGD. I was hopeful. He encouraged me to inform him immediately if anything like this ever happened to me again. He also stated that the current JGD board would soon be replaced, and that the only karate event for which a foreigner could be legitimately excluded was selection to the Japanese national team. Otherwise, any member of the JKF was eligible to participate in any events sanctioned by the JKF. Well, I was a member of the JKF through the Jitsu Gyo *Dan,* the *Tōkyō* City Karate Federation, and the JKF Wadō Kai.

The following year, I made the best eight again in both divisions of the Jitsu Gyo *Dan* tournament and qualified to attend the national Jitsu Gyo *Dan* championships in *Tōkyō*. However, the sad irony was that I was unable to participate, as my company had a job for me that week that would take me out of *Tōkyō*. However, change had been achieved and the Way was paved for other non-Japanese practitioners to participate in all events approved by the JKF without discrimination.

I also entered the Shibuya Ward Championships (all styles), the East Japan and the All Japan Wadō Kai Championships, and finally, the 1st World Wadō Kai Championships at the Budokan. I tended to place in the top 3 in the Ward tournaments and for five consecutive years in the "Best Eight" in Wadō Kai events. The average age of the women was approximately twenty-two, and in the Wadō Kai tournament, there were typically around thirty-five participants in the kata division. One year, there were two individuals aged over twenty-five years in the division, of whom only one (me) was aged over thirty-five years.

Guseikai (Serendipity) *Dōjō*, Sugamo, 1990

In the summer of 1990, I met Katsuyuki Kawano, who spoke relatively fluent English. He appeared at the Arakawa *dōjō* one night and started talking to me whether I liked it or not. He had lived in Australia for a year and was in his early thirties. He trained with Toshiaki Maeda and occasionally with someone named Takagi, who was a dentist and had no relation to Fusajiro Takagi. Kawano suggested that I train with Dr. Hideho Takagi, as his *dōjō* was located in a primary school gym near where I lived. Training was held on Sunday evenings at Seiwa

Sho Gakko (primary School) in Sugamo and at the Nippon Dental University in Iidabashi on Mondays, Wednesdays and Fridays. The days were convenient and would not conflict with training with Mr. Arakawa, but I wasn't sure that I wanted to commit to another *dōjō*. However, one evening I wanted to talk to Kawano san, and he said I should meet him at the Dental School *dōjō* that night. I went there, deliberately without a gi, to meet Kawano san and watch the class. I had heard conflicting reports about Dr. Takagi's teaching methods, so I wanted to see for myself whether they were true.

Kawano san saw me standing at the door and told me to dress in my gi and join in. I gesticulated not possible, due to not having a gi, and that I would just watch. However, he walked over to a man with a mustache and pointed towards me. The two came over to me, and Kawano san introduced me to Takagi sensei, who immediately also invited me to participate in the class. I said that I did not have a gi. He walked away, and a young man with a brown belt (Toya was his name) disappeared and returned with a gi and a fusty, slightly slimy, cotton belt that had once upon a time been black but was now brownish, with faded orange embroidered kanji indicating its owner. I could understand enough kanji to know that the name on the belt was "Takagi." The gi was embroidered with the same kanji. I realized that both belonged to Takagi sensei and it fitted me perfectly. I succumbed to my fate and was shown to another cockroach-infested room full of sweat-stained, unwashed judo and karate gi covered with various species of mold, towels, cloths and worn-out bits of kendo armor. Some institutional green lockers were covered with patches of rust and layered with years of undisturbed grime. Inhaling lungfuls of mold spores and heavy dust motes due to the humid summer air, I stepped out into the *dōjō*.

The uninsulated *dōjō* on the top floor of the dental school absorbed the day-long summer sun. The temperature inside the room was ~ 40°, even with the windows open. It had a *tatami* area for *aikido*, a *shinden* for obeisance to the kami sama, and five rows of names calligraphed on old pieces of lacquered wood hanging the entire length of the room. I recognized one that looked like Toru Arakawa. Since it was under the 8th *Dan* list, it had to be Toru Arakawa, whom I was already training with.

The training was fairly unstructured, but Dr. Takagi was nothing like the bully I had been led to believe. He immediately pounced on me as soon as I joined the line and started fixing things, but nicely. I loved it. More input, correction, and learning. By the end of the class, I knew I had to leave the YMCA classes with Mr. Ichimura. I would now study *Wadō Ryū* seven days a week; four days with Takagi *sensei*, and three with Mr. Arakawa. Surely, I would learn about *Wadō* if I could do this for a few years!

After class, Takagi sensei drove Kawano-kun and me to a restaurant. Takagi sensei asked where I lived. I told him. He then said that Sugamo is close where I live, so I can drive you home! Good god! In a city the size of *Tōkyō*, my fate serendipitously led me to live two minutes away from where Takagi sensei taught, and not only that, his home! Get this: I lived one stop away from Ohtsuka Station on the JR Yamanote Line, where the Toden Arakawa Line was just about 50 yards away. Surely, I was doomed.

I trained with Dr. Takagi and developed a relatively close friendship with him. That is to say, if I found myself in any kind of trouble in Japan, I would have no hesitation in asking him to help. He was a 7th Dan in the Wadō Kai, and I have not met anyone quite like him. I had been confused between technical and moral competence in the past. It had taken a while to understand that years of karate training and technical understanding is no guarantee of moral standards, ethical principles, or just basic goodness. One might enthusiastically repeat, "seek perfection of character" seven times a week, but the only objective achieved by such behavior was likely to be the realization that no amount of seeking is unlikely to develop perfection.

Dr. Takagi was technically remarkable, sincere, and ethical. From what I understand, he was born during World War II and was sent to

Manchuria for safety because his father was an army dentist, as was his grandfather. He lived under these circumstances until 1952 when he was 10 years old. When he and his siblings arrived in Japan, they were immediately separated and sent to different schools. At that time, all Japanese children underwent a health check before they were allowed to enter school, and he was assessed as being too weak to participate in sports. Takagi sensei was not happy about this as he particularly enjoyed basketball and all the things 10-year-old boys generally liked to do. However, in the interval between the physical exam and entrance to a school, he was assigned to one that assumed that for some reason, his health report must have been up to standard. Fortunately for him, the health report disappeared in a morass of post-war bureaucratic bungling, so he managed to play lots of basketball after all. He made it through all the games and conditions of school without mishap and started training in Wadō karate at Nippon Shika Daigaku under Hironori Ohtsuka…. and never stopped. His eldest daughter, Miho, was about to enter the doctoral program at Nippon Shika Daigaku, where he was now teaching karate. It looked like she would continue the family tradition. His eldest son was a dental technician, and his youngest son Hidemasa was nine years old. Mrs. Takagi waited for 10 years before they could marry, until he had completed his studies and internships. A small man, about 5'5", who wears 1970s clothes and has hair cut in the 1970s of sideburns and drives an immaculate 1970s Nissan model that completes the image He has a ready smile, an unruffled demeanor that rockets blood pressure, and a wicked sense of humor. I saw him once with a bunch of Persian karate practitioners who demanded 5th Dan certificates because they had flown all the way to Japan and intended to train in *Tōkyō* for a week. His response? A smile and a complete refusal to comprehend the slightest suggestion of English.

"Just put on your gi and practice with us." Smile.

Arguing with a smile flummoxed such people. He is open-minded and unconditionally accepting of all who show up at his *dōjō* regardless of style or affiliation. There are no tests to pass, no egos to overcome. All a stranger has to do is wear a gi and practice, and that was all that was needed to be taken seriously unless a person decided otherwise. I never heard him say a negative word about anyone. He certainly had opinions, and he occasionally expressed them.

He also became my dentist, like all the other students in the *dōjō*.

In 1992, he and his youngest son, Hidemasa (Ma-kun), along with 24 of his students, spouses, children, and grandparents, visited Vancouver for sightseeing and a *gasshuku* (summer camp). I and several friends helped me to arrange a schedule. With the help of Kikuma, we arranged a sunset cruise down Indian Arm, complete with Japanese food, golf games, and sightseeing. Through the help of James Johnson and Karate BC, a *dōjō* was available and accessible for training every night from the moment they arrived. A day trip to Victoria, on Vancouver Island with training space kindly accommodated by Frank Hussey (Shotokan), whales at the Vancouver Aquarium, and ice cream at Lion's Gate Bridge. People kindly took time off work to transport the group around in vans. The week passed quickly and left an indelible impression on our Japanese visitors: Vancouver is some kind of paradise and Canada is a beautiful country that could fulfill dreams. The impression that Takagi *sensei* left has continued in annual exchange of gifts and visits from Canadians to Japan and vice versa. Takagi sensei attended the 1995 Nana Kai Ki (seven-year Buddhist commemoration of a death) for Makoto Gima, (an original founder of the Japan Karate Federation) to which 12 Vancouverites also attended, including James Johnson. Thus, Dr. Takagi's *dōjō* lived up to its name, Guseikai. It could be translated as the "serendipity group," the "potluck club," and the accidental group. The name was suggested to Takagi sensei by Mr. Eiichi Eriguchi, the founding General Secretary of WUKO, who preceded Fusajiro Takagi. It is taken from a Buddhist sutra, about which Mr. Eriguchi was knowledgeable. It says, in a convoluted way, that life is short; seize opportunities before they disappear. Sometimes, the Guseikai *dōjō* is so crowded with visiting foreigners that Japan becomes the minority. At other times, there are only one or two. On Sunday nights, sometimes the world would show up at the *dōjō*. On a typical Sunday evening, I watched as Takagi sensei worked with a group of 1st-year female university students while three Persians and two Englishmen practiced kumite drills. At a corner, a latecomer was busy reviewing basics in a corner. Ma-kun, Yoshie *san* and I practiced trying to refine Chinto kata. Everyone received useful information from *sensei* before the class ended. After training on Sundays, everyone were welcome to walk over to Dr. Takagi's minuscule house and squeeze into a six **tatami** living room, a chaotic testament to a family of five, one cat, years of karate training, dental predecessors and karate students crowded into a space of about 100 ft2. A table centered in a middle tatami "living" room became a *kotatsu,* (a low table) with an infrared lamp below and a futon cover or heavy blanket covered by a rigid Formica tabletop in the winter. Cats and small dogs like to spend many cozy hours underneath them, so humans have to take care of where they place their legs. You can sit on a tatami or carpeted floor and draw the futon or blanket up to your chin. On two walls are windows, a TV with a remote, books, display cabinets, piles of washing, cat food, pens, pencils, pieces of correspondence, and newspapers. School uniforms, blazers, shirts, and ties hung from ledges around the room and the remaining space was stacked with souvenirs from abroad or gifts from international visitors. Persian paintings and silver-plated copper platters, dental certificates, karate certificates, plaques, commendations, photographs of his parents, his wife's parents, banners and flags from karate tournaments, medals and trophies that his children have won in various karate competitions, small garbage cans, ceramics from Yasukuni Jinja (The only metal Shinto shrine dedicated to the war dead in Japan) in the form of whatever animal represented the current year, and metal wine goblets given by Mr. Seiji Nishimura after a trip to the USA were identifiable in the chaos. Mrs. Takagi ran back and forth, replenishing food, beer, and glasses for the visitors. A typical domestic bombsite. We informally squeeze together around the table, sometimes two or three deep, and poured beers or wine for each other as soon as a glass was half empty. The aging cat picked her way daintily among us, refusing to accept attention from anyone other than

Takagi sensei, whose role in her life is to open windows on demand. Our motley crew sat and talked about anything. Sometimes, I had no clue about the topic because I didn't have sufficient Japanese to keep up with the conversation. However, I never felt left out, and I presume no one else did either, regardless of whether they were university students, English teachers, salaried workers, people who have just started karate training or are old-timers. There was no formality, conversation was never crude, and it always continued until just before midnight when everyone left to catch the last train, and I bicycled home within two minutes on Jizo Dori. I had never visited the home of a Japanese karate instructor in Japan before meeting Takagi sensei. He clearly loved karate and anyone who loves it, too. I trained with him for seven years, during which he refused to accept *dōjō* fees from me because I was already paying training fees to Arakawa sensei. He always warmly welcomed anyone I brought to his *dōjō*. That often included taking them out for dinner and merriment after class, and a place on the floor at his home

Around 1992, 40 German and Swiss people came to *Tōkyō* to train and compete in the All Japan and World Wadō Kai championships. Naturally, they all came to the dental *dōjō* in Iidabashi, and a *kata* seminar was arranged for them over a weekend. I also attended this seminar, which happened to be the last time any of us ever trained at the dental school.

The xenophobic janitor complained to those in charge of the facility that too many foreigners were using the *dōjō*, which was meant for exclusively for Japanese dental students of karate and other types of *budo*. Dr. Takagi was told that if he wished to continue using the facility, no foreigners would be allowed to join the classes. Dr. Takagi did not argue. He simply expressed thanks for the use of the facility for over thirty years, and never returned. He quickly acquired space at the primary schools, Hosei, Nishi Sugamo, and, Seiwa Sho Gakko, all of which were within walking distance from where I lived. Talk about serendipity! I didn't really appreciate yet that I was training with two pre-eminent Wadō Kai icons seven days a week… and that I could walk within a few minutes to training on four of them. Considering the size of Tokyo and its population, serendipity must have been pulling strings.

Tanya's Wedding 1995

Tanya Petrovic was a member of the Yugoslavian National Karate Team whom I met at the Fukuoka Women's' event in 1990 decided to marry Robert Ropret, in Japan. The previous year, she had won the All Japan Wadō Kai championships and placed 2nd in the World Wadō Kai Cup. She remained in Japan after the tournaments and stayed at Dr. Hakoishi's hospital in Morioka for a few weeks, then with me for a few weeks. She enjoyed her stay and made many friends. She trained with Arakawa sensei and Takagi sensei, and learned some useful English phrases from me that she became very proficient in applying…She finally settled on a Buddhist ceremony in Morioka, complete with a wedding kimono and wig. However, before that, because I could not go to Morioka due to work, she wanted to do a civil ceremony in *Tōkyō* so that I could attend.

Tanja, in a yellow silk, off-the-shoulder short dress, gold shoes, and bouquet, arrived at the Kita Ku Ward Office accompanied by future husband Robert and my roommate Katya. She was met by Hiroko Noguchi (secretary of the JKF), Takagi sensei, me, and Zdravko Pavicevic, the Chargé d'Affaires of the Yugoslavian Embassy, his wife Branka and daughter, Maria.

We began completing the forms, with Takagi and I acting as witnesses for Robert and Tanja, respectively, while the ward staff scrutinized the passports and certificates of marriage eligibility issued by the Yugoslavian Embassy.

However, the pursed lips, and noisy sucking of air and stares at the passports by ward office bureaucrats indicated that this was not going to be as simple as it should have been.

Sure enough. The ward office staff patiently informed us that they could not accept the application for marriage because the current guidelines for such events stated that Japan does not recognize *Shin* (new) Yugoslavia as a country. In contrast, it did recognize *Kyu* (old) Yugoslavia. So sorry they bowed, by Tanja's passport was issued in 1994, indicating that she was a citizen of a nonexistent country, whereas Robert's passport, issued in 1990, proclaimed that he was a citizen of Yugoslavia. Ergo, Robert could marry in the ward office, whereas Tanja could not marry Robert. Zdravko went ballistic and demanded that the staff call the Ministry of Justice and the Ministry of Foreign Affairs. The staff politely informed him that it was impossible to phone these Ministries. Zdravko exploded with frustration and asked several times why it was impossible. Well, the answer was very simple. No one at the Ministries would answer any phone calls because they were all at lunch until 1 p.m.

We all decided to leave before Zdravko suffered a heart attack. We left the ward with the matrimonial documents signed and stamped by Takagi and me, attesting to the fact that we witnessed the non-wedding of Tanja and Robert. We all posed in front of the ward office for photographs as though the event had proceeded as planned. We then went to Ohtsuka for a celebratory lunch at a French Bistro Juillet near Takagi sensei's dental clinic. Tanja threw her bouquet, and Zdravko's daughter, Maria, caught it. Several beautifully presented courses of delicious *nouvelle* cuisine were accompanied by liberal quantities of Sancerre wine and much laughter over the absurdity of the situation. Just before dessert, Takagi said he had to leave briefly to take care of an emergency and would return as soon as possible. After the dessert and more glasses of wine and cognac ordered by Zdravko were polished off, Takagi sensei rejoined the revelries for coffee and photographs of the memorable occasion. Thus, the wedding feast ended, and Zdravko asked for the bill…which never came. Zdravko asked again, and the bar-tender simply walked away. Only then did I realize why Takagi sensei had left to attend to an "emergency".

He had already paid the bill for the lunch as a non-wedding gift, which cost approximately $1000. He was horrified by Tanja and Robert's experience at the Kita Ku Ward Office, as it should have been a memorable milestone in their lives. Zdravko berated himself because his plan had been to pay for the lunch Of course, Dr. Takagi refused any offers of money from Zdravko, who was at a total loss in terms of how to repay him. So, the un-betrothed couple returned to Morioka for a Buddhist wedding and I offered a suggestion to Zdravko.

It happened that Takagi sensei had a birthday on the following weekend, I invited him along with Katya, Zdravko, and his family to the *Tōkyō* American Club for brunch. Takagi sensei asked if he could bring Ma-kun, and I said of course. The point was it was a buffet, and it was impossible to pay unless you were a member. I also suggested that he take Maria to see Takagi sensei professionally because he had mentioned before that she needed serious dental work that would cost thousands of US dollars. This was because Zdravko was a consul representing a foreign country and was not eligible for Japanese health insurance, which also covered dentistry. He was thrilled. After brunch, Takagi sensei drove us to an Okinawan Goju Ryū *dōjō* in Yotsuya run by Aragaki Shuichi, where he had agreed to teach 12 Gima Ha Shoto Ryū practitioners from Vancouver, whose leader was James Johnson.

Mrs. Aragaki opened the *dōjō* for us and Takagi sensei handed her a present.

I wished I could speak more Japanese, as the more I learned about Takagi, the more I felt privileged to know him as a dentist, karate instructor, and friend. He exemplified the meaning of the word sensei!

Dental Notes

Foreigners who live in Japan tend to avoid dentists or go to those recommended by others who have some experience.

I was no exception. I was aware of the nature of Japanese dentistry and its esthetic standards, or lack thereof. Before leaving Chicago, I had visited a dentist for several weeks, undergoing a complete overhaul of old fillings and some preventative work. All covered by dental insurance provided by the company. However, it was now four years later. Time for an oral checkup. Japanese dentists without rubber gloves, moving from one patient to another without washing hands, fillings without anesthesia ....

I first went to a Japanese dentist recommended by the foreign community in *Tōkyō*. Dr. Yamaguchi had trained in Milan and New York, and his business card said that he was a Doctor of Dental Surgery (DDS) and a Medical Doctor (MD). His office was located in affluent Nishi Azabu, near Roppongi. I scheduled an appointment and drove to his office, which had an underground parking lot. I parked next to a limited-edition white convertible Cadillac with gold-spoked and white banded wheels. I guessed that it belonged to Dr. Yamaguchi. I entered the muted gray waiting room of his clinic and was asked to have a seat on a leather sofa. I was served a cup of green tea and given English Vogue magazines to read while listening to Mozart and waiting for Yamaguchi sensei to appear.

After sufficient time had passed and I had finished the tea, I was ushered into a room full of polished hardwood and a lone dental chair. Yamaguchi sensei emerged, a man of about sixty years, and two deferential nurses tucked me up in a blanket and fastened on a bib. I told Dr. Yamaguchi that I had not seen a dentist for four years and thought I should have a checkup. He examined my teeth and took some X-rays with a great deal of fussing and muttering in fluent English while the nurses reverently fluttered about nodding their heads sagely and repeated, *"Ah so desu ne?"* (roughly implying the discovery of something that required attention).

Dr. Yamaguchi went to great pains to point out a slight shadow on the X-ray, an upper left tooth. Another X-ray was taken of said tooth and more detailed explanations were given about problems, causes, possible treatments ....

Dr. Yamaguchi exited the room, and I was guided once more to the waiting room. After ~ 10 minutes, another porcelain cup of tea arrived, and furious rapid typing was audible through the opaque glass window of the assistant's area. Another 10 minutes passed, and I was presented with a bill for today's "treatment," which was around US $250, and a sheet of paper describing three choices of treatment for the tooth with the shadow on the X-ray. A root canal was the basic treatment in all three estimates, and the differences lay essentially in whether the crown would be made of platinum, yellow gold, or a mixture of metals. The quoted prices were $ 4,000, $ 3,500, or $ 2,500, respectively, and he did not accept the national Japanese medical and dental insurance provided by my employer. Cash only. I thanked him profusely for his time and advice and left with no intention of returning.

Although I had been training with Takagi sensei for about three years by then, I had never seen him in his professional capacity. I had thought that I should separate karate from dentistry, but Toya kun said that I should see Dr. Takagi because he treats everyone in the *dōjō*. Now was the time for an appointment at Takagi Dental Clinic, located on the 5th floor of the Chiko building, opposite the north exit of Ohtsuka Station. Not a fashionable part of the city teeming with upscale foreigners and a location that included no less than 30 dental offices all within walking distance of each other. Not a custom Cadillac in sight, but bicycles belonging to Takagi sensei and Mrs. Takagi (who did the accounting and, of course, had a "mama-chari" [literally "mother's chariot"]) leaned on a wall of in front of the Chiko building. A tiny elevator slowly creaked up to the 5th floor, landing where a sliding door opened directly into the *genkan* (entryway) of the clinic. There, outdoor shoes were exchanged for green plastic slippers before stepping onto the raised floor of the clinic. Three dental chairs occupied the room, flooded with natural light due to two large windows on the walls. I was a little early for my appointment, which was the first after lunch, so I made myself comfortable on of the green plastic bench seats and thumbed through the pictures of a Japanese magazine and intently studied pictures of the Japanese imperial household.

Takagi sensei appeared on cue at 2 p.m. and I was led to the center chair. Slippers were removed, and the chair back lowered to horizontal. He asked if there was anything particular bothering me. I gave him the same story I had given Dr. Yamaguchi, but did not mention anything about my experience with him. Takagi sensei then took some X-rays and brought them over to a backlight so that I could see them. He said that everything was generally OK, but pointed out one filling that could do with being investigated. He said that if it was not bothering me, it could be left for a little longer, and that the only way he could clearly tell whether or not there was a problem would be to remove the crown and take a look.

The tooth was not the same one that Yamaguchi had singled out, so I asked Takagi about it. He said that the shadow was most likely caused by an old amalgam leaching mercury, and that it could be replaced, but it was certainly not urgent.

He asked me if I had dental insurance, and I produced my card. He asked me what I wanted to do, and I said to fix the tooth that he thought needed fixing, replace the mercury amalgam on the other, apply whatever preventive procedures he thought necessary and clean and scale my teeth.

After taking the old crown off the tooth he had singled out, he discovered that a root canal was indeed necessary. He gave me the same choice of metals as Yamaguchi for the crown, and I told him to make the choice as he was the expert, not me. He said that in terms of performance, it didn't really matter, but some people preferred the colour that matched their general choice of jewelry. I drew his attention to my watch. An articulated band of matt steel and gold links. I left it to him. He chose platinum. I thought, oh dear....

I went to his dental office once a week on Saturdays for several weeks and saved to make sure I had enough money to pay for several procedures and two platinum fillings.

The moment finally arrived. I had 100,000 yen (approximately $ 1,000) with me and was prepared for a trip to the bank. Mrs. Takagi handed me a bill. I stared at it in shock and questioned the numbers. Mrs. Takagi looked at it and said no, that was correct. I owed 478 yen, which was about $5. There was no mistake. The bill was indeed 478 yen. She thought from my reaction that I considered it expensive and asked me.

No! Quite the opposite. Aren't there a few zeros missing?

Takagi sensei then scrutinized the bill.

No, that is correct.

I don't understand. Surely it should be more.

It is, but you have insurance.

Ah. Well, but if I did not have insurance, how much would this treatment have cost.

Oh, very expensive.

How expensive?

Mmm, about 10 times more.

About 5,000 yen?

Yes.

Then, I showed him the estimate from the Yamaguchi clinic.

Dr. Takagi laughed and said something to the effect that where there is a demand, there is a supply.

I went to him for all dental needs thereafter and recommended everyone I knew to do the same.

Among the reasons why foreigners are suspicious of Japanese dentists for many reasons are clinical hygiene, low technical and esthetic competence, and a lack of understanding of Japanese. Embassy staff must pay cash and obtain reimbursement from their home country's insurance programs. Dentists are often selected upon the recommendation of a friend or long-term resident who can speak Japanese. People like Dr. Yamaguchi, who have trained or practiced abroad, particularly in the USA, know the cost of dental work and are aware of the salaries and benefits given to the expat community in Japan. Consequently, they charge a substantial "comfort premium" that primarily consists of offering English-speaking staff, playing soothing classical music, and providing English magazines.

Other patients of the Takagi Shika In (dental clinic) included the family of a local karaoke bar where the *dōjō* members always went after winning or losing a tournament and the owner of a boxing gym across the street, who also owned a conglomerate of brothels, which had existed for 350 years since the Yoshiwara was the red-light licensed quarter of old Edo (*Tōkyō*).

Two years later, after another series of visits to the Takagi Shika In, involving yet another chunk of platinum and another root canal, I was never even given a bill. My protests were redundant. I made even more effort to recommend him to everyone I knew. After all, this is how his family was educated, fed and housed.

WUKO World Championships Mexico City 1990

To pass the WUKO exam once is insufficient. In addition, only three members of the RC were present in Fukuoka. The qualification has to be maintained by judging at as many WUKO-sanctioned international events as possible and attending refresher theory courses every two years. It has male and female, individual and team *kata* and *kumite* divisions. I expressed my desire to join the Canadian contingent, and my application was accepted by the NKA. I flew to Los Angeles and joined the group from Vancouver.

I had never been to Mexico City before and was relieved to find that we would stay in an international standard hotel with filtered water and air. James was now the president of the NKA and the leader of the Canadian delegation. He warned me not to eat outside the hotel and to drink nothing but bottled water.

I hoped to have time to visit Aztec ruins, pyramids, and museums, but there was so little time. The Museum of Anthropology was reportedly within walking distance, so there would perhaps be an opportunity to see something beyond the sulfurous miasma that polluted the air. The air was densely particulate due to the exhaust belching from the rear ends of decrepit Volkswagen Beetles in endless traffic jams that scarcely moved for miles and miles. So much for pollution control. Only even-numbered license plates were allowed on the road on certain days of the week, and odd-numbered plates on the others. A red digital smog index announced through yellowish metallic fog the amount of nitrous and sulfurous effluent we breathed. If I was going to be affected by anything in this acrid environment, it was not going to be the water or the food.

The hotel was located 30 minutes from the venue and private buses had been arranged to pick up the competitors and the officials and convey them to the venue. At first, I sat in the front of an elderly, non-air-conditioned bus that limped onto the freeway on balding tires. However, the air in the bus was drawn from the outside and so the atmosphere in the bus consisted entirely of petrol exhaust and putrid air. By the time I staggered out of the bus, I was dizzy, with a greenish-grey pallor and difficulty breathing. Fortunately, the bus arrived at the venue about one hour before anything started, as I needed a full 30 minutes to recover from the drive. Sitting at the back of the bus was not helpful, as motion sickness and a dose of the shakes were added to my discomfort throughout the week. So, I had no desire to step outside the hotel once I had immersed myself in its conditioned air.

I attended the referees' seminar and managed to pull through it with sanction to function on the floor. The following day was a *kata* seminar and exam, which I intended to watch, as being a lowly 3rd *Dan*, I could not participate in it. Alex Sternberg, Jaap Smaal, and a few other experienced referees convinced me not to waste my time attending the seminar, but instead to accompany them to the National Museum of Anthropology, which I learned is one of the best in the world. I allowed myself to be convinced and walked for 15 minutes through a park to the museum. I was not sure if I could make it without fainting. I staggered into the cooled entranceway to the museum and sank onto a bench for 30 minutes, unable to even stand. Of course, everyone kindly chided me for being a wimp, but it was evident to all that I was not joking. I suppose that the noxious level of pollution conspired with the altitude to wreak some kind of personal havoc. Still, I vowed I would never visit Mexico City again if it could be avoided. As soon as I could stand, I joined the group that had taken off with a guide. That was the only free time we had throughout the week. The museum was incredible. Anyone visiting Mexico City should at least visit that place.

Over camarones and vino rosso with James, I clarified that I did not intend to leave Japan soon, and he was living with a woman who had pancreatitis that worsened by the day. Well, maybe it was better to have James on my side, but distanced by separate obligations. We thus arrived at an understanding.

At the referee seminar, I had the opportunity to renew my acquaintance with Jo Pledge, an American woman I had fought against in one of Mr. Ozawa's tournaments in Las Vegas. She was going to attend the seminar and maybe try the exam. I fervently prayed she would pass and encouraged her to continue to try if she did not. As for me, a Japanese instructor residing in the USA, I raised an objection to my presence and complained to the referee council that I did not believe I was qualified to be there in terms of Pan-American qualifications. Dr. Hakoishi deftly side-stepped this concern by claiming me as a member of APUKO, the Asia-Pacific region of WUKO (renamed Asian Karate Federation in 1992). Something else for me to take care of later, but a minor detail compared with the next obstacle.

Arriving at the site on the first day of the tournament, I was assigned to a ring controlled by Mr. Yamazaki. Good news, he had been fair and just in New Orleans, so I knew I could trust him to give everyone in the ring the same opportunities to work the ring.

The morning was women's *kumite* events, and I was relieved to learn that I was seeing the action and reacting appropriately in the ring. I served as the mirror judge to several referees from around the world, with varying levels of ability, experience, and personalities, throughout the morning, and was satisfied with my performance. I was doing my best and felt confident that it was good enough to maintain the status I had already earned in Fukuoka in front of the WUKO Referee Council, Directing Committee, Technical Committee, referee panels in each ring, spectators, and most importantly, the athletes. That is to say, I made no more or less mistakes than anyone else on the floor.

We broke for lunch, during which a rather envious referee said:

"You are lucky, Norma. After lunch you will be able to have a break."

"What do you mean?" I asked.

"Well, it is the men's events after lunch."

"So?" I asked.

I reconfirmed that I had no intention of taking any break. Despite the foul atmosphere and peculiar lighting inside the arena, I had enough stamina to run around the ring for the remainder of the day's events.

Mr. Yamazaki motioned to me that our panel was ready to go back into action, so I wondered what the Dutchman was talking about.

Mr. Yamazaki put me in the ring with Mr. Murayama from Mexico to judge the first of the afternoon fights: The *men's lightweight* division. We were about halfway through the match when a commotion caught the attention of the entire arena. The French member of the Referee Council was bounding across the mats with his characteristic gait, waving his arms wildly about and shouting at the top of his lungs. I just knew it was focused on our ring, and as he approached, he demanded that the fight be stopped. Arms flapping like a wounded crow, I finally figured out what he was saying.

Arretez! Yame! Halte! (Stop! In three languages!)

He pointed and gesticulated at me.

Ce ne pas possible! Les femmes ne pas arbitre les hommes! (This is impossible. Women cannot judge men!)

Mr. Yamazaki sprang up from his controller's chair and asked him in English what he was doing meddling in his ring.

The French member continued expostulating, using as much body language as possible to convey the fact that he wanted me ejected from the ring. Such as yelling and pointing at me. Total public humiliation.

Mr. Yamazaki told him that he did not understand French and that if the Council member would kindly speak in Japanese or English, then perhaps they could have something to discuss. Someone materialized to translate. My heart rate rapidly increased. All eyes that were not fixed upon refereeing or judging other matches were focused on our ring. The athletes were confused, too, and I felt bad for them since neither they nor their coaches had expressed any displeasure at having me judge their match.

Mr. Yamazaki put up a good resistance, but finally he said:

"I'm sorry, Norma, you will have to sit down till this is sorted out. I can't make this person understand anything. He thinks the rules say that women cannot judge men. What nonsense.

If I didn't think you could do the job, I wouldn't have put you in the ring."

I thanked Mr. Yamazaki for his support, then in a gut-churning rage, sat down ringside, arranged my face, and controlled myself by carefully contemplating the most appropriate way to address this situation.

The first thing to do was practiced deep breathing to calm myself. The second was to address this appropriately, as it could take years before female officials could judge all human athletes. Suitably calmed after a few minutes, I looked for Canadians.

"Please find James and tell him Norma needs to talk to him RIGHT NOW! An urgent matter."

Having the president of one's national federation voice the question and lodge a complaint, if necessary, to the appropriate bodies would be the correct procedure. Furthermore, it just so happened that the President of the Canadian Federation would challenge a wrong until it was rectified, without fear for his personal status, perceived or otherwise, if he thought there was merit to the complaint. He was certainly not a coward and did not act like one.

James figured I had a case, so he told me to return to my ring while he sorted out this horror.

I saw him exchange words at the RC table. As he left, the Scotsman, the American and the Japanese thumbed frantically through the Competition Rule Book, the policies, procedures, and anything they could find in writing to prove that women *"were forbidden"* to judge male athletes. Perhaps there was some hitherto unknown clause buried under a section entitled Discrimination, or perhaps under Ignorance. At any rate, by the time my body temperature had returned to normal, the RC evidently failed to find the mystery rule, and I managed to keep a straight face when the American member of the RC descended from his celestial perch above the row of administrative tables and stated in front of Mr. Yamazaki and the rest of the referees and judges in my ring:

"Norma, you are a WUKO judge. You are qualified to judge anybody.

Thank you."

So, Mr. Yamazaki summoned me to be his mirror judge for the very next match, which publicly confirmed his support.

After about three matches, the referee, judge and arbitrator were rotated, and so it was with some surprise that I saw the French member of the RC man lumbering towards me again, although without the fluttering and flapping of feathers.

What now.

"Je suis tellement désolé. Je croyais sincèrement qu'il existait une règle disant que les femmes n'avaient pas le droit de juger les hommes." (I am so sorry. I sincerely believed that we had a rule stating that women do not have the right to judge male athletes).

I could hardly believe my ears. He apologized not once, but twice. He apologized again, afraid that I had misunderstood him.

I could not help but give a wry smile and said,

"Merci beaucoup…. c'est rien." (Thank you. It is nothing)

I accepted his apology because he was willing to admit his error, but a member of the RC of an international sports governing body who did not know the rules was unreasonable. Who was responsible for putting people in positions that wield considerable power over others? Incompetence was not an issue, but sex was. I voiced this many times afterward: a ring controller has the right not to select a person to work as a referee or judge in the ring if that person is deemed incompetent and/or ignorant of the rules, and the RC has the right to refrain from qualifying incompetent candidates in the first place. Referee and judge incompetence can lead to the wrong athlete winning and furthermore, endanger athletes. I argued that the sex of a referee or judge does not compromise athlete safety or diminish the ability to select the right winner. Totally absurd. Being identified at birth as male or female has nothing to do with competence.

I later discovered that a woman had qualified as a referee at the continental level but hit a glass ceiling that had prevented her from taking her skills to the World Championships. A notable member of the WKF RC later stated:

"She was good enough to referee the women, but not men and not at the world level." She was not "allowed" to challenge the WKF referee exams, and she believed it. There it was. The unwritten rule that prevented women from becoming WKF officials. No wonder no one could find it.

Why did the EKU RC qualify her at the highest level of kumite referee and kata judge in Europe then stopped her from going any further?

What sort of a comment is that? If a woman was "good enough" to referee/judge women in WKF continental events, why would she be unable to referee/judge the same women in WKF World events?

I later talked with some members of the British team, who kindly supported my efforts. However, they had been *told* that women in Europe could not aspire to referee or judge at the WKF World Championships and they believed it. No one questioned this?

I vowed that I would fight every obstacle in my path until these men would be forced to accept that being male does not guarantee perfect judgment making and that sex has nothing to do with competence. I could not understand the benefit to the WUKO by having no female officials. Athletes in national teams who train passionately for years and sacrifice almost everything to compete in WKF events deserve competent male and female officials from different countries who speak different languages and adhere to various belief systems. The prevailing attitude was all the more difficult to believe, as key supporters of the "only males can judge and referee" school of thought came from a country that was run by a powerful female leader at the time! Maybe his domestic front was also run by a powerful female leader. I pondered, trying to find an explanation for blatant sexism.

I soldiered on

The championships in Mexico City were extremely stressful. My judgments were expected to be flawless because if a male judge or referee made errors, then the following reasons would be justified:

Having an off day.

Caught a cold.

Wife having a baby.

But they would only be pertinent to that individual. If I made the same errors, it would not only be me who would be labelled as incompetent; it would be assumed that all women were incompetent, had off days, colds and migraines. Thus, the future of women in judging or refereeing at world events might be compromised, as the next woman to try would have to overcome this extra hurdle. In any event, I was awarded Referee B and Judge B certificates at the post-competition briefing.

At the party after the event, many men and women from several nations approached me, kindly voiced support for my efforts, and ventured positive opinions. This helped the gram of aspirin I had just swallowed to distract me from the tension headache that enveloped my head like a vice.

On the following day, the first of a weeklong series of cluster migraines hit me just as the Canadians checked in at the airport to return home from Mexico City.

Someone told me that people with migraines tend to get them more frequently in Mexico City. I suppose something had to catch up to me, as I had eaten outside the hotel and drank orange juice with shaved ice in it, probably made from local water. However, I never suffered any digestive disturbances that some of the other Canadians experienced. Air pollution and high altitude might have been factors.

As for the Japanese instructor who voiced concerns about my qualifications at the start of the week, I sent him a letter saying how much I respected his karate, how I had only been able to learn a particular kata from him at a seminar many years ago because he taught it so well, and how I was mortified to learn that perhaps there was some misunderstanding on his part regarding my right to judge at WUKO events. A list of places, dates, and achievements where I had officiated should have resolved any lingering confusion.

He later injured himself during a demonstration using a long sword, and I sent him a condolence card. At Christmas that year, I received an elegant card from him that included a pleasant message, so his misapprehensions had been relieved... at least for the time being.

APUKO Championships, Auckland, New Zealand, 1991

I attended the last Asia Pacific Union of Karate-Do Organizations (APUKO) Championships before the region became divided into Oceania and AUKO (Asian Union). The JKF permitted me to judge essentially as a representative of Japan, since, of course, Canada was part of PUKO (Pan-American Union of Karate-Do Organizations). This was the first time I had traveled to New Zealand, and it all looked rather familiar, with emerald-green rolling hills, misty rain, and thousands of sheep, all contributing to the natural climate change. The city of Auckland also had the feel of an Americanized Aberdeen in decline, with "For Sale" or "Rent" signs in many windows, people hanging out on the main street, and garbage swirling about listlessly in a cool, damp breeze. Many aboriginal people were unemployed, and resentment bubbled just below the surface. The unemployment rate that year was 17%, and the economy was not in good shape.

At this tournament, I was both excited and scared when Dr. Hakoishi told me to referee after a few rounds of judging. I was worried when I had to referee a match between male competitors from Iran and another Middle Easterner, both of whom were becoming emotionally involved in their match. At first, when I stepped onto the mat, I was concerned that they would object to a female referee, but they showed no outward signs of such sentiment. However, it was a difficult match for me to control and at one point, I had to step in between them with both arms yelling *"Yame"* as loudly as possible to stop the match. It worked, but some small bones in my right hand cracked as a result. Never mind. Ignoring the immediate swelling, I stood at the designated spot and waited for the competitors to calm down. It took a while for them to understand that I was not going to allow them to restart the match, then I penalized both of them. I thought that the competitors might not react well to this, but they accepted the judgments with exemplary politeness. However, when I assumed the position to continue the match, my right hand would not straighten, and the fingers could not be kept together.

These apparent trivia are important in the demeanor of a referee and such lapses in form are invariably criticized by someone without better things to do. After the bout, I submerged my hand in ice and got on with the job for the rest of the day.

The President of the RC of the Karate Do Federation of the Islamic Republic of Iran approached me, ice and all. I was so sure that he was going to say something derogatory, so I braced myself and was astonished at his question. Would I consider going to Tehran to do a referee course for their women? He explained that many people, including himself, were religious, but not fundamentalist, and did not necessarily agree with the way their country was being run. He said that women used to practice karate with the men before the revolution, and continued to practice, but separately from the men. This meant that they could attend a referee seminar, for example, but they were forced to cover themselves from head to toe in black chadors, which severely hampered their ability to move. If I could go there, they could have a seminar without chadors. I immediately wanted to go, of course, and I told James over a phone call about the exchange. He advised against it because he thought it would be too dangerous. I said that maybe if Dr. Hakoishi or someone went, I could go as his tea girl.

The remainder of the tournament passed relatively uneventfully, at least for me.

I met Ros Storey in Auckland. She attended the referee seminars but did not try the referee or judge examinations. Her husband, Greg, spoke fluent Japanese, and both studied what I think was Shito-ryū. I was delighted to find another woman interested in refereeing, but unfortunately, from this standpoint, they later came to Japan to set up an Australian consular office in Nagoya and Ros did not continue with this aspect of karate.

JKF 4th Dan exam 1992

In late 1991, I thought it was about time to take the JKF 4th Dan examination, which was a prerequisite for judging kata in the World Karate Federation (WKF), replacing WUKO. The JKF recognized Dan certificates from the four major karate styles (Shito Ryū, Wadō Ryū, Goju Ryū and Shotokan) within the federation. I had Dan certificates issued by the JKA, and the rule was that the JKF technical committee automatically accepted the validity of 1st–3rd Dan certificates issued by its style members. An automatic equivalent JKF Dan certificate could be issued up to 3rd Dan. Theoretically, I was eligible to try the 4th Dan test.

However, the JKF examiners refused to accept my JKA Dan certificates because they had not been issued by a Japanese instructor in Japan. They were bona fide JKA Dan certificates signed by world-renowned Shotokan authorities and countersigned by Masatoshi Nakayama and Zentaro Kosaka, but they had been issued outside Japan. Realistically, they hadn't been issued outside Japan. They were issued in Japan and mailed to their final destinations in Scotland and Canada. I was told that I must pass the JKF examination for 1st Dan, wait for six months, then attempt 2nd Dan and pass, and finally attempt 3rd Dan six months after that. If I passed all of these, I would have to wait another six months before attempting 4th Dan. What lunacy. However, I believed in the credibility of my Dan ranks and trusted the technical competence of those who issued them, so I followed their instructions exactly. If I failed, I still had the JKA certificates recognized everywhere else in the world, and if I passed, I would be one step closer my goal.

I followed this course to the letter and passed JKF 1st, 2nd and 3rd Dan examinations within the required time frames.

Finally, no more excuses could be given, and I was given the go-ahead to attempt 4th Dan in Chiba, along with 54 other individuals, in November 1992. The exam was very simple. You had to show kata from two styles of karate and fight with persons to the left (younger) and right (older) of you in the lineup. A panel of 7th and 8th Dans from different styles scrutinized the candidates; then, the judgment is sent in the mail to your member organization two or three weeks later. I performed the Wadō *kata Chinto* and the *Shotokan kata Chintei* (Unusual hands) I liked the similarity in the words, as it confused the grading panel, who assumed that the foreigner had made a mistake. However, the dissimilarity in the two kata is a good representation of the respective styles, and *Chintei* is an advanced Shotokan kata that is not commonly seen during Dan tests. Mayumi Nobetsu of JKF Goju Kai also tried 4th *Dan* on the same day. We had met in New Zealand in 1990, and she remembered me. It turned out that she knew another friend of mine here in *Tōkyō* through teaching English, and her birthday was on the same day and month as mine, except she was ten years younger. Her brother also tried 5th *Dan* that day.

We all passed. Now, the way was clear towards kata refereeing and the possibility of attempting 5th *Dan* soon.

World Championships, Granada, Spain, 1992

With reasonable confidence that I could actually get the job done and that no other officiating gremlins would appear out of the cracks in the rules to haunt me, I prepared to judge at the World Championships in Spain.

Visions of fat, succulent olives, liters of Rioja wine, and the chance to visit the Alhambra were not minor factors in my decision to attend this event, which turned out to be extremely well organized. Even the referees and judges were given a warm welcome dinner, liberally washed down with private label Rioja. The label was the tournament logo, designed by a local artist. Each of us was given a commemorative ceramic plate with the same design, which the president of the Spanish Federation later said was rather inexpensive; however, the value of that plate in terms of the memories it conjures up was invaluable.

I arrived late for the referee seminar, on account of my leaving *Tōkyō* three days later than planned, to attempt the JKF 4th *Dan* exam on 15th November. I needed this qualification to even be eligible to join in the *kata* seminar, but I would not be able to do so because it started in Granada on the 16th and there was no way to get there by departing *Tōkyō* on the evening of the 15th. I reasoned that the *Dan* exam was more important and that I could obtain kata judge qualifications at another WUKO seminar/exam. If I had not attempted the *Dan* exam that time, the opportunity would not have come again for another year, which would then delay various other events by one year.

I left Japan the day after the 4th *Dan* exam without knowing the result.

I received flak from more than one individual for my late arrival, but did not mind explaining that 4th Dan was more important to my karate career than their opinions. Although I arrived in the afternoon of the first day of the seminar, the RC did not permit me to participate. The rationale was that if they allowed me to participate, then they would have to allow others who had arrived late to do so as well. This would not do, since everyone knew well in advance the date, time, and location of the seminar. This was fair enough and punctuality is a reasonable requirement of attendees. I watched the seminar nonetheless, and derived considerable benefit from it, without the tension associated with active participation.

Despite my non-attendance at the seminars, my qualifications from Mexico City were still in effect, so I was valid enough to be assigned to a ring for *kumite* and I displayed my skills sufficiently.

I found myself with a group of Europeans and my ring controller was a Spanish gentleman with whom I could not converse. He did not speak English.

The day wore on reasonably well with no major *faux* pas in my ring, when suddenly a member of the RC came over to my ring and had words with the Spanish gentleman. I immediately knew it concerned me from the glances in my direction through severely convex spectacle lenses. Sure enough, I was removed from the ring in the middle of the match, thus confusing the Egyptian athlete and his opponent.

A new twist in the fascinating saga of women in karate refereeing. Another new unwritten rule…Women may not referee Arabs! This was quickly altered to Islamic male competitors.

Well, in the name of whom this time?

I thought this one out, with a lot more control than the Mexico City scenario. Obstacles were becoming a predictable feature of every international event I had attended so far.

The Egyptians had not complained.

The Iranians had not complained.

Furthermore, the Egyptians had fielded female competitors. Gosh, if this logic were true, then surely men, particularly infidel men, should not be allowed to referee Islamic women.

If it were the Iranians, why would they have supported the idea of my visit to Tehran?

I checked with the officials of the Islamic countries, and none of them admitted to making a complaint. Dr. Hakoishi informed me that this whole issue was nonsense, stating that the RC had not received any formal complaint, but advised me to wait until this matter was resolved before judging any further Islamic competitors.

It was not too long before Dr. Hakoishi returned with a Spanish translator and told the Spanish gentleman that there were no barriers to my judging Islamic competitors, but that I may not judge competitors from Japan or Canada.

This was also nonsense, as officials are not permitted to referee or judge athletes from the same country and national federation as themselves.

Pursuant to this provision, the countries I should not be judging are the U.K. and Canada, for which I have passports.

Suppose I cannot judge representatives of the country in which I have only a residence permit, then I should not be allowed to judge the USA, for which I have a green card, so I have the right of permanent residence there, as well as Japan, where I only had a work permit.

Someone was responsible for this new step in the dirk dance, and I doubt it was an Islamic male. A simple process of elimination pointed a very accusatory finger. There was nothing to be gained from further investigating the source of this "new rule," so I accepted the momentary proviso that I might not judge Japan and filed it away for further consideration.

No sooner had the Spanish gentleman, who had been informed of the inconsistency of his perceived rule had he stopped another match I was judging, having apparently forgotten the information received less than ten minutes before. This time, I fought him visibly by refusing to step off the mat and left it to my assembled peers to tell him again that the word was official. Norma is allowed to judge Arab male athletes. The match continued, with me corner judging, wondering what would happen next.

JKF Wadō Kai 4th *Dan* Examination 1993

However, another approach also offered a substantial challenge. Takagi sensei suggested that I try 4th *Dan* in the Wadō Kai.

Dan certificates are important in terms of having sufficient documentation to support any opinions or claims a woman might have or make against her in the WUKO environment. For example, if someone disagrees and challenges a *kata* score, it is better to support their opinion with as many credentials as possible.

There were, as yet, no women judging or refereeing in WUKO, and I was determined to show the world that women can and will be qualified, competent officials. I am not sure how many WUKO officials held 4th *Dan* certificates in two or more styles at that time.

With trepidation, I studied in earnest for the JKF Wadō Kai 4th *Dan* exam. This was more rigorous than the JKF exam, as there were more components to be scrutinized, and there were new routines to be learned.

I did not have a very clear grasp, for example, of the 10 Kihon Kumite kata of Wadō Ryū, and I was sure I would forget which one was number six, or start attacking with the wrong foot and totally ruin my partner's chances of passing. However, the 4th *Dan* examination includes any two of the first nine Kihon Kumite routines.

The gym at *Tōkyō* Agriculture University (known as Nodai) was cool on a blustery March morning. A number of lads in military university uniforms and with shaved heads were gathered at one end of the room. As the gym began to fill, the uniformed folks would occasionally snap to attention, slap thighs with rigid hands, and bow collectively with a resounding "Ossu!" For a moment, I thought I had stumbled into a JKA *dōjō,* but I was assured that this was, indeed, the site of the JKF Wadō Kai shodan *shinsa* (*Dan* examination). The eager young militarized junior recruits were from Koku Gakuin University (国學院, Academy of National Studies that aims to study and preserve at Japanese culture and traditions) and their behaviour reflected its nationalism. They are the only group within Wadō Kai that I have seen behaving like that, and I was glad to discover later that such behaviour is not encouraged by others in the JKF Wadō Kai.

Eight people tried 4th *Dan* that day. The exam included basics, a kata decided for you by a panel of 7th and 8th *Dans,* a kata of your choice, free sparring, and two *kihon* kumite routines selected by the panel. A short thesis on something relevant had to be submitted in advance. Since mine was in English, I doubt if it was ever read, although Takagi sensei asked me to explain the gist of it. Perhaps not surprisingly, I wrote about the desirable qualities of a karate sensei.

The examination committee of the JKF Wadō Kai delivered their results within an hour. Out of the eight who tried 4th *Dan,* only four passed and

I was one of them. I was very happy about this and enjoyed the personal satisfaction of having worked towards this goal and achieved it.

Second time around. Marriage to Matt Yoshida, Tokyo 1992

Marriage 1992

I met Matt at the *Tōkyō* British Club. He was rather shy and socially awkward, although his English was fluent, with an American accent. His name was Masatsugu, and was called Matt at the suggestion of some World War II veteran. Matt was one of the first Japanese to be awarded a Fulbright Scholarship to study in the USA, where he went during the 1950s. I had thought Matt was in his 40s, but he was actually 50. He was not exactly my type in any sense of the word, as we had few common interests and he was neither an entertaining conversationalist, nor blessed with or much humor. He enjoyed tennis, going to church, keeping track of his stocks and shares, and fine dining. What he had in his favor was timing.

I met him at the same time as a German expat, from whom I had accepted an invitation for dinner. A pleasant meal at a favorite Indian restaurant was followed by some dancing in a Roppongi disco. The more whisky this man consumed, the more obnoxiously he became, insisting that I sleep with him. When words were not having the desired effect upon bringing me to his wife's bed, he became physically threatening. I managed to fight him off by parking my car within walking distance of his home and sprinting distance of a police box. He refused to get out of my car, so I told him he can stay in my car if he liked, because I am about get out and walk to that little building about 25 yards ahead. I informed him that it was a *"koban"* (police) box, got out, and slammed the door of my little RX7 and started to walk, not run—towards the police. This prompted him to haul himself out of my car and stagger off towards his home. I had never before experienced such intensity, such an overpowering need for conquest that physical violence was a viable choice of persuasion. This was a man whose face had been published in a press release in the Japan Times newspaper by the prestigious German automobile company that he worked for as President of its Far East operations! My skin crawled.

On the following day, I returned from work and found seven messages on my answering machine, demanding that I talk/visit/sleep with him that very evening because he only had a limited amount of time—as his wife would return from her holiday in a week! Clearly, this man was mentally ill.... A man whose face had graced the Japan Times newspaper, in a press release from the prestigious German automobile company that he worked for as President of its Far East operations! My skin crawled when thinking about visiting the *Tōkyō* British Club where this maniac might show up looking for me. But I was the Vice President of the Board of Governors at the time, so it would not bode well if I avoided it.

Matt had been out of town when this incident occurred, and when he returned, he invited me out sometime, perhaps to play tennis. This was sufficiently innocent, so I accepted, even though I was not particularly interested in tennis. This was soon followed by red roses arriving at the office and invitations for dinner. I explained the issues with the German fellow, who I had not seen since the last incident. Matt was understanding, empathetic and kind. I was in no danger of immediate physical or psychological aggression.

We became an item and attended many of the expat social events in *Tōkyō*, such as the St Andrew's Ball, the American Chamber of Commerce Ball, Embassy Parties, chic dinner parties, etc. Before long, he pressured me to move into his palatial apartment in Hiroo, one of the prestigious areas of *Tōkyō*. My little apartment contrasted with his empty four-bedroom three-bath luxury condominium, and I was sad when he told me he had been alone for several years. He said that his first wife had walked out along with, the contents of their joint bank accounts, the furniture and three children. A big shock to him, as he had not seen it coming. (I should have listened more closely...).

Pressure to marry became intensive. I resisted it. He was a church goer (when I go it is rarely to a church) and he didn't want to live "in sin" (Another red flag missed). He said:

"How am I supposed to introduce you to people?"

How about:

"..... and this is Norma", or "Norma Foster?"

My name was sufficient as it had worked quite well for several years in three English-speaking countries. Of course, what he wanted to say was:

"....and this is my wife." (Note the absence of a name and the inference of possession.).

I suppose that I was unusually vulnerable for a while after the experience with the German fellow and missed the proprietary nuance in Matt's second statement, which led me to start yielding to his pressure. He wasn't much of a conversationalist, but then, I can speak enough for two. He didn't have much of a sense of humor, but then, how important is that? He was ruthless, which was not immediately obvious, but hidden behind a facade of bonhomie. I supposed that was a good quality to have in a business that sold American car parts to Japanese auto makers. A swagger in his walk hinted at arrogance. But these were not obvious.

I was thirty-nine years old at this point. Here was someone who was eager and willing to marry me and subsequently give me the world on a platter. Holidays in luxury hotels of the Far East. Promise to stop working. A life of leisure and plenty dangled itself before me, at the cost of a marriage certificate. But I was not ready to stop working and had no desire to so. I could not visualize myself as a no-name, trophy wife.

Matt faked interest in karate, even going so far as to work out in a class that I taught. He changed his image a little, buying new clothes and visiting a hairdresser instead of a barber.

I took him to visit *Kikuma* and Carol at *Kikuma's* mother's house in Meguro, *Tōkyō*. Carol had her daughter, Maya, with her, who had not yet learned to drink milk from bottles. During the visit to the Yamaguchi home, Matt seemed dreadfully uncomfortable, but he didn't say anything until after we had all eaten dinner at the *Tōkyō* American Club.

"That was disgusting the way Carol fed Maya," he said.

"What do you mean?" I asked.

"That was disgusting of her to do that in front of us," he explained.

"What?" Was I hearing right?

"Feeding the baby."

"Did she?" I asked.

"Yes."

"Well, you must have been searching for it then, I don't remember seeing any exposed flesh. Why do you think it is disgusting anyway?" I asked.

"My friends would never do a thing like that", he said.

"What? They don't feed their children?" I asked.

"Not in public."

"She wasn't feeding her child in public; she was feeding her in the sanctity of her husband's family home."

I had to let that one go for the time being, I was mortified by his attitude to a natural activity. However, it was to be repeated many times in the future and a mental gap slowly widened.

I should have seen the signs. Hindsight, of course, is clear

I contemplated the situation and agreed to marry him. After all, I had nothing to lose. It might be a Good Thing to be married for a second time before the age of 40, so I accepted Matt's proposal. Letters were written to everyone on the planet who mattered to me, announcing my intentions. I sincerely tried to convince myself that I was doing the Right Thing and that I should conform to the expectations of society regarding how a woman on the brink of Middle Age should behave.

We signed papers in the Minato Ku Ward Office and had lunch at the Prince Hotel. The attendees were the eldest of his two daughters, Emi and Yasmin, who came from Los Angeles for the event and Shawna. Pictures show me with a pale face under an absurd hat several sizes too large and Matt with a Cheshire cat grin.

He talked a lot about "love". I did not, as I was still trying to convince myself that this was right and that this was how life was supposed to be and that I would grow into the role.

As time went on, it became obvious that what he thought he wanted in a wife was indeed what he had married. Initially, he had said that he wanted to spend his life with a North American female who was active, independent, intelligent, attractive, and have a drivers' license. Had he placed an ad in the newspaper for the job, I might have looked like an ideal candidate. Unfortunately, the ad might have been misleading because those qualities were not at all what he was really looking for in a mate. He was looking for a "prize" that he "deserved", because he had "worked hard" all his life. The prize was to be the American Dream of the 1950s, a Caucasian wife who prepared and served food at specified hours and said grace before eating. A wife who shed her apron the moment the doorbell announced the imminent arrival of her hard-working husband, kissed him at the door, and handed him a glass of chilled white wine, wearing perfect makeup and coiffed blonde locks.

They would sit down together at dinner, immediately wash the dishes, then watch TV together in a state of marital bliss every single weekday of this idyllic American life (think Norman Rockwell images). Conversations would revolve around how much he loved her, and she would respond by saying how much she loved him, and everything would progress as it did in romantic movies of the 1950s. On the weekends, they would play tennis together, grace the tables of high-end restaurants together and go to church .... together.

None of this was me. I thought I had married a Japanese businessman, but in fact I had married a conservative American whose attitudes were a generation removed from mine. Not only that, but an American with a Japanese face living in a fantasy world, conditioned by a homestay experience with a conservative Swedish Protestant family in 1950s Wisconsin.

I had made a terrible mistake.

This man was not what I thought he was, and here he was, besotted… and *"in Love"*.

Initially, he was easy-going, generous, and did not mind my continuing to work or my involvement in karate. However, within months of the marriage, a conservative, inflexible and obsessive-compulsive creature emerged. I would often wake up in the morning to find him crouched at the bedside, staring at me. Bizarre. He was condescending and patronized me. He considered people who were important to me as nameless, faceless entities and referred to them as *"your little friends"*, which made me simmer with repressed anger. I tried to bury this increasing fury and commit to the decision I had made of my own free will. No one is perfect, including you, I kept repeating to myself like a mantra. Try to see the good sides, tolerate the qualities you don't find appealing, and adapt. Give and take. Listen to the endless stories about successful sales calls. Brakes and airbags. Eventually, he would recall that I really did work.

And what did you do today in your little job? That quaint British company that you go to every day?

In the face of increasing pressure to explain why I married him, to stop work, to give up my identity to become a trophy wife, I became quite ill.

This initially manifested as I traveled in the car with Matt, who drove me to the Hirōo subway station, where I would catch the Yamanote line train to the office. My skin would literally crawl with goose flesh. Then I would start to shake. More than once, I had to have him stop the car so that I could open the door and reverse the flow of breakfast into Azabu gutters. One day on the packed rush hour subway in the middle of summer, I turned completely cold, sweat broke out in rivers down my face, down my back. Jelly knees. I staggered off the train at the next stop, swayed into the toilet and collapsed by the sink on legs no longer able to support me. People came into the toilet, but ignored the kneeling foreigner with its arms draped around one of the sinks. I could see the headlines.

"Foreigner dies in Kasugai rest room."

"I thought she was having a hangover." said a passerby.

Waves of nausea, skin cold and clammy. After about 10 minutes or so, these symptoms had subsided sufficiently for an upright posture to be shakily assumed and to catch another train to the office. Equilibrium was slowly restored throughout the day.

The stress of living with a man I disliked became intolerable around the time when acute appendicitis attacked me during karate class with Mr. Arakawa. I did not know that was what it was. I went to the changing room, slid down a wall to the floor and stayed there for a while, then returned to the class. Everyone looked at me oddly. After class, I returned home on my scooter, which had replaced the RX7. I told Matt that if this was not gone by the morning, I would go to the hospital. However, I woke up during the night with extreme abdominal pain and Matt rushed me to Hiroo Metropolitan Hospital After imaging and spinal anesthesia, the appendix was removed and pickled for a take-home souvenir of Japanese medical expertise.

The removal of said organ that had actually been complaining for almost one year, incidentally, coincided precisely with when I was first married, and the period of sweats and chills abruptly ceased. I tried to concentrate on being the kind of wife Matt wanted, but I just could not do it. I had to leave him and have the freedom just to be me.

He went on a business trip to Osaka for three days. I left his apartment with a spaghetti pot, a cedar *tansu* (chest of drawers) and my wedding ring, which Matt told me that he gave it to me to spite his first wife.....!

He was surprised when I left him. He could not understand it. Wasn't he the best husband in the world? Didn't he understand me better than anyone? Didn't I have a diamond ring? A jewelry collection purchased at airports? Why wasn't I happy? After all, he would buy me anything.

He asked why I was so ungrateful. Many women would just jump at the chance to marry him.

"So why did it take eight years to find a third wife?" I asked.

He rationalized by blaming other people. It wasn't his fault, it couldn't be my fault, we would have been happy had Shawna not lived with us during the first 6 months of the marriage …….

No, we were both to blame. No one else was responsible for the loathing and disgust that overwhelmed me when I woke up every morning in his executive luxury apartment. He believed he wanted a specific kind of person. However, when he got it, he realized that he couldn't cope with it and wished for something different. He then set about trying to change me into something that would fulfill *his* needs and fantasies.

He wanted me to be his tennis partner, but he had to win all the time. It frustrated him immensely when he didn't, yet I had only played a handful of times. So, he needed someone who enjoyed tennis but was not as good as he was.

I did not want him in my karate class, where he refused to listen to any explanations, commands or requests, and usually stared at me with a rather vacant, lovelorn look.

(My wife is a karate instructor)

I had made two serious judgment errors. One was in the assumption that I had married a Japanese man, and the other was in thinking that I could conform to someone else's vision of what I ought to be.

He talked of moving to Detroit. No! I did not come to Japan to end up in a Detroit suburb. Especially when Matt would be the focal point? No! I could not go to North America with this man. It was better to leave him now, after only one year of marriage, than to string it out for longer; then we would all lose.

I went back to live in my minuscule apartment and breathed easier. Who knew that freedom could exist in 54 m2. We divorced within a year.

JKF 5th *Dan* Exam 1995

By the time I could attempt 5th *Dan* in the JKF, the euphoria that I felt from passing any Wadō Kai exam had long since disappeared. I started to feel that the more I practiced, the less I understood, and if I did not understand anything by now, would I ever? Furthermore, if I really did not understand anything, how could I have the gall to present myself for a 5th *Dan* evaluation? I became mired in a downward spiral of self-deprecation. I have no glib answers to questions about karate and cannot even execute an effective foot sweep, bend my ankles sufficiently, or stand properly in shikodachi (四股立, four directions stance; resembling a squat).

The 4th and 5th *Dan* examinations would undoubtedly be held in a freezing venue cannot and I was concerned about Raynaud's syndrome manifesting itself or my lungs going into spasm in the middle of the *kumite* part of the exam. However, the examination would not wait until I started to believe in myself and my level of understanding improved, and the venue would never be tailored to fit my annoying physical needs. So, I decided to go ahead and present myself to more scrutiny in Oyama City, Tochigi, in November 1995.

Forty-two and 86 putative 5th and 4th *Dans* assembled in the new, beautiful, and unheated Oyama City Budokan for formal introduction to the board of examiners. The candidates were split into one court for 5th *Dan* and another for 4th *Dan* examinations. These exams were held annually, and the numbers were increasing.

We were called into the examination gym in groups of 10. In any JKF *Dan* examination, you are compared with peers within a similar age-grade. The youngest are evaluated first, and the oldest last. This way, the twenty-nine-year-old ex-WKF world kumite champion did not fight with a sixty-year-old who has never competed. Candidates were asked to perform a JKF *Shitei* (listed) *kata* and a *tokui* (favorite) *kata*, and fight the person to the left and right of you in the line. My number in the age line was 18 among the 86 candidates.

Although I was wrapped in Lycra from the waist down and wearing a ski undershirt below my heavyweight gi, and despite the tracksuit top and the gymnastic shoes, my feet were frozen, and my legs turned red and purple while sitting through the first 14 kata presented by the seven candidates in the group. By the time I stood up, my legs were shaking, partly from cold, partly from nerves. Furthermore, by the time I started the first kata, which was *Seishan* (十三; meaning 13), my legs were not just shaking; they positively vibrated throughout the first set of slow *Seishan dachi* (Seishan stance) so the examiners had a chance to deduct points for nervousness as well as for less-than-perfect stances. I finally got into stride by the 7th move, after which I was mad enough with myself to channel some focus into the kata. Unfortunately, Mr. Yanagida was one of my examiners, a national coach and Wadō Kai video star. He had just recently spent a great deal of time at a Wadō *kenshukai* (training/research group) correcting my Wadō *hanmi nekoashi dachi* (half front-facing cat stance), muttering that it still had too much of a Shotokan influence. Having reclaimed sufficient control over my extremities to actually crescent kick my hand with a heart-warming slap and follow it up with a reasonable facsimile of a reverse punch at the end of the *kata*, I realized that I just might, after all, have enough energy to plough through Jion (Shotokan) without collapsing halfway through. For safety, I had taken two puffs of theophylline from a new inhaler prescribed by a concerned general practitioner in Vancouver. He would be thrilled to know that I had used the thing at least once.

I'm sure that Mr. Abe from the JKA in Shiroganedai (Minato ward, *Tōkyō*), who was sitting on Mr. Yanagida's right, thought that there was decidedly too much Wadō influence in the *kiba dachi* (horse stances), which are prominently featured in Jion. I could see scores just tumbling down in a negative cascade. I also managed to raise my left hand far too high in the first of the *soete uchi* (添手内; supporting inside hand; move 25), then lowered the right. The JKF version required the fist to be at the level of the mouth of an opponent the same size as me, and my left hand had a mind of its own when the rest of the body is on autopilot.

So, I unconsciously did what I had done in that move since 1972 and corrected it to the 1995 version on the other side. I'm sure the faux pas was not missed.

My fights were better than those I did for my 4th *Dan* exam. The first fellow I fought was about 5' 8" or so, maybe about 70 kg, stiff-muscled, aggressive, and no one called *yame*! (stop). All he had was an easily identifiable right reverse punch that I could see coming and throwing in a *kizami* to the face first. Of course, he kept coming with the reverse punch anyway, but it was OK because I had demonstrated *sen no sen* timing. The next opponent I had to fight weighed about 80 kg, and I faced him with more trepidation than I had the first. However, he was considerably slower, and though he applied a wider repertoire of techniques, including a whole lot of kicks to my head, they were easy to block or step in, loaded with a reverse punch. I demonstrated essentially *go-no-sen* timing and even managed to include a couple of kicks myself. I was particularly thrilled when I managed to reverse-punch him in the back as he over-reached a roundhouse kick, which put him in a state of mubobi (ム ボ ビ; no self-defence).

However, I did not stay to watch his next fight, so I don't know if he was just slow or whether he was not used to fighting with a female.

Speaking of women, only one other woman was among the 5th *Dan* hopefuls that day. Her family name was Yamakage. She was in her 50s, and she practiced Goju Ryū. She was also possibly the first woman in Japan to become a nationally qualified referee. She was supportive, and we often exchanged sympathetic smiles throughout the wait. As I came off the floor after the kumite, she gave me an encouraging smile and said the Japanese equivalent of "way to go!"

It was kind of her. Among the four women tried 4th *Dan*, one was Junko Ide, who was already a 4th *Dan* in Shito Ryū and a member of the Japan National Coaching Squad. Junko was a successful national team member for many years, returning to Japan with several WUKO gold medals. She then married a Goju practitioner, who established the company called Champ.

I wondered how long it would take before a woman sat on the JKF examination panel (by 2024, it still does not have a woman on the panel).

I later discovered that I was the first foreign woman ever to even try 5th *Dan* in that system, as until recently, it was not allowed. Well. Another first, and this one totally unconscious. I was also the first foreign woman to fail 5th *Dan*, as confirmed by mail about three weeks later.

The reason I failed was that I did not sufficiently understand the basics. That is, I could not move smoothly enough or use my muscle strength properly. My legs were weak. My initial disappointment was like finding out your mate has ditched you for a more attractive version. I was angry with myself and disillusioned. The fact that 90% of all 4th and 5th *Dan* candidates failed did not justify my failure.

Although logically, I understood precisely why I had not passed, I was also angry at a system that allowed me to proceed so far within it with such glaring deficiencies. How did I ever reach 4th *Dan* when such fundamental flaws must have been obvious? My anger was palpable as I mentally castigated all of my teachers throughout twenty-eight years, only to discover that I do not understand the basics? Several people had plenty of opportunity to see that, well, including me, of course.

I quit blaming my teachers for my incompetence. I needed to ask, but what do I ask? If I could not perform a simple front punch by now, was there any point in continuing?

As 1995 and training for the year came to a close, I settled down to reading Minamoto Musashi, the most famous Japanese samurai who authored the book *Gorin no Sho* (The Book of Five Rings). His life had been colorfully dramatized in an NTV television serial that elicited plenty of things to consider. Musashi had endured much frustration when he had followed his path for many years and failed to find the right answers. At the point towards the end of Eiji Yoshikawa's highly novelized account, where Musashi pulls at the sleeves of the garment worn by the Zen priest, Guro and begs him to give him a word of advice, he is at the *nadir* of despair. The priest shrugs him off and says he has nothing to give Musashi. There are no words. The priest sets off on a journey, and Musashi follows him, unwanted and unbidden, ignored by the priest and his companion. After several days, Musashi implored him to just give him one word. The priest picked up a fallen branch, drew a circle around Musashi, and walked away. Musashi was immobilized by a range of emotions. Finally, he realized that the circle represents the universe when expanded, and when diminished to a dot, it represents consciousness, and that he himself is the universe. What he had searched for was within himself all along.

Inspiration! The capacity to progress or not is personal. No need to be angry or disappointed. Just figure out the root of the problem, then set about fixing it. Nothing deep, nothing unusual. Just more training of the entire body…, including the brain. Might as well get started. It is said that learning begins only after 1st *Dan* is achieved. I do not believe this. Satori for me was the realization that I had planted my feet on a pathway that has no end.

The Tōkyō British Club *Dōjō*

A demand for karate classes arose among the TBC members, who ranged in age from thirty to fifty years. Some of them had children who wanted to practice, too. Now my roommate practices Shotokan karate, but I thought Wadō would be more suitable considering the age range. Wadō is more natural than Shotokan in that movements are more natural, not exaggerated, and a great deal of effort is not required to execute them correctly. Shotokan has a rigid framework into which every shape and type of body must precisely fit, whereas Wadō allows the frame to fit the body. For example, I never heard Wadō instructors say things like, "Your back foot in a front stance must be at 30 degrees to the forward direction of the movement". Rather, I heard statements such as "Your foot should be no less than 10, and no more than 40 degrees to the forward direction of the movement, depending upon your ankle flexibility". As I gather, Shotokan was designed for the

Japanese and requires considerable hip and ankle flexibility to make, maintain, and move in deep, long stances. Face-level roundhouse and back kicks, along with their respective variations and for generating impact force through maximal rotation through the axis located at the hip, involve a lot of energy, muscle strength, and stamina. Great physical education for schoolchildren, but I could not be responsible for introducing people aged in their 50s and 60s to this style of karate. After all, if they wanted to build stamina, they could go running. If they want to build strength, they can lift weights. If they want to develop flexibility, they could do yoga. None of the people who joined the TBC club did any of that.

Wadō concentrates on deflecting, avoiding, and going with the flow. Its major features relative to Shotokan, if observed by an outsider, are higher, more natural stances, faster punches, relaxation, and body shifting. It might appear limited compared with Shotokan, as the teaching focus is concentrated upon a smaller repertoire of techniques and fewer kata. I understand that the founder of Wadō, Hironori Ohtsuka, believed that trying to perfect 13 kata was enough of a lifetime challenge.

Finally, I described this rationale to my roommate and said that if she agreed that I teach Wadō, I would join her in opening a *dōjō* at the TBC. I didn't think the students would be around long enough to worry about the fact that there were only 13 kata in the system instead of the 25 practiced in Shotokan. For whatever her reasons, she agreed.

It was made quite clear in ads that our objectives in teaching would be to give people a taste of something Japanese, but in a user-friendly, English-speaking environment. I would introduce them to some Japanese terms and some behaviors common to all *dōjō*. Thereafter, if they gained a level of proficiency and felt comfortable, they could continue studying karate in a totally Japanese environment elsewhere.

Most of the students who joined this class did so because they spent all their time in an English-speaking, foreign environment, rarely communicated with Japanese people, and did not have the time to learn the language or to study something with a Japanese tradition. So, this class would help give them a taste of something that they could pursue further by themselves, either in Japan or in their home countries. Most of the students were on a two–to–three–year stint in *Tōkyō*, so the turnover would be fairly fast.

Much to my surprise, about 20 adults signed up, and about 10 children! The pub floor was not big enough for all these, so we had to split the class.

We had Hideho Takagi come and teach as a guest instructor, along with Mayumi Nobetsu. Through Mayumi, Katy met Kazuo Takahashi, a JKA 3rd *Dan* who ran the Marunouchi *dōjō* in the center of Tōkyō.

Katy suddenly talked of nothing but the virtues of this Takahashi for weeks. Her current love interest became bored hearing about him every five minutes and finally let it be known he had heard enough. Katy went to the Marunouchi *dōjō* and underwent a new lease of life. She had no respect for Wadō whatsoever. She mentioned that Wadō "left her cold," and so for the past year, she had shown up to Dr. Takagi's *dōjō* on Sunday nights and "stretched". Suddenly, Katy talked about this beautiful *dōjō*, with an ofuro (Japanese bath) and a proper changing room for women, a varnished wooden floor, and at least two attractive men. One was Takahashi himself, and the other was called Odawara, who spoke Portuguese and Spanish and had lived in Africa for a while. Much of her conversation revolved around praising these men and their spirit, devotion to karate, sincerity, etc. According to her, these were "real karateka" who trained in karate because they loved it and not for competition. Well, I thought competition for people aged in their forties or fifties in Japan is virtually nonexistent, so anyone in this age group would likely practice for reasons other than competition. In fact, most people practicing karate anywhere do not do so because of competition. In British Columbia, Canada, for example, only 10% of the provincial membership is involved in competition. That includes judges, referees, administrators and other volunteers as well as athletes.

Suddenly, Katy had all the time in the world for training. She rearranged schedules and joined the new JKA that arose out of the ashes after the original JKA split. Before she set off for class, her nails were manicured and polished, and workaday clothes were exchanged for silks. The lipstick came out of cobwebs as Katy stepped out in designer finery to the Marunouchi dōjō several times each week. Her current love interest just sighed and shrugged his shoulders. A passing fad. She would get over it.

"Oh, we must have Takahashi sensei and maybe Odawara sensei teach at the TBC. They are so-o-o-o great; it is good to see such wonderful Shotokan; you will really like them."

Well, I figured Katy trained under Nishiyama sensei and elsewhere in California, and she had seen many instructors at summer camps that I had also attended. I considered that she understood quality, so I listened to what she had to say and agreed that Takahashi sensei should come and teach a class at the TBC. Since he was around fifty years old, according to Katy, it would be good for the *dōjō*.

I went out of town for two or three weeks, during which Katy taught at the TBC.

I returned to find that not only had she had Takahashi sensei instructing for two consecutive weeks, but that she had taken him out to dinner at TBC expense and wanted the TBC to provide him with a new karate gi in gratitude for teaching! Furthermore, he was willing to teach all the time, and everyone just loved him. Also, she had scheduled him to teach again so that I could meet him and proposed that we take him out to dinner again at *dōjō* expense? Well, I figured if Katy is willing to spend our *dōjō* purse on dinners for this man and buy him gi, he must be something amazing.

But I was uneasy. Had she promised this Takahashi sensei that he might eventually teach and take over the TBC karate group? After all, Katy said that he spoke English, and when I pointed out that we had made a rule that *dōjō* members had to be members of the TBC itself, she indicated that Takahashi was interested in joining it. Katy was quick to assure me that it was not her intent to have Takahashi take over the TBC *dōjō*. She just thought having him as a regular visiting instructor would be a benefit.

We had never spent such sums of money on any of the other people who came to teach. We all, including Katy and I, put 4,000 yen into a kitty every month and we had amassed a reasonable sum. Suddenly, we were being awfully generous towards this Shotokan 3rd *Dan*. Why had we not been equally generous with Mayumi, who was a 4th *Dan,* or Takagi sensei, a 7th *Dan*, both of whom had taught as guest instructors?

Were we really only willing to go out of our way to treat male JKA 3rd *Dans* with special attention? The rationale behind Katy's decisions was becoming clear. Her behaviour, body language, and tone all considerably altered when Takahashi sensei was in the vicinity.

After my three-week absence, all the students were suddenly practicing Shotokan! *Pinan nidan* had morphed into *Heian shodan*. Clearly, an effort had been made to deliberately change the style of the beginners. Perhaps Katy had given him permission.

Finally, I met Kazuo Takahashi as he came to teach at the TBC *dōjō*. I stood in line and trained in his class. He presented a basic standard Shotokan workout and made quite a show of doing a lot of pushups and sit-ups afterward, for "stamina." He frequently repeated the words "power" and "stamina" throughout the class as he demonstrated overpowered techniques that lacked flow, grace, and effectiveness. He performed front punches with a huge leap accompanied by a thundering *kiai* and a heavy stomp on the floor, which awed the students but did not impress me. I would bet that a fifty-year-old should be past caring about trying to impress people and should be looking into his inner self for some meaning beyond bodybuilding. However, he had taken the time to come all the way over to Ebisu and shared his vision of karate with us. Time is precious in *Tōkyō*, as getting anywhere can be laborious. Obviously, he had given up the greater part of a Saturday to teach, so

I was certainly willing to be gracious by buying him pints at the bar upstairs, talking to him, and trying to understand his interpretation of karate.

He invited me to his *dōjō*, along with any other TBC students who wished to go …. any time. The underlying message was palpable: "Come to my *dōjō* and see what real karate is about." Katy wanted him to teach again next week, but I pointed out that Takagi sensei was scheduled to teach, so if Takahashi sensei wanted to train in the class, he was welcome. Style notwithstanding, Takahashi was 3rd *Dan*, and Takagi was 7th *Dan*; nothing more to say.

I decided to visit Takahashi's *dōjō*.

Katy was so excited, describing to me a person called Odawara, how the men's changing room isn't big enough for all the men who practice, so they go into the *ofuro*, then dress and dry themselves outside on the tatami where the judo people practice. What nice butts; how marvelous that almost everyone in the *dōjō* spoke English; how intelligent everyone was because they are all so high in the Marunouchi hierarchy, etc.

Sure enough, it was a beautiful dōjō, and located right down the Mita subway line around the corner from Tōkyō Central Post Office. Very convenient, as we lived on the Mita line.

Shoes off at the door, bow, and enter the tatami floor. Step off the tatami onto a perfect, gleaming wooden floor. A scroll in a tokonoma (alcove) calligraphed "*Jaku nen fu do*," which had something to do with a Bodhisattva suspended at an angle of about 30°, a set of horns, and a first aid kit. The other end of the *dōjō* had a *makiwara* and a heavy bag. Kendō armor lay in breastplate-sized cubes, and shinai and all manner of sticks were crammed into a bucket in the corner. A standard *shinden* (small shrine) with the usual offerings to *Shintō kamisama* (gods) was located high on the long wall. One side of the room was covered in sliding wooden doors about shoulder height, which let in the hot, sultry vapor that passes for air in downtown summertime Tōkyō. The atmosphere redolent of toil, tatami and sweat indicated what to expect in this *dōjō*. Spirit would run high, people would put 100% effort into everything, 100% of the time and we would stand in lines, all doing the same series of movements. Lots of *kiai* would reverberate off the sliding doors, and we would all push and pull together—as one wave—in the moving Shotokan.

I followed Katy to the changing room, and she showed me the ofuro. Wow! A bath and a relatively clean changing room. Although it was the size of a postage stamp and full of kendo gi hanging on three walls, it also had a sink and a mirror. Truly amazing. While changing into gi, the unmistakable sound of a rhythmically pounded makiwara (a plank of flexible wood covered with sailcloth and tatami straw) reverberated through the walls. It was Takahashi sensei. Stepping out of the changing room, I bowed to him; he bowed in return, then continued punching the makiwara. We were early, so I drifted to a corner and began to stretch and warm up a bit. No techniques and no smacking anything. The class began to fill up, then Takahashi sensei called to start the class. We all lined up from left to right. The class included several black belts, and Katy stood at the far-right end of them. I filled in on her right, as she had the right of way at this *dōjō*, having trained here before me. She then did a soft shoe shuffle and ended up on my right. Hierarchies.

Seiza! Mokuso!

Mokuso Yame! Junbi Taiso!

So, we all stretched and warmed up. I asked Katy who was Odawara sensei. She said he had not arrived yet, but I would recognize him as soon as he walked in the door, and I did. A salaryman aged about mid-40s, shaven head to disguise encroaching baldness, size 5 gi. He was about 5' 7" and weighed about 75 kilos. He had a pleasant smile and, otherwise, was rather unremarkable.

As he stepped onto the floor. Katy rolled her eyes and feigned ecstasy. I raised my eyebrows; it didn't sit well with me. I could not see a valid reason for her attitude.

Basics consisted of the usual Shotokan combinations, namely, only those required for the Shodan examination. Nothing new, but it was nice to go through these familiar combinations that remained buried in muscle memory. We worked up a good sweat doing those, then lined up opposite someone for kihon kumite, or basic sparring. The first exercise was basic gohon kumite (five-step sparring), where an opponent step forward five times with a straight punch or kick per step to a named target. The defender steps back five times, performing the same appropriate block, then, on the last one, immediately throws a reverse punch to the opponent, and both hold the last position. This means that if the last punch was towards the face, it would stay there, as though frozen in a snapshot, and the defense side would block and counter with the reverse punch to the stomach. The purpose of this type of exercise is to develop a sense of learning the optimal distance required to attack and defend, how to control a technique that has forward momentum and centrifugal force, and how to block accurately. If this drill is practiced with several opponents who differ in height, weight, proportion, strength, speed or karate experience, it can teach a lot about applied basics. It can also provide insight into the psychological nature of the opponent. Soon, people who are insecure, arrogant, kind, shy, honest, sexist, egotistical, helpful and respectful become easy to identify.

I have always found it difficult to look people straight in the eye for extended periods unless I am talking to them. Maintaining eye contact for no reason other than waiting for whoever happens to be in control of the class to stop talking usually causes me to stifle a giggle. After all, what is the point of standing scowling at an opponent in an endless state of readiness while the key-counting boy is busy explaining to an inferior how many ways he has screwed up. I simply try to look at my opponent directly at the appointed moment, hopefully with a neutral facial expression. So, as the bicycle chain of opponents revolved around the room, I found myself face-to-face with Takahashi sensei. Bow. Ready.

"Gedan Barai kamae!" (Prepare to execute lower sweeping block) yelled

the teaboy.

"JODAN!" (face level) he yelled again.

"Hajime!" (Begin!)

So, I looked Takahashi in the eye, and despite his intimidating scowl, shouted "JODAN" so that he knew I was going to attack his face five times, and proceeded to take the first step forward. He stepped back into a long, low front stance and blocked in a manner clearly designed to break, rather than deflect arms, so I allowed my next punch to bounce off his arm to avoid massive bruises from elbow to wrist. The third and fourth were the same, and in the fifth, I launched a little faster off the mark than the others, which caused Takahashi sensei to miss-time the block. However, I did not touch him. This apparently enraged him because, as I stood there, frozen in suspended animation, with the last punch out there at face level, he unleashed a reverse punch to a target on the wall way behind my mid-section. Just a shame that my abdomen was in the way of whatever imaginary makiwara he was punching. The force of the blow sent me reeling backward a few feet, but fortunately, he had not caught me in the solar plexus, so the effect was to unbalance and shock me. So much for trusting your opponent. I realized that he aimed to teach me a lesson, although I wasn't sure exactly what, or really, why. After all, he had nothing to prove to me, and if he was really excited about using a stationary partner who he outweighed by about 25 kg as a punching bag, then he had clearly had issues. I squared up to face him again, and a supercilious smile flitted briefly across his face. Now, I had to be on the defense, because I knew that this was not a play, owing to unwritten rules for visitors. Sure enough, he came at me with as much power as he could muster, aiming well beyond my head. I smiled, which no doubt enraged him even more. I smiled because the drill simply could not function under such conditions, and unless I did something that the drill did not call for, such as moving to the side, he would simply pulp my face. For example, if I moved to the side, he would give me a hard time for not doing the exercise correctly. The exercise was pointless. Of course, he could make mincemeat out of me. There would be something seriously wrong with him if he couldn't. This made me smile again. There was nothing I could do but smile. At his last face punch, I blocked and countered with a reverse punch to his midsection, with the intent to stop the punch at skin touch. It never got there, as he dropped his outstretched punching arm into a *gedan* block, thus neutralizing my theoretical counter, and slammed another reverse punch into my ribs. I looked at him with horror and perplexity. What exactly was he was trying to do? Whatever it was, I knew it was not going to enhance my understanding of the finer aspects of Karate Dō and might land me in hospital with a few broken ribs.

The human bicycle chain revolved again, and this time, I found myself in front of Odawara sensei. I had somehow considered that he might be a bit more and intelligent than Takahashi, but I was soon to find out otherwise.

By this time, the class was practicing *kihon ippon* kumite, which is basic, one-attack sparring. The attacker tells the defense side what attack is going to come and then launches it. The defender steps back, forward or sideways, blocks and counters the attack, and both hold their final positions, just like in gohon kumite.

This holding of the final positions is supposed to demonstrate all the qualities embodied above, including *zanshin*, a state of awareness that danger still lurks. The moves are stylized and are a means of teaching Shotokan beginners basic fighting principles.

So, there I was facing Odawara sensei, and the first thing he did after settling into a front stance with *gedan barai* (lower sweeping block) in readiness to attack my head was to arrange his facial expression to resemble a gargoyle. The corners of his mouth turned down, and all visible tendons radiated stiffly from his neck towards his shoulders. People who carry a lot of muscular tension to class are usually very difficult to do these types of exercises with, as they tend to be rigid at all the wrong times in all the wrong places. When blocking people like this, a regular Shotokan block from a smaller muscle mass simply does not work, and all that happens is you bang wrists and leave with bruises as souvenirs. To avoid getting injured, it is critically important to time the defense to move out of the line of attack without using a block at all or to deflect the punch well before its complete extension. Odawara sensei attacked with a very tense and consequently slow face punch, so I sidestepped it, performed a side snap kick, and followed it up with a reverse punch that stopped short of skin touch - a fairly standard Shotokan maneuver. For whatever reasons that are still beyond me, instead of maintaining his position, he threw a spinning back kick that propelled me clean off my feet and sent me sprawling on the *dōjō* floor about five yards backward. Breath totally knocked out of me; heaving, coughing and spluttering, I picked myself up. Whoo! Tears just sprang unannounced to my eyes and started rolling down my face. Not even a perfunctory oops, sorry. What the hell? This was simple abuse. Had that happened in free sparring, then it would have been perfectly acceptable, but this was not free sparring. I was clearly being taught an unwelcome lesson. Who was trying to prove what? And to whom? I had never been treated like that before or after in a Japanese *dōjō*.

They did not treat Katy this way. They never touched her with a technique. They were gentlemen. They played by the rules. I understood that nothing like this had happened to Mayumi either, and subsequent events have proven likewise, as several foreign women have gone to that *dōjō* and never experienced the abuse inflicted on me. I had never met Odawara sensei until that night; it was surely not a personality issue. So, what was it? Katy remained curiously silent about the issue and claimed to know nothing about it. So, of course, I returned to that *dōjō* several times to confirm what I thought was true. Simply, these two instructors felt it necessary to "put me in my place" and clarify stylistic superiority. But why? I will never know.

I quit going to that *dōjō* after about half a dozen times and refused to have Takahashi sensei or anyone associated with his *dōjō* anywhere near the TBC again. After all, if that was how he treated me, how could I entrust him with the well-being of my students?

Odawara sensei, his wife and family left for Mexico City, and Takahashi sensei seemed not to fall for Katy's charms. Her enthusiasm for training at that *dōjō* soon dwindled. The constant stream of Marunouchi consciousness that poured forth from her mouth slowed to a trickle and everyone settled back into their normal respective relationships with Katy before discovering the Marunouchi *dōjō*. As for me, that experience remains the only serious blot during eight years of training in Japan.

One of The JKAs' 1994

I decided to investigate the new JKA premises in Ebisu, just up the street from the bowling alley that served as its former HQ. After the split, the Mizuno faction of the JKA moved to Shiroganedai in Minato Ku, and the Nakahara faction relocated to Ebisu. The latter had been granted the rights by the Tōkyō Civil Court to the JKA name, the red rising sun on a white crescent logo, and the use of the prestigious Nippon Budōkan for their All-Japan tournament. This was appealed by the Mizuno faction in the spring of 1995. I think they lost, but these details were not my concern.

The new JKA *dōjō* looked bright, cheerful, and friendly, with an umbrella stand and potted plants providing decorative touches to an otherwise utilitarian first-floor office. A friendly fellow in a gi dealt with my questions about membership. I had quickly visited before and collected a membership after watching a class.

I noted that his name was Naka, a single Chinese character on his bleached white gi. He was around thirty, pleasant, and had a wide, infectious grin. I learned that he lived not far from me, had Sakunosuke as his first Shotokan instructor at Takushoku University (Takudai), and had trained with Hideho Takagi sensei from primary school through high school. Naka sensei knew that I trained with Sakunosuke from my KUGB record book, then mentioned in an oblique way that he was a *"henna hito"* (strange person), to which I responded, 'Hai…*chikan desu"* (Yes, he is a pervert). We were on the same page. Upon entry to Takushoku, he switched to Shotokan, as he decided he wanted to become a karate professional, and the JKA was the only way to become a karate professional at that time. I remember that one of Ingrid's favorite sensei at the old JKA was called Naka, and I guessed this must be him. At any rate, this exchange was encouraging. He asked who I trained with in Tōkyō, and I told him. He was pleasantly surprised and asked me why I wanted to join the JKA. I told him that I had to maintain an understanding of the Shotokan Kata Jion and Kanku Dai, as I needed to perform kata from two styles in the era of Shitei kata examinations and elimination rounds in international championships. I decided to train there when I discovered that he would be teaching the next class.

The one-hour class upstairs in the shiny new *dōjō* started with terse orders from a teaboy to line up, kneel down, meditate, bow here, bow there, stand up, warm up. No one seemed to walk anywhere; they ran, even if it were only a couple of yards. It would look as though it were the most important undertaking ever attempted. Perhaps someone would die if they failed to reach that key spot in front of the mirror, just there at the far right of the fairly small room. Everyone was deadly serious, intent and tense. Shoulders were up around their ears, and it seemed that relaxation never entered their training or their vocabulary. There were several foreigners in the class, many of whom must have been reincarnations of Funakoshi himself or thought they had their own minds and spent the entire class scowling and trying to stare down opponents. Macho egotism filled the room, barely dispelled by Naka sensei, whose excellent workout and humorous approach to teaching failed to loosen knots in several shoulders. I wondered how much Dr. Takagi had influenced Naka's communication and teaching style.

Mostly, I felt comfortable enough there to consider training there regularly. After a few weeks of evening practice at several *dōjō*, I had the opportunity to experience as many of the instructors as I could. I concluded that Tanaka, Osaka, Shiina, Naka, and Ogura sensei were the best I could learn from. Some of the others retained the arrogant nonchalance that was a major feature of the JKA before the split, and some were just too compulsively nit-picking to make it worth the one-hour trek there and back. If the only feedback was to adjust the angle of the open knife-hand in a static blocking position by one or two degrees, then was it worth the train rides plus the $120 per month for *dōjō* fees? I then planned a schedule that included training with Arakawa sensei and Takagi sensei in the Wadō Kai, as well as the JKA instructors mentioned above.

It seemed to work as long as Heian kata were avoided.

I began to know some of the practitioners better. There was Beverley from Australia, who left Japan every three months for a tourist visa renewal, a chore she had repeated over 12 times. She was a 3rd Dan in her mid-30s with a spectacular mane of thick, straight red hair down to her waist. Beverley worked as a hostess in a bar owned by one of the JKA instructors, and she trained mostly at Aoyama Gakuin, a prestigious private university. She had a history of injuries, many of which were directly caused by her instructor, with whom she had made the mistake of sleeping a few times. She had teeth replaced, stitches in her face, a broken jaw, massive bruises that were so bad she could hardly walk, and a host of other minor injuries sustained while being a punching bag for the JKA sadist that she respected and called sensei. That she was treated like this was shocking, but that she chose to endure it and go back for more was more so. No one needs to be systematically battered to learn karate. Regardless of style, morality, nationality, sex or treatment, Beverley's life was karate. She once said that in Australia, her only job prospects would be waiting tables if she did not have karate. However, now she was experienced enough to run her own *dōjō* when she returned to Australia, and the fact that she was not selected to participate in the brutal JKA instructor course, although disappointing, would not radically affect how she would be perceived in Australia. She was a talented fighter with good kata, who had devoted years to refining her karate. Only one other subject held any interest for her: men. There always seemed to be someone asking her if the hair elsewhere on her body was the same color as that on her head, why her breasts weren't any bigger, how old she was or if they could have a quickie in some back room. She might have been quite flattered at the attention; underneath the veneer of outrage, she expressed when recounting the scandal of the moment with unbridled enthusiasm at the top of her Australian voice.

Nonetheless, Beverley was honest and sincere about her karate training. She left Japan on the verge of disillusionment with her dream, perhaps because she found that her dream was a nightmare. At the age of 36 years, she behaved like a teenager, and consistently competed in tournaments populated by 20-year-olds (and doing rather well), training in a university *dōjō*, being promiscuous with several instructors. This behaviour in a woman aged 36 years was looked down upon and it did not net her any respect… but perhaps she had lost respect for herself. When she returned to Australia for the last time, she was very depressed. She went to Thailand for a few months, then returned to Australia with a baby.

Another serious female practitioner I encountered was Judy, who hailed from Alaska. A tiny, muscular 26-year-old, she was a 2nd Dan when I met her. She would quake with fear whenever the instructor's footsteps threatened to come her way, and she understood very little Japanese despite her two-year stay and constant daily attendance at the *dōjō*. She was shy, but that changed after consuming a beer or two. She had distinct notions of what respect was all about and demanded a certain number of bows, whether or not it was called for in the context of the class. When she became annoyed, which was often, she would sulk for several hours, which was no fun for anyone around her. If, during training, her opponent was faster than her or more skillful, she would retreat into herself mentally and not look that person in the eye. If beaten in a tournament, she would cry and sulk in the stands for hours. If she made it to the podium, she talked about it endlessly. She was naive, extremely insecure, stubborn and hypersensitive. She trained very diligently and sincerely, but had yet to learn some fundamental truths. Mind you, I had to learn some of those myself at the same age.

Several Japanese women trained in the Ebisu *dōjō*. They covered a range of ages and karate experience, from beginners to experienced and the gracious Mrs. Osaka. Having raised her children to university level, she worked for Mitsubishi and trained at least twice each week. Truly egoless on the floor, it was delightful to practice or socialize with her. Her smiling, unusually freckled face and softly curling hair naturally attracted people toward her. Although she did not speak English, and even if one didn't understand any Japanese, her assertive, generous nature seemed to shine so transparently that language was not a barrier. She must have been in her late forties, but she ran could have been easily mistaken for a much younger person.

Hiroko Abe sensei ran a "Ladies Class" on Tuesdays. She was the first woman to graduate from the JKA instructors' course. Abe sensei was a mass of disarticulated joints, and she had a peculiar gait, indicating severe lower back or hip problems, no doubt related to her participation in the JKA instructor course and the brutal version of Shotokan that she had practiced for decades.

By the time I went to her Tuesday classes, she must have been around fifty-something. She sported a crew cut and wore men's shirts and jeans most of the time. Her notion of formal was pressed slacks and an Oxford button-down broadcloth instead of lumberjack plaids or summer T-shirts. When not in the *dōjō*, she wore a single discreet circular earring in one ear.

Abe sensei and her sister, who was divorced with a child, shared a beautiful modern home on land inherited from their parents. The split-level house was formed into a duplex in the fashionable Shimo Kitazawa area of Tōkyō. The ground-level garage door led to a gleaming dōjō, with showers for both men and women, a perfect wooden floor, bars, mirrors, and other equipment, including closed-circuit cameras. Here, she ran her own classes, where she gained a reputation for being a stickler for correcting the most trivial of technical infractions. Like Masahiko Tanaka, her senpai, she rode a motorbike to the Ebisu *dōjō* in warmer weather. This was notable because she was the first woman I had ever seen riding on the front seat of a motorbike in Tōkyō.

Farewell party for Beverley, Tōkyō 1995

Katy and I hosted a farewell party for Beverley at my apartment, and I was not in a party mood. However, this had been planned by others for quite some time, and invitations were sent, so there was no pulling out. The guest list included Takahashi from the Marunouchi *dōjō*, to whom I was not inclined to extend hospitality, several JKA louts whom I had never met, several JKA students I did not particularly care about, and sycophant foreigners to fawn over the instructors who attended the gathering. My small apartment resounded with these acolytes bowing loudly, yelling "Osss" every time someone a Japanese person with a dan rank that exceeded theirs showed up. I called it "gratuitous ossing" and worried about the neighbors. A particularly diligent sycophant called Ingmar was in Tōkyō on a scholarship to study for a Ph.D. in Japanese linguistics at the University of Foreign Languages. She spoke Japanese and English fluently, along with several European languages. Wearing a very short black Lycra dress, she sat at the feet of the gods all night, danced only with gods, and stared straight into their eyes with beckoning and sultry smiles. Her act was interesting to watch, as the fifty-something-year-old gods with whom she danced became increasingly drunk and furthermore, charmed by her behaviour

William, a Canadian who had just been accepted into the instructors' course, vied with Ingmar to wait hand and foot upon the exalted and confirm every drunken pronouncement with an "Ossu"! Obviously, my guests confused my apartment with a *dōjō*.

Mr. Osaka, who was so inebriated that he could hardly stand, but not so much as to ignore the pressure on his bladder despite the attentions of Ingmar, was helped to the tiny room that housed the convenience. The space of ~2 ft3, was just sufficient for one person and a ceramic flushing device. It was festooned with books; prints hung on the walls, shelves holding ever-accumulating piles of magazines, a Thai metal sculpture of a dancer letting loose an invisible arrow from a bow, and a wooden monk watching over the proceedings. A tall ceramic vase encircled by a dragon held extra rolls of paper, and somewhere in between the library and the gallery was the best that the Toto company had to offer in the way of human waste disposal. After a rather lengthy period, Osaka sensei emerged rather uncertainly from our Museum of Oriental Culture and Library and toilet, clutching a book while shaking his head.

He plopped down onto the back room tatami rather loosely and opened the book. It was Karate Dō Shitei Kata, and consisted of images of compulsory kata from each of the four major styles recognized by the JKF. These kata would be implemented for the first round(s) of competition. Osaka sensei performed the Shotokan kata described in the book. (It was finally removed as a way to select those who would proceed to the next round during 2013). Within hearing distance from William, Ingmar and anyone else who was paying attention, he slurred (in Japanese):

"No-o-ma!

How can you do this?"

"What sensei?" I asked.

"The toilet. I found this book in the toilet."

"Yes, sensei. That is where it is kept," I replied.

"No-o-ma."

"Look. This is me", he pointed to the side snap kicks in Kanku Dai.

"I cannot do this now and here I am, in a toilet?"

William hastened to console him by saying,

"Of course, you can still kick like that, sensei."

I told him to stop lying to the man. I said that he was drunk, not stupid, and indeed, he does exist in our toilet.

I laughed and said that we all had to get old, even JKA instructors.

"Sensei, the book is in the toilet because being in the toilet should not exclude a

learning opportunity.

A wonderful feature of karate is that it can be studied anywhere, anytime.... even in a toilet."

He was drunk enough to take this answer seriously and faced William, who was totally aghast. Osaka sensei tried to focus his eyes on William and expounded upon what a fine person I was, how serious, how diligent, etc.

At this point, I had to leave the room laughing ..., I could not stand it anymore, and William said I should obtain Osaka sensei's autograph.

I declined and went about cleaning up and trying to remove all remaining hangers-on, as it was now around 3 am, and the hostesses needed to sleep.

I later learned that the esteemed Osaka sensei, while inebriated, was unable to find public convenience, so he sprayed the entrance to Myogadani subway station late one Saturday night with the metabolized remains of an excess of beer and whisky. However, although the story was probably authentic, I was not there, so I cannot confirm it personally. Ingmar succeeded in charming the pants right off Osaka sensei and became his paramour for quite some time.

Wear and Tear, 1995

I flew back to Vancouver for surgery on my left knee. The problem was similar to that encountered almost a decade before. Frazzled meniscus. The wizards at the UBC Sports Medicine Clinic, this time represented by Bill Regan, put me under the knife at 8.30 am, and by noon, I was walking without sticks into a favorite Italian restaurant for lunch.

Unfortunately, this time, it took a lot longer to recover, probably because I was now about a decade older, and there was soft cartilage under the kneecap, which did not bode well. For the first half of 1995, although walking was not a problem, everything else involving the knees was. Though I attended the International Budō seminar in Katsuura in March of that year, it was with half a body. Seiza and kicks were impossible, and shoes had to be worn throughout Kanazawa sensei's karate class to ensure that sliding and torquing on a cold hardwood floor were avoided.

In May, I accompanied Takagi sensei to Basel, Switzerland, where I, as well as Takagi sensei, were guests of Georges Santiago and Elena Mores. There was training every evening, and my knee would blow up and sound like crunching biscuits. Every evening was a round of ice and aspirin, and every morning, the knee would refuse to bend beyond 90°. A return to Vancouver for a checkup confirmed that the kneecap was becoming locked, rigid and that flying at 35,000 feet with the knee bent for nine hours was one of the worst things I could have done. A horrified Dr. Regan told me what to do, which was simple enough. Keep the knee moving, or keep it locked straight. Manipulate the kneecap manually and isometrically tense the thigh muscle often. It should conform sufficiently for another few years of use before the arthritis sets in.

The other knee was beginning to show signs of osteoarthritis, so I was careful with the snap kicks on that side, too.

Was the cause—karate or a genetic predisposition? My father had cartilage problems in his knees, and so did his father. In fact, my father's cartilage problems were sufficient to keep him out of the Royal Navy, or so he claimed. I supposed that karate had exacerbated the tendency, if there was one. Regardless, I had the personal goal of trying and passing at least one 5th Dan exam in Japan before I left, so the ice and aspirins continued for a while.

Vancouver 1984 National championships. The day I beat the gold medal athlete to win a bronze due to aggregate scoring system

International Budō Seminar, Katsuura

Every year during March, a weekend seminar is held at the International Budō University in Katsuura. It is like a PE college, except that martial arts are the main focus. These include judo, *kendō*, karate, sumo, *kyudō*, *naginata*, *aikidō*, and *jukendō*. The degree program includes sports medicine, kinesiology, biomechanics, martial arts literature, history and philosophy, as well as a variety of sports.

In conjunction with the Ministry of Education, the Budō Gakuen targets 100 foreign practitioners of martial arts. The objectives are to introduce foreigners to a martial art other than what they currently practice and a smattering of the more esoteric, deeper aspects of *budō*. For instance, Eugen Herrigel's landmark book on archery has been critiqued, along with various translations of the Book of Five Rings, written by Miyamoto Musashi. The ways of sitting in Zazen have been dissected for hours, while restless foreigners who can barely sit still on hard wooden benches wait for the moment to actually get up and go practice something.

The seminar draws a diverse crowd of individuals from all over the world who have devoted decades of their lives to the pursuit of a single martial art. Some take themselves very seriously, while others take themselves normally. Regardless, there is such a worldwide gathering of knowledge, expertise, and anecdotes that may be difficult to find in one place, and the opportunity to study a different version of a kata, a new application, style or a new martial art is precious.

Because it is subsidized by the Ministry of Education, the entire weekend, including lectures, practice, accommodation and food at the time costs ¥5000 or so, which is an amazing bargain, considering that one dinner for an average Tōkyō restaurant can cost around the same. The first year I went, I was delighted to find that I knew some of the attendees, among whom were some Vancouverites and Hakoishi sensei, who was responsible for teaching the karate portion that year. By the end of the weekend, all of us were well acquainted, and if not, the skits at the closing banquet filled any remaining gaps in camaraderie.

It was heartening to see world-renowned martial artists shed their controlled dignity long enough to provoke peals of international laughter. The second time I attended, Kanazawa taught the karate section, and at the farewell party, he performed a wonderful song and dance routine that called for much leaping about in the air. The energy and abandon with which this light-footed sixty-year-old karate legend was hurling himself about was a fitting relief from a three-hour lecture on *"ki"*.

Tōkyō, 1996

Still in Japan. Through association with the JKF, JKF Wadō Kai, the JKA in Japan, and Karate Canada, I tried to maximize these opportunities to study with various instructors of different styles and to attend as many karate events as possible. Thus, I refereed at Goshi Yamaguchi sensei's Japan Gōjū tournament, at a goodwill match between Canadian and Japanese practitioners of Gima Ha Shoto Ryū in Ojiya, Niigata, and at Bunkyo and Shibuya Ward tournaments in Tōkyō. I have attended Wadō *kata* seminars in the bowels of Meiji University, Shotokan and Shito Ryū seminars in the Yoyogi Olympic facility, and competed and placed in several local tournaments.

I participated in Shinto weddings, Buddhist funerals, shrine burning, *bonenkai* and *shinenkai,* tolling bells to welcome the new year, and a Buddhist ritual purification of a new house. I enjoyed the congratulatory ceremonies for Yamaguchi sensei becoming the *soke* of his group, for Mr. Arakawa reaching the venerable age of sixty *(kanreki)* and for Tsuyama sensei receiving JKF 8th Dan. An invitation to the Nana Kai Ki, or seven-year commemorations of the passing of Makoto Gima, provided another opportunity to participate in a unique Japanese ceremony.

These experiences are memorable.

In the future, having gained more referee experience and qualifications, I wanted to go to other countries and help encourage women to become involved in refereeing. Perhaps eventually, female officials will become a normal part of the standard WKF tournament image. My experience in British Columbia indicated that women shy away from officiating for many reasons, and since fewer women than men practice karate, the pool of potential female officials is also smaller. Nevertheless, I would like to impact this so that a women's WKF event would consist of 50:50 ratios of female athletes, coaches, and officials.

Canada seemed a reasonable place to start, as that is where my strongest base of support has been and continues to be. I think there is a lot of room for growth in Canada with respect to women's karate.

I established a trust fund in British Columbia to help women in karate; it was called the YF fund. It was not a lot of money, but there is enough to provide results if wisely invested in improving skills. This money could be used to stimulate more interest in refereeing among women and conduct referee seminars around the province.

Three Wadō groups were recognized within Karate Canada. These were headed at the time by the following sensei: Tatsuo Suzuki, Hironori Ohtsuka II and Mr. Ryutaro Hashimoto. These groups are spread across the country and sadly do not communicate much with each other. Perhaps forming a uniquely Canadian group of Wadō practitioners would prevent further fragmentation and lawsuits as seen in other countries. No one should be prevented from studying and learning because of political feuds that occurred long ago among people who are no longer with us. Knowledge should be shared and enjoyed by those who wish to share and receive it, as it is not the property of one or a chosen few.

Furthermore, it is important that those who are in positions of authority within karate organizations should understand that more women will practice karate, stay for the long term, and become coaches, officials, and leaders in general. This means that women must be taken seriously so that what happened to me one weekend in 1994 will not happen to others.

Pusan, Korea 1994

Korea fielded a team in the Fukuoka Women's Cup in 1993, and they did not do well. They presented a version of Bassai in the team kata competition. The technical level was far below what was expected in an international event—that—the chief referee had to call a meeting of the judges, of which I was one, to discuss how to score it. The team completed the kata without any flaws in directions and sequences. All three performed the same movements, but without synchronicity, understanding of the kata, the impression of fighting multiple opponents, focus, balance, continuity, or anything else that the rules state are key features for a kata to score. They were like white belts who were completely out of their depth among world-class competitors. The judge from France wanted to give a zero; I wanted to give the lowest score within the range of 6 and 8 that was due to the team, because this was a "semifinal". In actual fact, it was not necessary to run three rounds of kata because the total number of teams did not exceed 16. In this tournament, 16 teams would be eliminated to eight; then another kata would decide the final placings. I felt that a score of zero would be too harsh and only humiliate the girls. Scores between 6.0–6.2 were sufficient to put them right at the bottom end of the scale, but without punishing them.

The two Japanese judges agreed with me, so the scores were set at no more than 6.2 and no less than 6.0.

The kumite was also an embarrassment to Korean karate, as clearly, these girls had not been coached properly. They did not understand the rules, and all of them lost their first match within 60 seconds.

I felt sorry for these girls and decided to ask the president of their federation where they trained and if I could help in some way. I discovered that the president, Do Mo Jung, lived in Pusan, which was not far from Fukuoka. Less than two hours by air from Tōkyō. I asked him what style the girls were studying, and he said it was Shotokan. I said that I had studied Shotokan and that, though I was just a WKF judge, perhaps I could help these girls so that the next time they represented their country, they would be able to do so at least feeling comfortable with the rules and what would be expected of them. Mr. Jung thought my proposal was a good idea. Then I told him I needed to seek the permission of the Canadian Federation president. James Johnson did not object to the idea.

However, time passed, and a Christmas card arrived from Mr. Jung, which pointed out that I had not "fulfilled my promise" of visiting Pusan. Therefore, I arranged to go in the spring during a long weekend.

Mr. Jung met me at the airport and said he had brought his car. First of all, he forgot where he had left it, and the little dark blue Daihatsu was very difficult to find in the pitch-black parking lot. Mr. Jung also had difficulty navigating his way out of the airport and ended up driving down a dead-end lane with a no-entry sign clearly pasted at the entrance, and was cheerfully ignored by my host, who spoke to me in Japanese. I do not speak Korean, and he knew little English, so Japanese was the lingua franca.

After driving around in circles for about 40 minutes, we ended up back at the airport terminal, and he finally asked someone the way out. To accomplish this, he stopped and asked me to roll down the window on my side of the car. He then leaned on my thigh and let loose a rapid fire of Korean to a passerby. I resented this and shifted in my seat. We finally made it out onto an open road where his driving skills seemed to endanger every other driver on the road except himself, as he would drive in the fast lane below the minimum speed limit. Large trucks hurtled down on us with screeching brakes and honking horns that would eventually cause Mr. Jung to swerve into an adjacent lane, regardless of oncoming traffic. He was the most terrifying driver I had ever experienced, so I asked him how long he had been driving.

"About thirty years," he replied.

The route to the hotel seemed to be endless, and I tried to discuss subjects relating to his karate, the Korean Federation, and karate in Korea as opposed to Taekwondo. However, a typical conversation ran like this.

"How many people do you expect to show up at the seminar tomorrow?" I asked.

"Oh, don't worry about that now.

Foster san, I don't understand why you are not married".

"Oh, don't worry about that, Jung san. So, getting back to the seminar, where will it be held?" I asked.

"My dōjō. Foster san, human beings need not only food and water for life. Must have

sex. Otherwise, get sick," he said.

"As you can see, Jung san, I am perfectly healthy. As to your dōjō, how many students do you have?" I asked.

"Not so much. You know, in Korea, a man can be married, still, it is OK to have another woman."

"Thank you for your insight into Korean culture, Mr. Jung. About the seminar tomorrow..." I diverted.

"Seminar tomorrow. Let's go dancing tonight," he proposed.

"No, thank you. I am very tired, as I have come straight from my office today, and I would like to get settled into my hotel. Thank you. If you can kindly tell me what time the seminar starts and what you wish me to teach, I will prepare a schedule."

If no dancing, how about drinking?

I was already regretting my decision to come here, but no flights out of Pusan were available at that time of night, so I was locked in this disagreeable situation. And it was all my own fault.

At the hotel, he offered to share my room for the night. I refused as politely as possible. He said that his wife wouldn't mind.

I pointed out that his relationship with his family was not my concern and if he wished to stay in the same hotel, it would not be in my room. I had to shove him away from the door because he kept trying to squeeze into the room. I finally slammed and locked the door.

I was disgusted and angry with his behaviour. This was the President of the Korean Karate. What did he think when his girls completed their performance? Did he think that I offered to go to Pusan on the pretext of a sex tour with him as an obliging stud? I shuddered to imagine what fantasies he had envisioned.

The next day, he appeared at 1 pm and took me to his dōjō, which was close to the hotel. No one was there. Finally, one student arrived wearing a tracksuit. He sat down in the outer office and started to smoke. I asked Mr. Jung if I could call the Canadian President so that he would know where I was. I told Mr. Jung that it was important to check in so he would know I arrived safely. No problem. The request did not faze Mr. Jung.

After 30 minutes, another fellow shuffled in. He and Mr. Tracksuit scuffed off to change into blue and red *doboks* (Taekwondo uniforms), respectively. They started kicking a heavy bag from the ceiling of the padded *dojang*. This place was clearly geared to Taekwondo. The floor was covered with filthy, gouged foam rubber with taped lesions all over it. An aging couch with disgorged grey stuffing near the entrance, conveniently located near a TV and an overflowing ashtray, should spectators become bored with the activity on the floor. A weight training system rusted heavily in a large alcove on one side of the room, and the walls were decorated with Taekwondo posters. Eventually, an assortment of colored polyester *doboks* (cotton uniforms) with ankle-length pants and jackets with several patches tied up with calf-length belts joined the class. By 3 pm, there were about eight men and no women. I asked Mr. Jung if more people would be coming. No, that was it, so I could start teaching the class now. I guess this was not for the benefit of his female students, after all.

We did Shotokan basics. This was news to each of the students, most of whom were very fit, well-muscled, flexible, and willing to try hard, but they had been schooled in Taekwondo. Mr. Jung said that they were doing Korean Shotokan and told me not to answer any questions if they asked.

"So, what is Korean Shotokan, exactly?" I asked.

"Moo Duk Kwan", he replied.

Mr. Jung had learned Shotokan in the 1960s, so he learned the names of the Shotokan forms and the sequence of moves. He claimed that he tried to keep the Shotokan that he learned "pure", meaning he taught some *kata*.

However, he had also studied some brands of Taekwondo for the past thirty years. He also said that he had no teachers from Japan since the

1960s and had studied by himself.

The girls who had represented Korea at the World Cup were his students. Furthermore, his dōjō was the sole member of the Korean Karate Federation. OK, now I understand everything.

His students asked me to teach them Kanku Dai and Bassai Dai. First, I asked them to show me their versions. One fellow was particularly adept. He might have been around twenty years old and had a positive outlook. The *kata* were recognizable as named but might have been acceptable in a Korean event in the deep south of the USA.

We spent several hours on Bassai Dai. At the end of the class, I asked if anyone had any questions. One person asked about a technical point in the kata and another about a *bunkai*. However, when another asked if I understood anything about the history of karate, Mr. Jung told me in Japanese not to answer that question. Presumably, he did not know any of it.

Talk about the mushroom principle! The students were kept in the dark and fed nonsense to avoid exposing the fact that their teacher understood very little about Shotokan karate. After the class, Mr. Jung presented me with a 4th Dan Taekwondo certificate along with another certificate that says I have permission to teach the style. A nice pair of souvenirs with no value.

I suggested to Mr. Jung that all the students go out with us to eat or drink or whatever, but it was not to be. Mr. Jung had other plans.

There was something unusual about someone who deliberately kept his students away from a visiting instructor, so I tried to insist on spending some social time with the students. However, my intention fell on deaf ears.

He drove me to a small, dimly lit room on the second floor of a cabaret-type place that was all dark wood and stained plush red velvet seats and banquettes. The place reeked of stale cigarette smoke, spilled beer, cheap perfume, and mold. A long, narrow table filled up most of it, and subdued red lighting fixtures covered with dust caused me to have an immediate coughing fit. I was introduced to the occupants of the room, of whom three each were males and females and aged below fifty years. The males appraised me as I was introduced and given bowls containing slices of raw ginseng and honey to dip them in. Cherry Brandy was produced for me, and the party continued on its merry way. The loudest of the women spoke some Japanese, and the quietest of the men spoke some English. Thus, communication was established.

The fun wore on until about 1 am, by which time the conversation had been reduced to the basest levels of humor, with the Mama san eventually baring her left breast and offering it to the person seated next to her to squeeze. The group began speculating about it, and I deftly avoided asking very rude personal questions for about ten minutes. After exhausting that line of entertainment, everyone stood up and prepared to leave. I was so grateful to get out of this suffocating den and looked forward to returning to the hotel, which did not happen. The party was now going to continue in a room in another part of the basement of the same building for Korean karaoke.

So now I had to sing. I sang. So did everyone else, with great gusto and feeling, until about 3 am. The party for Mr. Jung and his former high school buddies finally shuddered to a stop, and I was taken back to my hotel; another offers from my host to stay overnight in my room was deftly thwarted.

He decided that I would teach class the next day for two hours, then I would accompany him to a high school reunion.

Once again, I met all the characters from the previous night, this time wearing baseball caps and playing ball games in a dusty dirt field. I was taken to a stall covered by an awning, where unidentifiable meat buzzing with flies was slapped on a plate by bare hands, along with some kimchee.

I then asked for some time out to go shopping for *omiage* (presents) to take back to Japan, since I was having such a good time here in Pusan.

Fortunately, this netted some escape from this lecher, and off I went to visit the downtown area, blessedly, alone. The streets of Pusan were filthy, dusty, and decrepit. The shops were mean, and the merchandise was cheap. Inside the one and only department store was another world of experience—air conditioning, cleanliness, uniforms and excellent customer service.

Given that Pusan is only three hours by ferry from gleaming, pristine Fukuoka, few Japanese visitors were evident. Given the manners of most Japanese people, service levels that must be the best in the world, a taste for branded goods, fashion and aesthetics, it is easy to infer why they might not shop in Pusan.

Having obtained some souvenirs, I returned to the hotel to enjoy reading a book in peaceful solitude. No sooner had a few pages been turned than the phone rang. My host kindly inquired as to what time I would like to eat. No hurry.

He came to collect me about two hours later and told me that we were going to go on a short sightseeing tour. I was recklessly driven to a less mean side of the city in the Daihatsu that stopped at a curved beach near a Hyatt hotel. Unlike Japanese beaches, all kinds of recreational activities were in full swing, with people doing gymnastics on parallel bars wearing suits and ties, couples walking along the water edge, picnics, ball games and children running around in the setting sun. The beachfront in the waning light looked very romantic, and Mr. Jung wasted no time in asking further highly invasive personal questions and offering himself to relieve me of whatever frustrations he had decided I must have.

He took me to eat raw fish in a restaurant by the water's edge. You choose your fish, and then the staff catches and cuts it up for you, just like Japanese sashimi. Unlike Japanese sashimi, it is eaten wrapped up in a shiso leaf, accompanied by a pungent miso-based brown sauce and a whole raw garlic clove. Mr. Jung washed down this delicacy with Korean rice wine. After that, he insisted on going for a drink or two in the Hyatt. I wondered when torture by lascivious bonehead would end. He wished to go to another drinking venue, but by now, I understood that the only words Mr. Jung understood were black and white and that he literally had to be slapped in the face with them; otherwise, he would just grin and continue his line of inappropriate questions.

I demanded to return to the hotel and stated that I wished to sleep unaccompanied. Finally, he got the message, not before informing me that instead of doing any karate on the following and mercifully last day in his presence, he took me to visit a historic site about two hours' drive from Pusan! The thought of being in a confined space for a total of four hours with this loathsome creature was almost inconceivable, and so I asked him if he would not rearrange my flight back to Tōkyō instead of wasting his valuable time out on a workday to go sightseeing. He looked pained and insisted.

The next day, I packed my bags and checked out of the hotel by the time he arrived. He tentatively offered to pay my hotel bill, with not too much enthusiasm. I paid it myself as I was not going to be obliged to him.

Thus started one of the most foul days of my life. Completely in the control of this worm for about 12 straight hours, I thought death was going to arrive in the form of an 18-wheeler, if not by choking to death due to the close proximity to this man in his suffocating little Daihatsu. Most of the day was spent white-knuckling and removing the right arm of Mr. Jung, which tended to accidentally fall off the steering wheel, onto my left thigh.

Most of the day was spent with Mr. Jung, getting quite lost because he was ignoring direction signs, so that he was forced to lean on my thighs several times to ask people for directions.

The site was the tombs of the Shilla dynasty kings, a huge preserved and reconstructed historic area consisting of a village with several stone Buddha carvings, artifacts, tumuli, temples and shrines. The day could have been so interesting, but Mr. Jung cast a pall over it and a gathering lightning storm further diluted the enjoyment of the site. However, I collected enough information to perhaps return there one day under more agreeable circumstances.

After a two-hour drive to Pusan in a powerful thunderstorm, followed by a two-hour traffic jam from the edges of the city to wherever he was taking me, I finally found myself checking into a hotel that was located quite near the airport. My flight the following day left at 7 am.

I obtained the key to my room and walked towards the elevator. Mr. Jung said:

"I will help you with your baggage, then maybe we could go to a disco?"

"No, thank you, I can manage myself." I replied.

"Meet here, then we go to disco."

"No disco. Thank you for the offer." I kindly refused.

"How about dinner?"

"No, thank you. You have been most kind, but you must be very tired after the long drive and sightseeing and frankly, I am not terribly hungry.

What about a drink then? Coffee, maybe?"

Thank heavens the elevator arrived as I entered it alone and turned to face Mr. Jung for the last time.

"Foster san, are you sure you wouldn't like even a snack.........?"

I was so incensed over the weekend, disgusted with the scenario, and so angry at myself that it was interfering with my ability to breathe.

I was never so grateful to arrive at Narita airport. I had returned home from an alien experience. If it had been North America, a sexual harassment lawsuit would have been lodged. In Korea, nothing unusual had happened. Mr. Jung, at times, seemed rather perplexed that I had refused every single one of his endless unwanted advances.

James Johnson also had no sympathy and thought it rather naïve of me to imagine that I would go to such a country alone and expect to be taken seriously.

Therefore, I learned a few new lessons from the experience. Karate traveler Tip 1: always visit another country for karate purposes, accompanied by a male unless women are organizing the visit.

Reflections on Meiji Dōri beach, Sugamo

Sometimes, during hot weekends, I would sit out on my balcony on the crossroads of Meiji Dōri and Naka Sen Dō, catch some rays and listen to cicadas and crows compete with motorbikes, scooters, cars, trucks, fire engines, police vehicles and ambulances that hurtle through the intersection called Nishi Sugamo. During "Traffic Safety Week", police would blow whistles every time the stoplights changed color. From 8 am until 5 pm, seven days a week, shrill blasts would be added to the cacophony .... and...... just in case you forgot the time, loudspeakers attached to trees would emit electronic chimes followed by a feminine voice admonishing the entire ward that, "This is the Kita Ward Office. It is 6 o'clock, and time to return home. Do not lose anything and do not forget anything." Quiet moments for reflection in a hectic life.

The eight years that I lived in my tiny apartment gave me plenty of opportunities to practice karate with several instructors with a range of personalities and teaching styles.

It was not until training at the JKA in Tōkyō that I became acutely aware of training differences in that environment. The air was thick with palpable tension. There was a changing room for women that was large enough to linger in and have a chat, yet no one spoke to each other or smiled at each other. The students perhaps did not try because they were scared of a language problem, but there was no excuse for the foreigners, who mostly spoke English as their first language. While waiting for a class to finish and the next to begin, if a Japanese instructor walked by, women would stop doing whatever and respectfully bow with a loud "Ossu" and look at him straight in the eye like a suppliant waiting for a pat on the head. Once on the floor, the intent of some foreign male students was apparently to impress various sensei with their power, strength, and total muscle tension. That type of individual rarely considered the height, weight, sex or experience of any person they had to work with, and quite often, a smirk of satisfaction could be seen fleeting across their faces, having actually smacked some Japanese 8th *kyu* white belt in the face or a foreign woman in the chest. If an 85 kg 2nd Dan with about seven to ten years of experience feels good about displaying physical or technical superiority over an individual with only a few months of training, then I think that they are not practicing karate. Malice is dangerous and the atmosphere in the dōjō was air. It only takes one unsupervised individual in a class to produce a learning experience that one might not have bargained for after paying for a little plastic card with the world-renowned symbol on the front. The microcosm in which these egos thrives allegedly has a system of checks and balances that are supposed to maintain equilibrium in Japan; a hierarchy.

This works very well in Japan, since everyone has been born into it, played in it, schooled in it, works, lives and thinks in it. Every aspect of a Japanese person's life is influenced by their position in a number of groups. Everyone is a senpai (senior) to somebody, a *dohai* (same level) to some and a kohai (junior) to others. If you are female, you defer to everyone. Social status is reflected in the correct use of the language, manners, levels of politeness, respect, and obsequiousness, as well as in body language. For example, the depth of a bow and the length of time during which the waist is bent, efforts to carry bags, open doors and the like.

It is common for one 8th Dan to call another "Hako-chan" (chan is an affectionate suffix given, for example, to children, pets, very close friends), when "Hako-chan" is, in fact sixty-two years old, a doctor and an 8th dan, but is junior to another 8th dan because he arrived at university one day after the other … forty years ago. Abbreviating names can also be another means of showing affection and position in the hierarchy.

If "Hako-chan" talks about the other 8th Dan, he might call him Arakawa sensei. It is assured that each knows his place in the hierarchy. There is no question that the relationship is carved in stone, even if the senior person had remained at 3rd Dan while the junior went on to achieve 8th Dan.

When a student surpasses a teacher, the teacher is forever referred to as *"sensei"*. Thus, your junior high school arithmetic teacher is called Suzuki *sensei* by his ex-student Takahashi kun, regardless of the latter obtaining a PhD in string theory and becoming a Nobel laureate. Suzuki *sensei* might well consider that Ta-kun (affectionate suffix for males and individuals involved in group activities) has done quite well for himself, but it does not change the inviolate nature of the relationship hierarchy.

There has to be a way of tempering the egos of the Ta-kun so that they do not negatively affect the harmonious status quo of a group. Similarly, it is quite possible that when Ta-kun attended junior high school, he was subject to or inflicted *ijime* (bullying), a common occurrence in Japan, where outlets for individual expression are scant. Sadly, individual expression of bullied students is exhibited too frequently in the form of suicide by hanging. A note might remain to tell the tale, but it is too late. What happens to bullies when they go to high school, university and then onto a corporate job? What happens to their victims as they travel their life course? Where does the arrogance go? Bullying, however, is not only an individual activity. "Harmonious" groups use bullying for entertainment.

During the early 1990s in Japan, the media were full of the story of a man who established a boarding school for fourteen to eighteen-year-olds with learning disabilities or who dropped out of school. He seemed to be reasonably successful until two of his charges were found dead in a locked railway cargo carriage. They had been there for three straight days or thereabouts, without food and water, at the height of the summer. They had died of heat exhaustion. The temperature inside the carriage was ~ 50°C. They had been caught smoking cigarettes. This was against the school rules and so the teacher defended his choice of punishment as being adequate for the crime. Despite his vigorous defense of his teaching methods in court, he was jailed for a long time, and his school was closed. I wondered what kind of a creature this teacher was. Typical of media in Japan, no personal details were published in the English press.

Also, in the early 1990s, a teacher killed a junior high schoolgirl by closing the school gates on her neck as she tried to run into the playground. The teacher's defense? His action was justified because his job was to ring the school bell and close the school gates at 9 a.m. The pupil was one minute past 9 a.m. and late. He was only doing his job, and it was not his fault that the girl was late. Fortunately, the court thought otherwise.

On a more mundane level, a foreigner visiting the JKA was changing out of her gi, which exposed Victoria's Secret underwear. This caused an envious university student wearing a black belt to comment, "It must be nice to wear whatever you want under your gi. My senpai only allows us to wear white underwear." Yikes!

I wondered about teacher training in Japan? I don't know. I understand that schools and universities in Japan are places where young people go to absorb facts and learn to fit in with a group. At the cost of personal development, independent thought and social skills, Japan is indeed a harmonious society, which is safer than many and strictly policed. But what of young folks with repressed hopes or dreams? Do they have any? Did they ever have any? Do they now? What happens to them when they are put in positions of authority?

Nevertheless, trouble tends to be avoided during social interaction in Japan. People will smile when faced with a difficult situation and, more often than not, remain silent. Foreigners can sometimes wade through this attitude and trample all over small sensitivities with loud mouths. Do the Japanese bow to the overbearing, self-righteous, noisy, insensitive foreign ego? Does the foreigner feel empowered?

Here in the Ebisu shrine to the god of modern karate, the attitudes were poised to continue into the 21st century. What would Funakoshi have thought? Did he have a sense of humor? Was he a compassionate teacher? He seemed to be, according to his books. He even said that karate would benefit weak people, such as women and children. Given the times and the environment in which Funakoshi lived, he was a visionary. He was not a big man; all photographic evidence suggests that he was under 5 feet tall. I have difficulty pairing a power ego with Funakoshi based on available translated reports. I like to think that he would have been appalled at the two horrifying incidents described above.

At any rate, the Shotokan was established by a teacher, presumably a man of humility, compassion, and ambition. How was his art of protecting the weak from the strong and the victim from the oppressor translated into the strong conquering the weak and the oppressor taunting their victim?

Was there a fundamental flaw in the art, the teacher, the process of dissemination, the system, or the students?

Takushoku University

This was the source of a generation of Shotokan instructors. I wondered if an entire generation of karate instructors were lost during World War II. There is a gap between the colonization of the Western world by the Takudai graduates of the 60s and the Funakoshi generation of founders. And what of the Takushoku graduates now?

Takushoku is a private university in Tōkyō. It does not rank among the top 20 most prestigious Japanese schools. The main campus is in the Bunkyō Ku, and a satellite campus is in Hachiōji city.

It was originally named the Taiwan Association School and was established to contribute to the development of Taiwan. It was renamed as the Oriental Association Vocational School in 1907 before gaining its current name in 1918. Takushoku translates as "development and industrialization" as well as "colonization," that is, of Taiwan and Korea, which Japan had intended to "industrialize".

Given the rise of Japanese nationalism before the end of World War II, it is easy to imagine that barbaric activities that passed for karate training continued into dōjō during the early post-war period. Kindness, compassion, tolerance, humility and wisdom were unlikely features of military conscripts. The Japanese government dissolved the university at the end of WWII due to its powerful support of militarism. Obviously, it reopened later, as it had 1,000 international students, five faculties and graduate schools. It also houses the Institute of World Studies, and is the only university think-tank in Japan for international relations and security.

Its karate club was founded around 1924, and many world-renowned karate instructors and athletes emerged from it.

However, a student died as recently as the late 1980s in the Takushoku University dōjō because he failed to present his senpai with a suitably clean and pristine karate gi. The dōjō that produced some of the most renowned and respected Shotokan karate masters had finally reached its nadir.

So that was the legacy, innocent followers of karate dō in the 1960s and early 70s. We thought they were some kind of gods. We low-income earners with a need for inexpensive exercise had no idea that universities are not all created equal and that what we were being taught was post-war right-wing fanaticism disguised as culture. Inscrutable Japanese! Mysterious Asian philosophy! Perhaps they had to be inscrutable because if anyone got close enough to anyone to scrape their mental surface, they were unlikely to hear the sound of one hand clapping.

Everyone was a samurai descendant. None were sons of grocers or leather tanners. A real samurai, right here in your living room with the doilies and Earl Grey tea. And we believed it, lock, stock and barrel. Due to basking in the glory days of colonization by Shotokan, we were all *"samurai"* too. We were part of the continuum and the more we trained and the more abuse we tolerated, the more we became part of our own mythology. See how noble, righteous and strong we are!

Look at the punishments and bruises endured, wisdom obtained, and obstacles overcome! We are karate practitioners, heirs to a noble art, a strategy for life. Look! She who passes by on the street is a guardian of exotic secrets.

A Black Belt!

Whispers behind hands, sideways glances and reflections in store windows.

It was all a facade. The supreme master of the moment might have just graduated from JKA instructor school, having started training at Takudai. How could we know that he had perhaps only four years of training, admittedly on a daily basis, but in the pseudo-military, quasi-homosexual environment of a sadomasochistic, university boy's club?

What did they learn about social interaction? What did they know about foreigners? What did they know about women? What did they know the behaviour in other cultures? What did we know about Japanese society and culture? Not much. We did not know that we were being colonized and were victims of our delusions.

A Japanese woman is your mother, daughter, wife, relative, or personal slave. In the company where I work, the women always eat lunch together regardless of age or position in the company. Usually, they bring their lunches in tiny boxes or buy them locally and eat them in a small room in the office. All the men go out to one of several local restaurants every day. The women are responsible for making sure there is hot water in the Thermoses for tea and that the coffee in the machine is hot. Some of them serve tea to the men in their division. Interaction is allowed within the guidelines of the job—still, neither group can contemplate a purely platonic relationship with a coworker of the other sex that might include lunch. If such individuals are seen going to lunch, the assumption is always that there is romance/impending marriage in the air. Since many people meet their future spouses at work, they are generally rather discreet about their relationships.

Sexual abuse of female office staff only emerged from the closet during the early 90s. Some senior managers of "traditional" Japanese companies cannot see anything wrong with overt sexual advances to junior female staff, who are supposed to smile good-naturedly in their company uniforms and accept that being groped is all part of the job. Hmm....

A complaint from women in the Kobe Osaka area that they were being harassed by perverts on trains was ignored. The railway management pointed out that a poster designed to prevent such activity would upset the male paying passengers on the trains and make them feel *uncomfortable*. This was the 1990s.

Thirty years ago, the attitudes would not have been much different. Put a Takushoku boy who has spent his life among female relatives or slaves and all his free time in a ramshackle building stinking of yellowish, tattered gi permeated with mildew, sweat and blood in Paris, London, Hamburg. Consider that in the 60s, to be called a "playboy" in Japan was a compliment and that the word *"lolikon"* (Lolita complex) was much bandied about. The latter refers to the fascination of the Japanese male with prepubescent girls, which continued well into the 90s and beyond. This might explain why women of marriageable age sound and act like young girls, as that is what seems to attract putative mates.

Did the expat Japanese karate instructor cope? Well, *"gaman suru"* (perseverance), of course, he did. There was no choice. He could rarely go to Japan, as that would be an admission of defeat, but his soul and return societal conditioning never left Japan.

The first order of business might be not to acquire the local language but rather to acquire a wife. Preferably Japanese, so that rice can be cooked, and children propagated to carry on the samurai bloodlines, undiluted by foreign genes. Contacts would help to find a space to become a dōjō. A sympathetic local with pretensions to Japanese understanding might help out, becoming enslaved in the process for at least a few years until the mystique had worn off, or enough teeth had been lost, sacrifices made and unrewarded.

Having set up a Japanese microenvironment consisting of a dōjō and a home complete with a wife, the new expat performed demonstrations, and a native speaker perhaps marketed him. Soon, the difficult times were history, and students flooded the gates of dōjō, ready and willing to believe that everything that was yelled by the master was the truth, the whole truth and nothing but the truth. Verbatim! Enthralled, naïve karate practitioners were ready to absorb anything from a Japanese "authority".

Having set up a quasi-cult with a reasonable following and a supreme being at the helm sometimes led to earthly rather than godly activities such as fraud, embezzlement, sexual harassment, and lies. All of these have been tolerated at one time or another and even when exposed, the instructor, especially with a Japanese face, has often been charismatic enough to retain a reasonable following.

For example, a karate instructor in Ontario, Canada, was charged with fraud in the early 1980s. He was caught in a scam that involved printing lottery tickets that he sold to his students. The prize was a trip to Japan and the proceeds of the lottery would be used to pay for the travel expenses of the so-called founder of the style group to visit Canada. A check of the bag that contained the winning number revealed that it contained only tickets with the same number as the winner…. who was absent and, in fact, did not exist. Even when this low-level fraud was exposed, students continued to follow this master, who went on to perpetrate more abuses on his loyal students, including issuing fake black belt certificates and giving his students titles in organizations such as the World Karate Federation (WKF), of which neither this "master" nor his organizations were members. Yet members of the organization he established still regard him as a saint. Perhaps he was repaying Canadians for isolating him and his mother in BC camps during WW II. This person passed away in the year 2000… but I still have the newspaper report about the fraud.

I had to consider that morality in Japan is a different concept from what is embraced by Western Christian democracies. Activities considered corrupt according to Christian morality help Japanese society to flow smoothly. Much obsequious fawning over superiors, playing on sympathies for favors, and massive abuse of funds that a Westerner would consider bribery, in Japan, is considered an advanced thank you for ensuring one's success. When people get married, the guests give money to attend the reception. The closer you are to the bride or groom, the more you pay. But the donations help to pay for the event. When invited to a funeral, the attendee signs in, and a monetary contribution is noted in a ledger. This again balances the cost of the funeral.

Huge amounts of money flow from lay Buddhist corporations (a fine contradiction, "religious corporation") to political parties. Middlemen increase the prices of domestic consumer goods so that the Japanese pay more for a Sony TV than a North American, and huge taxes are levied on imported goods that the country cannot or will not produce for itself. Unreasonable taxes are levied on rice so that Japanese consumers pay the highest prices in the world to greedy farmers who know perfectly well that this is an unrealistic situation, but, naturally, wish it to continue. How many ways can I defraud my fellow countrymen and women? Let me count.

Maybe it is reasonable to fool happy foreign followers by bestowing fake qualifications and titles for fees, of course. After all, where is the harm? Everyone is content. Everyone is a winner. The Japanese sensei makes money—hand over fist—and the students continue paying for more unenlightening, expensive seminars, to substantiate their titles and grades with worthless certificates.

When the organization became large enough, with acolytes numbering in the thousands and scattered over a continent, the successful instructor might then ask the Japanese *honbu* for an assistant.

The assistant might be located in the master's foreign HQ *dōjō*, or be sent to a region far from it. In any case, the following was likely to happen.

The assistant would invariably chafe under pressure from the Japanese master and the *honbu* (headquarters), who expected money to roll in and defect from the *honbu* to start his organization or would be used by the master to generate more money while he participated less and pocketed the income.

Among the JKA instructors in the UK during the 70s, these situations would occurred frequently and eventually led to the formation of several factions, each headed by a Japanese instructor, which ultimately fragmented the once unified group. Several of them left the JKA but continued to teach until their death. Now, having seen the behaviour of Japanese instructors in their country, there was no incentive for a 1st Dan to continue training under the yoke of any Japanese instructor when he could start his own club or organization within minutes of achieving 1st Dan. In Scotland, we often requested a guest instructor to run a seminar and have the instructor reconfirm the details, including costs. We would meet him at the railway station only to find that his assistant would step off the train. We were expected to pay the assistant and treat him exactly as if he were the master. This happened several times, and though the assistants were competent instructors in their own right, we felt cheated as our expectations were not met. Furthermore, the assistant was presumably supposed to go back and report to his senior and hand over all the loot gained by this misrepresentation and his work. I imagine that the assistants did not feel very good about this sort of activity either, as at least two of those who came to Aberdeen started their own organizations, and two left the country.

The temptation not to take advantage of a potentially highly lucrative situation must have been challenging. I do not see anything wrong with making a living from karate, or any other martial art. There is no need to fool people.

How many dōjō are there with a karate instructor who has not, at one time or another, had an intimate relationship with at least one student or who has never made disparaging or sexually harassing remarks about a student under their control? More than we might think – remember the Dōjō Kun?

This is all about abuse of power. Mishandling money or having close personal relationships with students constitutes the dark side of pyramidal hierarchies. Karate practitioners are no less or more noble or moral than any other group. I believe that they might even have more scope for abuse than a non-martial art or sport due to a structure that is based on Japanese militarism. The issue is further compounded in the West by the professor, who, in his free time, says, "Call me Jim; we're not in the classroom now". I think this confuses people. Sensei here, Jim there.

We call this person sensei (teacher) inside this room, but Fred in another room, so he must oscillate between being an authority figure one minute and a regular guy the next.

Now, what about Fred's girlfriend, a student who has trained for a few years, is anxious to please sensei in any way, shape, or form for reasons not necessarily associated with the love of technical improvement?

Some dōjō contain 20%–100% women and girls, taught by men throughout the world—a great opportunity for power abuse.

Here is an example. Justine was an extremely attractive, petite woman in her late twenties who had started training in karate in Florida. Her mother was French Canadian, and her father was American. Early on in life, Justine's mother decided she was done living with her husband and four children and returned to Quebec. Justine was the eldest of the four, so at age thirteen or so, her life became that of a mother to her three siblings, and who knows what her relationship with her father was like. For several years, she persevered, finished high school in the USA, then went on to university. Finally, she graduated with a master's degree. By the time she found a dōjō in Montreal, she was already 1st *kyu* (brown belt). The instructor of the dōjō was Japanese, not much older than Justine, and she found him quite attractive. He was already involved with a 1st kyu (brown belt) student in the dōjō, but soon transferred his affections to Justine. They were similar types in a way. She even physically resembled what his female alter ego might look like. Justine was a tiny, Caucasian version of her instructor, with high cheekbones, cornflower blue eyes, and an athletic physique. She was far more intelligent than Emmeline, the current girlfriend, and, therefore, a better intellectual match for the *Sensei*. She studied diligently under this instructor, grading to 2nd *Dan* in his organization in the early 1980s. Eventually, she moved in with him. Neither of them had much money, but she had learned how to conserve finances from her childhood days and was frugal in every sense of the word. She could prepare delicious meals out of scant ingredients, design and sew her own clothing, and thus was nonchalantly chic on a very strict budget. Living together would not cause financial hardship but rather alleviate it for both of them. A one-bedroom apartment would be sufficient. He had little in the way of possessions, and she mostly owned books.

He discovered a better opportunity out west and decided to move there. He did not tell anyone about the fact that he would be followed by his girlfriend until about the day before she arrived and that allowances would have to be made. He had a peculiar attitude when discussing her. He said that he made it quite clear to her that if she decided to accompany him out West, he would not be responsible for her if she wanted to accompany him. The message should have been loud and clear.

She arrived, followed a month later by her possessions, apparently shipped by moose. He made her the secretary of his new dōjō, which already had a secretary, but he felt he could trust Justine more. This did not go down well with the displaced secretary. Justine lacked people skills and fiercely guarded her relationship with her sensei. Any attempts at friendliness from anyone in the dōjō were immediately interpreted as threats. She interpreted this as "trying to get closer to sensei through friendship with me", or the person is "only trying to be friendly with me because I am sensei's girlfriend. Eventually, people stopped trying, and she and her partner became very isolated. People would invite them to parties, such as those around Christmas. Either Justine or her sensei then invariably questions who would participate, how many would be there, what the dress code would be, what kind of people they would be, what time would be best to arrive, how long they should stay, whether a gift was expected and if so, what to bring. These were hardly embassy functions where a diplomatic incident might result from wearing the wrong tie. The key was to determine whether or not the participants included karate practitioners; if so, this couple would invariably decline invitations. Over time, they alienated themselves from the students and only contacted someone if they needed something. People did not like to feel used, so their social life dwindled to a few enduring sycophants.

Despite being fluently bilingual and educationally qualified, Justine failed to secure suitably remunerative employment, so it was left to sensei to earn the income that would bankroll his preference for status cars, elegant clothing and other image enhancements. Pressure on the karate organization to support him financially increased, while communication between either he or Justine and the group became ever more fractured.

Justine notwithstanding, this instructor approached at least five other female students with the line, "No one else understands me except you". It worked on two of them for a while.

The three that this approach failed to charm told me about it and were quite shocked.

One was very confused, she had given this man unconditional respect, and one day drove him home after training because he did not have a car at the time He put his hands on her knee and asked her to come into his apartment for tea. She refused and asked him about Justine. He replied that Justine was not available at the moment. She was disgusted at the thought of being a temporary stand-in for Justine, but was perhaps torn by some attraction to the man. When she asked me what she should do, I told her that she had better quickly sort out her feelings for this man and for karate and figure out where she wanted to put him in her life. I said that if she liked him, go ahead and have an affair, but consider the consequences and how long she could expect such a relationship to last. Looking at the worst-case scenario, she would be history as soon as either Justine reappeared or something more to his liking showed up. In that situation, I asked her to think about how she would feel taking orders from him in the dōjō. Could she continue training with this man after she had satisfied his temporary needs?

She made her decision and avoided one-to-one situations with him, but continued to train under his guidance. She soon quit karate. I later discovered that she had a history of an affair with another karate instructor at an earlier stage in her karate career, which left her rather bitter and with a low opinion of that person. The effect of that experience influenced her decision to join and train with Justine's boyfriend in the first place. It must have seemed like deja vu.

On the other hand, the relationship between Justine and her sensei ended with her departure from Canada. She spent time abroad, becoming trilingual. The sensei returned to Japan and had nothing more to do with Justine, having found far younger playmates.

Tōkyō, December 1995

There I was, bundling up to go to training for that second attempt at 5th Dan when an inebriated Osaka phoned up to invite me to join Takahashi, Katy and Taniyama at an *izakaya* (local, inexpensive tapas/drinking establishment) in Sugamo. I regretted that I was on my way to training but might be able to join them afterward, if they were still there. Osaka sensei had finally found that my claims to passing the D level (lowest) of the JKA examiner, judge, and teacher exams were true. It had taken him just one and a half years to confirm this and issue a little plastic card, which had cost me about $500 Canadian at the current exchange rates. I wanted that card as a receipt. Mr. Osaka seemed to feel quite guilty about this, the depth of such feelings being, of course, directly associated with the amount of alcohol consumed. The thought of spending a couple of hours in a smoke-filled *izakaya* with a Japanese trio unable to string words together without slurs and blurs did not fill me with excitement. However, I would have liked to see Osaka sensei torture himself over the incompetence of the JKA bureaucracy. By the time I arrived there, he had staggered off, so I had to go to the JKA to collect my $500 card later during the week. That was when I decided my days with the JKA were over.

Thanks to Hiroko, the following week found Katy and I seated in the VIP section at the Nippon Budōkan, between Joesefina Vequillas, executive assistant to the Philippine Karatedo Federation. We were introduced formally to the assembled masses of the Budōkan as being from the El Salvador Karate Federation.

Everyone knew she trained with Mr. Nishiyama. Here we were, just in time for an obento (boxed lunch) courtesy of the JKF and a movie about Ryoichi Sasakawa, another arch-enemy of Nishiyama sensei and the financial base of the JKF and WKF, who had passed away earlier in 1995 at the age of 92 years. Before the massive video production extolling the contributions of the late Mr. Sasakawa to furthering worldwide interest in karate, Eiichi Eriguchi sensei, who was celebrating his 80th birthday, provided a speech about Mr. Sasakawa, a Class A war criminal turned philanthropist.

Eriguchi sensei's speech was delivered with his usual flair and energy, which continued even into his walk off the podium, down onto the floor, and back onto the VIP section. Not a wobble or a hesitation. No bending of the upright back, even though he was already fighting cancer and was quite frail. Manuel Vequillas, President of the Philippines Karate Federation, said that Eriguchi sensei was a bomber pilot during the war and his missions included the Philippines. And here we all were, he mused, old enemies, new friends. Eriguchi sensei walked over to me and, while shaking my hand, expressed surprise that I was busy being introduced formally to an assortment of ambassadors and Japanese politicians.

He then whispered in my ear, *"Do you think everyone could hear my speech well enough?"*

I said that as far as I could see, no one had any difficulty understanding his speech, as his voice was sufficiently powerful. It is probably just as well that my Japanese is not subtle enough to add that the PA system was also quite powerful.

All joking and concerns about the source of the Sasakawa billions apart, I could not help feeling that I was witnessing a piece of karate history. I was there! I was a part of it. I was thrilled just sitting in the warm Budōkan, with the lights off, watching this mini-documentary about the history of the JKF and WKF, in the company of people who were involved in the founding of these organizations. I also considered whether good, bad, or imperfect, I was a part of this era and that I had a contribution to make to the karate world.

I was happy to see three women were refereeing, which meant that—surely—it will not be too long before more Japanese women would become WKF referees and judges. They officiated with dignity and had an intimate understanding of the rules. Since Ms. Emiko Yamakage passed 6th Dan in Gōjū Ryū this year, it will soon be difficult for Japanese in positions of authority to use Dan grades as an excuse for not presenting women to the WKF as potential officials.

I enjoyed watching the kata divisions and observing the officials, to see if my armchair judgments coincided with theirs, as well as their general demeanor, gestures, and style.

Because Shito and Shotokan stylists tied for 2nd in the women's kata competition, they each had to perform a tie-breaker kata. The Shito stylist executed a notable Suparimpei (108 hands) and received a score of 26.2. Suddenly, the Chief judge was called to the scoring table and a discussion ensued, while the chief referee walked to the other side of the ring and conferred with someone else. He walked back to the scoring table and called the corner judges. No announcements were forthcoming, and the athlete remained standing at the finish line of her kata. More discussion followed, and the judges returned to their seats. The Chief judge stood up again and conferred with Hakoishi sensei, who the corner judge seated to his left, and a member of the WKF RC for several years.

All five judges then crossed their hands above their heads, which meant "cancel the previous decision". The Gōjū athlete was finally allowed to leave the ring. She had been disqualified. No announcements or explanations. The Shito stylist stepped into the ring to perform her tie-breaker kata. Her score was irrelevant because the silver medal was already hers unless she did something really odd.

Unfortunately, the Gōjū athlete selected the same kata for the tie-breaker that she had already performed in the first round, which was, and still is, against the rules. It was obvious to the audience that Japan's most experienced and qualified judges, including a member of the WKF Referee Council, had made such a mistake. You see, only 12 female and 13 male athletes competed in that particular kata division, which left no room for excuses. The lack of information might have been quite humiliating to the athlete, who was left standing alone in the middle of the ring with all eyes on her, wondering what she had done. Did someone tell her about the competition rules? Had she read them? Did she know, or had she only practiced two kata without considering the possibility of a tie? I don't know. If she did know the rules and only knew two kata, then that raises some questions about the JKF and WKF, as this athlete had scooped a silver medal in the World Championships in Frankfurt earlier in the same year.

It also raised a concern about the nature of subjective judging. To generate a tie, scores must be within a very small range. We junior judges were always being told to avoid this type of situation by spreading scores over a reasonable differential. One judge scored 8.8 for three out of four athletes in the men's kata final, which was hardly a fine example of differentiation.

I wondered how to change this. Everyone, including the spectators, athletes, and judges, expects that scores will be in a certain bandwidth. That includes the Referee Council. However, the judges are placed in a lose-lose situation. If your score differs from those of the other judges, your opinion is challenged, and your ability to judge and your personality will be questioned. So, the messages are conflicting.

"Please try to widen the gap between scores," says the RC.

So, you do.

"Why did you give such a stupid score," says the RC.

So, you don't try to widen the gap.

"Another time-wasting tie-breaker," says the RC.

Anyway, the gold went to the right person.

Katy and I left clutching our JKF socks, mementos of the 23rd All Japan Championships, to change for a party at the Metropolitan Hotel, Ikebukuro, to celebrate the 20th anniversary of Guseikai Takagi dōjō and honor Eriguchi sensei's 80th birthday.

I presented Takagi sensei with a commemorative plaque from Karate BC and Eriguchi sensei with some Canadian smoked salmon. Karaoke at Lonshan in Ohtsuka until the wee hours of the night, but I left due to clouds of second-hand cigarette smoke becoming rather repressive. It really was the most enjoyable tournament day I've ever had in Japan.

Tōkyō, January 1996

It is the year of the rodent. Japan has its 8th prime minister in seven years (Ryutaro Hashimoto) and the Heisei Emperor has ascended the Chrysanthemum throne. I hope Ryutaro Hashimoto will be successful and not forced to resign due to scandals or the failure of some policy or procedure.

Besides being a Kendō 5th dan, he was the President of JKF Wadō Kai. It would not be detrimental to the cause of karate to have a successful prime minister among its ranks.

Speaking of 5th Dans, I now understand why I failed. Toru Arakawa clarified it through action and voice. Satori! Inspiration! Now I have something clear to concentrate on, think about, analyze, break down, and start building up all over again.

When moving forward in a front stance, I lean forward with the upper body first in an effort to generate momentum. It therefore looks as though my butt is sticking out. All my movements look slow, heavy and labored. There is no snap, crackle, and pop. Unfortunately, no one noticed that last year or any of the preceding 27 years.

It finally dawned on me that Nishiyama sensei had already said (more than once) that all movement is generated from the floor. In other words, the back foot pushes while the front foot pulls to initiate movement. This prevents a forward-leaning posture that reduces impact force. Furthermore, the sole of the foot being in pulling contact with the floor ensures stability during the transition of a left (or right) foot stepping into a right (or left) front stance. The backbone must remain naturally vertical, and the physical center of gravity will remain at the same height throughout the forward progression. The muscles of the upper body that are not in use until the moment of impact must remain relaxed and tense simultaneously with those of the rest of the body, only at the moment of impact.

You would think that after 27 years of training, I'd be able to put these principles into practice. Well, as Arakawa sensei said, "If you can fix that and that, then you will become godan" (5th degree black belt).

Good lord! Another twenty-seven years? Can I wait that long?

Simply being told to "make ankle soft" doesn't work. I wanted to ask these 8th dans to make their eyes turn blue.

Don't they know that flexibility is joint-specific and genetically inherited? Apparently not. Nevertheless, I am working on it and will continue to do so. Inflexible ankles confer a life-long struggle to apply the natural laws of the physical world within the framework of karate.

To move forward in a front stance, you can raise your heel, or you can pivot the ball of the front foot before you start to move. If you do not do either of those things, your butt will stick out and your center of gravity will rise or change direction and you will lose in a competition (technical incompetence) and fail dan exams (aesthetics). Something needs to be done. We should not wallow in failure, become discouraged, blame others, or say nasty things about examiners, referees, and judges. We need to face and overcome deficiencies and stay motivated. It is worth a try.

Tōkyō, Spring 1996

Several people over the years have asked me what I have learned from practicing karate, and I can't answer it. Separating the effects of karate training from the effects of aging and life experience is impossible. I have always been independent, curious, stubborn, and cynical since in my childhood.

Subjectively, of course, I might say that karate has given me self-confidence, but I think plenty of that already existed before I ventured into it. I can attest to the effects of kata competition, where you are alone in a ring and you might stumble, trip, forget or miss sequences, or fall, as a means of increasing self-confidence.

One day, I forgot the movements of the kata Unsu just about halfway through. It was too bad because the level of the competition was so low that the audience hushed when I started to perform this kata. At the moment a black hole descended, there was a collective intake of breath, which I realized was from the audience. I walked back to the starting point, bowed, and walked off the ring, having learned more than if I had simply won a medal. I learned that people tend to be sympathetic regarding a mistake. In other words, people want to see good things rather than bad. I also learned that the world will not stop turning because of anything I do or not do, as I am just not that important in the cosmos. Thus, I learned that being upset over losing a competition was futile and, by extrapolation, being upset over anything is likely to be pointless, so why waste the energy? Better to channel it into a positive pathway.

Nothing like doing something alone in front of a crowd to increase confidence. Now, I do not blush, stammer, or even hesitate if someone asks me to sing a karaoke song or do something silly in front of an audience. Some may consider this a conceit, but I think it is simply believing that a global upheaval is unlikely due to a fluffed line in a song or a failure to show the 8th dans whatever the heck it is they want to see. If you make a fool of yourself, there will only be laughter, which will not last long, is not harmful and will soon be forgotten.

Through practical experiences with "self-defense" in Aberdeen, Honolulu, Mexico City, Pusan, Nagoya, and Tōkyō, I discovered that I had indeed learned some emotional control. It is a long way from total, but then emotion makes us all human. I still found talking to my mother and some members of my family extremely difficult. I have little patience with them.

Continuous karate training has undoubtedly maintained a reasonable level of health and fitness over the past five decades, and it is far less expensive than other activities. However, I have learned that men are simply humans, and those who profess lofty ideals might not have lofty morals. The discovery that no man is a god undoubtedly arose from being taken advantage of, allowing it to happen, realizing my role in it, becoming angry, and then accepting that I have only myself to blame. There are choices to make in life, and only one person is responsible. Some mistakes I have made more than once, but never more than twice. Sometimes, it takes a while for things to sink in. Like a kata competition, life is a one-person meandering stream that one can, to some extent, control. I like to think that I have authority over mine. I chose to come to Japan because I was motivated by karate. It turned out to be a very good choice.

I am very independent, often alone, but rarely lonely. I enjoy my own company and do not feel a need for another person to fill a gap in my psyche or be the father of my children, so to speak. There is so much that remains unknown in the world. New places to visit, new friends to make, and new experiences to discover. I walk on the streets of Tōkyō, Bangkok, Seoul or Los Angeles with the same confidence that I walked with on that summer day so long ago in Prices Street Gardens. I can look at myself squarely in the mirror and not flinch. I am blessed with several close and long-term friends whose support is beyond words. I met most of them through participation in karate. Several of us have different ideas, but we have a similar vision. We all have had different life experiences, but we move broadly in the same direction, so we can reach out and touch each other heart to heart any time.

Karate itself is a kind of friend. It is non-committal, but subtly guides you when you abuse it or embrace it. After an absence, it welcomes you back. Diligent training comforts you with the familiarity of repetition. If you are depressed, it can provide a crutch; if you are happy, karate amplifies it. When you are young, you can acquire skills, coordination, fitness, and self-confidence and test your mettle against others in competition. When (if) you mature, karate offers many facets, such as teaching, officiating, coaching, administration and simply practicing it because you love it.

For those with a different bent, there are cultural and philosophical aspects of *budō,* Zen, Buddhism, Shinto, history, Japanese tradition, culture and language.

For me, karate represents humanity. The bad, good, ugly, and their baggage. An endless source of fascination. There is nothing more important about karate than the people involved with it, and I have the great good fortune to have valuable and cherished friends.

Sun City, South Africa, 1996

The 1996 WKF World Championships were held in Sun City, South Africa.

I hoped to see more women participate as WKF officials. However, none were present except me. I saw a woman dressed perfectly as a referee: a navy-blue blazer made to measure, the perfect collar on a white shirt sporting a Windsor-knotted official tie, tailored grey pants of the right length, dark socks, and black patent leather slip-on shoes. About my height and short red hair. I watched her work at the score table for the ring and she was very competent. No one else working the table was dressed like an official. I had to speak to her, and I did during a break in the action.

I asked her why she was not on the floor, and she told me that women were not allowed to officiate at WKF events.

"Well, I am here, which rather contradicts that, don't you think"? I said. She told me that she had a Kumite Referee A and a kata Judge A certification. Her name was Gudrun Hisatake, and she was clearly not Japanese and then it suddenly dawned on me who she was. I had cut a report out of Black Belt magazine about a Hawaiian man who refereed a very difficult kumite match between two athletes who allowed negative emotions to interfere with the fight. There came a point when he called *"Yame"* with the appropriate gesture, but one athlete became enraged and lost control of his actions. The referee called *"Yame"* as before and but the athletes refused to stop battering each other. This occurred three times. Finally, the referee stopped the match by doing something that should never be seen in an amateur non-contact bout. He stepped between the fighters and punched the more aggressive one so hard in the face that it sent him to the floor. Both athletes were given *"Shikaku"* (disqualification), which prevented them from further participation in the event. This was in a national USA competition. I think his given name was George, but I knew his family name was Hisatake. Gudrun was his wife. They met and lived in Germany, where he had been stationed in the US military during WWII. He died suddenly at the age of thirty-nine, and Gudrun, now in her sixties, had continued her involvement in karate and never married again. I mentioned the incident to her, and she confirmed it. I told her to have a chat with Tommy Morris (Carluke, Scotland), Chair of the WKF RC. She did. I would love to have been a fly on the wall. At any rate, she never controlled score tables in any other WKF events as she functioned as a referee and judge. I was so-o-o happy for her because her love of officiating was associated with enduring love for her husband.

Wherever I am located, I will be training, trying to deepen my understanding of karate. While engaged in this never-ending quest, I hope to meet even more people with similar interests. Because of karate, I am privileged to have met many remarkable individuals, of whom several have become close and valuable friends. The affection and esteem in which I hold these individuals reaches far beyond any that I hold for most of my blood relatives. As such, I regard many of these friends as my family, which encompasses a range of views, likes, and dislikes, ages, abilities, styles, and grades. As in many families, there may be happiness, sadness, loss, discord, closeness, distance, or affection, but the underlying thread is humanity and concern for others. It is important to try to learn tolerance, develop flexibility, care, and disregard geographic origins and political viewpoints, sex, race, religion, or class. It is also key to develop the ability to think independently and try to make the best choices, regardless of the popularity of the decision. I think all of these things can be taught through participation in any martial art. What a person does with the information, like anything else, is a matter of individual personality.

But… karate can be practiced in a dōjō, beach, backyard, living room, or inside your head, and of course, while in the toilet. Karate is a personal journey.

Time out with Dr. and Mrs. Takagi

During training, Takagi sensei noticed that my retracted punch was a bit low. So, I asked him where it ought to be. He said, *"oppai"* (at the level of the nipple[s]).

So, I looked confused and pointed out that when women age, things such as *"oppai"* might not be where they were when they were younger due to gravitational effects.

This does not usually happen to men unless they are obese. So, what to do?

With an impish grin, he retorted, well, in that case, anywhere the *"oppai"* happen to be will have to do… and walked away.

On another day, I received a phone call asking me if I was free to go to a party.

"When?" I asked.

"Tomorrow, 5 pm."

"Where?" I asked.

"Some hotel. Don't worry, I will drive, so meet at our house."

"Dress code?" I asked.

"Business attire would be acceptable."

So, I left work early and went to his home. Takigawa, one of his students, and I sat in the back seats, and Mrs. T. sat in the front. We arrived at a very expensive hotel in Roppongi. When we entered the hotel, we were directed to a party that was in full spring. We all signed a fat guest book, then entered a line of people waiting to bow to all seven members of the welcoming host family, starting from the youngest to the matriarch, who wore the largest diamond I had ever seen on a finger. We were ushered into a vast ballroom full of men in business attire. One long side of the rectangular room consisted of a buffet that included every possible type of food. The Japanese version of Frank Sinatra sung on a podium, accompanied by a live band, and several stunning girls dressed like waitresses pushed carts of appetizers and endless bottles of single-malt Scotch whisky, brandy, rum, vodka, gin, various brands and types of beer, and wines. Finally, I asked Takagi sensei about the reason for the party, which surely held over 1,000 guests. He said it was the 350th anniversary of a business called "Kadoebi" (Corner shrimp). Then I asked him what kind of business it was as it was obviously very prosperous.

Prostitution.

I asked how he came to know these people.

Well, he taught one of their sons karate and fixed their teeth. The business also owned a boxing ring near sensei's dental practice, and he would also fix boxers who were smacked in the teeth...

The company had been around since the heydays of the Yoshiwara, a red-light district in Edo (An old name for Tōkyō).

When it was time to leave the event, everyone lined up to bow to each member of the family as they presented gifts to all. As we were driving back to Ōhtsuka, Mrs. T decided to investigate the gift bag and found that the contents were associated with a saucy night in "Sleepless Town" (Kabukichō, the entertainment district in Shinjuku, Tōkyō): a towel, toothpaste, a toothbrush...and a phone card with a picture on it. They were the size and texture of a debit card and worked like one, but only for telephones. Mrs. T scoffed and said something to the effect of, "Ugh, same as the last time," and tossed it back in the bag.

So, I rummaged through my bag and found the same contents, including a phone card with a picture.... of a stallion mounting a mare, with a focus on the fully erect male shaft required for the task. More laughs and a discussion of equine anatomy until we reached Ōhtsuka.

Time out with Hakoishi sensei

I had heard a rumor that the Wadō style included a version of the kata "Unsu" (cloud hands), so I investigated who knew it and was directed to Dr. Hakoishi. I talked with him and asked if this was true. He said that Hironori Ohtsuka had presented it publicly and that he had a poster of the demonstration... but he could not find it. I said I would like to see it and learn it. He invited me to visit Morioka, where he lived (Iwate prefecture, about four hours north of Tōkyō by shinkansen). So, I accepted the invitation. It was during the winter, so he told me to bring skis in addition to karate gi. I knew that he instructed ski instructors. He also played rugby into his early 80s and competed in karate in senior kumite and kata well into his 70s until the Wadō Kai canceled the division, presumably to save the dignity of the competitors. He took me to his hospital, where all were covered in immaculate green tiles, and the operating room housed outdated medical devices. Some were possibly from the 1950s. He said he had closed the hospital and only tended to geriatric patients with orthopedic problems. He took me to a small room with a tatami floor where many surfaces supported a large stuffed wildcat with gleaming golden eyes and sharp white teeth, waited to leap, various large stuffed species of birds, and a few deer heads sported large antlers. Thick medical tomes in German lined one wall, and a few English language books were strewn about the tatami floor He had taught himself German and had recently started to focus on English. This was his man cave in the heyday of his career, when he would live in the hospital in case of problems with surgical patients. Impressive. Then he told me to change into ski clothes, and we skied on Mount Iwate with his girlfriend. He was surprised and impressed when he looked at my skiing style and identified it as Japanese and said that my level was about 2nd Kyu in the Japanese ranking system. Wow! All due to Kikuma. Après ski consisted of eating *udon* (thick, wheat-flour noodles) at his favorite noodle shop. I learned that his girlfriend was a master of Ikebana. Thereafter, we all went to his house, which he was very proud to show off. A total man cave with a dead bear splayed out on the floor as a carpet, a state-of-the-art Bang and Olufsen sound system with four-foot-high Tannoy speakers, more stuffed heads of animal trophies with and without horns and antlers that stared eternally into …. shotgun barrels? Of course, he also had an impressive collection of guns and a katana.

I was having a fine time, but asked when I might see and learn something about Wadō Unsu. Oh, too late today… tomorrow. OK. So, he drove me back to his man cave, where my belongings were left and opened a cupboard containing a futon and its foam and cover and assured me that I would be safe. The door of his den can be locked from the inside and the entrance to the hospital will be locked during the night. I wondered if I could sleep with all the dead animals brought back to life by taxidermy, another of Hakoishi sensei's skills.

Well, I managed to sleep perfectly well in the room, which was definitely one of the most unusual personal spaces I have ever seen, let alone sleep in.

At 9 a.m., Hakoishi appeared and took me out for breakfast; then he said he had something to do, but would show me the kata after lunch. Er, I was leaving on a 4:00 p.m. train to Tōkyō, and time was running out.

Eventually, at about 2.30 that afternoon, he took me to the Iwate University dōjō, and we worked on it for about 30 minutes before I had to return to his hospital to exchange gi for clothes. Bottom line… I never learned this elusive kata, but I recall that it closely resembled the Shito version.

Hakoishi sensei provided a lecture one year at the International Budō Seminar in Katsuura. The theme was to impart to a gaijin (foreigner) audience what Budō meant to each of the 8th Dan instructors of the various martial arts presented at the seminar. Most of these iconic teachers delivered their speeches in Japanese and would drone on and on, boring the audience, most of whom did not understand Japanese. Hakoishi sensei lectured in English, so the audience straightened up and paid attention. He talked about a situation in which he had slipped in snow and found himself unable to climb out of an icy river in the middle of a dark, frosty night. He thought about how easy it would be to let himself die by fully immersing himself in the freezing water. However, he fought the impulse to choose death and finally managed to climb out of the water. He attributed his decades of studying Budō to giving him the strength to live. Everyone was impressed by this very personal story. He asked if anyone had any questions. Katy immediately raised a hand and asked what he was doing outside in the middle of a snowy night in the first place.

He said that he had woken up in a pool of diarrhea that had soiled the sheets and his sleepwear, and he wanted to clean it all outside due to the smell. Everyone, including Hakoishi sensei laughed...but they did not know the whole story. He had colon cancer and was on medication that disrupted his digestive system.

Hakoishi decided that he wanted to ski at Whistler Mountain in British Columbia, Canada. He arrived with Tanizawa sensei from Hokkaido and checked into a hotel. He called me and told me his itinerary. I was to meet him and Tanizawa sensei in the Roundhouse Lodge (altitude 6,069 ft). I had to work in the morning, so we planned to meet around 1 pm.

I reached the Roundhouse at ~1.30 p.m. and could not find them. I knew that he would be on very steep, mogul-infested black runs, which were beyond my skiing skills, but I skied a few runs, hoping to meet him at the bottom of the gondola. Didn't happen, so I drove home and called his hotel. Tanizawa sensei answered the phone and said that Hakoishi sensei had been injured. I asked, "How? Is he OK? Can he speak?"

"Yes", replied Tanizawa sensei. He passed the phone to Hakoishi sensei, who sounded somewhat remorseful and not his usual happy self. He had gone off-piste, that is, out of bound areas where skiing is forbidden. Such areas have warning signs and are often inaccessible. Some people like to ignore such information. Of course, that is where he wanted to ski. He skied off a cliff and bounced his way from a considerable height to finally land at the bottom of a ravine. Tanizawa sensei was unable to reach him, and he was covered in blood leaking from his head. There was no way to contact the Ski patrol as no one would be patrolling there, and phones were not yet smart. So Hakoishi sensei found his skis and poles then started climbing. He reached the top of the ravine, then, of course, had to ski down to the nearest gondola to take him to the base of the mountain and find first aid. It must have been an unusual sight—seeing two elderly gentlemen skiing down the mountain, one with blood all over his head, face, and stained ski clothes.

He giggled when he said, "Stich stitch, many, many stitch—my head is like a hat"! The skin of his skull had almost been completely ripped off, but enough was still attached to reunite it with the skull using 110 stitches. He really was extraordinary. He encouraged me in my efforts to become a WKF official and sided with me against some serious strife later.

He conquered cancer and lived for another twenty-five years thereafter. He passed away in June 2022 from Alzheimer's disease.

Vancouver 1997

I returned from Japan and was faced with shocking attitudes and activities that sent me spiraling down a rabbit hole. Certain individuals here at home did everything in their power to wipe me off the face of regional, national, and international karate for a decade. However, that is another twenty-eight years of tales that await the telling.

Explanations:
Karate Technical Terms

Dan	段	Black belt ranks.
Dōjō	道場	Anywhere Karate martial arts are practiced
Dōjō Kun	道場訓	Code of ethics; moral principles and behavior
Gi	道着	Clothing worn to practice karate and some other martial arts
Heian Pinan	平安	Forms studied before black belt
Karate-dō	空手道	Karate Way as both a martial art and philosophy of life.
Kata	形	Pre-arranged sequences containing all karate techniques
Kiai	気合	Shout at moment of impact
Kihon	基本	Basic techniques
Kumite	組手	Sparring or fighting practice with an opponent.
Kyu	級	Grades Student grades or ranks below black belt.
Obi	帯	Belt
Rei	礼	Bow; expresses respect, courtesy and humility
Senpai	先輩	Senior student in dōjō
Sensei	先生	Senior student in dōjō
Shodan	初段	First-degree black belt
Zanshin	残心	Continued state of alertness after moment of impact

Important primary school teachers

Donald Matheson: Excellent teacher; compassionate, much loved by all

William Robertson: Headmaster who admitted me to Sciennes primary school

William Sinclair: Retired army colonel, genius with children; humorous and sensitive

Impactful people

Andy Holmes: Gifted JKA Shotokan Karate teacher (Vancouver, BC, Canada)
Antonio Espinos: President, World Karate Federation for > 30 years (Madrid, Spain)
Bob Nash: JKF Wadō Kai student of Hideho Takagi (Sammamish, WA, USA)
Cedric Rodgers: Talented Shotokan practitioner and teacher (Little Rock, AR, USA)
Fusajiro Takagi: JKF President; Keio University, Shotokan (Japan).
Hideho Takagi: Distinguished JKF Wadō Kai teacher, student of Hironori Ohtsuka
Hidetaka Nishiyama: Renowned JKA Shotokan teacher (Los Angeles, CA, USA)
Hirokazu Kanazawa: Legendary Shotokan technician and teacher (Japan)
James Johnson: President of Karate Canada, WKF Committee, Shiseikai
Jeannie Parker: Taekwondo student (Houston, TX, USA)
John Allen: JKA Shotokan Karate teacher (Aberdeen, Scotland)
Mike Scales: Shotokan Karate instructor (Coquitlam, BC, Canada)
Osamu Ozawa: World renowned JKA Shotokan instructor (Las Vegas, NV, USA)
Reza Salmani: Outstanding Shotokan technician (Dubai, UAE)
Ronnie Watt, O.B.E.: Prominent Shotokan instructor (Aberdeen, Scotland)
Tanja Petrovic: Uber karate athlete and amazing coach (Belgrade, Serbia)
Toby Threadgill: Sōshi of Shindō Yōshin Ryū Jiu Jitsu (Evergreen CO, USA)
Tommy Morris: WKF Technical Committee Chair for 30 years (Carluke, Scotland)
Toru Arakawa: JKF Wadō Kai teacher, WKF TC member, student of Hironori Ohtsuka
Yoshiaki Ajari: JKF Wadō Kai teacher (Berkeley, CA, USA)
Minobu Miki: Shitō-ryū, instructor, WKF referee (San Diego, CA, USA)
Takayuki Mikami: JKA Shotokan instructor (New Orleans, LA., USA)

Organizations

JKA: Japan Karate Association; Global Shotokan organization
JKF: Japan Karate Federation; National sport governing for all karate styles in Japan
WKF: World Karate Federation; IOC- approved international governing body sport karate
WUKO: World Union of Karate Organizations - original name of WKF

Founders of karate styles and other martial arts

*Shotokan 松濤館 Karate style founded by Gichin Funakoshi (Okinawa)

*Wadō-ryū 和道流 Karate style founded by Hironori Ōhtsuka (Japan)

*Shitō-ryū 糸東流 Karate style founded by Kenwa Mabuni (Okinawa)

*Gōjū-ryū 剛柔流 Karate style founded by Chojun Miyagi (Okinawa)

*Judō 柔道 Japanese martial art founded by Jigorō Kanō (Japan)

†Kendō 剣道 Japanese swordsmanship (Japan)

†Shindō Yōshin Ryū Jiu Jitsu 新道楊心流 Integrated martial system founded by Katsunotsuke Matsuoka (Japan)

Regarded as *modern (gendai 近代; post 1868) and †ancient (koryū 古流; pre 1868) martial arts

This book can be the perfect gift for everyone:

Scan this QR code to get your copy of the book.

If you'd like to share your thoughts or feedback with the author, please connect via:

 canadajkfwadokai@gmail.com

 www.canadajkfwadokai.org

www.ingramcontent.com/pod-product-compliance
Lightning Source LLC
Chambersburg PA
CBHW071227070526
44583CB00017B/2081